WHEN CHARLIE MET JOAN

WHEN CHARLIE MET JOAN

THE TRAGEDY
of the
CHAPLIN TRIALS
and the
FAILINGS *of*
AMERICAN LAW

Diane Kiesel

UNIVERSITY OF MICHIGAN PRESS

ANN ARBOR

For questions or permissions, please contact
um.press.perms@umich.edu

Published in the United States of America by the
University of Michigan Press
Manufactured in the United States of America
Printed on acid-free paper
First published February 2025

A CIP catalog record for this book is available from
the British Library.

Library of Congress Cataloging-in-Publication Data

Names: Kiesel, Diane, author. | Michigan Publishing (University of
   Michigan), publisher.
Title: When Charlie met Joan : the tragedy of the Chaplin trials and
   the failings of American law / Diane Kiesel.
Description: Ann Arbor : University of Michigan Press,
   [2025] | Includes bibliographical references (pages 375–82) and
   index.
Identifiers: LCCN 2024043181 (print) | LCCN 2024043182
   (ebook) | ISBN 9780472133581 (hardcover) | ISBN 9780472222001
   (ebook)
Subjects: LCSH: Chaplin, Charlie, 1889-1977. | Barry, Joan,
   1920-2007. | Motion picture actors and actresses—United
   States—Biography.
Classification: LCC PN2287.C5 K54   2025 (print) | LCC PN2287.C5
   (ebook) | DDC 791.4302/80922 [B]—dc23/eng/20240923
LC record available at https://lccn.loc.gov/2024043181
LC ebook record available at https://lccn.loc.gov/2024043182

Cover images: Charles Chaplin, 1944, and Joan Barry, 1943,
© mptvimages.com.

You don't have to be a genius in Hollywood to fall afoul of your normal allotment of traps and snares, but if you are a genius and worth twenty million dollars or more, if you have a roving fancy and can afford to indulge it . . . you're almost a cinch to be headed for the front page.

FLORABEL MUIR, *HEADLINE HAPPY*

My means of contriving comedy plot was simple. It was the process of getting people in and out of trouble.

CHARLIE CHAPLIN, *MY AUTOBIOGRAPHY*

He's an artist, he has no common sense.

THOMAS WELLS DURANT, TALKING ABOUT CHAPLIN TO THE FBI

For Georges G. Lederman

CONTENTS

ACKNOWLEDGMENTS

An author needs many helping hands, and I was lucky enough to get them. I am grateful to the entire team at the University of Michigan Press, from Elizabeth Demers, the former editorial director, who saw promise in this book, to acquiring editor Katie LaPlant, who guided it to completion with the help of fellow editors Madison Allums, Haley Winkle, Annie Carter, Juliette Synder, Michael Hylton, Anne Taylor, and publicity manager Danielle Coty-Fattal. I owe whatever success I've had in my writing career to my experienced, savvy, tireless literary agent and dear friend, Colleen Mohyde.

I thank the librarians, archivists, and historians who provided information and guidance with patience and extraordinary skill. My early research took place during the COVID-19 lockdown of 2020 and early 2021, and by some miracle they kept information flowing to writers. In no special order, I thank Mary Huelsback, Wisconsin Center for Film and Theater Research; Louise Hilton, Margaret Herrick Library; Beth Williams, Cunard Archives, University of Liverpool; Thomas Philo, California State University at Dominguez Hills; Nancy Enneking, Getty Research Institute; Terri Garst, Los Angeles Public Library; Jessica LaBorzetta, American Heritage Center, University of Wyoming; Kenneth Cobb, New York City Municipal Archives; Curt Hanson, University of North Dakota Special Collections Library; Carolyn Waters and Kirsten Carleton, New York Society Library; Dan O'Brien and Claude Zachary, University of Southern California, USC Special Collections; John Cahoon, Los Angeles County Museum of Natural History Foundation; Ellen Jarosz, California State University at Northridge;

David Fort, James Huntoon, and Amanda Weimer, National Archives and Records Administration; Dorissa Martinez, Richard M. Nixon Presidential Library and Museum; Douglas Thompson and John Signey, Redondo Beach Public Library; John Fox, FBI historian; Melanie Locay, New York Public Library; and David Conolly, Theatre of Arts, Hollywood.

I want to thank attorneys Bridget Rohde and David Ostwald for clarifying points on federal criminal procedure and real estate law. Attorney Gary Rosen was my invaluable adviser about copyright.

After eighty years, all the players in the Charlie Chaplin–Joan Barry drama are long gone, but some of their surviving relatives kindly shared their memories of their loved ones and family photos: Joe Irwin, Loyd Wright III, Kenneth Marx, Marcia Winn Tingley, Linda Shawhan Shewak, Henry M. Willis III, Anne and Michael Schnoebelen, Tony and David Hecht, Barbara Jacqua, Father Al Scott, James Danis, Janalee Johnson, and Steven Dye.

I thank fellow writers and friends for their suggestions, edits, support, friendship, and shoulders to cry on: Heath Hardage Lee, Kitty Kelley, Gary Marmorstein, Vanda Krefft, and David Smith.

There are some beautiful photos in this book, thanks to the generosity of photographer Joan Marcus; Andrew Howick of mptv Images; Bill Psoras, principal of Newtown High School in Elmhurst, New York; and Kevin Fitzpatrick, Shepherd of The Lambs.

Angelica Salazar, building manager of the General Services Administration in Los Angeles, devoted a good part of a beautiful summer day to giving me a private guided tour of the Federal Building, where the Chaplin Mann Act trial took place in 1944.

Finally, I owe much to the grace and bravery of Joan Barry's two surviving children, Stephen Seck and his half sister, Carol Ann Berry. Carol Ann was on the front pages of newspapers around the country from the moment she was born and has done her best to craft a meaningful and private life on her terms. I thank both Stephen and Carol Ann for trusting me enough to allow me to enter their lives and for extending patience and candor in response to my many questions.

INTRODUCTION
"THE BEST SHOW IN TOWN"

In 1915, he was famous. In 1944, he was infamous. Charlie Chaplin, the silent screen's "Little Tramp," was beloved by movie fans until he starred in a real-life courtroom drama in which he was accused of transporting a woman across state lines for immoral purposes in violation of the Mann Act, then known as the "White Slave Law." Admirers who once stood in long lines at movie houses to cheer his films stood in long lines outside the federal courthouse in Los Angeles clamoring for his head. The trial and its aftermath damaged Chaplin's reputation and contributed to his exile from the United States, the adopted country he had called home for forty years.

War-weary Americans, tired of reading about Hitler's carnage, eagerly devoured the headlines about the scandal. Like the Lindbergh baby kidnapping trial that preceded it and the O. J. Simpson murder trial that followed, the Chaplin courtroom spectacle was labeled as yet another "trial of the century." Or as ace New York *Daily News* crime reporter Florabel Muir wrote: "The Chaplin show, while it lasted, was the best show in town."[1]

The show's leading lady was red-haired ingenue Joan Berry. In tearful testimony at the standing-room-only trial she claimed to have been seduced by the unparalleled director's promise to make her a star with the glamorous new surname "Barry." She became Chaplin's protégée and mistress in a volatile relationship. But neither movie nor marriage followed, so pregnant and alone, Joan became famous by tattling to the newspapers about their affair. Hot off the presses, the story fell into the hands of scandal-loving readers, including FBI Director J. Edgar Hoover, who was disgusted by Chaplin's louche attitude toward sex and his "parlor pink" political ideas.

Joan's plight also attracted a rapt audience of ambitious federal prosecutors who recognized the career-building benefits of bringing down a man with Chaplin's reputation. Overlooking her foibles, they put Joan on their own stage—the grand jury. Her testimony led to Chaplin's multiple indictments in which he was accused of paying for her to travel from California to New York and back for sexual trysts. Chaplin was also charged with conspiring with cronies to convince a Beverly Hills judge to run her out of town when she wouldn't stop her harassment campaign against him. He faced the terrifying prospect of decades behind bars.

As if that weren't enough, Joan claimed Chaplin was the father of her daughter, born in October 1943. When he refused to marry her, she dragged him into court for another round of public humiliation in a paternity trial. Although Chaplin avoided jail when he was acquitted in federal court, in a tragicomic turn straight out of one of the Little Tramp's silent films, he lost the paternity case even though science proved he could not have been the child's father.

Before it was over, Chaplin would spend three years in legal purgatory. The experience left him bitter, which played out in his 1947 film, *Monsieur Verdoux*, in which he starred as a bigamist and serial wife murderer. Meanwhile, Cold War politics turned to the right, and the presence in the United States of the left-leaning, sexually adventurous British-born comic made Uncle Sam's blood boil. When Chaplin, who was not an American citizen, went to Europe for the premiere of *Limelight* in 1952, the Joan Barry trials and his Communist sympathies provided the excuses the government needed to bar him from American soil for the next twenty years.

Joan Barry would not emerge unscathed either. Her courtroom performances brought notoriety, not stardom. Her appearances on the witness stand would be her only moments in the spotlight. Afterward, she briefly became a lounge singer in third-rate nightclubs, but her break with Chaplin was the end of any serious showbiz career. Her violent mood swings, histrionic outbursts, and repeated suicide threats, which should have been red flags, were exploited and ignored until she had a breakdown and was locked away in a mental hospital and estranged from the child she claimed was Chaplin's.

At its most basic, the story of the Charlie Chaplin–Joan Barry trials is an entertaining yarn about Old Hollywood. But eighty years later, when viewed in a new light, the trials raise serious issues about the power of celebrity, Cold War politics, the media frenzy surrounding high-profile court proceedings, and the sorry history of the Hollywood casting couch.

The trials had a lasting impact on the law. In 1945, jurors in California courts could reject blood-type evidence in paternity cases. But once Chaplin was ordered by a judge to pay twenty-one years of child support for a daughter who was not his, the miscarriage of justice couldn't have been more obvious. Not long after, blood test results negating the possibility of fatherhood became irrefutable evidence in all courts until the more exact science of DNA was developed late in the twentieth century.

Appreciation of the hysteria that surrounded the trials requires an understanding of Chaplin's outsized reputation. Chaplin was Hollywood's first superstar, recognized the world over as the Little Tramp. A creative genius, he made such classics as *The Kid*, *The Gold Rush*, *City Lights*, *Modern Times*, and *The Great Dictator*. Newspaper publisher William Randolph Hearst called him "the poet of the screen."[2] Chaplin's talent was such that three years after walking onto his first film set in February 1914, he was able to win a staggering million-dollar contract, over $26 million in recent dollars.[3]

Although barely five foot six—by some accounts shorter—Chaplin was handsome and blessed with a sexual magnetism that was catnip to women. He may have had as many as four wives (*may have* because scant proof exists of his third marriage to leading lady Paulette Goddard) and countless love affairs. Twenty-one-year-old Joan Barry was one of those affairs; she was pretty, vivacious, and gifted with some talent.

Government officials were not as enamored as the ladies. Chaplin lived in the United States for forty years, but like an unappreciative houseguest, the silent star did not hesitate to speak out against his host. His hypocrisy was galling; enthralled with the Bolshevist Revolution, he decried American capitalism while keeping a close eye on his millions. Early in World War II, he took to microphones across America urging the Allies to open a Second Front in Europe to help the Russians defeat the Nazis, which later was interpreted by the government in the Cold War years as supporting the Communist cause. Federal investigators searched relentlessly since 1922 for evidence he was promoting Communism.[4] While neither his politics nor his sexual proclivities alone were sufficient to bring him down, in tandem they provided the hook that the government could seize to silence him.

United States of America v. Charles Spencer Chaplin started with jury selection on March 21, 1944. Charles H. Carr, the ambitious U.S. attorney who had made his name investigating corruption in movie studio unions, led the prosecution. Chaplin hired Jerry Giesler, known as "the Magnificent Mouthpiece," the high-priced, high-profile defense lawyer as famous in California's courtrooms as Chaplin was in the world's movie houses.

The trial was not a Chaplin production, but he couldn't have cast it better if he had tried. Joan's appearance was first-rate. "If his schooling was responsible for her performance," wrote the *Chicago Daily Tribune*'s Marcia Winn, "she did him credit."[5] Chaplin's own weeping on the witness stand rivaled his 1921 star turn in *The Kid* and solidified his reputation as the world's greatest actor when it mattered most.

On April 4, 1944, after a long day of deliberations, the jury returned a verdict of not guilty, and the courtroom erupted in cheers. By then, Joan's nervous volatility on the stand, the weakness of the government's case, and Chaplin's inherent charm had turned the jury and the public—which had been riveted by the spectacle—in his favor. The Department of Justice ordered Carr to cut his losses and drop the remaining cases.

But Chaplin was not out of the woods yet. A paternity trial began in December 1944 and, if anything, was more salacious than the criminal case. Joan spewed titillating details from the witness stand about their sexual liaisons that weren't relevant during the criminal trial. Once more, the newspapers had a field day. Even so, it ended with the jury hung in favor of acquittal. Chaplin had an eleventh-hour opportunity to settle but considered Joan and her mother, Gertrude Berry, to be a pair of shakedown artists and refused to budge. At the retrial, the jury found in Joan's favor, and Chaplin was ordered to pay child support for her daughter until the girl turned twenty-one.

The Little Tramp remained a polarizing figure. Legislators took to the floor of Congress to denounce him, veterans' groups called for boycotts of his movies, and the government continued to gather dirt on him. In 1952, the other shoe dropped when immigration authorities barred him from the United States, citing his moral laxity and questionable loyalty to Uncle Sam. He and his wife, Oona O'Neill, daughter of playwright Eugene O'Neill, moved to Switzerland, where they raised eight children. Chaplin's popularity in Europe never diminished.

The world has turned many times since the Chaplin trials. Today, the extramarital affairs of Hollywood stars don't lift an eyebrow and single

mothers are ubiquitous. It is understood that the nation's Cold War obsession with Communists in Hollywood destroyed lives as well as careers.
Chaplin's creative brilliance is recognized as unsurpassed in the history
of film—regardless of one's politics. In 1972, when he was a feeble old man,
Chaplin was invited to return to America for an honorary Oscar and was
greeted with the longest-standing ovation in the ceremony's history as
he shuffled onstage to receive it. He died five years later, his reputation
restored.

But the world is still turning. Today, allegations of sexual misconduct levied against powerful men in Hollywood and elsewhere can end a
career—no matter how illustrious. In the early 1990s, director Woody Allen
faced allegations—never proven—that he sexually abused a daughter of his
romantic partner Mia Farrow. He married another of Farrow's daughters
following an affair carried on behind Farrow's back. When the story broke,
most of Hollywood sided with Allen, whose directorial talents and relationships with his leading ladies were equated with Chaplin's. But when
the allegations resurfaced in the twenty-first century, Allen was judged
more harshly, and some of his former Hollywood supporters backed away.

Then in 2020 and 2022, powerful Miramax producer Harvey Weinstein
was convicted of rape and sexual assault in New York and Los Angeles after
years of sotto voce talk about his improper conduct with women, although
in 2024 the New York conviction was overturned.[6] Weinstein became the
poster boy for the #MeToo movement that forced Hollywood to face its
history of abusing women. Today, the Academy of Motion Picture Arts and
Sciences might have second thoughts about bestowing a special Oscar on
Chaplin and some of the movers and shakers in the industry might not be
so quick to stand up and cheer for him.

In the 1940s, Joan Barry was considered an angry stalker and conniving gold digger. She drove poor Chaplin crazy with unhinged behavior
that Hollywood would later depict in movies like *Fatal Attraction* and Clint
Eastwood's lesser-known *Play Misty for Me*. Her claim that Chaplin fathered
her child was not true, and why she made it can never be known. But after
the trials, she spent years in a psychiatric hospital, making it likely she
suffered from undiagnosed mental illness when she was involved with
Chaplin. Today, rather than being dismissed as manipulative, she might
be considered a vulnerable woman who was exploited by a man who held
the power and control. Upon reflection, her doomed relationship with
Chaplin might evoke more sympathy than scorn.

This is not a biography of Charlie Chaplin but a look at a chapter in his life about a series of trials that captivated the public and had dire consequences for everyone involved. Today's readers may choose to reassess the Chaplin-Barry cases in the light of a new century, changed politics, advances in science and the law, and a new sensitivity to gender-related power imbalances.

PROLOGUE
"ANYONE WHO HAS EVER SEEN
A FILM IS IN YOUR DEBT"
OSCAR NIGHT—MONDAY, APRIL 10, 1972

The cloud cover made it feel cooler than it should have for an April morning in Southern California.[1] But by afternoon the sun was strong and felt good, the way it had years before on his tennis court at his Sunday afternoon soirees. Back then, all Hollywood would turn out: Doug Fairbanks and his wife, Mary Pickford, Greta Garbo, Gary Cooper, Paulette Goddard, Errol Flynn. And later, an ingenue who would one day be known as "Joan Barry."

All Hollywood would turn out on this night too. The stars of the 1970s: Jane Fonda, Jack Lemmon, Walter Matthau, Gene Hackman, Jack Nicholson. Some of the big names were strangers to him now, although he was no stranger to them. He was the one-and-only Charlie Chaplin, the most famous silent film star in the world. Back in the day, he commanded a fortune from the studios and set women's hearts on fire as the handsome, beloved character, the "Little Tramp," although Chaplin called him the "Little Fellow." But time and circumstances—both beyond his control—had turned him into a tired, feeble, and barely recognizable old man. At the invitation of the Academy of Motion Picture Arts and Sciences, Chaplin, now eighty-two, summoned what stamina he still had to travel nearly six thousand miles to accept an Oscar for a lifetime of achievement in film.

Chaplin had left the United States in September 1952 for London aboard the luxury liner *Queen Elizabeth* with his young wife, Oona O'Neill, and their growing brood of kids to promote his latest film, *Limelight*, and to enjoy a European vacation. Once the boat was out on the Atlantic Ocean, the government pulled up the gangplank. He would not be allowed back into the country where he'd lived and worked for forty years. No less than the attorney general of the United States decided that the reentry permit of Chaplin, a British citizen, should be revoked.

Now nearly twenty years later, Chaplin and his adoring Oona, who never left his side, made their way in a limousine to the Dorothy Chandler Pavilion in Los Angeles for the Oscar ceremony. But the waiting journalists were disappointed when he was whisked inside through an underground garage. Only actress Candice Bergen, on assignment for *Life* magazine, was granted access to capture Chaplin's every move with her camera.[2]

At the time of his forced exile, the press could be hostile. "After living in the United States forty years, Chaplin has openly joined our enemy, the Soviet slave masters," wrote the editors of the *Saturday Evening Post*.[3] Hollywood gossip columnist Hedda Hopper wrote: "Good riddance to bad company."[4] But the winds, ever part of California's unstable climate, had shifted by the 1970s. With America's unpopular war in Vietnam raging and the sexual revolution in full swing, a new generation at the helm of the Hollywood studios was no longer beholden to the censors or consumed with Uncle Sam's fight against Communism. Counterculture movies like *The Graduate* and *Easy Rider* had replaced middle-American crowd-pleasers like *The Sound of Music* and *How the West Was Won* as box office hits. Liberalism was in vogue.

Quietly, feelers went across the ocean: could Chaplin be coaxed to return to be honored by Hollywood? The thaw began a year earlier, ignited by an unlikely source—comedian Bob Hope, a GOP favorite famous for entertaining American troops abroad. Hope, who rose to stardom winning a Charlie Chaplin look-a-like contest as a child, contacted President Nixon's ambassador to Switzerland, the patrician Shelby Cullom Davis, suggesting it was time to let bygones be bygones and welcome the Little Tramp home.[5] Given Chaplin's advanced years and failing health, the ambassador agreed that "from the standpoint of public relations" and "in line with the president's wish to heal the wounds within our society," the time was right. In a secret cable sent on March 5, 1971, Ambassador Davis forwarded Hope's suggestion to Attorney General John Mitchell. The door was opened.[6]

The hard sell to a wary Chaplin came later. Daniel Taradash, president of the Academy, which hands out the thirteen-and-a-half-inch bronze Oscar statuettes, begged Chaplin to return. "Anyone who has ever seen a film is in your debt," Taradash wrote to Chaplin in January 1972. "Your thirty-seven hundred fellow artists in the Academy are anxious to express this in our tribute."[7] Chaplin agreed to come, but up until the last minute he harbored doubts. He hardly slept a wink on the long flight from Europe. He was afraid he would be shot on sight once he arrived in America and vowed that if so much as one protester showed up at the airport, he would turn around and go home—award or no award.[8]

On the afternoon of April 3, Chaplin haltingly emerged from Eastern Air Lines Flight 810 from Bermuda, where he'd taken a brief holiday. A police escort swooped in to take him to a suite at the Plaza Hotel in Midtown Manhattan.[9] By nightfall, he and his wife were the guests of honor at a swanky private party for sixty at the East Sixty-Seventh Street townhouse of his wife's dear friend Gloria Vanderbilt Cooper (later to be Gloria Vanderbilt of designer blue jeans fame). He was greeted at the door by her five-year-old son Anderson, a polite, blue-eyed boy in a white ruffled shirt and dark velvet jacket (later to be Anderson Cooper of CNN fame). Chaplin dined on his second steak of the day (he'd enjoyed the first on the flight) and made small talk with Truman Capote, Sen. Jacob Javits, Lillian Gish, and George Plimpton.[10]

The next night, he was feted at the Film Society of Lincoln Center. A banner was strung across Philharmonic Hall depicting Chaplin as the Little Tramp. It read: "Hello Charlie."[11] New York City mayor John V. Lindsay gave him a medal while twenty-eight hundred stage and screen luminaries cheered. Later, a champagne reception for one thousand paying guests degenerated into chaos as they jostled one another in a futile attempt to rub elbows with the great man and grab plastic flutes of bubbly.[12]

Onward, Chaplin traveled to California, where he prepared to accept further amends from the crowd that once snubbed him. He was awarded a brass star on Hollywood Boulevard's nineteen-block "Walk of Fame," an honor denied him for a dozen years.[13] And on April 10, the biggest prize of all—an Oscar.

Stuffed into a tuxedo, his once lithe figure long gone, Chaplin lurked backstage during most of the interminable Academy Awards program. Joel Grey, in a tuxedo shirt with ruffles down the front and a bowtie as wide as a dinner napkin, crooned about Old Hollywood in a creaky, overproduced opening number. Jane Fonda, as much of a thorn in Hollywood's side then as Chaplin had been in his day, was awarded the Oscar for Best Actress for her role as a tough but frightened prostitute in *Klute*. She appeared onstage in a severe black Chairman Mao–style pantsuit and had the good sense to grab her golden Oscar without grabbing her soapbox. "There's a great deal to say, and I'm not going to say it tonight. I would just like to really thank you very much."[14]

Television viewers from 30 million homes watched. How different from the first Oscar show in May 1929 when Chaplin's best friend in Hollywood, Douglas Fairbanks, then the academy president, presented him with a special award for producing, directing, writing, and starring in *The Circus*. On that night, there was an audience of 250 at the Roosevelt Hotel in Hollywood and newsmen couldn't have cared less.[15]

As the 1972 Oscar ceremony drew to a close, the houselights dimmed and the audience was treated to a fifteen-minute compilation of Chaplin's greatest film moments. Afterward, Chaplin emerged onto the darkened stage. The audience cheered, yelled, and leaped to their feet. "Bravo, bravo!" came shouts from every corner of the auditorium. They screamed his name and did not stop for three minutes. Struggling—and failing—to hold back tears, Chaplin waved, smiled, and thanked all the "wonderful, sweet people" who genuinely seemed to love him.[16] The orchestra struck up "Smile," the theme song Chaplin wrote for *Modern Times*, the last of his movies in which he appeared as the beloved Tramp.

Chaplin had not heard so much yelling directed at him in Los Angeles in nearly thirty years—on February 14, 1944, to be exact. But then, it was from inside the drab hall of a federal courthouse, those who were yelling were not "sweet people," and there was nothing to smile about.

ONE

THE CIRCUS

Charlie Chaplin's face was taut with tension, and his blue eyes were focused straight ahead as he emerged from the elevator in the Los Angeles federal courthouse and walked the gauntlet of gawkers to the U.S. marshal's office. "Here he comes," shrieked some of the mostly women who lined the 150-foot-long hallway. Hisses and boos filled the air. Some tried to swat him with rolled up newspapers or their purses.[1] At least forty reporters and cameramen elbowed one another for space.[2] One woman screamed a single word: "Rat." Others picked the awkward moment to beg for autographs. Chaplin ignored it all.[3]

Getting arrested and heckled was not how Chaplin had hoped to spend his first Valentine's Day with his teenage bride, Oona O'Neill. But he'd been indicted by a grand jury and ordered to surrender. On the morning he did so, February 14, 1944, it was sunny and chilly.[4] Carrying a tan topcoat over his arm and wearing a wool sweater under a light blazer, Chaplin entered the new Art Moderne–style Federal Building for what would feel like the longest half hour of his life.[5] At his side was the high-powered, high-priced lawyer Jerry "Get Me" Giesler, the go-to guy for the rich and famous in deep, deep trouble. And Chaplin was in deep, deep trouble. Years later, Giesler would recall, "The trial of Charlie Chaplin carried with it the heaviest weight of public loathing for a client I've ever had anything to do with."[6]

Chaplin was to be booked on charges that he violated the Mann Act by transporting his former girlfriend and protégée, Joan Barry, across state lines for immoral purposes and conspired with cronies to run her out of

California in violation of her civil rights.[7] Joan had also given birth to an out-of-wedlock child she claimed was Chaplin's, but that was a matter for the civil courts to decide later.

Without his trademark Little Tramp costume—tiny mustache, coal-rimmed eyes, scruffy clothes, derby hat, huge shoes, and bamboo cane—Chaplin was unrecognizable. Those who didn't work at the movie studios or frequent Hollywood's posh supper clubs might not know that the handsome, exquisitely dressed man with the deep blue eyes and thick white hair was their favorite silent screen bum. By nightfall, the press would take care of that. Photographs of Chaplin getting fingerprinted on the salacious charges would be plastered on the front pages of newspapers everywhere.

Had Chaplin really been a tramp he would have been hauled to the courthouse in handcuffs by burly FBI agents and probably locked up until his trial started. But as a movie mogul he could afford to enlist Giesler, whose reputation and slick negotiating skills spared Chaplin that humiliation. The day after the grand jury voted a true bill on February 10, Giesler entered his appearance as Chaplin's lawyer. U.S. Attorney Charles H. Carr gave Chaplin the courtesy of allowing him to travel the thirteen miles from his Beverly Hills mansion to the downtown courthouse to surrender like a gentleman.[8]

Once at the courthouse, Chaplin failed to appreciate that he was not directing this production. As flashbulbs from news photographers' cameras exploded in his face, a visibly annoyed Chaplin complained in his practiced, proper British accent, "My word! This is really tough." Giesler, in a stage whisper, replied, "And from here on, it will get nothing but tougher."[9]

Chaplin may have been lulled into thinking this day would never come. As the grand jury investigation dragged into its fourth month, Giesler scoffed at the idea that charges would stick. "The whole thing is absurd," the lawyer said.[10] Reporters took their cues from the celebrity attorney they'd nicknamed "the Magnificent Mouthpiece."

Giesler's predictions were usually as good as money in the bank, but this time he turned out to be dead wrong; the U.S. attorney was determined to plow ahead. Carr was new and itching for a high-profile case—even though his bosses back in Washington were not enthusiastic about it and Attorney General Francis Biddle warned him to proceed with caution.[11] Besides, Los Angeles County District Attorney Fred Howser had investigated similar charges against Chaplin less than a year earlier and couldn't make them stick. But that didn't deter Carr.[12]

The Valentine's Day fingerprinting got off to a shaky start. Chaplin balked at being photographed for the newspapers. "I won't do it," he protested. "I'll stand on my constitutional rights." Florabel Muir, the salty crime reporter for the New York *Daily News* who broke the story about the Joan-Charlie scandal and was no fan of the London-born comic, snapped back, "You mean your constitutional rights as an alien?"[13]

Giesler stood up for his client. "No warrant has been issued and there is no reason why he should be photographed." This encouraged Chaplin to climb on his soapbox. "I want to go on record," he began, until Giesler pulled him aside and reminded him of the danger of ignoring his other constitutional right—to silence. It didn't sink in. "Under duress . . . ," Chaplin continued. Again, Giesler yanked Chaplin away.[14]

Chaplin, who built his own film studio in 1917, had directed more than sixty movies by 1944 and was used to being the boss.[15] Giesler had been around this block with famous clients before. He was apoplectic when defending Errol Flynn for rape the year before and caught him flirting in the hallway with a teenage redhead who operated the courthouse candy stand. (It was Nora Eddington, a future Mrs. Flynn.)[16] "He called the actor aside and softly gave him holy hell. Like a good little boy, Flynn went back into the courtroom to await the verdict," wrote Los Angeles *Evening Herald and Express* reporter Agness Underwood, who had witnessed the tongue-lashing.[17]

News of Chaplin's griping reached the sixth-floor sanctuary of Carr, who came flying down to the marshal's office, his angry red face matching his flame-colored hair. "He'll be fingerprinted or I'll send the marshal out after him with a warrant," he fumed. Giesler calmed Carr down, assuring him Chaplin wasn't objecting to being printed, only to having it photographed.[18] The cameramen ignored the fuss and kept snapping pictures.[19]

With no choice, Chaplin stepped into the fifth-floor office of Deputy U.S. Marshal George V. Rossini, a former furniture salesman with ten years as a marshal.[20] While Chaplin had been sniping at the photographers, one of his coconspirators, Beverly Hills Police Lieutenant Claude Marple, slipped in to quietly get printed and get out. Giesler tried to muscle Chaplin ahead, but Marple's lawyer stood his ground—first come, first served.[21] The great Chaplin would have to wait his turn.

Marple played a minor role in the Chaplin conspiracy indictment, which was separate from the Mann Act charges. Marple had booked Joan for vagrancy after she faked suicide in a parked car on New Year's Eve in 1942. Carr believed the vagrancy arrest was trumped up at the behest of Chaplin and part of a conspiracy to get her tossed out of Beverly Hills.[22] Getting the bum's rush out of town was known in the vernacular as being "vagged" or given a "floater." It was a popular practice in 1940s Beverly Hills to get rid of undesirables as a favor to the elite.[23] Marple was outraged at getting caught in the Chaplin-Barry web. "I've been on the police force for 18 years and I've never been in any trouble before—not even a traffic tag," he groused.[24]

Also waiting his turn to be printed was Marple's boss, Detective Captain William W. White, who was charged with improperly influencing the judge who presided over Joan's vagrancy case to banish her as a favor to Chaplin. After Joan was released from jail and told to leave town, White escorted her to the train station, where he slapped one hundred dollars and a ticket to New York into her hand—both provided by Chaplin.[25] The money and the ticket were passed to White by another coconspirator on the finger-print line, Robert Arden, aka Rudolf Kligler, a Chaplin pal and shadowy Austrian refugee. What he was still doing in the United States in 1944 was anybody's guess; he had been deported in 1930 for overstaying his visa and was arrested in 1941 after sneaking back into the United States illegally.[26]

Chaplin's tennis pal Thomas Wells "Tim" Durant, another coconspirator, had introduced Joan to Chaplin in 1941 and had done Chaplin's bidding throughout their romance and its demise. Durant was a tall, handsome New England Brahmin who had been given a seat on the New York Stock Exchange in the 1920s as a wedding present from his father-in-law, E. F. Hutton. After divorcing Adelaide Hutton in 1936, Durant drifted to Hollywood.[27] By 1940, he had been nominally employed at United Artists, partly owned by Chaplin, and was informally the great man's financial adviser, tennis buddy, and late-night dinner companion. The FBI had a low opinion of Durant; agents believed the rumors floating around Hollywood that he was Chaplin's pimp.[28]

Regardless of Durant's outsized role in Chaplin's life, his role in the conspiracy indictment looked small. Of the twenty-two overt acts alleged by the government, Durant was named in only three. On May 7, 1943, allegedly on Chaplin's orders, Durant called the police to have Joan arrested when she showed up at Chaplin's home to break the news she was pregnant. To further the conspiracy, Durant allegedly hired a lawyer for Joan on May 11, 1943, who would keep her from talking to authorities and keep a lid on the burgeoning scandal, but when the effort to keep matters quiet appeared to have failed, he instructed the lawyer on May 12 to withdraw from the case and allow Joan to languish in jail.[29]

The two remaining coconspirators—Police Judge Charles J. Griffin, who ordered Joan to leave town as part of her sentence when she pleaded guilty to vagrancy on January 2, 1943, and Jessie Billie Reno, the women's matron in the Beverly Hills jail who supposedly falsely told Joan that no attorney could be called for her to help with her case—were scheduled to turn themselves in the next day.[30]

The colorful cast of characters, the unprecedented crowd, and the media madness threw veteran marshal George Rossini off his game. The burly, expressionless lawman grabbed Chaplin's delicate fingers in his own meaty paws and, after rolling them in pungent black ink, placed them on the booking card. It was a slow, laborious process—taking at least twenty minutes for each suspect—but this time it didn't go well. A shaken Rossini apologized to higher-ups because the fingerprints of Chaplin and his codefendants were "the poorest he had ever taken." He feared the commotion had so ruined his concentration that the prints would be useless.[31]

Chaplin was also shaken by the ordeal. He fumbled with the fountain pen he used to sign the print card, attempting to dip it into an inkbottle that still had the cap on it—a Little Tramp moment that brought a small smile to Chaplin's lips.[32] After signing the card, he couldn't get out of the courthouse fast enough. But first, he slipped into the men's room to remove the ink from his fingers with a gasoline-covered rag supplied by Giesler.[33]

The next morning, pictures of the diminutive Chaplin being fingerprinted by the large, double-chinned Rossini, with Giesler watching over them like a hawk, would appear in newspapers in large cities and small towns across America.[34] The Chaplin fingerprinting shared front-page space with reports of the Allied bombing of the world's oldest monastery at Monte Cassino to drive out Nazis who were bunkered there.[35]

As the accused were exiting the courthouse, prepared to go their separate ways, only Tim Durant seemed to appreciate there was a victim involved—or at least was the only defendant astute enough to signal to reporters that he was sympathetic to her. "I'm so sorry for Joan," Durant said as he left the courthouse with his lawyer.[36]

TWO

"FEATHERING HER NEST"

Joan Barry, the woman for whom Durant said he felt sorry, was born Mary Louise Gribble in Detroit on May 24, 1920, to Gertrude and James Alfred Gribble. In childhood, she shuttled between cities and schools; in adulthood, she drifted between jobs and sofas in the living rooms of friends and the beds of lovers, husbands, hotels, and mental hospitals. She bounced from coast-to-coast in search of love and security, which she never seemed to find, with her overbearing mother, whom she never seemed to shake, at her heels.

As she pursued stardom, she used the name Joan Barry. Although she would later hobnob with some of the richest and most famous men in the world, she came from working-class stock. Her mother was born Gertrude McLaren in New York City on December 13, 1899.[1] Gertrude was one of seven children born to an Irish immigrant, thirty-three-year-old Catherine Timmons, sometimes spelled "Katherine," and her forty-year-old husband, Robert McLaren, a Scottish bricklayer.[2] Tragedy struck on December 5, 1903, when Robert died of pneumonia.[3] With only an eighth-grade education, Kate McLaren supported her large family as a matron at the Manhattan Barge Office, where immigrants arriving from Europe first entered the United States.[4]

Joan's father, James Gribble, was born on October 4, 1897.[5] His father, William Gribble, and his mother, the former Mary Louise Patterson, lived in Brooklyn with their five children.[6] Mary Louise took her own life on

January 23, 1914, by inhaling carbon monoxide fumes from a gas lamp in the family's Brooklyn tenement.[7]

Joan's parents were married in New York City on August 22, 1919, shortly after James was honorably discharged from the army, having served two and a half years as a private. He was a twenty-one-year-old machinist, and Gertrude was a nineteen-year-old stenographer.[8] They relocated to Detroit, where James worked as a machinist for an engineering company.[9]

Joan told FBI agents investigating her involvement with Chaplin that her father had committed suicide before she was born, a victim of World War I shellshock.[10] But Joan was rarely a reliable narrator. Five years after Joan's birth, James Gribble was still very much alive and had returned with his family—which included another daughter, Agnes, born in 1923—to New York City, where he worked as a car salesman.[11] He *did* commit suicide, but not until December 10, 1926. He shot himself in the head with a .25-caliber German automatic revolver—perhaps filched from a dead enemy soldier on the battlefield—at the family home at 531 West 148th Street in Manhattan.[12] One can only imagine how much little six-year-old Mary Louise may have seen, heard, and suppressed.

A year after her husband's death, Gertrude Gribble married thirty-five-year-old John Berry, a traveling salesman, who would turn out to be a traveling bad check artist, with a criminal history going back to 1909.[13] In early 1930 the couple and Gertrude's youngest child moved to Cleveland, Ohio, leaving Joan with Grandmother McLaren to finish the fifth grade at St. Rose of Lima in Upper Manhattan.[14] Mary Louise took her stepfather's last name and was a good student, with a B average in her academic courses and a B+ in conduct. At the end of the school year she joined her family in Ohio, leaving no forwarding address with the nuns at St. Rose's.[15]

During the Depression, the Berrys returned to New York and Mary Louise attended Newtown High School in Elmhurst, Queens, where she was known as "Mary Lou Berry." Her classmates described her as "charming, young and fair with the loveliest red hair."[16] It is not clear when or why she started calling herself "Joan," but her mother always called her "Mary."[17] Joan developed a long string of aliases—Joanne Berry, Joan Barratt, Mary L. Barratt, Bettie Booker, Mary L. Spencer, Catherine McLaren, and Mrs. Mark Warner; some she may have been trying on for size, while others helped her evade hotel bills, prying landladies, and, in some instances, the law.[18]

After graduating from high school, Joan had vague dreams of movie stardom but no clue how to achieve them. But her classmates were right; she was striking at five foot five, a voluptuous 125 pounds, with thick auburn hair, fair skin, and freckles. Male FBI agents, who would spend a considerable amount of time in her company during the Chaplin investigation, were both fascinated and wary. They described her as "vivacious" with a rapid speaking voice and a "very nervous" manner.[19]

As with many a starstruck teenager, Joan's dreams were fed by images of Hollywood glamour peddled in the pages of popular movie magazines like *Photoplay* and *Modern Screen*. The fan magazines featured stories about heartthrobs like Tyrone Power and Clark Gable. They chronicled the enviable life of Myrna Loy, star of *The Thin Man* movies, who, like Joan, was a beautiful redhead.[20] Joan knew she was never going to be "discovered" waiting tables at the restaurant on West Forty-Seventh Street in New York City owned by her uncles, Daniel and Arthur McLaren, or typing in some dull office, so soon after graduating, she left on the first of many back-and-forth journeys to Hollywood.[21]

Her first foray into California in 1938 was a failure. She found a three-dollar-a-week room in a boarding house in West Hollywood and began dating Mark Warner, the possibly married owner of a downtown shoe store who was likely supporting her.[22] Her pious Catholic mother would have been mortified had she known.[23] Joan still attended mass regularly in California, no matter how far she strayed from the church's teachings. Still, no amount of prayer could make her a star. She had no studio connections, no theatrical training, and so little money she could neither pay her rent nor afford decent clothes.[24] She pinched a dress from the May Company department store a week before Christmas and was arrested, prosecuted, and placed on a year's probation. At sentencing, the judge told her to go home, and she did.[25]

Back in New York City in 1939, she settled for a humdrum job in the typing pool at the Chubb insurance company. That lasted until May 1940, when she again heard the siren call of Hollywood. This time, she came prepared to get her foot in the door of a major studio. Her mother's sister Agnes McLaren, dead since 1924, had been married to Moe Marx, also long dead, whose nephew, Sam Marx, was a producer at MGM. Marx would make *Lassie Come Home* and some of the Andy Hardy movies starring young Mickey Rooney during his long career.[26]

Marx came to Hollywood from New York after his 1928 marriage to Marie Josephine Simard, a Ziegfeld girl. In 1930, his childhood friend

Irving Thalberg, who ran MGM with L. B. Mayer, hired Marx as a story editor. After Thalberg's early death in 1936, Mayer made Marx a producer.[27] Marx had an uncanny eye for talent; he was responsible for hiring F. Scott Fitzgerald as a twelve-hundred-dollar-a-week screenwriter, but Fitzgerald's drunkenness was by that time so severe he didn't last long.[28]

Joan lost no time seeking out "cousin" Sam. On a quiet Saturday in June 1940 she talked her way onto the gated MGM lot and into Marx's office to beg a screen test, playing on their distant family connection. Marx invited Joan to join his family for dinner in Laguna Beach. Over the meal, she admitted she had no acting experience and was broke. Marx told her the same thing the judge did after her shoplifting conviction—go home.[29]

This time, she didn't listen. Two nights later, as Marx and his wife were parking their car after seeing a movie, they stumbled over Joan's seemingly unconscious body on the sidewalk near their home. Marx dutifully picked her up and revived her. Her performance was hardly Oscar winning; she woke up too fast for it to be anything other than an attention-getting stunt. Joan cried that the Marxes were her only friends in Hollywood; she also claimed she had taken an overdose of sleeping pills because she wanted to die.[30] Joan's suicide attempts—real and feigned—and her wild mood swings were routine, yet nobody she came into contact with in Hollywood seems to have advised her to seek psychiatric care.

Marx gave in and ordered the screen test. Later, he was surprised to learn from the test director that Joan had artistic "fire." But turning that "fire" into marketable talent would require a makeover and a year of acting lessons, which MGM wouldn't fund. Once more, Marx advised Joan to go back to New York, and again it fell on deaf ears. After the screen test, Joan showed up at Marx's home at 601 North Foothill Road in Beverly Hills in a taxicab with an angry driver who'd chauffeured her around aimlessly before learning she had no money. Marx slipped the driver five dollars with instructions to take Joan home. A month later Marx received a phone call from Joan's landlady, who said she'd skipped out on the rent. Fed up with his distant cousin, Marx told the woman he knew nothing about it and hung up.[31]

Joan had moved on to greener pastures. She found a six-dollar-a-week room in a house she shared with occasional B-movie actress Ann Baldwin. Baldwin played bit parts in small-budget movies produced by Republic Pictures, such as *Wall Street Cowboy* in 1939 starring Roy Rogers and the aptly named *Forgotten Girls* in 1940.[32] Through Baldwin, Joan met

California oilman Jean Paul Getty, who was instantly smitten.[33] It would be a life-changing acquaintance for her, but there was one small wrinkle. In November 1939 Getty had married his fifth wife, Louise Dudley Theodora Lynch, known as "Teddy." Teddy was a lounge singer who aspired to the operatic stage and spent the early years of their marriage taking voice lessons in Europe while ignoring creeping fascism and the impending world war. With their red hair and shapely figures, Teddy and Joan could have been sisters, but Joan came from the wrong side of the tracks while Mrs. Getty was the well-connected, Paris-educated niece of financier Bernard Baruch.[34]

Getty was a skirt chaser. Although he claimed he did not "purposely start romances," he justified them, saying he had "many good women friends, and I felt that just because I was married was not a reason for me deliberately to avoid those women."[35] The FBI, which kept a close eye on Getty during the war because of rumors he was a Nazi sympathizer, took notice. Getty "is constantly 'chasing' women, regardless of his marital status," one agent wrote.[36] Getty was no Tyrone Power. When he met Joan, he was forty-eight, with reddish-brown hair, gray-blue eyes, a pencil-thin mouth, and a perpetually dour expression on a craggy face that he'd had surgically lifted. But he was five foot ten and a fit 170 pounds, wore well-tailored suits, and bragged that women were attracted to his "old-fashioned gallantry."[37] Undoubtedly, they were also attracted to his old-fashioned money. His father, George Getty, had been an attorney who in 1903 invested $500 in an oil rights lease in Oklahoma and struck oil. When he died in 1930 he left his widow and Getty, his only child, in excess of $25 million ($387 million today), which kept growing because of young Paul Getty's own business acumen.[38]

For years Getty kept meticulous diaries in little ringed leather binders. He filled these tiny notebooks with his cramped penmanship, providing quotidian evidence of his art buying and womanizing. Between September 1940 and May 1942, Getty saw Joan close to one hundred times in Los Angeles, Mexico, and Tulsa. In the notebooks, he referred to her as "Joan," "Joanne," "JB," or, for whatever reason, "Bear." The diaries stop short of describing sexual contact with Joan or with any other woman—including his wife, Teddy—for that matter. Getty steadfastly denied he and Joan had a sexual relationship, but few believed it.[39]

On one of their first dates, September 19, 1940, Getty took Joan to the Los Angeles Coliseum to see presidential candidate Wendell Willkie.[40] Joan was on Getty's arm at the popular LA dining spots of the day: Perino's, the Brown Derby, Chasen's, the Cock'n Bull, Romanoff's, and the Biltmore Bowl. He showed her off to important friends, including former U.S. senator William Gibbs McAdoo and U.S. District Judge John Francis Thaddeus O'Connor, known by his initials, J. F. T., and called "Jefty" by those who knew him.[41] The bachelor O'Connor, like Getty, quickly fell under Joan's spell. At an intimate lunch in the judge's apartment, he gave her an autographed copy of the book he wrote about serving as FDR's comptroller of the currency, *The Banking Crisis and Recovery Under the Roosevelt Administration*, a title unlikely to set a woman's heart on fire.[42]

Getty dated Joan in California until late November 1940, when he and his cousin, Howard "Hal" Seymour, climbed into Getty's Ford Mercury and drove to Mexico City at the invitation of Senator McAdoo to celebrate the inauguration of Mexican President Manuel Avila Camacho.[43] After Getty left California, Joan returned to New York ostensibly to visit her dying grandmother and to later attend her funeral.[44] But it's also likely that with her MGM screen test a bust and Getty not around to pay for meals, she was unable to make ends meet in Hollywood.

While Getty lingered in Mexico well beyond the president's inaugural festivities of December 1, 1940, Joan feared she was losing whatever hold she had on him. She phoned him on December 17 and, according to Getty's diary entry, "had nothing to say except that she hoped I would soon be in New York." Two days later she called again, looking for money. "I am afraid she has telephonitis as well as always being in financial difficulties," Getty grumbled, but he wired her emergency cash just the same.[45] Then, on December 23, 1940, Joan strolled into the lobby of Getty's hotel in Mexico City, her surprise visit probably funded by the money he'd sent.[46] Joan later would claim that Getty invited her to the Avila inaugural, which doesn't explain why she didn't arrive in Mexico until long after it was over.[47]

Joan showed up with a girlfriend and spun a tale about being en route to China to get married via Mexico City, where her future husband's brother supposedly lived.[48] She often used the "I'm getting married" ruse to incite jealousy in suitors who were insufficiently ardent. Getty later insisted he used the opportunity to remind her that *he* was already married and suggested she go back to New York.[49] But if their relationship was as platonic as he claimed, why would she have needed the reminder? Notwithstanding, Joan hung around through Christmas, and Getty seemed in no hurry to get rid of her.[50]

Getty introduced Joan to a life she coveted but couldn't afford. He brought her and her girlfriend to a Christmas Eve party at A. C. Blumenthal's place and treated them to holiday dinner the next day. Alfred Cleveland Blumenthal—"Blumey" to his friends—was a fifty-five-year-old entrepreneur on the lam in Mexico from former business partners, process servers, an ex-wife (Ziegfeld Follies showgirl Peggy Fears), and the IRS. Blumey's career as a real estate broker and theatrical producer had been in its heyday in the 1920s when he helped mogul William Fox expand his local theater holdings into a chain of nine hundred theaters in North America and the United Kingdom.[51]

The day after Christmas, Joan and her friend left for Acapulco, but Joan returned to Mexico City alone on New Year's Eve, without further mention of any future husband waiting in China. She and Getty rang in the New Year at the Ritz Hotel. Three days later, Getty drove her to the railroad station, where she boarded a train for El Paso, Texas.[52] Getty started supporting his "friend" Joan to the tune of $150 a month, or $2,600 in today's dollars. These payments continued until Chaplin put her under contract. Known for being a tightwad, Getty nonetheless also "loaned" Joan $600 to buy a car.[53]

Getty remained in Mexico for months. Joan called him every few days from New York until, on February 3, she returned—uninvited—to Mexico City. Meanwhile, Getty's south-of-the-border entourage was growing. His close friend and attorney, David Hecht, arrived from New York City.[54] Getty considered developing nine hundred acres of Acapulco beachfront into a resort and needed Hecht's legal help. Beautiful German actress-in-exile Hilde Kruger, rumored to have been Hitler's girlfriend, was also there. Joan fantasized that Getty would divorce Teddy Lynch to marry her, but it was Kruger whom Getty wanted for his sixth wife. Getty also wrote to one of his former wives, Ann Rork, and invited her to join the party in Mexico. She declined because she was in an ankle-to-hip cast following a ski accident.[55] Unfortunately, Getty's pipe dreams about Kruger were going nowhere because she only had eyes for Hecht.[56]

Hecht was born to a poor Polish Jewish immigrant family. He was short, dark, and not particularly handsome, but he wore a tuxedo well and women found him fascinating. He was single, living at the Pierre Hotel in New York City (owned by Getty), and a brilliant lawyer. A 1930 graduate of Columbia Law School, where he was editor of the law review, Hecht had represented Getty since 1936.[57] He was a formidable attorney but a soft touch. Within months of meeting Joan, she hit him up for a $200 loan, crying that her father needed an operation and her sister had run off with the money for it. Joan never paid him back.[58] Stung, Hecht dismissed Joan as a gold digger, believing she only chased Getty for the purpose of "feathering her nest."[59]

For the next six weeks, they frolicked through fancy dinners, parties, and an Artur Rubinstein concert. Getty put Joan's experience in the Chubb typing pool to good use by having her prepare papers for the beachfront deal.[60] But for all Getty's big talk about not letting marriage cramp his dating style, he grew anxious that his wife would catch wind of his fling with Joan.[61] Part of working for the oil millionaire was doing his dirty work, so Getty left it to Hecht to tell Joan to get lost. The attorney dutifully complied, but Joan didn't want to hear it.[62]

On March 1, 1941, Getty, cousin Hal, and Hecht left Mexico City and the ladies behind to enjoy five days of male bonding in Acapulco. But the next day, as the trio was headed to the beach, Joan popped up again. She had ditched Kruger at a party at two thirty that morning and hired a chauffeur to power-drive 236 miles so she could join the guys.[63] On March 13, after they were all back in Mexico City for a final week, Getty put Joan on a train to the States. A few days later he caught a boat to California, the long party finally over.[64]

A month later in California, Joan and Getty picked up where they left off. They spent most evenings together without incident until, on May 17 while dining at Ciro's, Joan became jealous of a woman who caught Getty's wandering eye, which led to an argument. They fought over money on May 26; Joan was never able to hold onto it. Four days later they sat in her car for two hours and argued again—over what, Getty never said. When they were "at last talked out," he took her for a hamburger.[65] In between skirmishes, Getty was supportive of Joan's career, driving her to perfunctory interviews at Fox studios, where she was given lines to rehearse but no roles. For her twenty-first birthday on May 24, 1941 he had planned a romantic sail to Catalina Island, two hours off the California coast, but when the day came, Getty (a serious hypochondriac) claimed his stomach hurt too much to go. Whether that was true or whether he was sick of their bickering is unclear, but he did treat her to dinner at Romanoff's as a consolation prize.[66]

Getty was unable to get rid of Joan, but the problem soon would take care of itself. Before she left Mexico in March, Joan made one final Hail

Mary pass at Hollywood. Either Joan, desperate for movie stardom, or Getty, desperate to get rid of her, convinced Blumey, whose name still opened studio doors, to send a letter of introduction on her behalf to anyone in show business who could make her famous.[67] Blumey complied. Joan Barry would never make a movie in her life, but thanks to the A. C. Blumenthal letter she would become more famous than she could have imagined.

THREE

THE LOST LITTLE TRAMP

In May 1941, Charlie Chaplin was adrift. A year earlier, he'd made his first movie in nearly five years and his first complete talkie, *The Great Dictator*. Released in October 1940, it was popular with audiences but suffered with some critics, who disliked the film's lengthy closing speech calling for peace and unity delivered by Chaplin as a Jewish barber mistaken for Adenoid Hynkel, a stand-in for Hitler.[1] Once dubbed "the first genius of the silent drama," Chaplin was now saddled with mixed reviews that stung: "an undefinable something was missing"; "Communist propaganda"; "sinks to sophomoric moments and even to dullness."[2]

After the movie wrapped, there were no new ideas percolating in Chaplin's restless mind. The more or less happy decade he'd spent with Paulette Goddard, his leading lady on- and off-screen, had come to a crashing halt. His only true friend in Hollywood for more than twenty years, Douglas Fairbanks, had died of a heart attack in 1939.[3]

Chaplin had long suffered from frenetic bursts of creativity followed by deep wells of depression. Producer Sam Goldwyn recalled that when Chaplin was in one of his black moods, he would "sit motionless in his room" for hours.[4] Today, that behavior might trigger a diagnosis of bipolar disorder, especially with his family history of mental illness. His maternal grandmother, Mary Ann Hill, and his mother, Hannah Hill Chaplin, cycled in and out of what were then called "insane asylums."[5]

Most stories about Chaplin's youth focus on his poverty, which provided the authenticity for his Little Tramp character and explained why

Chaplin could be tight with a dollar once he made it big. But Chaplin's family was comfortable when he was born on April 16, 1889, in South London. His parents made a decent living onstage.[6] Yet, by 1895, the family was on a downward slide, first to smaller, shabbier apartments, then to the workhouse, largely due to Chaplin's mother's madness and his father's alcoholism.[7] It taught Chaplin that the rug could be pulled out from under a man in real life as quickly as it could in a slapstick movie.

Charles Chaplin Sr., Charlie's father, had been a popular music hall singer in Victorian England.[8] There were some five hundred music halls in turn-of-the-century London, which staged variety shows at prices the working classes could afford.[9] Hannah, who performed as Lily Harley, married Charles Sr. in June 1885, when she was just shy of twenty years old and he was twenty-two, but their marriage didn't last. Four years later, she gave birth to their only son, Charlie.[10] Just weeks before they'd married, Hannah had given birth to Sydney, or Syd, as he was called, who was the son of another man. During her marriage to Chaplin's father, she had an affair with a fellow stage performer, Leo Dryden, and gave birth to his son, whom Dryden raised.[11] Chaplin had no memories of living with his father, and Charles Sr. only supported his family sporadically.[12]

As the twentieth century approached, Hannah Chaplin would be institutionalized repeatedly.[13] Her breakdowns were precipitated by depression, violence, hallucinations, and incoherence.[14] Her condition may have been hereditary, but at least one contemporary medical diagnosis suggests syphilis, which, if true, could have caused the symptoms she suffered as well as headaches, altered behavior, and dementia.[15] When she improved, she was released to eke out a living—which by then consisted of taking in mending and selling off her old stage costumes—but without today's antipsychotic medications or a social safety net, she would decline, and the family would shuffle off to the workhouse, an institution alluded to with dread in Dickens's novel *A Christmas Carol*.[16]

The British workhouses, a product of the Poor Law Amendment Act of 1834, were supposed to feed and house the destitute but served mostly as punishment for poverty. They were overcrowded, unsanitary, and brutal. Food was scarce and the death rate was high. Inmates, as the residents were called, were put to work breaking rocks.[17]

Even worse for seven-year-old Charlie was his forced separation from his mother by welfare workers who whisked him and Syd off to the Hanwell School for Orphans and Destitute Children. The school provided clean clothes, decent food, and an education, but it was a cruel place that Chaplin loathed.[18] Syd hated it, too, but escaped because he was old enough to join a navy training program.[19] Chaplin recycled the most traumatic events of his life for his movies, and social service functionaries like those who stuck him in Hanwell would get their due in his 1921 classic, *The Kid*, and again in 1936 in *Modern Times*, where they were portrayed as heartless destroyers of the family bond.

The vicissitudes of his mother's illness, his father's absence, and the lack of government assistance would haunt Chaplin for the rest of his life and leave him in a state of permanent insecurity. When Chaplin was nearly nine, he was released from Hanwell to his mother, then in one of her lucid periods. But the revolving door of mental hospitals and the Lambeth Workhouse continued to spin; months later, in September 1898, Hannah was locked in a padded cell at the Cane Hill Asylum, and child welfare workers were demanding that Chaplin Sr. step up to support his son.[20] The elder Chaplin's idea of stepping up was to put young Charlie to work as a clog dancer with "The Eight Lancashire Lads," where the boy earned half a crown a week, or about 2.5 shillings at a time when a rental apartment was about 5 shillings a week.[21] The exhausting gig lasted two years, until Charlie came down with debilitating asthma.[22] Chaplin Sr.'s boozing finally killed him in 1901. He died penniless at the age of thirty-seven of cirrhosis of the liver.[23]

Utterly alone, little Charlie hustled. He sold flowers, newspapers, and old clothes on the streets. He ran errands for a shopkeeper and worked as a glassblower, a printer, a receptionist in a doctor's office, and a dance instructor. What he did not do was attend school regularly; as he approached adolescence, he was barely literate.[24] Visions from Chaplin's uncertain childhood were splashed across the screen in the misfortunes that befell the Little Tramp. He seemed to come from nowhere, live with no one, and have no place to go. All of the resourcefulness that Charlie used to survive on the streets of Edwardian England was embodied in the Tramp character he created. The Tramp could eat by pinching food from a vendor's cart (*A Dog's Life*). He could cheat in a prizefight by slipping a horseshoe into his boxing glove (*The Champion*). And he could pose as a foreign dignitary to impress a girl (*Caught in a Cabaret*).

Eventually, Syd returned from life at sea to take care of Charlie. With their scant education and lack of marketable skills, the Chaplin brothers turned to the occupation in their blood—the stage. Shy, undersized

Charlie made the rounds of the theatrical agencies as his parents once had done. In 1903, Charlie landed a role as a pageboy in the popular play *Sherlock Holmes*. Because Charlie's reading skills were poor, Syd fed him his lines so his little brother could memorize them. Meanwhile, Syd scored a job with Fred Karno, director of the Fun Factory studio, England's leading producer of music hall comedy sketches, and convinced Karno to take on Charlie.[25]

At Karno's Fun Factory, nineteen-year-old Charlie found romance for the first time with fifteen-year-old Hetty Kelly, a fellow vaudevillian. Always impetuous when it came to women, he proposed four days after they met. She pooh-poohed the idea, arguing they were too young; she later died in the 1918 worldwide influenza epidemic.[26] Future biographers attributed Chaplin's lifelong obsession with young girls to his subconscious desire to resurrect that lost love with Hetty. There may be a grain of truth in that, but it may also be that his traumatic childhood stunted his emotional growth and that his mother's illness and the family's resulting financial ruin attracted him to young, vulnerable women he thought he could rescue in a way he couldn't save his mother.

While on tour in the United States with Karno, Charlie starred in the popular skit *A Night in an English Music Hall*, where he played a drunken dandy who stumbles into a theater after the curtain goes up and tries but fails to quietly take a seat in the audience. Mack Sennett, head of Keystone Pictures and dubbed "the King of Comedy," claimed to have "discovered" Chaplin when he saw the skit in 1912 at the American Theatre on Forty-Second Street and Eighth Avenue in New York. Sennett tracked him down and offered him a one-year movie contract at either $125 a week, if you believe Sennett, or $150 a week, if you believe Chaplin.[27]

Although he signed the contract, Chaplin was underwhelmed by the Keystone comedies.[28] They had minimal plots and invariably ended with the actors being chased by the Keystone Cops and ducking cream pies. "We made funny pictures as fast as we could for money," Sennett later wrote.[29] Sennett spewed out 140 movies a year.[30] Despite his distaste for them, Chaplin was a visionary who saw the untapped potential of the medium. He mastered the technical skills of moviemaking. With that foundation, he harnessed his innate talent, boundless curiosity, and unique worldview to create comedies that surpassed everyone else's and paved the way for the development of modern cinema. As Chaplin biographer David Robinson explained, "The crucial point of Chaplin's comedy was not the comic occurrence itself, but Charlie's relationship and attitude to it." This set Chaplin apart from other early cinematic funnymen and "was the essential factor in Chaplin's almost instant and world-wide fame."[31]

It wasn't until after the release of *Making a Living*, on February 2, 1914, that Chaplin developed the beloved Little Tramp, whom Chaplin always called the "Little Fellow," by donning oversized pants, an undersized jacket and hat, a bamboo cane, and a little black mustache.[32] Chaplin biographer Joyce Milton summed up the Tramp's appeal: "The character personified the eternal loser, struggling to keep up appearances and preserve a modicum of human dignity."[33] In his only year at Keystone, Chaplin made thirty-five movies and directed nineteen of them.[34]

With Sydney driving the contract negotiations and renowned copyright lawyer Nathan Burkan on hand with legal advice, Chaplin's career took off.[35] In 1915, he moved to the Essanay Film Manufacturing Company of Chicago for $1,250 a week and the promise of a $10,000 bonus.[36] In 1916, he signed with the Mutual Film Corporation for $10,000 a week and a $150,000 bonus, with the understanding he'd deliver twelve pictures.[37] In 1917, he accepted a $1 million deal with the First National Exhibitors Circuit, a whopping $26.6 million today. That same year, he built his own film studio on the corner of North La Brea Avenue and Sunset Boulevard in Hollywood and took pride in knowing he now had to answer to nobody.[38] In 1919, he formed United Artists with Fairbanks, Mary Pickford, and D. W. Griffith to distribute their films without a middleman.[39] Chaplin became one of the wealthiest and, because of the ubiquity of the movies, best-known men on earth.

Out from under "the King of Comedy," Chaplin could do what he wanted, which was to stop cranking out silly slapstick with lightning speed and start developing movies with pathos and plot—as well as a lot of laughs. The glacial pace at which he moved drove his UA partners crazy because they needed product to distribute to make money, and it infuriated his leading ladies eager to be seen in his next movie to further their careers.[40] But Chaplin, the gloomy genius, needed time to develop character and plots and do as many takes as necessary to achieve perfection.

Chaplin's own enigmatic personality did—and did not—resemble the Little Fellow's. Pickford called him an "obstinate, suspicious, egocentric, maddening, and lovable genius of a problem child. . . ."[41] He was a left-handed, chain-smoking, violin-playing loner, who supposedly slept with two thousand women.[42] Wealthy beyond his wildest dreams, he saved pencil stubs.[43] A relentless autodidact determined to make up for lost schooling, Chaplin waxed eloquent to a journalist about his imagined ideal day: "I go to my library and live with the great abstract thinkers—Spinoza, Schopenhauer, Nietzsche and Walter Pater."[44] Yet strewn over his bed were copies of *True Detective*.[45] He had a hair-trigger temper, would explode when things didn't go his way, and, despite all his money, short-changed Uncle Sam on his taxes.[46]

Chaplin's first order of business at Essanay was to assemble his own stock company, filled with actors willing to accommodate his eccentric directing style. For the male roles, he chose actors who'd had film or vaudeville experience. But his pattern for the next thirty-five years would be to select young, inexperienced, and unknown leading ladies. He wanted to mold them to his way of doing things and if they were so inclined—and they usually were—to sleep with them. The first was nineteen-year-old Edna Purviance, a petite San Francisco secretary with wavy blond hair, a gorgeous smile, and big blue eyes.[47] She was the perfect protégée—she knew nothing about acting and Chaplin could play Pygmalion to her Galatea. Their first movie, *A Night Out*, was released in February 1915.

Chaplin and Purviance shared an easy, on-screen chemistry in thirty-three movies.[48] They shared off-screen chemistry too. She once made him very happy, and he seriously considered marrying her.[49] But they drifted apart, their relationship undermined by Chaplin's wandering eye, Purviance's jealousy, and her drinking habit.[50] But their parting initiated another Chaplin pattern: taking up with girls barely out of adolescence. At age twenty-nine, he married seventeen-year-old actress Mildred Harris because he thought she was pregnant. Although still working alongside Chaplin, Purviance learned about the September 23, 1918, wedding by reading about it in the newspaper.[51] Heartbroken, she poked her head out of her studio dressing room the day after and whispered, "Congratulations," to Chaplin as he walked by.[52] Whether out of loyalty or guilt, he kept Purviance on his payroll until she died in 1958, even though she never made another movie for him after *A Woman of Paris* in 1923.[53]

As happened in his romances, Chaplin grew bored with Harris. Further, the pregnancy turned out to be a false alarm. Harris did get pregnant eventually and gave birth to a severely deformed son, Norman, who died within days, but it did nothing to solidify the marriage.[54] By November 1920, they were divorced.[55]

Chaplin was a selfish and cavalier lover. In 1926, he described his ideal woman in an interview with *Vanity Fair*: "I am not exactly in love with her, but she is entirely in love with me."[56] Georgia Hale, who costarred with Chaplin as the dance hall girl in *The Gold Rush*, also had a romance with him and described it as "whimsical, imaginary and unreal." She complained that he could turn his affections "off or on with the bat of an eye. And he did."[57] His only true love was his craft. "Charlie doesn't really care about anything but his work," remarked his second wife, Lita Grey. "He hates anyone who interferes."[58]

It would have behooved Chaplin to be more careful with women in light of the Harris disaster, but instead he became more reckless. Like in his moviemaking, where he started with the germ of an idea and developed the story as the camera rolled, in life, he went where his adventures took him, with no thought about endings or consequences. In 1924, with her mother looking over her shoulder, Lillita McMurray, fifteen, signed a contract to play the original dance hall girl in *The Gold Rush*. She'd caught Chaplin's eye when she was twelve and had a supporting role as the angel vamp in the dream sequence of his earlier gem *The Kid*.[59] Over the objection of his longtime cameraman, Rollie Totheroh, who found nothing photogenic about the chubby-cheeked adolescent, Chaplin plowed ahead, changing her name to "Lita Grey" and preparing to make her a star.[60]

But Chaplin hadn't shot more than a few scenes when he seduced her and she became pregnant. Panic stricken, Chaplin tried to buy her off with $10,000 and the address of an abortionist, and when that failed, a $20,000 dowry she could bestow on some other groom. But Grey's uncle, a lawyer, threatened to have him prosecuted for statutory rape, so in November 1924 their secret shotgun wedding took place in Empalme, a dusty Mexican town six hundred miles from Los Angeles.[61] Afterward, on the bleak train ride back to California, the thirty-five-year-old groom told some of his guests, including his attorney Nathan Burkan, "Well, boys, this is better than the penitentiary; but it won't last long."[62] He was right; they divorced in 1927 after she bore him two sons, Charles Jr. and Sydney. The dissolution of their union was so acrimonious that he refused to mention her by name in his autobiography, devoting just three sentences to their miserable marriage.[63]

Lita, on the other hand, couldn't say enough about it. Her forty-two-page divorce complaint contained allegations so salacious about Chaplin's sexual preferences and his multiple extramarital affairs that it was hawked on the streets for twenty-five cents a copy.[64] The nearly $2 million it cost him in alimony, child support, and legal fees to get out of the marriage, plus the humiliation of having the world know about his fixation on oral sex, sent Chaplin plunging into another of his depressions, this one so profound that he fled to New York for seven months, suffering a nervous breakdown in his lawyer's Fifth Avenue penthouse overlooking Central Park.[65]

Burkan extricated him from his marriages to Harris and Grey and protected the actor's fortune in the process. In the first divorce, Harris had sought an injunction to stop Chaplin from disposing of the distribution rights to *The Kid*, which she contended were community property, until Burkan negotiated a $200,000 settlement.[66] The second, with Grey threatening to make public the names of Chaplin's lovers, including "a prominent motion picture actress" (William Randolph Hearst's mistress, Marion Davies), was more problematic. Temporary receivers from the Los Angeles County Court took control of Chaplin's bank accounts and safe-deposit boxes and posted guards at this studio while Chaplin ducked service of the divorce papers by slipping aboard a train for New York.[67]

With big brother Syd watching over Chaplin's financial interests, it was left to Burkan, connected to New York City's Tammany Hall, to take care of his legal ones. When Chaplin sued an author for writing a magazine profile of him without his consent, when the IRS slapped liens against him for back taxes, and when a U.S. marine filed a copyright infringement suit against him claiming authorship of Chaplin's World War I hit *Shoulder Arms*, Burkan took care of all of it and still had time to represent mobster Frank Costello in federal court for running a $25 million liquor-smuggling ring during Prohibition.[68]

And just as his personal life was spinning out of control thanks to the Lita Grey revelations, his professional life fell into turmoil. On October 6, 1927, Warner Brothers' eighty-nine-minute movie *The Jazz Singer*, starring Al Jolson, had its New York premiere. The film had only a few lines of dialogue and five songs, but the public went wild.[69] Chaplin wanted nothing to do with "the talkies." As a silent screen icon, the Tramp had universal appeal, but once he spoke, the spell would be broken. More to the point, if the Tramp were to talk, would it be in the working-class dialect echoing the social strata from which he came or in the King's English that the striving Chaplin struggled so hard to perfect?

Bucking the trend, Chaplin soldiered on in silence, which was one advantage of owning his own studio. Four years after *The Jazz Singer* opened, Chaplin stubbornly released another silent tour de force, *City Lights*, in which a blind flower girl mistakes the Tramp for a millionaire. But the tumultuous decade had taken its toll. After finishing *City Lights* in January 1931, Chaplin closed up shop and left on an extended trip to Europe and the Far East with his brother. He would not return to Hollywood for a year and a half, leaving behind girlfriend Georgia Hale without so much as a postcard.[70]

The hiatus didn't help. A month after returning, Chaplin was still moping over talking pictures, the worldwide economic Depression, and a dry spell for female companionship after Hale had rightfully told him to get lost. To cheer him up, UA president Joseph Schenck invited him aboard his 138-foot yacht, usually populated by an available young woman or two. Chaplin went, hoping to find a new love interest there.[71] He did: the beautiful, vibrant (and, at that time, gum-chewing, platinum blond) Paulette Goddard, a divorcée in her early twenties, which by Chaplin's standards was too old. But Chaplin, in his own way, was ready to settle down.[72] At forty-one and middle-aged, Chaplin finally had met a grown woman who was smart, fiercely independent, and ambitious. In his unreliable, heavily self-censored autobiography, Chaplin would base their attraction on their mutual "loneliness."[73] But they had much in common; she was exactly like him, minus the clinical depression.

Goddard would become Chaplin's muse, leading lady, lover, best friend, and *maybe* his wife. Rumors of a marriage surfaced almost immediately after they began dating. But for a reason known only to them, they refused to confirm their marital status. Nevertheless, she moved into his Beverly Hills mansion at the top of a winding road at 1085 Summit Drive.[74] Best of all, she became a loving stepmother to his sons. Charles Chaplin Jr., who was six when Paulette came into their lives, said of her, "We lost our hearts at once, never to regain them through all the golden years of our childhood."[75]

Goddard's first steps on the professional stage had been in Flo Ziegfeld's legendary chorus line. She didn't last long; shortly before her seventeenth birthday Goddard eloped with Edward James, the wealthy president of the Southern States Lumber Company in North Carolina. A few years later, in 1932, she filed for divorce in Reno, Nevada, citing "mental indignities," and walked away with a $375,000 settlement, or $7 million today.[76]

She drove off into the sunset toward Hollywood in a new Duesenberg.[77] When she met Chaplin, she was under contract to the Hal Roach studio, producer of the *Our Gang* comedies and Laurel and Hardy movies, where she was being groomed to be the next Jean Harlow. Chaplin had more refined ideas for his new lady friend. He bought out her contract, signed her to his studio, dyed her hair back to its natural brunette, and wrote a juicy role for her in *Modern Times*.[78] The movie was inspired by Chaplin's growing radicalization through friendships with left-leaning intellectuals and socialist émigrés. Although funny, the movie exposed the evils of capitalism.[79] It would be the last appearance on-screen of the Tramp, who in the final frame walks off hand-in-hand with Goddard. It was Chaplin's belated acknowledgment that talking pictures were here to stay and that it was time for the Little Fellow to retire. He might also have been trying a mature relationship on for size.

Goddard lit up the screen like a firefly in *Modern Times* as a scruffy, homeless waif using her wits and charm to survive. "[T]here is unusual promise in her work—perhaps more than in the instance of any other Chaplin leading woman," wrote critic Edwin Schallert in the *Los Angeles Times*.[80] With the release of the film in 1936, Goddard's career was smoking, and in a town where youth in women was paramount, she needed to strike while it was hot. But Chaplin, who moved like a snail, hemmed and hawed for an idea for his next feature, "Production Number 6," oblivious to Goddard's desire to get back on-screen. Instead, he planned a surprise five-month trip to Hawaii and the Far East for the two of them and Goddard's mother, never once communicating with his sons while he was gone.[81] He claimed he and Paulette got married there, although no marriage certificate has ever surfaced.[82]

A year later, not one reel of film had been shot on "Production Number 6," and Chaplin still hadn't a clue what it would be about.[83] Tired of waiting for inspiration to strike her man, Goddard did what none of his prior protégées dared; she signed a contract with Selznick International Pictures, determined to keep her career going with or without Chaplin. David O. Selznick was in the midst of a highly publicized, worldwide search for an actress to play Scarlett O'Hara in *Gone with the Wind*, and Goddard desperately wanted the part.[84]

For most of 1938, Goddard was laser-focused on Scarlett, much the way Chaplin was when he was making a movie. She made nine screen tests—more than any other actress—and was Selznick's first choice for the most coveted role in Hollywood history.[85] Popular wisdom has been that the ambiguity of her marital status with Chaplin caused her to lose it. It was, after all, the 1930s, and Selznick couldn't afford to invest millions in a female star whose possible sinful living arrangement might hurt ticket sales in the Bible Belt. But if Selznick had misgivings about anything other than Goddard's suitability for the role, it's more likely he feared locking horns with the notoriously difficult and litigious Chaplin, who still expected Goddard to star in his next movie. In the end, the role went to Vivien Leigh, whose own affair with the very married Laurence Olivier didn't stop Selznick from signing *her*.[86] Finally, on September 9, 1939, ten months after Goddard's last screen test to play Scarlett O'Hara and the same month that Hitler invaded Poland, Chaplin began shooting what would become *The Great Dictator*.[87]

A year later, on October 15, 1940, warp speed for Chaplin, *The Great Dictator* premiered simultaneously at two New York theaters, the Astor and the Capitol. H. G. Wells, former New York governor Alfred E. Smith, Franklin D. Roosevelt Jr., Mayor LaGuardia, and Mr. and Mrs. Joseph P. Kennedy turned out to see it. Chaplin greeted the celebrity-filled audiences and the fans with Goddard at his side, her dazzling beauty enhanced by Chaplin's gifts of a huge diamond solitaire ring and a pair of matching heart-shaped earbobs.[88] After eight years of playing the coy game of "Are-they-or-aren't-they married?" Chaplin proudly introduced Goddard as his wife.[89] The couple posed for photographers in the lobby of the Astor at the start of the picture and dashed six blocks north to the Capitol in time for the opening credits under a "lights-and-sirens" police escort.[90] Crowds lined the streets between Broadway and Eighth Avenue to catch a glimpse of the celebrity couple.[91] Later, they danced cheek to cheek in a New York City nightclub, Chaplin in a tuxedo and Goddard in a glimmering gown.[92] It was like a fairy tale.

And that's what it was. Five days after the premiere, Goddard quietly went back to California alone.[93] Chaplin rented a posh apartment on the East River and remained in New York for four months.[94] While Chaplin dithered in New York, Goddard packed up her belongings and moved out of the home they'd shared for nearly a decade. As Chaplin would later bemoan, once Goddard was gone the house was "very sad."[95]

The loss of Goddard was a staggering blow on top of others that had piled up over the last twenty years. In spite of all the money, fame, adulation, and artistic success, Chaplin was headed into what today would be called a full-fledged midlife crisis. At fifty, his doppelgänger, the Little Fellow, was gone, and he had no on-screen persona with which to replace him. Too young to retire, he needed to begin the grueling work of going back to the drawing board to develop a new idea in this new medium of sound pictures, which was not his forte.

Control, so important to Chaplin, seemed to be slipping away. Certainly his marriage to Goddard, if indeed it was that, which had been his only successful one so far, had collapsed, and there was nothing Chaplin could do about it. When it was finally over, he said, simply, that it was "inevitable" that he and Goddard would part.[96] But it wasn't inevitable to Goddard, who puzzled over the breakup for years. She told a newspaper columnist in 1969, "We never quarreled. . . . Then I just went one way and he another. . . ."[97]

About to head back to California, Chaplin, who never knew how any of his pictures would end when he started them, was ready to go wherever real life took him. But at loose ends in this sad and lonely state, he was a sitting duck for trouble. The next scene should have been obvious. He was about to meet a new protégée, and history would repeat itself, but this time there would be a stunning plot twist and an even unhappier ending.

FOUR

"A BROOKLYN STENOGRAPHER"

Chaplin left his unhappy house on the cloudy Sunday afternoon of May 25, 1941, to give the eulogy at a memorial service for Doug Fairbanks, who was laid to rest beneath a new $40,000 marble mausoleum at Hollywood's Memorial Park, two years after his death of a heart attack. At the cemetery, Chaplin escorted Fairbanks's young weeping widow, Lady Sylvia Ashley, on his arm. Although Fairbanks was linked in the public mind with Mary Pickford, their sixteen-year marriage had ended in divorce three years before Fairbanks's death. Chaplin's own wife, Paulette Goddard, was nowhere to be seen among the fifteen hundred mourners.[1]

The mercury hit 81 degrees, but the heat didn't wilt Chaplin, who was resplendent in his flawlessly fitting, dark wool suit and doused in Mitsouko, the musky women's fragrance he always wore.[2] In his remarks about the dashing star of *The Thief of Bagdad* and *Robin Hood*, Chaplin called Fairbanks "the epitome of knightly courage and romance." He bid his friend farewell by reciting lines from *Hamlet* inscribed on the casket: "Good night, sweet prince, and flights of angels sing thee to thy rest."[3]

Fairbanks's memorial service was a sign that another chapter in the story of Old Hollywood had come to an end. Outside the insular universe of movies and make-believe, life also was moving on, for better and for worse. Just ten days earlier, New York Yankee Joe DiMaggio began what would be his historic fifty-six-game hitting streak, a 1941 record never to be broken.[4] Europe was at war and Chaplin's native London had just emerged from the Blitz—eight months of nightly aerial bombing by the

Nazis that began in September 1940 and lasted until May 1941, leaving nearly twenty-nine thousand civilians dead.[5]

After leaving the cemetery, Chaplin unwound on his tennis court with Tim Durant.[6] The two had bonded over their mutual love of the game and the months they'd spent together in Pebble Beach in 1938 when Chaplin was paralyzed by writer's block after *Modern Times*.[7] Durant's pedigree couldn't have been more different than Chaplin's. A Connecticut Yankee, Durant was a bon vivant with a Yale degree and connections to the uber-wealthy.[8] In his early forties, Durant was six foot two and athletically fit at 160 pounds, while Chaplin was a decade older, nearly a foot shorter, and getting thick across the middle.[9] Following their game, they showered, dressed, and were chauffeured to Perino's, an Italian restaurant on Wilshire Boulevard popular with the movie colony, for a double date arranged by Durant. One of the women, Joan Berry, was anxious to meet the great director.[10]

For Joan, whose twenty-first-birthday cruise to Catalina the day before had been ruined by Paul Getty's bellyache, an intimate dinner with Charlie Chaplin was a dream come true. By this third go-round in Hollywood, she was forced to face a harsh reality: the town was flush with women waiting to be "discovered" for the silver screen. Without the backing of a powerful studio head, she hadn't even been able to score the standard six-month, seventy-five-dollar-a-week, renewable option contract. Lucky "option girls" landed roles as extras in crowd shots while awaiting their big break; the not so lucky ones were passed among producers as window dressing for cocktail parties and stag events until the next new crop came to town.[11]

More than eighty years later, with none of the players still alive, how Joan Berry became Joan Barry and ended up on Charlie Chaplin's casting couch comes mostly from the files of the Los Angeles County District Attorney's Office, the Federal Bureau of Investigation, and the Immigration and Naturalization Service—agencies that investigated Chaplin during the four decades he lived in America. But law enforcement didn't start looking into Chaplin's behavior involving Joan until the summer of 1943, two years after they'd met and a year after they'd separated, by which time those interviewed had scores to settle or reputations to protect. Chaplin never spoke to the DA or to the FBI, probably on advice of counsel. Chaplin wrote about Joan Barry in his autobiography, published in 1964 and described by one of his biographers, Peter Ackroyd, as a "self-serving account replete with inaccuracies and evasions."[12] Ironically, Getty's contemporaneous diaries seem more reliable about the Barry-Chaplin romance because they were written without any thought they'd ever be public. Getty's main worry at the time was sanitizing them from his wife's prying eyes.

Joan's first interview with the FBI wasn't until she recovered from the birth of her daughter, who was born on October 2, 1943. Her account of how she met Chaplin is rambling, repetitive, and in some aspects as unbelievable as parts of Chaplin's autobiography. She told agents that when she returned to California from Mexico in 1941, Durant dutifully contacted her thanks to the A. C. Blumenthal letter. She said she played hard to get, which is hard to believe given that she was jobless, broke, and desperate to be in pictures. When she finally agreed to meet Durant for a drink, she said he tried to steal a good-night kiss. That part was certainly true; she was young and pretty, and men in Hollywood felt entitled to take advantage of starstruck ingenues. She said she pushed him away because she was not that kind of girl—at least not with men she didn't think were as wealthy as J. Paul Getty, for whom she still carried a well-lit torch. She said Chaplin's name never came up that first night.[13]

Durant spoke to investigators from both the Los Angeles County District Attorney's Office and the FBI. He said Joan was a relentless, and ultimately annoying, aggressor. She called him and raced over to his house as soon as she hit Los Angeles. She made a good impression, he said. In other words, she was attractive enough to be introduced to Chaplin.[14] Yet despite vetting her for the great director, Durant took umbrage whenever government investigators suggested that he was Charlie's pimp. "My main function was to keep women away from Chaplin," he snapped.[15]

Joan was so excited about her first date with Charlie Chaplin—whom she called "Charles"—that she couldn't keep from gushing about it to Getty, who made a note of it in his diary.[16] On the big night at Perrino's, Durant and his date bowed out early, leaving Chaplin and Joan behind, where they sat chatting at their table until closing. Afterward, Joan said Chaplin's chauffeur drove the couple to and from the beach for hours while they continued talking. Joan dropped Getty's name, complained that Hollywood was "a cruel town," and fell back on her wedding ruse, claiming she was returning to New York. Chaplin stroked her ego, praising her nascent acting ability and claiming he could tell she had talent just by hearing her talk.[17] For his part, Chaplin wrote in his autobiography years later that they had a charming but uneventful evening and that he had no intention of seeing her again.[18] Nonetheless, she said he gave her his phone number, a fact Chaplin implicitly confirmed in his autobiography by writing that shortly after meeting him she called him to invite him to lunch.[19]

A week after they met, Durant brought Joan to Chaplin's Sunday afternoon tennis party. There, she sipped tea poured from a sterling silver pot, picked turkey finger sandwiches and crumpets from a three-foot-tall platter, and mingled with the A-list movie crowd.[20] Joan continued dating Getty while Chaplin kept company with other women, among them Goddard, Carole Landis, and Hedy Lamarr.[21]

But Joan's romance with Getty was on the rocks. The night after her first date with Chaplin, she and Getty dined at the Brown Derby, and they got into an argument about money—she needed it and he didn't want to give her any. Getty described the dispute as so "unpleasant" it left him tossing and turning all night.[22] It upset Joan, too, sending her to Durant's apartment at three o'clock in the morning in a state of hysteria and possibly drunk to cry on his shoulder, although she barely knew him.[23] A week later, Getty sent her a dozen roses as a peace offering.[24] The following Saturday night, June 7, Joan had a seven thirty dinner date with Getty at Lindy's but cut it short after an hour to see Chaplin.[25]

Between films and with plenty of time on his hands, Chaplin invited Joan to join him on Wednesday, June 11, 1941, a beautiful day with sunny skies and a warm breeze, for a ride to an auction in Goleta, about an hour north of Los Angeles.[26] While the chauffeur kept his eyes on the road, Chaplin kept his eyes on what he strangely described in his book as Joan's large "upper regional domes," which he could easily ogle because of her "extremely low décolleté summer dress" that "evoked my libidinous curiosity."[27] In plain English, he couldn't keep his hands to himself. Joan spent most of the ride fending him off, using "boyfriend" Getty as the excuse and reiterating her plan to return to New York.[28]

But those "domes" did the trick. The night after the auction Joan phoned Getty with the exciting news that Chaplin was going to offer her a movie deal.[29] Mixing business with pleasure, they began dating regularly, although Chaplin blamed the romance on *her* persistence and habit of popping over to his house unexpectedly at all hours.[30] Regardless, they enjoyed each other's company. While Getty was out on the town on June 19, 1941, with his third ex-wife, Fini, he saw the couple at Mocambo's, then the new Hollywood nightclub where live exotic birds flapped around during performances.[31]

Joan's signed her contract on Monday, June 23, 1941—a standard, six-month, seventy-five-dollar-a-week contract with the Charles Chaplin Film Corporation—using the name "Joanne Berry."[32] Joan promptly repaid "Charles" with sex. "I might add here that Chaplin's success in this regard was due to his verbal persuasiveness," she told the FBI. He supposedly told her he was madly in love and tagged her with the pet name "Hunchy."[33]

Falling head over heels with impressionable young women was Chaplin's modus operandi, which may be how he lured those two thousand women into his bed. British journalist Alistair Cooke, who befriended the comic in the 1930s, wrote that whenever a woman attracted Chaplin, "he would soon be as deep in intimacy as Macbeth was in blood." Cooke attributed this to Chaplin's "egocentricity" and his need to wow women "with . . . his charm, humor, talent, knowingness, and—which was a little less impressive to anyone used to thinking—his intellect."[34] Proving Cooke's point, dancer May Reeves, Chaplin's companion in Europe from April 1931 until March 1932, wrote in her autobiography that they ended up in her hotel suite the first night they met and the morning after Chaplin told her, "I love you as I've never loved anyone."[35]

Regardless of what Chaplin told Joan, to the world he still had a wife, and despite Goddard having moved out of their house, they remained on friendly terms. On June 30, a week after Joan signed her contract, the *New York Times* ran a photograph of a relaxed and contented-looking Paulette and Charlie enjoying an after-dinner coffee at a restaurant on Santa Catalina Island with the headline "Mr. and Mrs. Charles Chaplin On Vacation." Joan told investigators that Chaplin took her away to Catalina on his yacht, the *Panacea*, a week after she signed with his studio, which is belied by the picture. Chaplin did spend four days on the boat between July 6 and 10, 1941—which may be when he took Joan.[36]

When Chaplin chose leading ladies with little or no acting experience, it was because his insightful eye saw something unique in them. Yet his enthusiasm for Joan Berry—soon to be "Barry"—left some industry insiders scratching their heads. Durant thought she looked like "a Brooklyn stenographer," and Alf Reeves, general manager of the Chaplin studio after years with him at Karno, found her ordinary.[37] Still, Durant believed Chaplin's interest in Joan was real. "He was genuinely fond of Miss Berry and sincerely interested in her career as an actress," Durant told FBI agents.[38] Durant claimed to have had qualms about Joan's emotional stability from the beginning. He said she was extremely jealous of anyone Chaplin associated with and, when the relationship wasn't going her way, threatened to run off and get married. "There were always scenes like that as time went on. Always very embarrassing and very disturbing."[39]

Once Chaplin signed Joan, he spent no small sum preparing her for stardom in "Production Number 7," which was as yet undetermined. In addition to her $75 weekly salary (raised to $100 six months later), Chaplin paid for three months' dramatic training with Max Reinhardt at $65 a month. He paid $500 to a dentist to straighten her teeth. He spiffed up her wardrobe with $1,186 (about $20,800 in today's dollars) in new clothes from the May Company, where she'd been caught shoplifting three years before. He gave her $180 for two months' rent for an apartment on Shirley Place in Beverly Hills.[40] But Joan lived beyond her means and continued to hit him up for cash—$150 here, $200 there—just as she had done with Getty and David Hecht.[41]

And like Goddard before her, Joan waited—and waited—for Chaplin to find a suitable vehicle for her still unproven talent. Unlike Goddard, whose burning ambition drove her to use the waiting time to her own great advantage—working so hard at dancing lessons that she was able to credibly partner with Fred Astaire in *Second Chorus* in 1940—Joan idled away most of 1941. To occupy her time, she let Getty entertain her. Throughout the summer and autumn of 1941, they went to the movies and the beach and made their way through LA's popular eateries: Mocambo's, the Ontra Cafeteria, Romanoff's, the Biltmore Bowl, the Cocoanut Grove, and Lindy's.[42] But Joan wasn't eating much as she waited for stardom. "She is dieting (or starving) for pictures," wrote Getty in his diary on August 24. "Weighs 124, normally 144."[43]

Soon after Joan signed with Chaplin, her mother, Gertrude, came from New York to live with her. Gertrude's nearly fifteen-year marriage to John Berry was on its last legs; his occupation as a traveling salesman turned out to be a cover for passing bad checks. The cops were looking for him and he was on the lam.[44] Gertrude had failed to do her due diligence before she married him in 1927. He had a rap sheet going back to 1909 that spanned half a dozen states. A bunco artist, John Berry had used multiple aliases to write bogus checks on nonexistent bank accounts, peddle stolen goods, and swindle hoteliers.[45]

But mother and daughter were like oil and water. The piously religious Gertrude was domineering and appalled by her daughter's promiscuous behavior with men. All they had in common was their shared love of alcohol and their penchant to go at one another when they had a few too many.

Nonetheless, Joan's mother was enchanted with her daughter's dazzling new Hollywood life and her connection to wealthy, powerful men. And Joan was only too happy to have her mom around for company. On occasion, Getty entertained them both and found Gertrude "charming."[46]

Joan tried to stay out of Chaplin's hair because he was updating *The Gold Rush* for the sound era, but they spent many nights together. "We were both very much enamored of each other," she told FBI agents.[47] So enamored that by September 1941 she was three months pregnant. Chaplin and Durant pressured her to have an abortion.[48] Durant, who arranged it, and Dr. Arthur Maurice Tweedie, who performed it, denied any involvement, but the evidence suggests they were lying.[49]

Dr. Tweedie was an abortionist with offices at 3326 West Fifty-Fourth Street in Los Angeles.[50] An obstetrician-gynecologist in California since 1914, by the 1940s his practice was strictly the termination of pregnancies.[51] He'd lost his medical license in 1937 for performing what were then euphemistically called "criminal operations," but it was reinstated two years later after his empty promise to stop doing them.[52] "In Hollywood, abortions were an open secret and everyone seemed to have a friend of a friend who could help," wrote Cari Beauchamp in *Without Lying Down: Frances Marion and the Powerful Women of Early Hollywood.*[53]

Actresses routinely had abortions; male studio heads insisted on them to protect their investments in the women's careers. Public relations flacks provided bogus medical excuses as cover. Jean Harlow, pregnant by William Powell, star of *The Thin Man* series, was hospitalized for a "rest." Jeanette MacDonald's abortion was labeled an "ear infection." Joan Crawford, Judy Garland, Ava Gardner, Lana Turner, and Dorothy Dandridge all had abortions.[54] The operation could be dangerous. It was performed with a long spoon-shaped instrument called a "curette" that scraped tissue from inside the uterus. Even a trained doctor could accidentally perforate the uterine wall, causing life-threatening bleeding or infection.[55] Joan endured two abortions by Dr. Tweedie. After the first, she needed to have her uterus "flushed out," probably because it was not completely cleared of tissue, and after the second, performed when she was only a few weeks pregnant in January 1942, she complained of excessive bleeding.[56]

But Joan was lucky; she survived. In June 1942, the Los Angeles County district attorney filed murder charges against Dr. Tweedie for killing a woman on the operating table. Later, he was quietly permitted to plead to lesser assault charges.[57] When District Attorney John F. Dockweiler sought court approval for the sweetheart plea deal, he said that because Dr. Tweedie's patient had died from anesthesia given *before* the procedure "the only fair conclusion" was that the doctor had not yet decided whether to perform the abortion.[58] With this tortured logic, the DA asked the court to spare the doctor a life sentence, and the judge complied, imposing a six-month jail term followed by three years' probation. Dr. Tweedie was being treated with kid gloves, although the state medical licensing authorities again revoked his license.[59] But recognizing that he'd had a close call, Dr. Tweedie burned all his patient records and ended his practice.[60]

The first time Joan visited Dr. Tweedie, she was so ambivalent about terminating the pregnancy that he refused to do it.[61] But Durant, acting as Chaplin's fixer, warned Joan that a pregnancy scandal would end her movie career before it started and warned Chaplin it could hurt him, too, given his shaky history with women.[62] Longing for stardom and a permanent place in Chaplin's life, Joan dutifully returned to Dr. Tweedie's. After the abortion, she recuperated on a cot at his medical office for about five days, cared for at night by a high school student nurse, Jeanette Voris. While there, Joan talked her ear off about her imminent stardom. "She was a difficult person. I recall that she was very high-strung and that she was very excitable and hard to manage," Voris said.[63]

Dr. Tweedie would forever deny performing an abortion on Joan Barry or on anyone else, hardly credible given his arrest, plea deal, and license suspensions. And Durant's denials that he had anything to do with any abortion were absurd; too many witnesses contradicted him. One of Dr. Tweedie's nurses recalled Durant visiting Joan at the medical office while she was convalescing.[64] Former Chaplin butler Edward Charles Chaney told the FBI that after Joan revealed to him that she'd had an abortion, he asked Durant about it, and Durant told him not to worry because, he explained, "That was paid in cash."[65]

After she recovered, Joan turned to Getty—although his diaries are silent about any abortion—because Chaplin was still busy updating *The Gold Rush*. And Chaplin was also busy with other women. On November 5, Getty spotted him at the Mocambo with Hedy Lamarr and Durant but no sign of Joan.[66] Nonetheless, by the 1941 holiday season, Joan and Charlie were together again. They dined together almost every night, either at Romanoff's or at Chaplin's home. He supposedly told Orson Welles that he was in love with her, and he extended her contract.[67] After taking her to a party in November at Jack and Ann Warner's, where Joan enviously eyed famous women in luxurious furs, she whined for one too. He sent Joan and her mother to the May Company, where they charged an $1,100 silver fox coat to Chaplin's studio account.[68] Like the rest of Chaplin's employees, Joan received a $1,000 Christmas bonus. He invited her to holiday dinner at his home, where she entertained his family by reading from the play *Shadow and Substance*, which he later bought for her movie debut. But before the tinsel came off the tree, Joan learned she was pregnant again.[69]

This time, there was no fuss about returning to Dr. Tweedie. But afraid her mother would find out, she used her Christmas bonus to send her mother to Reno to end her unhappy marriage to Joan's stepfather. Joan deposited Gertrude in Nevada on January 2, 1942, to establish the necessary six weeks of residency to be able to file for an uncontested divorce, and then Joan returned to California alone.[70]

Once again, Durant made the arrangements. Chaplin's chauffeur drove Joan to and from Dr. Tweedie's office on January 8. As soon as Joan walked in, Voris groaned, "Oh no, not again."[71] With Joan barely pregnant, the second procedure went quickly, without anesthesia. She insisted on going back to Chaplin's that same night, against Tweedie's orders. When it was clear she wouldn't listen, the doctor sent Voris with her. When they got to Chaplin's home, he greeted Joan with a hug. Joan went upstairs to the room that adjoined Chaplin's, which the household still called the "Paulette Goddard Room," while Chaplin and Voris chatted downstairs. Curious as to what they were discussing, Joan eavesdropped. She said she heard Chaplin say, "I know it's my fault, but then I suppose it is a 50–50 proposition. But . . . I will never let her go through it again. The strange part is that all I have to do is look at her and she gets pregnant."[72] Voris denied that the conversation took place when she later spoke to law enforcement officers. She said that Chaplin simply asked after Joan's health and made small talk about his plans for her career.[73]

A decade later, Voris told a darker version of the story to INS investigators looking to bar Chaplin from the country. She said that Chaplin had told her that Joan slept with other men, too, and suggested one of them may have gotten her pregnant. He also complained to the young nurse that while he was working hard to make Joan a star, she was ruining it by failing to "behave herself."[74] Voris was in high school when Joan had her abortions and must have been frightened to death by cops asking questions about her involvement in what was then a serious crime. When she spoke to the INS a decade later, Dr. Tweedie was already dead and too much time had passed for Voris to be prosecuted. She had far less to lose by telling the truth.

Whichever version of Voris's story is more accurate, Joan's is not credible at all. Having gone to great lengths to leave the abortion arrangements to Durant, Chaplin wouldn't have admitted to a high school girl whom he'd never seen before that he got Joan pregnant. The first time Joan told this to investigators was on January 7, 1944, two years after the fact. By then, Chaplin was married to Oona O'Neill and denied being the father of Joan's three-month-old daughter. Joan was jealous and probably angry. By telling the FBI agents that Chaplin admitted getting her pregnant twice and that he paid for her abortions, she was incriminating him in a crime.

But the mere fact that Chaplin had talked to Voris at all did not sit well. "Joan called up (Dr. Tweedie's office) the next day and was raising Cain. She was insanely jealous because I stayed about 15 minutes too long downstairs," Voris told investigators for the Los Angeles District Attorney's Office.[75]

After Joan's second abortion, Chaplin's concern about her health lasted about a week, but her convalescence at his Summit Drive home ended badly. She and Chaplin got into an argument about the abortions, and she said she would "not go through one of those things again." Joan claimed that Durant, present during the fight, told her he was sick and tired of her "antics" and slapped her. When she tried to hit him back, Chaplin grabbed her hands to stop her.[76] "This time that Tim hit me at Chaplin's is only one of many times," she said.[77] Durant countered by telling the FBI that Joan was a "psychopathic liar" and borderline insane. He attributed her allegations to the fact that she was "embittered" because he was counseling Chaplin to dump her.[78] That may be, but men who hit women rarely admit to doing so. And, because Durant knew she was telling law enforcement agents that he arranged for her abortions, it behooved him to do what he could to undermine her credibility.

Despite all the drama in his household, Chaplin finally finished updating The Gold Rush and sent it to UA in New York for distribution on January 14, 1942. With only a week or so of downtime, he turned his full attention to "Production Number 7," his showcase for Joan. By Friday, January 23, Joan had recovered sufficiently to go to Western Costume on Melrose Avenue, adjacent to the Paramount lot, to be fitted for maid's outfits for movie stills. Joan was photographed in thirty-two poses in simple work dresses. Her hair was pinned up in a bun and she wore little, if any, makeup. The overall effect is of a plain and simple girl with lovely skin—easily the look of a young Irish housekeeper.[79]

The following Monday, Chaplin directed Joan in a seven-hour silent screen test, photographed by his longtime cameraman, Rollie Totheroh. After looking at the 3,510 feet of film that Totheroh shot of Joan, Chaplin liked what he saw.[80] He was ready to plunk down good money for the rights to *Shadow and Substance*, the play Joan had read so beautifully to his family at Christmas, and make her a star.

FIVE

"ONE GIRL IN HOLLYWOOD"

Why Chaplin got such a bee in his derby about adapting Paul Vincent Carroll's play *Shadow and Substance* is puzzling. Written in 1937, the play is set in the parlor of the Dublin parish house of the self-aggrandizing, cantankerous Rev. Thomas Canon Skerritt. A rebel schoolteacher writes a blasphemous critique of the church under a pseudonym, which inflames parishioners who want to stone the author to death. While the canon wrestles with a more appropriate punishment, he takes comfort in Brigid, his simpleminded servant girl who talks to visions of her dead namesake, the martyred Saint Brigid.[1] The girl is either blessed or out of her mind.

Throughout the play, dim-witted church members drop in to bend the canon's ear about petty matters when he would rather be left alone to enjoy fine art and wines and bask in Brigid's devotion to her faith and to him.[2] It is unfortunate that Chaplin had tired of the Little Fellow because the slapstick potential of visitors coming in and out of the canon's parlor—perhaps through swinging doors—was enormous. Playing it for laughs, Chaplin could have reprised his sidesplitting 1923 role as an escaped convict posing as a man of the cloth in *The Pilgrim*.

Instead, Chaplin convinced himself that Brigid was a modern-day Joan of Arc and that *his* Joan was destined to portray her.[3] This was hardly a compliment. The playwright described the character as "possibly a little stupidlooking" and "obviously not mentally outstanding. . . ."[4] Chaplin's studio manager, Alf Reeves, agreed that casting Joan in the role was brilliant. He said she was "erratic, emotional, hard to talk to, and could easily effect a vacant stare in her eyes." He added, "[T]his last mannerism of hers was ideally suited for the part in the picture."[5]

Sinclair Lewis and Sir Cedric Hardwicke, the latter having starred as Canon Skerritt onstage, had pitched the play to Chaplin.[6] Author Paul Carroll drove a hard bargain for the rights: $20,000 in cash, clipper passage to the United States, and a three-to-six-month employment contract with United Artists.[7] With a war on, Carroll likely wanted out of Europe and needed a job to get a visa, but Chaplin wanted no part of a meddling playwright on set. Carroll settled for a flat $20,000—a staggering $318,000 in today's dollars—and nothing more.[8] The deal was closed on March 4, 1942.[9]

Immediately, Chaplin sent Joan to train for the part. From mid-March through June 23, 1942, she was enrolled at Max Reinhardt's acting workshop. Reinhardt, born in 1873 in Austria, was celebrated for his elaborate productions of Shakespeare, Molière, and the ancient Greek dramatists. He had fled the Nazis in 1933, and in 1937 he won his drama school in a Las Vegas poker game.[10] The school trained serious actors, and it infuriated Chaplin when he learned that Joan's attendance had been sporadic.[11] He thought she had innate acting ability that would blossom with an experienced teacher. "She has a quality, an ethereal something that's truly marvelous. A talent as great as any I've seen in my whole life," Chaplin remarked to his sons, Charles Jr. and Sydney.[12]

With his purchase of Shadow and Substance, Chaplin finally had a project for her, but after Joan's second abortion, he put the brakes on their sexual relationship—with occasional lapses—perhaps out of fear he'd end up in a third shotgun marriage. As her affair with Chaplin cooled, Joan shifted her attention back to Getty. She saw him briefly on January 19, 1942, but rekindling that romance was thwarted by his leaving California.[13] After the attack on Pearl Harbor, Getty felt a patriotic call to arms, but being forty-nine and plagued by physical maladies—real and imagined—his hope of becoming an officer in the United States Navy was little more than a pipe dream. He traveled to Washington, DC, to lobby military officials all the way up to Navy Secretary Frank Knox for a commission.[14] Knox convinced him he would better serve his country by stepping up production of military planes at the Getty-owned Spartan Aircraft Company in Tulsa, Oklahoma. Accepting the challenge, Getty determined to "take charge myself and get it working at top speed."[15] He immediately left for Oklahoma and remained there for most of 1942.[16]

With Getty gone, her sex life with Chaplin a fraction of what it was, and still no sign he would film *Shadow and Substance* anytime soon, Joan fell victim to her impetuosity. She circled back to Sam Marx at MGM to show off her new teeth and improved acting technique.[17] She asked Marx to give her a second shot at a screen test, but he refused because MGM would not test a player under contract to another studio. So on May 22, 1942, she wrote to Reeves instructing him to terminate her contract "inasmuch as there will be no activity here for some time, I perhaps could do better on my own somewhere else."[18] Her unilateral action shocked Reeves, who tried to stop her, going so far as to beg her mother to talk sense into her. But Gertrude Berry, surprisingly, stayed out of it. She told him that Joan was twenty-one and "if she wants to break the contract that is up to her."[19]

Coincidentally, two days later, on Joan's twenty-second birthday, a column by syndicated gossip writer Hedda Hopper appeared in the *Los Angeles Times*. It began: "This is written for just one girl in Hollywood. It may be you over there, you with the auburn hair."[20] Joan, with her distinctive red hair, had been seen hanging on Chaplin's arm at nightspots for months. Hopper was clearly fishing for a scoop; word had gotten out that Chaplin was to begin a new movie, and she was keeping her fingers crossed that the mystery redhead would take the bait and call her after reading her column.

Hopper's column prophesied that a package labeled "Fame" was coming to this unknown woman, courtesy of Charlie Chaplin. She wrote that the lucky lady would enjoy limousines and luxury. But she warned that as he'd done in the past, Chaplin would move on once their film was finished and her fledgling career would be over.[21] Hopper was at the height of her power in the 1940s—her column was published in eighty-five big-city newspapers, three thousand small-town dailies, and two thousand weekly publications.[22] A right-wing zealot, she loathed Chaplin's politics and was disgusted by his affairs with young women. It also irked her that unlike other cowed Hollywood personalities who lived in fear of her poison pen, Chaplin, as an independent producer, could—and did—ignore her.[23] For the moment, Joan ignored her too and left town.

On May 29, 1942, Joan showed up in Tulsa. Getty entertained her with dinners at Bishop's Restaurant on Main Street, a Tulsa institution, and took her to see the Bette Davis and Olivia de Havilland movie *In This Our Life*.[24] On June 2, he was glad to put Joan on an afternoon American Airlines flight to Los Angeles.[25] During her brief visit, she apparently never revealed that she had broken her contract with Chaplin, but Getty suspected something was up: she was thinner and more nervous than usual. She also tried to squeeze money out of him, which annoyed him after what he called her "grand lady" talk about her success in Hollywood.[26]

Meanwhile, now that she was a free agent, Marx set Joan up with a screen test at MGM. But after angling so hard to get it, she inexplicably skipped rehearsals and avoided setting a shooting date.[27] Marx came to regret reengaging with Joan. One day, she phoned him crying uncontrollably and threatening suicide. Fearing for her safety, Marx raced to her apartment and saw that her face was bruised. She accused unnamed persons at Chaplin's of beating her. While bitterly complaining about her treatment, Joan was diverted by a phone call. Deciding there was no emergency, Marx left.[28] The next day, Tim Durant called in an imitation "gangster style" warning him that Joan was "Chaplin's girl" and reminding Marx, "You're a married man and you had better lay off. I'm telling you to stay away."[29] The men got into an argument and hung up on one another. If Marx's claim about the Durant call is true, it tends to support Joan's allegations that someone at Chaplin's had assaulted her.

Meanwhile, Chaplin's public behavior was raising eyebrows in 1942. Shy and proudly apolitical ("I have never voted in my life!"),[30] Chaplin became the celebrity spokesman for a campaign to open a second European battlefront to help the Soviets defeat Hitler. It was a position widely supported by Communists, their sympathizers, and, in fairness, others who were neither. Chaplin's first opportunity to speak on the topic came in May when former U.S. ambassador to the Soviet Union Joseph E. Davies became too ill to address a rally in San Francisco. Chaplin agreed to a last-minute request to fill in from the American Committee for Russian War Relief. Fueled by too many glasses of champagne and irritation with prior speakers who voiced weak support for Russia, Chaplin greeted the audience as "Comrades!" It shocked both the crowd and the press and set the stage for future allegations that Chaplin was "Red."[31]

Joan's MGM screen test finally was scheduled for July 22, 1942. But on that day Chaplin gave another Second Front speech to sixty thousand union members in Madison Square Park in New York City via a long-distance phone hookup from the NBC studios in Hollywood.[32] Chaplin invited Joan to the broadcast studio to hear him speak, which caused her to miss the screen test. That was the last straw for MGM, which did not reschedule it. Joan seemed oblivious to the lost opportunity; she was elated that Chaplin had invited her to be with him during the broadcast and that they were on good terms again. That evening, Joan, her mother, Chaplin,

Durant, and Minna Wallis, a high-powered talent agent and sister of Hal Wallis of Warner Brothers, went to a concert of opera arias and duets at the Hollywood Bowl.[33]

If Chaplin really invited Joan to NBC and she didn't stalk him there, he might have been trying to put the kibosh on her MGM test so she could make *Shadow and Substance*. Chaplin's studio continued to pay Joan until September 26, 1942, four months after she broke her contract, which seems to indicate he still wanted her for the role. Joan may have become intolerable as a romantic partner, but they could still make a beautiful movie together. Chaplin had no love for Virginia Cherrill, his leading lady in *City Lights*. "I never liked Charlie and he never liked me," Cherrill told a Chaplin biographer fifty years after the film was finished. But *City Lights* was—and is—a triumph.[34]

But inevitably, the prospect of making *Shadow and Substance* became intolerable too. Chaplin claimed Joan turned his life into a "nightmare."[35] She drove drunk to his home in her Cadillac (bought by Getty) in the middle of the night, once smashing the car in his driveway. Chaplin hated the telephone and loathed unannounced visitors, but Joan phoned Chaplin constantly and showed up at his house frequently. When he refused to answer the door, she smashed the windows and broke in.[36]

At some point that autumn, Joan and Chaplin had it out. She wanted to leave Hollywood to return to New York with her mother and wanted him to pay their train fare and toss in another $5,000. Chaplin said he agreed to her demands and was happy to see her go.[37] Joan denied making any such demands. She said things were fine between them when "one day, out of a clear blue sky, he said, 'Joan, you can go to New York.'" She claimed he did so because he knew he was going to New York to make another Second Front speech shortly thereafter, which she interpreted as his wanting her to be there with him.[38]

Neither story is completely true. When Reeves showed the studio books to FBI agents investigating the Chaplin-Barry affair, there was no $5,000 expenditure for Joan. And things were rarely fine between them. Chaplin's butler Edward Chaney would later tell the district attorney: "[T]hey sit for 10 minutes and talk and get in an argument."[39] Joan needed love, constant attention, and reassurance and was getting none of that from Chaplin.

As he had done in past relationships, Chaplin initially had fallen head-over-heels for Joan and then quickly lost interest, leaving her to deal with the pain of rejection, multiple abortions, and the loss of the chance to become a movie star. Joan's attention span was equally short, and it was coupled with indecision, restlessness, and substance abuse. She couldn't decide between Chaplin and Getty, between the Chaplin Studio and MGM, or between California and New York.

Her restlessness was such that while in California between May 1941 and June 1943, she'd lived at the Ambassador, Biltmore, Beverly Hills, Beverly House, Hollywood Roosevelt, and Chateau Elysee hotels. When not in hotels, she moved between apartments and rooming houses, one step ahead of the landlord. When Chaplin was paying the rent or she was on salary to his studio, she lived in apartments on Shirley Place and Robbins Drive in Beverly Hills. When on her own, she landed in rooming houses on Hobart Street, Franklin Avenue, and North Sycamore Street. Minna Wallis compared her to "a little stray alley cat" everyone "felt sorry for." Yet when she repeatedly called Wallis in the middle of the night to cry on her shoulder about Chaplin, Wallis's sympathy evaporated. "She is a mad woman, really she is. I think she is a little cracked," Wallis told the FBI.[40]

But Sam Marx, who provided Joan with money, companionship, and possibly sex, was kinder. Having spent years at the most prestigious movie studio in Hollywood, Marx had seen how cruel the industry could be to women. She reminded him of a "typical girl who came to Hollywood for a film career and when the career slipped through her hands it caused her to do many things that she undoubtedly would not otherwise have done."[41] By the fall of 1942, Joan was more vulnerable than most; she was emotionally fragile and financially insecure with neither a career nor a wealthy man to support the lifestyle she craved.

Joan had been angling to return to New York ever since she cancelled her contract and her MGM screen test failed to pan out. Perhaps it was meant as a wake-up call for Chaplin to start focusing on her. Joan swept up her mother and left Los Angeles for New York by train on October 2, 1942, using one-way tickets paid for by Chaplin. He also gave Joan a check for $500, not $5,000.[42] Arriving in New York on Tuesday, October 6, Joan stayed for two days with her mother at her aunt Catherine McLaren's brownstone at 630 West 158th Street, a three-story building in the center of a hilly residential block in a neighborhood today known as Washington Heights.[43] On October 8, she checked into the Waldorf Astoria hotel. Joan later told the FBI that she stayed there at Chaplin's behest, suggesting—in her mind, at least—that he wanted to meet her there. It is more likely that

Joan checked into the Waldorf because she knew that's where Chaplin stayed when he was in New York.[44]

Once at the Waldorf, Joan placed a long-distance call to Chaplin in Beverly Hills, only to learn from the butler that he was on a date with gorgeous Jinx Falkenburg, Miss Rheingold Beer of 1940 and a supermodel before the term existed.[45] Infuriated, Joan worked the phones to scare up a man with whom she could make Chaplin jealous. She found one: David Hecht, the Getty lawyer she had cavorted with in Mexico.[46]

Hecht was still an eligible bachelor, living full-time at The Pierre, a luxury hotel. Slender, five foot nine, with thick dark hair that he combed straight back, Hecht wore black tie as often as other men wore a necktie. Dressed to the nines, he made the rounds of the chicest nightclubs in New York, enjoying the fact he would be seen on the town, which he thought would serve him well with wealthy clients.[47] It was at one of those nightclubs that Joan told Hecht the woeful tale of her roller-coaster romance with Chaplin. Hecht demonstrated a sufficiently strong shoulder to cry on to convince her to pack her bags and decamp for The Pierre.[48] She checked out of the Waldorf the next day and was given Room 3808–9 at The Pierre, where she stayed until October 25. Her bill came to $247.69, or about $3,920 in today's dollars.[49] As she was leaving, she instructed the management to send the bill to Chaplin, who returned it—unpaid. The hotel then presented it to Hecht, who wouldn't pay it either, signaling that whatever may have happened between them at The Pierre, his feelings for her didn't run deep.[50]

Chaplin and Durant left for New York by train from Los Angeles at 4:30 p.m. on October 12.[51] Chaney, Chaplin's butler, accompanied them, carrying a pocketful of blank checks from the Chaplin Studio in case the boss needed money. Arriving on October 15, the trio went straight to the Waldorf, where Chaplin and Durant checked into Suite 38-F, consisting of a living room and two bedrooms. The butler was stuck in a separate small room, 2615.[52]

Joan called Chaplin at the Waldorf as soon as he arrived and kept calling, but only Chaney would speak to her.[53] She begged the butler for a pair of tickets to Chaplin's Second Front speech at Carnegie Hall, which was scheduled for October 16. Chaney had tickets sent over even though seats were scarce.[54] Later, when U.S. Attorney Carr was considering whether to indict Chaplin for violating the Mann Act, these facts should have given him pause. If Chaplin lured Joan across the country for sex, he should have gladly taken her calls, reserved a room for her at the Waldorf, and set aside tickets for her to attend his speech.

Joan showed up at Carnegie Hall with Hecht on her arm. The program, scheduled to begin at 8:30 p.m., droned on for hours, with Chaplin not getting onstage until 10:45 p.m. He spoke for twenty-five minutes, extolling the virtues of Stalin's call for a Second Front. "[I]f Stalin wants it, the idea must be good," he proclaimed.[55] Joan and Hecht spent the evening bellied up to the bar and missed most of Chaplin's speech.[56] Later at the Stork Club with Hecht, Joan noticed Chaplin and Durant sitting with others and stopped by his table, where he introduced her to his guests and allegedly told her that he hoped to see her later that evening.[57]

For someone who supposedly wanted to see her, Chaplin made little effort to do so. Joan's calls to the Waldorf were making his flesh crawl, he wrote years later, and he was ready to instruct the hotel operator to block them until Durant's cooler head prevailed. He convinced Chaplin that if he blocked her calls, she would show up at the hotel and make a scene.[58]

Instead, Durant's solution was to invite her to join the two of them for dinner. On October 19, she cut short a date with Harry Cooper, her clothing salesman (to whom she owed $800, a bill Getty would eventually pay), to meet Chaplin and Durant at the 21 Club, the venerable restaurant at 21 West Fifty-Second Street, a few blocks from the Waldorf.[59]

Around midnight, they all returned to Chaplin's suite, where Durant bid the couple goodnight, went to his bedroom, and closed the door. According to Joan, the small talk turned to Chaplin's desire that she return to Hollywood to star in *Shadow and Substance*, and he offered her $300 to come back, which she said was insufficient. With this issue unresolved, Joan said they retired to his bedroom for sex. If true, was he tempting her to come back to California, trying to get her mind off his money, or just taking advantage of an opportunity? At about three o'clock in the morning, while Chaplin was escorting her back to The Pierre in a cab, she told him she was destitute. He agreed to give her money, and later that day Joan returned to his hotel, where he handed her an envelope with $300 inside. She ran to the Forty-Second Street office of the Southern Pacific Railroad, bought a train ticket to California, and was back on the West Coast by the afternoon of November 2, checking into the Beverly Hills Hotel later that day.[60]

Chaplin left the Waldorf and New York at 6:00 p.m. on October 27 and arrived in California three days later. Despite the alleged pillow talk about wanting Joan back as his leading lady, there is little evidence Chaplin intended to revive *Shadow and Substance*. His secretary, Catherine Hunter, spent only one more day—November 12—working on it, and by December 29 the production was officially shelved.[61] By then, Chaplin had moved on to an idea suggested by Orson Welles about a French serial killer who murdered rich lonely women by posing as a wealthy widower seeking a new wife.[62]

And if Joan came three thousand miles to be Chaplin's leading lady, she seemed in no hurry to get before the camera. She spent most of her time partying with socialite Joine Alderman, whom Joan and her mother had met in Palm Springs the year before. Alderman, the privileged daughter of an attorney, had been the manager of the Palm Springs Tennis Club and was now the hostess at the Beverly Hills Hotel.[63] Alderman for a long time had sponsored gatherings with prominent thinkers and artists. The weekly salons had featured such luminaries as conductor Leopold Stokowski, director Frank Capra, actor Basil Rathbone, and, ironically, Max Reinhardt and Charlie Chaplin.[64]

While out with Joine, Joan talked incessantly about her punctured romance with "Charles." To cheer her up, Alderman introduced her to new beaux including Jimmy McHugh, a movie songwriter known for *I'm in the Mood for Love* and *On the Sunny Side of the Street*, and Hans Ruesch, a wealthy expat Grand Prix auto racer sidelined by an accident.[65] Joan also continued to keep company with the married Sam Marx.[66]

But Joan would not leave Chaplin alone. Three days after returning to California she called Chaplin, who sent her mixed signals by asking her to dinner at Romanoff's with the proviso that she not drink beforehand. Yet on the night of their date, November 8, she spent four hours getting drunk with Ruesch before meeting Chaplin. Furious, Chaplin broke up with her for good.[67] Distraught, Joan took an overdose of sleeping pills back at her hotel. A doctor was summoned (probably by Alderman), Joan was revived, and a nurse was assigned to keep an eye on her. But Joan promptly escaped and headed to Summit Drive. She tried to break into Chaplin's house, and when she couldn't get in she lay outside the front door and then in front of one of the cars parked in the driveway, but nobody inside the house paid any attention.[68]

Figuring that Joan had probably headed to Chaplin's, the nurse called his house and was told Joan was outside, so she drove over to retrieve her. With Chaney's help Joan was loaded into the nurse's car, only to bolt again. She was then pulled off the lawn of Chaplin's neighbor, David O. Selznick, and taken back to the hotel.[69] The next day the hotel evicted her and was left holding a $249 unpaid bill.[70] When he called Chaplin for the money, the manager was told she was no longer under contract to the studio. As so often happened when Joan was out of money and out of luck, Getty came to the rescue and instructed his Tulsa attorney Claude Rosenstein to pick up the tab.[71] But even Getty had his limits: he refused to pay the Beverly Hills Hotel another $70 to cover the medical bills for her suicide attempt and would not make good on a $500 bad check she tried to pass off on a local clothing store.[72]

Joan's next stop was Elaine Barrie's sofa. Barrie was the fourth ex-wife of actor John Barrymore. While on a date at the Mocambo with Getty in April 1941, Joan had become ill and rushed to the ladies' room, where she met Barrie, who, seeing that Joan was in extremis, shoved a slip of paper with her name and number into Joan's purse. It is unclear where Barrie was living in November 1942 because she had recently sold the mansion she had shared with Barrymore in West Los Angeles. Joan stayed with Barrie just two days, during which time they phoned Chaplin repeatedly, but only the butler would take the calls. Joan also called Sam Marx, but he wouldn't speak to her either. Desperate and down to her last fifty-seven dollars, she boarded a bus for Tulsa and on November 17 checked into the Mayo Hotel there.[73] Before she left California, Joan bumped into Minna Wallis outside a bank in Santa Monica and told her she was going to Tulsa to marry Getty's lawyer, presumably David Hecht. It was her same old lie and one she probably hoped Wallis would pass on to Chaplin in the hope it would make him jealous.[74]

When she arrived in Oklahoma, Joan's first order of business was to write a heartfelt letter to "Charles." "My brain is in a turmoil," she wrote. "You were right—I'm crazy and inarticulate." She ended with the wish that he was with her and signed it "Good night, dear. Joan."[75]

Working the phone in Oklahoma, she called Getty to say she was in town on her way to New York. Getty was reluctant to see her because he was afraid she was looking for money.[76] Nonetheless, he conquered his fears and took her to Bishop's for another steak and then to a movie. The next day, Joan called Getty at his factory to say goodbye, but she didn't leave. Instead, she sat in her hotel room and wrote again to Chaplin to apologize for acting "unbalanced." She described the torture she felt because she couldn't get close to him and said she was on the way to New York to get married, with "no clothes, no car, no money."[77]

Joan lingered in Tulsa, where the weather was cold and dreary, seeing

Getty two more evenings, until Monday, November 23, when he put her on an afternoon train to Kansas City (with only three minutes to spare before it pulled out of the station), presumably so she could head to New York for the upcoming Thanksgiving holiday.[78] Through Rosenstein, Getty took care of bills she racked up in Tulsa.[79] But rather than go to New York, Joan returned to Los Angeles, checking into the Biltmore Hotel on November 26, Thanksgiving Day.[80] Alone on Thanksgiving, Joan pathetically placed a call to Chaplin's house, only to learn he was out of town. He had gone to Chicago to make another Second Front speech the day before, and from there he would be in New York to be honored at an "Arts for Russia" dinner at the Hotel Pennsylvania on December 3. He would not return to California until December 10.[81]

The day after Thanksgiving, Joan checked into the Ambassador Hotel in Los Angeles under the name "Joan Barratt." She remained there through December 7, running up a $226 bill. She whiled away the next few weeks cultivating a relationship with Ruesch and a new man, Lionel Vasco Bonini, a thirty-one-year-old Italian wine merchant who had fled from his home country in 1939 on the eve of war in Europe.[82]

On Thursday evening, December 10, the night Chaplin came home from New York, Joan and Ruesch were dining at The Players Club—a celebrity hangout in the shadow of the Chateau Marmont hotel—where Chaplin was seated at another table with a beautiful blond whom Joan did not know as well as with director King Vidor and his wife, Elizabeth Hill.[83] A few days later, "exceedingly upset," Joan went to a pawnshop, Rosslyn Loan & Jewelry at 459 South Main Street in Los Angeles, and purchased an automatic handgun. Whether she planned to use it against Chaplin, the beautiful blond, or herself is unknown. No matter because she promptly lost or misplaced the weapon.[84]

A few nights later, Joan and Ruesch returned to The Players Club. While they were on the dance floor, Joan noticed Chaplin having dinner there with one of his tennis buddies. At the end of the evening, after dropping Ruesch at his apartment, she drove to Summit Drive to force Chaplin to speak with her. Venturing up the steep hill to his house, she saw a light on and knocked at his door. This time, Chaplin answered, and they chatted on his sun porch, where Joan said he asked her to rate him as a lover. When she said Ruesch was better than he was, which she claimed to have said to make him jealous, Chaplin allegedly became violent and physically attacked her. "During all this time I was crying and from his actions and mannerisms, I believe the man was crazy at that time. He was insane. He was cursing me with all the words that he knew," she said. Despite what she described as a brutal beating, she never reported it to the police, never sought medical attention, never revealed it to any of her friends, and was able to drive home in her own car.[85]

If it really happened, it still wasn't enough to keep her away from Chaplin. In the days that followed, Joan called him daily, but he refused to speak to her. Increasingly agitated, Joan resolved to confront Chaplin one last time. But first, she went to the Hollywood Gun Shop at 5216 Hollywood Boulevard to buy an inexpensive, but reliable, .25-caliber German Ortgies pistol. This gun she would not misplace or lose. Like her father before her, she planned to blow her head off. She would do it at Chaplin's house. "[I was] thinking that when I got up there I would kill myself right in front of him."[86]

SIX

"I WANTED TO HURT CHARLES THE WAY HE HAD HURT ME"

While Joan contemplated her dramatic exit, another woman—or, more accurately, another girl—entered Chaplin's life, the beautiful, seventeen-year-old estranged daughter of Nobel Prize–winning playwright Eugene O'Neill. Dark-eyed, raven-haired Oona O'Neill was nomadic, popular on the New York nightclub circuit, attracted to wealthy, older men, and marginally interested in a movie career.[1] A lot like Joan, without the histrionics.

Oona was born in Bermuda on May 14, 1925, to O'Neill and his second wife, writer Agnes Boulton, who it was rumored had once had a fling with Chaplin.[2] Oona's parents separated when she was three—Eugene having dumped Boulton for actress Carlotta Monterey. The embittered couple battled over alimony, leaving Oona and her brother, Shane, with a prestigious surname and not much else. Eugene O'Neill remained on the margins of his children's lives—writing them occasional letters but showing little interest in seeing them. Eventually, he even stopped writing letters.[3]

Boulton and her children bounced around. Oona attended public and parochial schools in New Jersey and Key West, Florida, and a prep school in Warrenton, Virginia.[4] Agnes moved to New York City and enrolled Oona in the prestigious private Brearley School.[5] Busy with her own romantic adventures, Agnes exerted little supervision over her daughter's education or social life.[6]

With other underage girlfriends, Carol Marcus (future wife to William Saroyan and Walter Matthau) and heiress Gloria Vanderbilt, Oona made the rounds of nightclubs while still in high school. In 1942, Oona was named "Debutante-of-the-Year," a title bestowed by the Stork Club's legendary owner, Sherman Billingsley, as much to trade on her famous name as to recognize her charms. Her outraged father called her a "nitwit."[7]

Oona was admitted to Vassar, but she eschewed the dull academic life for the glitter of New York nightlife. On a rare visit to Tao House, her father's twenty-two-room home in the San Francisco Bay area town of Danville, she told her stepmother, Carlotta, that her goal was to marry a rich man (she would later claim she was only kidding).[8] O'Neill refused to have anything more to do with her once he learned she was skipping college.[9] For her part, Oona remained obsessed with winning her father's attention and was bereft over his rejection, which explains a lot about her attraction to Chaplin, who was her father's contemporary.[10]

After graduating, Oona dabbled in modeling and summer stock, making her stage debut in July 1942 at the Maplewood Theatre in New Jersey.[11] That didn't sit well with her father either, and when she asked him to pay for dramatic school he blew his top. He said that he'd heard through the grapevine that his daughter had no talent, and he considered her desire to go onstage a way to avoid the hard work of obtaining an education.[12]

That summer, Oona chaperoned Carol Marcus's visit to Sacramento to see her fiancé, Saroyan, then in the army. Agnes Boulton was living in Los Angeles and working on a screenplay, so Oona moved in with her, making the rounds of the studios and represented by Minna Wallis, the powerhouse agent who had discovered Clark Gable.[13] Surely the O'Neill name was the reason Wallis represented her, but even that couldn't launch poor Oona's career. She bombed her screen test at Columbia and fared no better at Fox.[14]

O'Neill and Chaplin met in November 1942. Chaplin later wrote a romantic we-locked-eyes-across-the-room kind of story about their meeting at a dinner party at Minna Wallis's (whose name he misspells as "Mina Wallace" in his autobiography), arranged so the agent could foist Oona on him to replace Joan in *Shadow and Substance*. Arriving early, Chaplin came upon Oona sitting quietly before the fire and was captivated by her beauty and serenity. At just seventeen, she was far too young to tackle the complex role of Brigid, Chaplin believed, but just the right age to become his next girlfriend. He was fifty-three.[15]

Chaplin's longtime cameraman, Rollie Totheroh, recounted a more down-to-earth version of their meeting. He said Oona had Chaplin in her sights before the Wallis dinner, and her determination to meet him was an uncomfortable reminder of how Joan Barry operated. O'Neill approached Totheroh on the street as he was coming back from lunch one day and told him she was a "debutante from New York." She said that she'd met Chaplin there and that he'd told her to look him up if she came to LA. And here she was.[16]

Fearing new trouble, Totheroh tried to steer her to studio manager Alf Reeves. But Oona was insistent—she only wanted to see Chaplin. When told he was not at the studio, she left. But within the hour, she phoned Totheroh to ask whether Chaplin had returned, and when told he hadn't, she found out where Chaplin lived and took a taxi to his house. "Next thing we heard, Charlie was going around with this Eugene O'Neill's daughter," Totheroh said.[17]

Whatever the truth, within two weeks of the Wallis dinner party, Oona was on the guest list for Chaplin's Sunday afternoon tennis parties—although her game was as bad as her acting ability. Chaplin's teenage sons engaged in a friendly rivalry to see which one would get a date with her first. Before long, a disappointed Syd realized it wouldn't be either of them. Her outsized devotion to Chaplin was obvious. Charlie Jr. wrote in his biography of his father that Oona "worshiped him, drinking in every word he spoke."[18]

Joan was none the wiser when she came creeping up the driveway to Chaplin's house with her gun in late December.[19] After she was dropped off by taxi after midnight, her plan was nearly thwarted when a car approached and she heard Durant bidding Chaplin good night. But she hid among the trees on Chaplin's lawn until he was inside.[20] She boldly marched to the front door and rang the bell, but nobody answered. She went to the back of the house and knocked, but when nobody answered there either, she smashed a pane of glass in the door to the library and let herself in.[21]

Sneaking upstairs, Joan tiptoed into the dressing room adjacent to Chaplin's bedroom and heard him flirting with someone on the telephone. In a jealous rage she burst into his bedroom pointing her gun at him. Startled, Chaplin quickly hung up and asked whether she intended to kill him. A moment later, he amended his statement: "Oh, I know, you are going to kill yourself."[22]

Maintaining his cool at the barrel of a gun, he motioned for her to sit down. Obediently, she parked herself on the bed, confessed she was in love with him, and cried because their relationship was over. In a star performance, Chaplin suggested that she still had a place in his heart and that he hadn't "gone out with any other girls," so she had no reason to kill herself—or him.[23] Calmly continuing the sweet talk, Chaplin sat down beside her and suggested she borrow a pair of his pajamas, stay the night, and revisit her plan to shoot herself in the morning.[24]

But outside the bedroom, the household was in a tizzy; the butler was yelling Chaplin's name from downstairs, and his sons were frantically pacing the hallway figuring out how to save their father from the intruder.[25] The Chaplin boys had come home from a holiday party and had seen the broken glass in the library door along with a pair of high heels and a woman's handbag on the lawn. Worried, they woke Chaney, who lived in the servants' quarters part of the house, and the three of them investigated. Chaplin came out of his bedroom and ordered his sons to go to their room and shut the door. To them, he appeared nervous.[26]

Joan stayed the night and woke up the next day, relinquished the gun and cried that she was broke. Chaplin dug into his pants pocket and handed her fifty-six dollars to cover her bill at the Beverly House Hotel. She later claimed that before she left Summit Drive that morning Chaplin had promised to pay her twenty-five dollars a week and revive *Shadow and Substance*.[27] If he really made those promises, it is hard to believe he did so for any reason other than to get her out of the house and avoid getting shot.

The next day Joan returned to Summit Drive and was given twenty-five dollars by Chaney, which she used to check into the Hollywood Plaza Hotel. Shortly thereafter, alone on Christmas with just two dollars in her pocket and an overdue hotel bill, Joan returned uninvited to Chaplin's house to wish him a Merry Christmas and pick up another twenty-five dollars, but behaving like Ebenezer Scrooge, he would neither see her nor give her more money.[28]

Joan got decked out and returned to Chaplin's on December 30, at which time she said they had dinner and sex in front of the fireplace. In Chaplin's telling, she never got past the front door that night. Regardless, they finished the evening the way they often did—arguing about Joan running through Chaplin's money. Afterward, Chaplin and Joan climbed into his Ford so he could drive her home. But once on the road, Joan told him she had no home to go to, which was not true—she had rented a room in the 1400 block of Sycamore Avenue in Hollywood. If she thought feigning homelessness would force him to let her stay with him, she was wrong.

By this time, Chaplin was seeing O'Neill. As they passed the Beverly Hills police station, Chaplin pointed to the entrance and snidely suggested she sleep there. Joan hopped out of the car, walked into the police station, and he drove away.[29] A light rain was falling.[30]

Sgt. Claude Marple watched from behind the desk as Joan sauntered into the station house wearing her beloved fur coat over an evening dress. She was neither disheveled nor injured. Marple said she told him she was "in trouble" but refused to elaborate about her problem and "kept crying and going on." She also told Marple that she had no friends or relatives in Los Angeles, no place to sleep, and no money. Periodically, she moaned, "Oh Charles, Charles." When Marple asked who Charles was, he got no answer.[31] Marple told her she couldn't sleep there, so she called Ruesch from the police station, who agreed to let her stay the night at his place. Marple and Jessie "Billie" Reno, a jail matron responsible for female inmates, drove her to Ruesch's apartment in Sulgrove Manor at 9709 Olympic Boulevard in Beverly Hills.[32]

Later that day, which was New Year's Eve, Joan hailed a taxi and went back to Chaplin's. Not wanting the driver to know where she was going, she made him drop her off at Selznick's property up the road. With no money to pay the fare, Joan left her silver fox coat behind as collateral. Joan rang the bell at Chaplin's house, but he was ringing in the New Year at Chasen's restaurant with his future codefendant Robert Arden and Arden's date, Lillian Harvey.[33] Max Watt, a security guard hired by Chaplin following the gun incident to protect him from Joan, answered Chaplin's door and pulled her into the kitchen, where he gave her a stern lecture: "Don't you know Mr. Chaplin is through with you, why don't you get it through your thick skull?"[34]

Meanwhile, the befuddled cab driver wandered into the house holding Joan's fur; his company would not let him keep it, and he wanted his fare. Watt promised the cabbie that the Chaplin studio would reimburse him. The driver left and Watt called Chasen's restaurant to report to Chaplin that Joan was back. Joan was present when he made the call, but had no idea who he was talking to. But while Watt was on the phone, she overheard him say, "Yes, she is here, what do you want me to do," and after a pause Watt continued, "all right, I will call the police."[35] Once Joan heard that, she slipped into the bathroom, turned on the water, yanked off her shoes, and held them as she dived out the window, landing fifteen feet below into a bed of ivy. She ran down the driveway, shoes in hand, leaving her fur coat behind and not stopping until she reached Ruesch's apartment.[36]

Ruesch, too, was out celebrating the New Year. Joan talked her way into his place by convincing the landlady, Elizabeth Hanni, that she was Ruesch's fiancée. Inside, Joan acted as if she owned the place, helping herself to Ruesch's pajamas, slippers, and liquor and inviting Hanni in for a nightcap. She bent the landlady's ear, telling her that she was madly in love with Ruesch but that they had quarreled earlier and he slapped her.[37] It might have been her way of explaining any obvious injuries she may have suffered in the leap out of Chaplin's window.

Hanni left after midnight. Joan continued drinking and began dialing. She called Chaney at Chaplin's to tell him she had taken fifteen or sixteen sleeping pills and wanted to say goodbye. "But I didn't take no notice of it," Chaney later told FBI agents, "because I've heard that talk many times, ever since she's been at the house it's always been pills, or getting drugs or something. I don't know whether she did or not, but they never killed her."[38] She left similar messages with Elaine Barrie's mother, the Beverly Hills police, and the Los Angeles *Examiner*. "I wanted to hurt Charles the way he had hurt me," she explained to the FBI.[39]

Still in Ruesch's nightwear, she went outside and climbed into the back seat of an empty Buick convertible parked in front of the apartment. At about 2:20 a.m., Sergeant Marple received a call from an unidentified woman—either Elaine Barrie or perhaps Joan herself—that a possible suicide was in a car outside 9709 Olympic Boulevard, the address where Marple and Reno had taken Joan the night before. He summoned an ambulance and jumped into a patrol car. Marple found Joan sprawled out in the parked car, appearing to be unconscious. But he wasn't buying it, particularly when he saw that she opened and shut her eyes. "[S]he was more or less putting on an act," he concluded.[40]

Doctors at Beverly Hills Hospital immediately recognized Joan's lame suicide attempt—which included dabbing her lips with a little iodine—as fake. Once in the emergency room, she begged for sleeping pills so she could end her life over Chaplin's unrequited love. One of the ER doctors called her a "ham."[41] Marple ripped into Joan, "[T]here is nothing the matter with you." He told her to go back to Ruesch's, but Joan changed her tune from the one she'd sung to the landlady—now she said she barely knew him and didn't want to impose. Out of ideas, Marple brought her back to the precinct and booked her for vagrancy.[42]

On New Year's Day, Det. Capt. William W. White arrived at the Beverly Hills police station shortly before eight o'clock in the morning to begin his shift and checked the overnight booking records. Uniformed officers locked up lawbreakers, and detectives questioned them if further investigation was necessary. Captain White summoned Joan from her cell for an interview.[43] To Joan's surprise, Robert Arden was there. Joan would later tell New York *Daily News* reporter Florabel Muir that she had hoped Chaplin would be there, ready to rescue her like a knight in shining armor. Instead, as Muir wrote, "she saw only his stooge, Robert Arden."[44] Joan had met Arden in 1941 at one of Chaplin's tennis parties when Arden would, in Durant's words, "barge up there to Charlie's" uninvited.[45]

Chaplin outsourced his unseemly business; had he set foot in a police precinct to spring Joan, his former protégée and lover, a stampede of reporters would have been right behind. Durant, Arden, and Wallis served as Chaplin's willing flunkies to solve his Joan Barry problem for him. In their zeal to protect Chaplin they attacked Joan as crazy, loose, and dangerous. As Arden left White's office, he murmured nothing more than a "hello" to Joan, but it was obvious that he had come as Chaplin's emissary and had dished dirt on her. How else would Captain White have known, as he did, about her late-night forays onto the Chaplin estate, her frolic in Mexico with Getty, and her relationship with the married Sam Marx?

Arden's explanation for his presence at the precinct was that he wanted to help his good pal Chaplin and spare poor Joan the ordeal of languishing in jail.[46] But, in fact, he was there to silence her. To that end, Arden came up with a plan—have the judge declare Joan a vagrant and run her out of California. "Possibly you could do us the favor," he told White, the "us" presumably being him and Chaplin. "[N]obody has any interest in harming the girl," he contended. "I believe her place is with her mother." As an inducement, he said Chaplin would pay her train fare back to New York and cover her outstanding hotel debts.[47] As Arden was leaving, he gave White the silver fox coat Joan had left behind when she took her leap out of Chaplin's window, along with the pistol she'd taken up to the house a week or so earlier. The coat was returned to Joan, and the gun went into the back of Captain White's desk drawer.[48]

In her interview with White, which now included Police Chief Clinton H. Anderson, a nervous and jumpy Joan spewed the tale of her broken romance with Chaplin. White had no sympathy. Speaking to investigators for the Los Angeles County District Attorney in the spring of 1943, he said that *she*—not Chaplin—was the little tramp. He said she was "a cheap little prostitute who was very attractive and who was apparently trying to crash the movies, but in failing to do so, had taken to making a living the best way she could."[49]

After a full day in jail with no opportunity to speak with a lawyer, Joan was brought before Beverly Hills City Court Judge Charles J. Griffin at 10:30 a.m. on Saturday, January 2, 1943. She was quite a sight in her fox coat over Ruesch's pajamas and a pair of Matron Reno's shoes to replace Ruesch's bedroom slippers. It wasn't a scheduled court day, but when a woman was arrested on a weekend, the court held a special session to avoid the city having to pay a matron seventy-five cents an hour to mind a female inmate longer than necessary.[50]

Before Joan entered the courtroom, Captain White cornered Griffin for a highly inappropriate private conversation to do Arden's bidding. The judge told White he would not allow Chaplin to run his courtroom.[51] Nonetheless, Judge Griffin did exactly that, ordering Joan out of Beverly Hills, which was as far as his jurisdiction extended. As Muir would later complain, the government of Beverly Hills worked hard to protect its own wealthy and privileged residents from outsiders.[52]

The fact that a man as famous and wealthy as Chaplin was taking an interest in this seemingly routine matter should have made Griffin—a judge with nearly seven years on the bench—think twice.[53] Nonetheless, the arraignment went forward, with Judge Griffin reading Joan the charges against her, telling her that she had a right to counsel—California offered indigent criminal defendants free lawyers as early as 1914—and that she was entitled to bail.[54] When he asked how she wanted to plead, Joan seemed mystified and started to cry. Joan would tell the FBI that Matron Reno had advised her the night before to plead guilty, suggesting she was likely to get a suspended sentence.[55]

Reno later denied giving Joan any free legal advice. Still, as a woman, Reno felt sorry for Joan and was wise to Arden's game. She knew his goal was to banish Joan before she could embarrass Chaplin. And like most folks in Beverly Hills, Reno was well aware of Chaplin's penchant for attractive young girls. Male police officers pegged Joan as insane, but Reno thought the young woman was distraught over the shabby treatment she'd received from the great comedian.[56]

Joan pleaded guilty to violating California Penal Code Section 647, Subdivision 3, which made "roaming about from place to place without lawful business" a crime. The judge sentenced her to ninety days in jail, suspended on the condition she get out of Beverly Hills, stay out for two years, and pay her outstanding hotel bills.[57]

As the twentieth century wore on, "status" crimes such as vagrancy would be struck down by the United States Supreme Court as unconstitutional.[58] But regardless of the legality of the statute, there was little to suggest Joan was a vagrant. Although her statement to the judge—that she had a screen test coming up at MGM through which she would earn a movie contract—was by then delusional, she *was* wearing a fur coat, owned a car, had a place to sleep on Sycamore Avenue, and up until a few days earlier was getting twenty-five dollars a week from Chaplin.

What Joan experienced in that Beverly Hills courtroom was the power of Chaplin's celebrity coming down on her head like a ton of bricks. Chaplin legitimately could have had Joan arrested when she showed up at his house threatening him with a gun, but the story would have been plastered all over the newspapers, subjecting their relationship to unwelcome scrutiny. Instead, at the end of his patience with her outrageous behavior and at the beginning of a relationship with O'Neill, he and his cronies hatched a plan to get rid of Joan and keep the budding scandal quiet. The police, the court, and Chaplin's gofers worked in tandem to set it in motion.

But it was never that easy to get rid of Joan. In the car with Arden after her release from jail, Joan revealed she didn't intend to go anywhere and the authorities couldn't force her. "I told her nobody cared what she did, she could jump in the lake here. She said she wanted one more try in the movies," Arden said.[59]

Arden bided his time. He paid her hotel bills and retrieved her belongings, which were being held by hotel managers as collateral against her debts.[60] Joan's resolve to stay in California didn't last. Within days, she called Arden to say she was ready to go home. To guarantee that she got on the New York train, Arden enlisted Captain White to escort her to Union Station in downtown Los Angeles. White brought his wife along to chaperone.[61] Chaplin had wanted Arden to be on hand to make sure Joan boarded, but Arden claimed the train's departure conflicted with his evening radio broadcast. More likely, Arden thought the police captain would be a more intimidating presence in forcing Joan onto the train. The Whites picked Joan up in a cab at seven o'clock in the evening on January 5, 1943, and stayed with her until she boarded. Captain White warned her not to get off at Pasadena because if she did "we'll only have to go through this trouble again of putting you back on the train."[62]

When Chief Anderson found out Captain White had escorted Joan to the train, he was livid, recognizing White had crossed an ethical line. Anderson was ready to fire him on the spot, but White's many years of loyal service to the Beverly Hills Police Department made him think better of it. The two were already at odds because a disgruntled White had been passed over for the chief's job, which Anderson had only held for a month prior to the Joan Barry debacle.[63]

The train went to New York through Chicago, where passengers heading farther east had to change trains. Once the train pulled out of Union Station, Joan had trouble finding her assigned berth. She enlisted the help of a Pullman porter, but it seems Joan's reputation preceded her. After depositing her where she belonged, the porter said: "You're the young lady that's not supposed to get off until Chicago."[64] Joan said nothing. But long before Chicago, when the train pulled into Omaha in the middle of the night, she quickly gathered up her few belongings and hopped off.

SEVEN

A LOST SOUL

Now that he had gotten rid of Joan, Chaplin was free to tend to his blossoming romance with Oona. As usual, he moved fast, albeit cautiously for once; they did not do the town. Having barely avoided a scandal with Joan, he didn't need a press flogging like the one he got during his 1927 divorce from Lita Grey by flaunting a love affair with another adolescent.

When Oona arrived in Los Angeles, she lived with her mother at 1074 West Thirty-Fourth Street. In March 1943, they moved into an apartment at 9850 Olympic Boulevard, closer to Chaplin's home and probably paid for by him given Oona wasn't working and her mother had no money to speak of. By the end of May, Boulton had returned to New Jersey, leaving her young daughter in Chaplin's hands.[1]

The press was silent about Chaplin's new romance until shortly before his marriage, an exception being an item in Ed Sullivan's column in the New York *Daily News* on January 18, 1943, not more than two months after Charlie and Oona met. Sullivan wrote: "Charlie Chaplin will pop the question to Oona O'Neill."[2] The fingerprints of Oona, the former teenage toast of the New York nightclub circuit, or of her mother, eager to secure her daughter's financial future, were all over the Sullivan column. The next mention was by Louella Parsons, the nationally syndicated gossip columnist, on April 8, 1943: "Charlie Chaplin turning the charm on Oona O'Neill, Eugene's daughter. . . ."[3]

Oona outlandishly claimed that as late as two weeks before they married, she and Chaplin had never so much as kissed.[4] Servants in the household knew better; they revealed to investigators that Oona was living on Summit Drive well before the wedding, while still underage.[5]

As Charlie and Oona's relationship ripened, Joan was waiting in the wings, ready to pounce. After slipping off the New York–bound train in Omaha, she checked into the Paxton Hotel on January 7, 1943, and languished there until January 11, again enjoying fine lodgings with no money.[6] The Paxton was a stunning example of Art Deco architecture, built in downtown Omaha in 1929 with four expansive dining rooms and a beautiful ballroom.[7] Beyond parading around the hotel in her expensive fur coat, Joan made phone calls to Ruesch and Chaplin, but at the Chaplin house, she never got past Chaney. She left Omaha for Tulsa and checked into the Mayo Hotel from January 12 through 23, sneaking away on January 18 for the elegant Muehlebach Hotel in Kansas City until January 21, without having checked out of the Mayo and leaving unpaid bills in both places.[8] There was a war on, and military men were hoarding train seats, but somehow Joan managed to ride the rails with ease as she crisscrossed the country in 1942 and '43.[9]

Before she had left California, Arden had advised her on how to end her financial troubles: Go back to Getty. Her visit to Tulsa meant she might have been taking his advice to heart. But now there was an impediment: Getty's wife, Teddy Lynch. She was back in the States, finally having escaped from Italy, where she'd been trapped since the early days of the war while taking singing lessons. With his wife stuck overseas, Getty was free to play the field and immerse himself with running the Spartan aircraft plant in Tulsa.[10] In what turned out to be terrible timing for Joan, Getty's wife arrived in Tulsa on December 21, 1942, and stayed until January 13. While there, Teddy and Getty celebrated Christmas like any ordinary married couple—putting up a tree, exchanging gifts (Lynch gave her husband two Scottie puppies, and he bought her a bracelet), and visiting family and friends.[11] Worried at the havoc that Joan might cause with his wife around, Getty hired the Burns National Detective Agency to keep her under surveillance. By tailing Joan, the private eyes discovered she was keeping company with a man dressed in a cowboy outfit.[12]

Soon enough, Lynch would tire of being Getty's hausfrau in Tulsa and would resettle in her husband's California seaside mansion to resume her singing career.[13] But with access to Getty and to his money cut off, Joan turned once again to Dave Hecht, who happened to be in Tulsa when she was there. Over cocktails, he grilled her about what she was doing in town.

"To figure out some things," she said.[14] Striking out with both Getty and Hecht, Joan called Chaplin's home and told Chaney she was about to be married. She also wrote to Chaplin from Tulsa to tell him the same thing, implying that because she had no income she was forced to trade sex for money.[15] By this point, it's unlikely Chaplin believed anything she said or cared about anything she did.

With no other options (except to go home to her mother or get a job), Joan went on a crime spree, albeit one she blamed on Arden for failing to deposit twenty-five dollars a week from Chaplin into her bank account as he had supposedly promised. At the Mayo Hotel on January 12, she cashed a check for ten dollars on a nonexistent account at the Bank of America. On Saturday, January 23, while shopping at Seidenbach's, an exclusive department store, Joan was arrested on charges of defrauding an inn-keeper. She had passed bad checks at the store and at the Muehlebach Hotel. In their arrest report, Tulsa detectives Riley Stuart and N. C. Williams noted, "This girl is a hot check artist."[16] When she was picked up for her alleged criminal activities in that city, Joan told Detective Stuart that J. Paul Getty was her "boyfriend," that she was there to see him, and that his local attorney, Rosenstein, would cover her debts. Yet when the detective contacted Rosenstein's office, the secretary volunteered that Getty and his wife had slipped out of town to avoid her. While in the custody of the Tulsa police, Joan kept mum about being pregnant, although Joan would later tell FBI agents that she already knew she was.[17]

Joan's criminal conduct landed her in the *Tulsa Tribune* and the *Tulsa Daily World*. The news traveled fast: Detective Stuart received long-distance phone calls from Chaplin's attorneys asking about Joan's activities in Tulsa—clearly the fact that she had not made it to New York was troubling.[18] Joan cooled her heels in a jail cell for a few days until Rosenstein came to the rescue with cash, after which the charges were dropped.[19] Like Chaplin and his cronies, Getty and his lawyer were anxious to get rid of Joan. The day she was sprung, Rosenstein bought Joan a $35 ticket to fly to New York via Chicago and gave her $125 in cash to spend once she got there.[20]

Joan returned to New York and played it safe for the next two months, living with her mother. But by March 1, she was back in Tulsa, steering clear of the Mayo and checking into the Tulsa Hotel under the last name "Barratt." If she was hoping to find Getty, she was disappointed; he spent most of the month with his wife in Los Angeles.[21] By this time, Joan was a lost soul. She left Tulsa on March 5 and returned to New York, where she checked into the Park Central Hotel and kept company with Ruesch (he had left California in January to pursue a writing career) and another wealthy pal, Donald Flamm, who had sold his radio station, WMCA, for $850,000 in 1941.[22]

On March 24, 1943, using her aunt's name, "Katherine McLaren," and Chaplin's Summit Drive address as her own, Joan checked into The Pierre. Two days later, a maid found Joan passed out on the floor of her room, possibly another of her suicide attempts. A doctor was summoned, Joan was revived, and the credit manager told her he intended to contact her mother. Joan warned him: "If you do, I'll jump out of the window." Instead, the next day she left the hotel through the front door and left behind an unpaid bill for $84.58. The hotel kept her luggage until the bill was settled a month later.[23]

Back in Tulsa on April 2, she stayed until April 6, when Rosenstein gave her $210. Using that money, she went to Kansas City to visit one Lt. Samuel Marsh, who had invited her to an officers' dance at Fort Riley.[24] On April 16, she returned to Tulsa, where Getty loaned her another $700. And with that, even Getty had had enough. His lawyer made her sign a release promising she would "never again request financial assistance from or of Mr. Getty, either directly or indirectly." The release also required her to affirm she had "no claim, demand . . . of any kind, character or nature whatsoever, known or unknown . . . against C.H. Rosenstein, or against J. Paul Getty, or his wife."[25] Rosenstein told Detective Stuart that Joan had told him she was pregnant but he didn't believe her until he read it in the newspapers a month later. Perhaps this is true, but as an attorney who knew that his fabulously wealthy client had fraternized with Joan, he must have been worried that Joan might be telling the truth, because he advised Getty to make her sign the release, which would hinder Joan's ability to sue for child support if the child turned out to be Getty's.

Back in Los Angeles on April 19, Joan checked into the Biltmore and repeatedly phoned Chaplin, anxious to give him the unwelcome news, but he never took her calls. Now about four months pregnant, Joan was ambivalent about giving birth. On April 20, she booked an appointment for a morning massage at the hotel beauty shop under the name "Mrs. Marsh." She told the masseuse, a woman named Helen Kirk, that she had married an army captain in Kansas and was pregnant. She booked a second massage for later that same day, supposedly to keep her girlish figure for her movie career. The proprietor of the shop wasn't buying it. Convinced "Mrs. Marsh" was trying to abort her pregnancy, she refused to allow the treatment.[26]

Easter Sunday, which fell on April 25 in 1943, was yet another holiday on which Joan was alone. She phoned Getty, who was in Los Angeles with his wife. After speaking with Joan for a few minutes, Getty handed the receiver to his wife, telling her someone wanted to talk to her. Teddy took the phone and heard a tearful woman on the other end. "Please make Paul call Charles for me." Confused, Lynch asked, "Well, who are you? And Charles? Charles who?" The woman replied, "Charles Chaplin, and I'm Joan Barry. Paul knows all about this, and he's got to get Charles to talk to me. I don't know what else to do. Please, please help me."[27]

Disgusted, Lynch handed the phone back to her husband. Getty had secretly listened in on the extension but made no mention in his diary about what Joan had to say, why he'd handed the phone to his wife, or what Joan had told him before he put his wife on the line. Joan had been visiting Tulsa with alarming frequency in early 1943, and Getty may have hoped that by showing allegiance to his wife, Joan would take the hint and leave him alone. Whatever was said, it worked. Joan's calls and unannounced visits to Getty's stopped. In her autobiography, *Alone Together: My Life with J. Paul Getty*, Teddy Lynch wrote that she promised Joan she would tell her husband to call Chaplin. But later that evening, the Gettys had a heated argument about Joan's call, during which Getty groveled to his disbelieving wife in his attempt to convince her that he had never had sex with Joan.[28]

It was time for Joan to face her pregnancy problem. With $1,000 given to her by Rosenstein—$16,000 today—burning a hole in her pocket, she checked into the Chateau Elysee in Beachwood Canyon, the Hollywood luxury apartment hotel built by the widow of silent film producer Thomas Ince. It was home to stars like Cary Grant, Katharine Hepburn, and Carole Lombard.[29] Ironically, Ince had died in 1924 following a party aboard William Randolph Hearst's yacht that included Hearst's mistress, Marion Davies, and Chaplin. The official cause of Ince's death was a mysterious heart ailment, but Tinseltown rumor had it Hearst accidentally shot him with a bullet intended for Chaplin, who was having a not-so-secret affair with Davies.[30]

The first call Joan made from the Elysee was to Chaplin, but she only got as far as Chaney. She told him she was married, was pregnant, and wanted Chaplin to contact the Beverly Hills City Court to get the judge's order barring her from town lifted. Chaney told her to call Robert Arden.

When she called Arden, he offered no help, told her he couldn't care less if she was married, warned her to get out of town, and hung up.[31]

Not too pregnant to party, Joan summoned her old crowd—Lionel Vasco Bonini, Joine Alderman, Marx, and Bill Castle, the future horror film producer—for evenings on the town, which quickly ate up her remaining cash.[32] Unable to hide her condition any longer, she told Marx she was pregnant, but he didn't believe her. But Maria De Garda, a new friend Joan met through Marx, *did* believe her, and when Joan revealed that Chaplin was the father, De Garda pressed her to tell him. On Thursday, May 6, Joan ventured to Chaplin's house, determined to break the news.[33]

It was a sunny spring day, with a high of 71 degrees.[34] Joan let herself into Chaplin's house through the back door and walked upstairs. Hearing voices in Goddard's old bedroom, she opened the door to find Oona lying on the bed naked and a fully dressed Chaplin standing nearby. Angry and upset, Joan ran downstairs with Chaplin following close behind. In the kitchen she demanded he make Oona leave, but he refused. Joan told him to meet her outside by the pool. Whether she told him she was pregnant is unknown, but what unfolded suggests that she did. He never showed up poolside, probably because he was pacing the floor or on the phone to Durant, in terror. Tired of waiting, Joan broke an ashtray and made a half-hearted attempt to slit her wrists, drawing blood. She could not have done much damage because Chaplin's chauffeur drove her to her hotel rather than to the hospital.[35]

Joan resolved to play her last hand. A year earlier, Hedda Hopper had written a syndicated column that was published on Joan's twenty-second birthday and dedicated to Chaplin's latest anonymous ingenue—her. It had prophetically warned she would be discarded and replaced; Joan had apparently been holding on to it. On Friday, May 7, Joan "popped up" at the frosted glass door of Hopper's office in the Guaranty Building on Hollywood Boulevard. Weeping uncontrollably, Joan revealed that she was the anonymous ingenue and said she was pregnant with Chaplin's baby.[36]

One can only imagine the barely contained glee Hopper must have felt when Joan dropped out of the sky with a scoop like this. Hopper was a self-appointed protector of family values who detested real and imagined Communists, philanderers, and Chaplin. Born Edda Fleury in 1885 in Pennsylvania to a butcher and his wife, Hopper ran away to New York City to pursue a showbiz career with $250 she stole from the cashbox in her father's store. Only twenty years old, she renamed herself "Hedda" and joined the chorus of a musical comedy revue where she met DeWolf Hopper, age fifty, known for reciting Ernest Thayer's poem "Casey at the Bat" onstage. She became his fifth wife.[37]

Hopper's husband was a serial cheater, which may explain why she hated philanderers so much. She divorced him in 1922, obtained custody of their only son—an actor who would one day play investigator Paul Drake in the popular television show *Perry Mason*—and had a middling career as an MGM contract actress.[38] In 1937, when she was fifty-three and her acting career was dying, she came back to life as a gossip columnist for the Esquire Feature Syndicate. An MGM publicity man had recommended her, saying he had no idea if she could write, but she certainly knew all the best gossip.[39]

Hopper sent Joan to her own physician, who confirmed the pregnancy. There were some who thought—particularly those in the Chaplin camp—that Hopper engineered Joan's next move. From Hopper's, Joan went to Summit Drive, where Chaplin, Oona, and Durant were having dinner and perhaps plotting damage control given what Joan had seen at his house the day before. When he learned Joan was at the door, Chaplin feared she might have returned to shoot him and went to pieces.[40] Refusing to let Joan in and leaving her marooned on the porch, Chaplin and Durant spent about ten minutes taking turns poking their heads outside to tell her to scram, but she refused to budge. Chaplin ordered Durant to call the police to have them remove her.[41] Joan had plenty of time to run before the squad car arrived, but she obstinately waited, raising suspicion that Hopper had instructed her to get herself arrested at Chaplin's to provide the news hook necessary to allow Hopper to blow the story wide open.

Joan was duly arrested and brought to the Beverly Hills precinct dressed in a white blouse, colored slacks, and a cloth coat. She was crying and claimed to be under a doctor's care, but for what, she wouldn't say. After she was booked for violating her probation by coming back to town and harassing Chaplin, she was put in the waiting room for Matron Reno to arrive. While there, she pulled a compact out of her purse, broke the mirror, and began slicing her wrists.[42]

Hapless Sergeant Marple was again working the desk. He saw Joan break her compact and stick something in her waistband. Fearing she could hurt herself or someone else with whatever she had shoved into her pants, Marple took her upstairs to the station house dressing room and told her she would have to change into jail clothes, which she refused to do.[43] Reno showed up, and she and Marple wrestled with Joan to force her into prison garb. Marple, a father of four, could see she was pregnant. When later under investigation for stripping a female prisoner, Marple said Joan "was fighting like a tiger all the time," leaving him no choice but to help Reno undress her. It took Reno an hour to subdue an angry, screaming Joan.[44]

After spending the night in jail, Joan called Hopper on Saturday morning, May 8. Hopper had been busy working the phones herself; she called Chaplin, who would not talk to her.[45] And then, because she was a gossip columnist and not a crime reporter, Hopper made one more call.

She dialed the number of the elegant Westmore Salon in the heart of Hollywood at 6638 Sunset Boulevard, an Art Deco beauty parlor that catered to the likes of Claudette Colbert, Marlene Dietrich, and Bette Davis. One of the white and gold phones jangled, and when an employee picked up, Hopper asked for New York *Daily News* reporter Florabel Muir, who was there for her weekly hair appointment. Muir came to the phone, and before she could say more than "Hello?" Hopper warned her to leave the salon and find a public pay phone. She didn't want to risk having the salon switchboard operators hear what she had to tell her.[46]

EIGHT

"A STORY THAT NEEDED MANY EARS"

Florabel Muir flew out of the salon, grabbed both her purse for nickels to pump into a pay phone and a towel to dry her soaking wet, fiery-red hair, ran to the corner drugstore, and dialed Hopper's number. Years later she would write, "What she told me almost dried my wet locks. It was that hot."[1] Hopper repeated Joan's tale about *l'affaire* Chaplin and the resulting pregnancy and she urged Muir to race to the county jail for the story of a lifetime.[2]

It made perfect sense that Hopper would share her scoop with Muir. Hopper was a gossip columnist and Muir, age fifty-four, was a hard-charging news reporter who had covered crime and the courts for the New York *Daily News* since 1927. Assigned to the Los Angeles and Holly-wood beats since the 1930s, she knew the district attorney, police captains, judges, and defense lawyers—all of whom feared her tenacity. Years after the Chaplin trial, Muir would be shot in the behind by a bullet meant for mobster Mickey Cohen.[3] Hopper knew Muir could handle the story and would work with her to be sure they both got the credit for cracking it wide open.

After hanging up, Muir called the Beverly Hills jail. She decided against visiting after a matron told her that Joan was so distraught after being sentenced to thirty days that she had to be sedated.[4] It wasn't until Tuesday, May 11, that Muir sent two female photographers to the county jail at the Hall of Justice, where Joan was being housed. But Minna Wallis had gotten there first and had warned Joan to avoid contact with the press.[5]

While Hopper and Muir were gearing up for the story that was sure to knock World War II off the front pages, the Chaplin machine was working to make sure it never saw the light of day. Under the guise of lending a helping hand, while keeping Chaplin's involvement hidden, Durant, Arden, and Wallis did their best to muzzle Joan. They hired a lawyer for her whom they could manipulate, pressured the Beverly Hills police and the judge, and waved money around to get Joan quickly and quietly booted out of town. Again. Their frantic actions made it apparent that when Joan had cornered Chaplin in his kitchen on May 6, she had dropped the bomb that she was pregnant. But Chaplin and friends had no impact on Muir; if anything, their actions made her more aggressive. When Muir got to the jail, she bumped into Wallis, whom she knew from covering Hollywood stars and their foibles. Wallis was startled to see her and asked what she was doing there.

"The same thing as you are—I want to talk to Joan Berry," answered Muir.

Wallis tried to discourage Muir. "Oh, I hope you're not going to write anything about this—it's a terrible case."

Muir told her she wouldn't have written anything about the case had Chaplin not decided to have Joan thrown in jail.[6]

As part of her campaign to discredit Joan, Wallis also called Hopper, first seeking to determine whether Hopper intended to "do anything about Berry being in jail," and to ensure that Hopper wouldn't, she told her she'd known Joan through her own friendship with Chaplin and in her opinion, Joan was "a terrible person—bad through and through."[7] At the jail, Wallis had suggested to Muir that J. Paul Getty was responsible for Joan's pregnancy, but Muir was skeptical. She asked Wallis how she knew Joan was in jail; Wallis said Hopper asked that she check on her. Muir called her a liar.

"I don't think that's true, because she sent me," Muir said.[8] With that, Wallis left.

Alone with Joan, Muir explained that Wallis's allegiance was to Durant and that she was no friend of Joan's. Besides believing that Hopper had sent Wallis, Joan had also convinced herself her arrest was part of Chaplin's master plan to make her a star. "I'm sure that Charles is only doing this to me to make me suffer so I can be a great actress."[9]

Muir called Hopper from the jail and handed the receiver to Joan. Hopper assured Joan that she had not sent Wallis and that she could trust Muir.

But Muir didn't trust Joan. She invited other reporters to hear the story. "Hers was a story that needed many ears besides mine," Muir later wrote in her autobiography, *Headline Happy*. She feared without other journalists on the story, she might be accused by Joan of misquoting her. [10]

The first thing Muir did was to ascertain whether Getty might be the father. Joan adamantly denied it, saying she and Getty had never been lovers—a statement that seems impossible to believe. Joan insisted she had conceived the December night that she had broken into Chaplin's home with a gun. [11]

Crossing what today would be an ethical line in journalism, Muir told Joan she would find her a lawyer to get her out of jail. Muir wanted Samuel (Sammy) Simpson Hahn, the diminutive celebrity divorce lawyer who often handled the legal problems of newspaper people for free. [12] But once again, Wallis beat her to it, having already retained Judge Cecil D. "Dutch" Holland, a part-time justice of the peace in Beverly Hills, to represent Joan. Unlike Hahn, Holland did not come free; he wanted $500. [13]

When Joan was arrested, she'd had $1.09, a compact, and a few worthless items in her purse, so she couldn't afford Holland's fee. [14] Judge Holland knew Wallis from having represented her when she got nabbed for speeding. [15] Through his $350-a-month part-time job on the bench, Holland had presided over small cases involving big stars behaving badly, like Errol Flynn, who once slugged a newsman who made him unhappy. [16]

After her unexpected and unpleasant encounter with Muir, Wallis had hustled over to Dutch Holland's office to hire him. [17] Durant insisted to the FBI that Wallis took it upon herself to hire Judge Holland and that neither he nor Chaplin had anything to do with it, which was preposterous. [18] Wallis, connected to Hollywood's A-list through her powerful brother, producer Hal Wallis, and her own job as an agent, had little use for a nobody like Joan—"bad through and through."

Durant misled investigators about his role as Chaplin's fixer. Durant willingly did Chaplin's dirty work for the heady satisfaction of a standing invitation to play on the great man's tennis court and the opportunity to be photographed next to him in evening wear at nightclubs and movie premieres. For Arden, an illegal immigrant whose position in the United States was precarious, service to Chaplin meant exposure to actors and intellectuals whom he could invite on his radio show and who might use their celebrity to convince the government to let him stay in the country. Wallis's motivation may have been as simple as her unrequited love for Durant. [19]

Once Wallis retained Judge Holland on May 11, he phoned his colleague Judge Griffin to speak privately about Joan's case. The line of people improperly vying for Judge Griffin's ear was growing. Besides his ex parte conversation with Capt. William White after Joan's arrest in January, Judge Griffin had again talked to the captain privately after Joan's latest arrest, when White told him how Joan had made a pest of herself during her latest visit to Chaplin's.[20] After their chat, Judge Griffin summarily sentenced Joan to thirty days in jail without the benefit of a lawyer or a hearing, which understandably sent her into an emotional tailspin.[21]

A few days later, Holland telephoned Judge Griffin to relay the news that Joan was pregnant and asked him "to consider a motion to modify her probation so that she can be sent to a sanitarium and afterwards out of the state."[22] Couching his suggestion as concern for Joan's welfare, Holland tried to convince the judge a sanitarium would be better for her health than a jail cell. Judge Griffin told Holland he might consider it if the lawyer were to come back with a doctor's note, which Holland did the next day.[23]

On May 12, the day the New York *Daily News* published Muir's story about the unorthodox case, the judge modified Joan's sentence so she could leave jail. Later that day, Judge Griffin bumped into Holland and a newspaper reporter outside the court clerk's office. There, Holland told Griffin, in the reporter's presence, that Chaplin was not the father of Joan's child and that the real father was not in the motion picture business. Judge Griffin suspected that Holland was acting more in Chaplin's interests than in Joan's, yet he did nothing to protect her.[24] Also on that day, in another effort to buy Joan's silence, Arden called the jail to offer Joan $5,000 if she left town. But by then it was too late; the judge had already ordered Joan's release and she was stashed away by Holland and Wallis in an apartment in Westwood Village under an assumed name.[25]

But Muir, ever the ace investigative reporter, quickly discovered Joan's whereabouts. But by the time she phoned the apartment hideout Joan had been moved again, this time to Santa Monica Hospital. As if in one of Chaplin's slapstick comedies, reporters rushed to the hospital, only to be blocked by nurses who insisted that Joan needed her rest. That didn't stop Hedda Hopper, who slipped in through a back door and marched into Joan's room. She and Muir hatched a plot to kidnap Joan until it became clear it would never work. Joan was incommunicado, "shot full of hop" as Hopper put it, and loaded with sleeping pills.[26]

Muir's story was splashed across page 2 of the New York *Daily News* on

May 12, 1943, alongside a photo of Chaplin, his ex-wife Paulette Goddard, and Durant. The scandalous headline read: "Ma-to-be, 23, Jailed; Blames Chas. Chaplin." Before twenty-four-hour cable news shows existed, newspapers published multiple editions, and Muir's article was prominently displayed in all of them. One interested New York reader was Joan's mother, Gertrude, who until then was in the dark.[27]

On that same day, two other major newspapers picked up the brewing Chaplin scandal. A headline in the *Chicago Daily Tribune* read "Girl Says Love For Chaplin Led to Term in Jail; Gets 30 Day Sentence for Annoying Star," and the *Los Angeles Times* ran a front-page story that read "Girl Gets Jail, Not Film Role; Screen Aspirant Who Made Scene at Home of Chaplin Sentenced." But only the New York *Daily News* touched the hot-button topic of Joan's pregnancy, and only Muir kept pounding away at the story. Her work raised the eyebrows of Harlan Guyant Palmer Sr., the publisher of the hometown *Hollywood Citizen-News*. Palmer, a former judge, had owned the midsize local newspaper since 1911 and used it as a platform to fight against illegal gambling and police payoffs.[28] What happened to Joan at the hands of Beverly Hills officials smacked of corruption to the muckraker.

In an editorial in the *Citizen-News* on May 15, Palmer questioned why Joan had been run out of Beverly Hills in January and who was paying for her expensive attorney and the pricey sanitarium. "Does Holland represent the girl, some friends of the girl or some friends of persons who may want to keep the girl out of Beverly Hills and away from newspaper reporters?" he wrote astutely.[29]

Team Chaplin tried to tamp down the story, but it was like putting out a forest fire with a watering can. Holland and Wallis told Muir that the protrusion in Joan's stomach was not a fetus but a tumor. Hopper's doctor confirmed Joan's pregnancy, Muir replied. Arden called Muir and Hopper claiming *he* was the father of Joan's child. When Muir reminded him that immigration officials would be interested in knowing that a man in the country illegally was fathering illegitimate children here, Arden quickly said he was only kidding.[30]

Making matters worse, the Joan Barry scandal shined a spotlight on Chaplin's romance with the underage Oona O'Neill. On May 17, a column in the *Hollywood Reporter* asked, "Isn't someone with the good of the business at heart going to coax that famous comic to relinquish his momentary hold on the seventeen-year-old dotter [*sic*] of that famous playwright?

85

Before the talking she's doing (or her family) catches up with him. And before we all get splashed with mud again."[31]

Meanwhile, Judge Griffin was getting nervous. He had given an interview to Palmer for the May 15 editorial in the *Hollywood Citizen-News*, but now he feared that he hadn't sufficiently whitewashed his role. On May 27, Griffin ran to Beverly Hills mayor Arthur L. Erb to share his case files to prove he had acted on the up-and-up.[32] He also wrote to Los Angeles County District Attorney Fred Howser inviting him to open an investigation to determine if there was any criminal conduct by those involved and promising his full cooperation. "[I]t is my desire to remove from the minds of any who are responsible for the proper enforcement of our laws any suspicion relative to the action of this Court in connection with this or any other case," he wrote.[33] The statement smacked of a guilty conscience.

Continuing his self-rehabilitation campaign, Griffin wrote to the Beverly Hills City Council to further excuse his behavior in Joan's case. "When she appeared in Court that morning, she was clothed in jail garb and not wearing any furs as stated in a recent newspaper article," he wrote to explain his vagrancy finding. He insisted that when he sentenced Joan he was "interested in the case" and "not in Chaplin's problems."[34]

Muir wasn't buying any of it. She barged into Howser's office demanding to know why he wasn't investigating Joan's abortions and Chaplin's affair with seventeen-year-old Oona O'Neill, which was taking place under the noses of Chaplin's teenage sons.[35]

Finally, on May 30, Mount Vesuvius exploded. Gertrude Berry swooped into town ostensibly to comfort her daughter, although her real motive was probably to broker a marriage deal or to secure Chaplin's money for her future grandchild. One can only wonder where the willfully blind Gertrude had been for the past four years while her young daughter aimlessly roamed the country with no source of income other than that which came from rich, older—and often married—men. Gertrude retrieved Joan from the hospital, and the two checked into the New Carlton Hotel in downtown Los Angeles. As usual, they drank too much and bickered, and Joan repeated an act from her repertoire of threats—to jump out of the window. In the midst of the drama, Joan slipped out of the hotel via the door to visit Chaplin while Muir and Gertrude headed to Hopper's sun-filled home at 1708 Tropical Avenue in Beverly Hills, with its lush gardens and landscaped in-ground pool, to plot their next move.[36]

While the reporters and Joan's mother put their heads together, less than a half mile away, Joan and Chaplin were in his backyard quietly contemplating the mess they were in. He had agreed to see her, perhaps to try to buy her off cheaply, but Joan got right to the point and made her demand: marriage. Having endured two disastrous shotgun weddings Chaplin had no intention of being bullied into a third. Plus, he now had Oona to contend with. He had a proposal of his own: he would support the child if Joan would agree to leave California and stop yapping to the press.

Disappointed that she would not be the next Mrs. Chaplin, Joan ran into his house in tears and bounded up to the second floor, perhaps looking for more signs of O'Neill's presence. In Paulette's old room, she found them—articles of women's clothing. She ran back outside and angrily accused Chaplin of living with O'Neill, which he denied. "You've got to protect me Joan," he supposedly complained. Recognizing that Joan might sue him, he allegedly said, "If you bring this into court . . . the newspapers will be after you, your picture will be taken—oh, it will be grand for a couple of months. Then people will forget it." Perhaps sensing he was getting nowhere, his tone darkened, Joan later said, and he threatened to blacken her name if she sued, even if it cost him his fortune to do it.[37] Before parting, Joan supposedly demanded $150,000 in lieu of walking down the aisle or into a courtroom, which she steadfastly denied. With no meeting of the minds, the afternoon ended with Chaney driving her back to Hopper's.[38]

There, Joan gleefully reported that Chaplin had promised that if she did what he asked, he might marry her once the publicity died down. Given Chaplin's desperation, he might have made that empty promise during the hours they spent at the pool, but it seems unlikely. Muir and Hopper didn't believe it either and spent the rest of the day trying to pound sense into Joan's head. "[W]e told her that she was listening to a lot of hogwash; that he was just trying to get her out of the state," Muir said.[39] Strangely, it didn't stop Muir from adopting Joan's irrational perspective when she wrote about their poolside parley. In Muir's article in the Daily News on June 2, "Joan and Chaplin Dine; Ma Visions Bridal Cake," Charlie and Joan "chatted gaily and seemed happy," according to "other diners" who were supposedly there. Muir also reported that Joan's mother was looking forward to a wedding.[40] As the apt title of Muir's future autobiography later revealed, she was indeed "Headline Happy."

Now that Joan's mother was in the picture, Muir shuttled Joan and Gertrude over to Holland's office. When Joan left to get something to eat, the two women ganged up on Holland. Gertrude asked Muir, in front of Holland, if he could be trusted. Muir was blunt: "I think he's a crooked b——d and I wouldn't trust him as far as I can see him. However, he's way out on a limb now and everybody's watching him."[41]

Cornered, Holland confessed. "I'll admit Minna Wallis engaged me," he said. "She made me the proposition that if I took her [Joan] out of jail and got her out of the state, Tim Durant would give me $500."[42] But Holland insisted that once he met Joan, his sole concern became her welfare.[43]

Gertrude was uneasy after they left Holland's office. "I think if I could talk to a priest, I'd get my mind straightened out on this whole thing," she said.[44] Muir took her to Blessed Sacrament at 6657 West Sunset Boulevard, but Gertrude didn't like the priest there, who she felt had given her the bum's rush. The next day, Muir drove her to see Father Michael Lee at St. Peter's at 333 South San Vincente Boulevard, off La Cienega. There, after a private talk with the priest, Gertrude emerged from the rectory all smiles. She announced to Muir, who had been waiting outside, that she would be hiring her own lawyer, whose name she kept to herself. "I think we need better advice than Holland can give us," she said.[45] The next day Muir was pleased to learn that John Joseph Irwin, a well-known Los Angeles lawyer, would be entering the case.

Gertrude Barry could not have made a better choice than John Irwin. Known as "Jack," Irwin was a deeply religious family man, respected within and outside the church. In 1943, he was thirty-five years old, smart, politically connected, and photogenic. Dark haired with wire-rimmed glasses, he stood about five foot ten and weighed 160 pounds.[46] Born in Michigan, he graduated from the University of Michigan and the Loyola University School of Law, skipping his third year. Before building a successful private practice, he had been, at twenty-eight, the youngest assistant U.S. attorney in Los Angeles history.[47]

Irwin's strong Catholic faith was the anchor for his personal and professional life. He was selected as a Knight of the Holy Sepulcher and handled legal matters for Los Angeles cardinal James Francis McIntyre. Over the years he would become an aide to then senator Richard Nixon, president of the Los Angeles Police Commission, and deputy to Los Angeles mayor Norris Poulson. Plus, he sang and played the mandolin.[48]

The Berrys were broke. Gertrude's ex-husband had declared bankruptcy in 1939 and for all she knew was in jail somewhere for passing bad checks. Joan's chance for a movie contract was nil after the notoriety of her relationship with Chaplin and the fact that she was six months pregnant. One of the roles of the parish priest was to act as a social worker to the faithful in need. Father Lee, who was close with the Irwin family, called upon the lawyer to lend a hand, knowing Irwin would see it as his duty to provide his professional services to a Catholic in crisis. Muir also stepped in. Feeling sorry for Joan and her mother, she let them stay at her house with the understanding they wouldn't tell anyone where they were. Muir didn't want her lawn covered with nosy reporters; plus, she now wanted to keep the juiciest details of the story exclusive to herself.[49]

Finally, in early June, Hedda Hopper, who had been operating behind the scenes since Joan appeared at her office door, let loose. In her syndicated column published June 3, 1943, she wrote her first words about the Charlie Chaplin–Joan Barry scandal, asking her millions of readers across America: "What is to become of that child and its mother, Joan Barry?" "Will her child have a name?" These questions, she insisted, "Hollywood has a right to ask and not only hope for an answer but demand one."[50]

In what amounted to perfect timing—perhaps planned—the same day the Hopper column appeared, Irwin filed a paternity suit against Chaplin in the name of Gertrude E. Berry, as guardian ad litem for Joan's unborn child, in the Los Angeles County Superior Court. He asked for $10,000 for prenatal care for Joan, $2,500 a month in support for the unborn child, and $5,000 in court costs.[51] At least some of the $5,000 would cover his costs in bringing the suit; Irwin's Catholicism didn't prevent him from seeking some money from Chaplin for his work. At a news conference to announce the filing, Joan wore "a blue maternity frock, a nervous smile, and a sprinkling of freckles." Joan demurely—and disingenuously—told reporters she was "not interested in any money from Mr. Chaplin for myself" but was "only seeking to establish the baby's paternity."[52] When served with the legal papers for the paternity suit the next day by a deputy sheriff, Chaplin said, "Well, I guess here comes trouble."[53] Chaplin was directed to appear at 9:30 a.m. on June 17 for a hearing before the Honorable William Baird to answer the allegations.

After weeks of trying to keep the story under wraps, Chaplin's attorneys, Loyd Wright and Charles E. (Pat) Millikan, came out swinging. Their client's version of the poolside lunch with Joan differed drastically from hers. Now Joan's alleged demand for $150,000 was revealed. "I am not responsible for Miss Berry's condition," Chaplin declared through his lawyers.[54] "Miss Berry states her unborn child was conceived in December last.

The first claim made upon me by Miss Berry was in May and was accompanied by demand for the payment of $150,000."[55]

After Hopper's column was published, powerful producers David O. Selznick and Sam Goldwyn, Chaplin's good friend, told her that taking on Chaplin would be "bad for the industry."[56] Hopper could afford to ignore them. But one man couldn't. Frederick Napoleon Howser, age thirty-eight, had been the Los Angeles County district attorney for a little over three months when the Chaplin scandal broke. The previous district attorney, John Dockweiler, had died while in office of pneumonia on January 31, 1943. Less than twenty-four hours later, Howser, a Republican state legislator, was chosen to replace him by local politicians in a closed-door deal.[57]

The new district attorney had to walk a fine line. After the scandal broke, he said, "If the law permits any prosecution we are going after it, even if it is a misdemeanor."[58] But the big-money movie producers were vital to Howser's political career, and he needed to stay in their good graces. The story had exploded, however, and it shocked the average reader, including Howser's ordinary constituents who needed a diversion from the constant war news. It was political poison for Howser to side with Chaplin against an obscure, unmarried woman who claimed the millionaire film producer made her pregnant and then abandoned her. Howser had no choice but to go full-steam ahead, or at least seem to be doing so. He unleashed his two top investigators, Herbert Grossman and Philip Tower, to start digging and see what they could find.

NINE

"SHOULDN'T WE RUN
THIS DOWN?"

District Attorney Howser's investigators fanned out over Los Angeles as fast as they could. The DA's agents had to get to witnesses before Muir plastered their stories all over the *Daily News*. The sleuths met with Joan on Saturday afternoon, May 29, at the New Carlton Hotel in the presence of her mother, a trying experience that resulted in Joan's usual hysterics and threats to jump out a window.

Joan's mother impeded the interview and demonstrated the exacting control she sought to exert over her daughter. She answered some of the questions the investigators put to Joan, and her presence inhibited Joan from telling the truth. With a straight face Joan denied having had sex with any of her slew of admirers.[1] She claimed to have spent 360 nights at Chaplin's during the first year they were together, obviously an exaggeration based on her whirlwind travel schedule alone.[2] She lied about when she last saw Getty, saying it was July or August of the prior year, when in fact Getty's diaries show they saw each other in Tulsa as late as November 1942, and possibly in January 1943, although Getty claimed they only spoke on the phone during her January visit.[3] Joan's mother was protective of Getty, perhaps because she knew he was giving Joan infusions of cash when her daughter was strapped. Joan casually dropped his name into the conversation in a benign context, for which Mrs. Berry admonished her. "Why do you bring Paul into it so much? That isn't fair."[4]

Mrs. Berry's fixation on money was apparent; she groused about how for Christmas in 1941 Chaplin had given Joan a silver fox fur coat and "a thousand dollars in cash" but how in 1942 all she got was a measly twenty-five dollars a week.[5] And, in discussing the early financial negotiations over Joan's paternity suit, she complained that if the baby died, her daughter wouldn't get any more money even though her career was "wrecked."[6] Unfortunately for Joan, Gertrude wasn't as skilled as Lita Grey's mother had been twenty years before when she brokered her daughter's marriage deal with a defeated Chaplin.

Because Joan had tattled to investigators about having seen Oona O'Neill in the nude at Chaplin's, they went to O'Neill's apartment on the evening of June 4, 1943 to see if she'd confirm it. The transcripts of the witness interviews have the names of the interrogators blacked out, but either Grossman or Tower got straight to the point.

"Has Mr. Chaplin ever made love to you?" one asked.

"Never," she said.[7]

"Never at any time kissed you?"

"Never," she answered.[8]

That was her story, and she was sticking to it. Threats of tossing her into the grand jury and indicting her for perjury did not faze her. The baby-faced teenager had nerves of steel and would admit only what she absolutely could not deny. Knowing Joan had seen her naked in bed at Chaplin's on May 6, she had to confess. But O'Neill's explanation was that she'd come up from the pool and was wearing a bathing suit with an open bathrobe over it when her rival burst in.[9] Neither of the men asked whether the suit was flesh colored.

Grossman and Tower next tried their luck with Dr. Tweedie, the abortionist. They arrived in the dead of night on June 5, pounding on the door of his home, waking him, his wife, and his irate adult son. "I don't do abortions," Dr. Tweedie snarled before turning on his heel to go back to bed.[10] The investigators reminded him he was still on probation following his conviction for killing one of his abortion patients on the operating table. Tweedie's angry son accused the DA's men of browbeating his father. In response, they warned young Mr. Tweedie that unless Dad cooperated, he would be summoned before the grand jury. "Will you tell the Grand Jury you woke him up at quarter to two?" his son asked snidely.[11]

Their strong-arm tactics failing, the investigators changed their style, assuring the doctor's son that his father wasn't the target. "[W]e have done him favors in the past, we feel he will cooperate."[12] Those "favors" included the generous plea deal the doctor was given by the district attorney—

despite the fact that a woman died at Tweedie's hands—a sure sign of the pervasiveness of the abortion trade in Hollywood.

Later that day, at a more godly hour and with a friendlier attitude, Grossman and Tower returned, but Dr. Tweedie remained uncooperative. He denied that he'd performed any abortions on Joan, but like Oona's predicament of having been seen in Chaplin's bedroom, he knew Joan had been seen in his medical facility, so he had some explaining to do. "[T]he name Joan Berry has a familiar ring to it," he said, vaguely. He said he recalled seeing her in his office "storming around about something." He thought the name "Tim Durant" sounded familiar, too, but, he said, "I am very sure I never met him."[13]

It had been a long, frustrating day for Grossman and Tower, and it wasn't over yet. Word had gotten out that they were popping up all over town because when they arrived at Minna Wallis's Beverly Hills home at about nine o'clock in the evening, she and her attorney, Herbert Freston, were waiting. Freston's job was to muzzle Minna. When Wallis referred to Joan as "a nut," Freston gently reminded her the investigators had brought along a stenographer who was taking down every word. The lawyer lamely tried to correct the record by asserting his client "doesn't want to make any reflections on the girl at all," except that she already had.[14]

On June 6, the investigators called on Durant, who claimed to know nothing about procuring abortions for Joan or maneuvering to get her ejected from Beverly Hills.[15] By five o'clock that afternoon, they were at Chaplin's to interview Arden. The mere fact that Arden's interview was conducted in Chaplin's home was a sign he wasn't going to cooperate. When asked if he'd ever slept with Joan, Arden refused to answer "without advice of counsel."[16] Questioned about his claim to Muir and Hopper that he was the father of Joan's baby, Arden said he had been misunderstood.

"I merely mentioned that the allegation that Charlie Chaplin was the father seemed rather without foundation since any one of a hundred men, including myself, at one time or another had enjoyed the somewhat doubtful favors of Miss Joan Berry," said Arden.[17] So much for needing a lawyer's advice before discussing whether he'd slept with Joan.

At eleven thirty that evening, also at Chaplin's house, Grossman and Tower interviewed Edward Chaney. The butler's allegiance, which would prove fluid over time, happened to be with Chaplin that night. He seemed to know little about the personal life of the man in whose house he'd lived and worked every day. He denied that Oona ever spent the night at his boss's home.[18]

Even Chaplin's teenage sons were not spared. In the office of Chaplin's attorneys, Wright and Millikan, with attorney Frank Doherty at their side, the investigators conducted a joint interview with the boys, hardly the most optimum setup as it allowed them to get their stories straight.[19] It may, however, have been the only way Chaplin would agree to allow his sons to be interviewed. The questions embarrassed the boys.

After both of them denied having seen Oona sleep over at their father's home, they were asked, "Have you ever observed your father in bed with another woman?"[20]

"Never," said Charlie Jr.

"With any woman?"

Charlie Jr. shook his head "no."

When investigators looked to his brother, Sydney said, "The same, no."[21]

The only woman the boys would admit seeing their father embrace was their "stepmother," Paulette Goddard.[22]

The district attorney was considering several possible criminal charges against Chaplin: that he'd procured illegal abortions for Joan, engaged in a sexual relationship with seventeen-year-old Oona O'Neill, and conspired with Beverly Hills police and government officials to run Joan out of town in violation of her civil rights.[23] Howser told reporters the investigation was initiated at the request of Judge Griffin.[24] But Howser's real motive for the investigation was probably his fear of Florabel Muir, who had browbeaten the inexperienced and reluctant Howser into doing something to stop the practice of violating the rights of the little people in tony Beverly Hills.

Regardless of what sparked the investigation, the grand jury was interested. On June 8 it passed a resolution directing Howser to keep going and to report back.[25] Deputy District Attorney Vernon L. Ferguson, the prosecutor in charge of presentations to the grand jury, told the jurors that they'd hear from him in a week if enough evidence existed to bring charges.[26]

As if the antics of Charlie and Joan couldn't turn into more of a farce, Joan's lawyer made public a telegram from a chaplain at the Camp Hulen army base in Texas saying that a soldier there was claiming he was probably the father of her unborn child. Joan sniffed at the news. "That is utterly ridiculous. I never was on intimate terms with any soldier and I never heard of this one."[27]

Meanwhile, Jack Irwin was proof of the value of an attorney with his client's interests at heart. He negotiated an agreement with Wright and Millikan, approved by Judge William S. Baird, under which Chaplin agreed to pay $15,800 for Joan's hospital, legal, and living expenses pending the outcome of a paternity test to be administered four months after her child's birth. The eight-page agreement placed the paternity action in limbo. Available paternity testing in 1943 couldn't identify a child's father but could rule out a particular individual. Joan agreed that if the tests showed Chaplin wasn't the father, she would drop any further claims. Still, Chaplin continued to deny he was—or could be—responsible for Joan's pregnancy.[28] Next, Irwin moved to vacate Joan's guilty plea to the vagrancy charge, asserting that she was never a vagrant under California law but was under the influence of a sedative and emotionally distraught when she took the plea and had failed to reveal to the judge that her mother was capable of supporting her.[29]

June 11, 1943, was a chilly day for Southern California with temperatures ranging only from the mid-50s to the mid-60s.[30] A visibly nervous Joan appeared alongside her mother and Irwin at the Beverly Hills City Courthouse in a blue coat, a blue dress with a pink collar, and matching pink shoes. Her fingernails were painted bright red. At the hearing, Joan said nothing other than to quietly consent to Irwin's request to Judge Griffin that she be allowed to change her plea to "not guilty." After accepting the new plea the judge agreed that, based on the facts as stated in Irwin's motion, Joan had not been a vagrant back in January and dismissed the case.[31] Once Judge Griffin dismissed the case, her original attorney, Judge Holland, withdrew as fast as he could. "[O]wing to my court duties, my private practice and other activities, I feel I cannot devote the time and concentration" to Joan's case, he announced.[32]

And there were more surprises. The same day Joan's case was dismissed, District Attorney Howser announced he was closing the Chaplin investigation without submitting evidence to a grand jury. In a press release Howser announced: "no evidence has been developed which justifies the initiation of a prosecution."[33] Moral outrage aside at the treatment of a powerless, pregnant woman who had overstayed her welcome in Beverly Hills, proving Chaplin and his cohorts guilty of a crime would be difficult if not impossible. Chaplin's supporters had stonewalled investigators at every turn, and Joan's hysterics would make any prosecutor wary of going forward. Howser also included in his press statement that he found "no irregularity whatever" in the judge's actions.[34] Although Howser was stymied in his ability to proceed, his exoneration of Judge Griffin's behavior was outrageous. The judge—who should have known better—engaged in improper one-sided communications with interested parties about a case before him and accepted a guilty plea from a frightened woman who was ignorant of the law and did not have the benefit of an attorney at her side.

It would have taken a crusading and confident prosecutor to pursue Joan's case, and Howser was neither. He'd been appointed to his job in a backroom deal and was widely perceived as ineffectual. The following year, when he ran for a full term as DA, the *Los Angeles Times* endorsed an opponent. In a scathing assessment, the paper wrote: "Neither by training, experience or maturity does he measure up to the caliber of the chief subordinates in his office."[35]

But the snooping by Howser's investigators raised another problem for Chaplin—what to do about Oona O'Neill? She wanted to be married to her wealthy man; Chaplin wanted to wait until he could establish his innocence, which would take until several months after Joan's baby was born and the blood test results were in.[36] Durant urged him to send O'Neill back to New York until the scandal subsided. Chaplin attorney Loyd Wright advised the same.[37] O'Neill may have been young, but she wasn't stupid. Given how quickly Chaplin lost interest in his lovers—not to mention he had probably had sex with Joan in December when she waved her gun around in his bedroom—Oona was not going anywhere without first becoming Mrs. Charles Chaplin. "I insisted that we get married immediately," she told friends.[38]

The Little Tramp hated walking down the aisle, and after so many failed marriages it's no wonder. Chaplin's friendly biographer David Robinson wrote that the couple fell in love at first sight and had talked marriage soon after they met, planning to do so after the filming of *Shadow and Substance*. Oona turned eighteen on May 14, 1943, and Chaplin had pulled the plug on the movie in December 1942, so they could have married by mid-May.[39]

At fifty-four, Chaplin finally may have found the love of his life with a teenager, but the timing of the marriage raises questions. They chose June 16 for their wedding, which was the date the grand jury was to have started considering criminal charges against Chaplin, had Howser not shut down the investigation. Surely, O'Neill would have been summoned to the grand jury, putting her in a quandary. If she told the truth, Chaplin could have gone to jail for years for having had sex with a minor, the fate he had narrowly escaped before by marrying Lita Grey. If she lied, she could have gone to jail for perjury. If they were married, the law protected her from being forced to testify against her husband.

Chaplin's former lover, Georgia Hale, claimed that Chaplin was in a panic about marrying O'Neill. Hale never married after her romance with Chaplin ended, and she carried a torch for the rest of her life, so her story should be taken with a large grain of salt. Nonetheless, in her autobiography, *Intimate Close-Ups*, Hale claimed that the night before he married O'Neill, Chaplin came to her small apartment at 1665 North Sycamore Street in Hollywood and begged her to run away with him. The ecstatic thirty-nine-year-old, knowing nothing about any wedding plans with Oona, agreed to go but said she needed a day to get her affairs in order. Disappointed, Chaplin abruptly left. Still, Hale was under the impression they'd begin their new life together the next day. But while Hale was walking outside the next morning, a neighbor excitedly told her she'd heard a report on the radio that Chaplin had just gotten married in Santa Barbara. Crushed, Hale said she felt "utterly deserted."[40]

The Chaplin-O'Neill marriage on the sunny morning of June 16 was hush-hush. The small wedding party included the bride, the groom, and two witnesses, Chaplin's secretary, Catherine Hunter, and former Hearst newspaper columnist Harry Crocker, who had played in *The Circus* as the handsome rival who wins the girl away from the Tramp. Having later worked as a publicity agent, Crocker's role was to control the press. What Chaplin didn't know was that Crocker was an FBI informant. A week after the wedding he told an agent in the Los Angeles FBI field office that a maid was threatening to blackmail Chaplin about O'Neill's presence at his house, perhaps another reason Chaplin made a rushed fourth trip to the altar.[41]

The wedding party started out in the wee hours of the morning— speeding in two cars to avoid the press—for the Santa Barbara County Courthouse, some eighty miles from Beverly Hills, for a marriage license. Later, there would be grousing to the federal Office of Price Administration because Chaplin drove so far and so fast to get married when the rest of the nation was subject to wartime gasoline rationing.[42]

At about 8:40 a.m., a visibly nervous Chaplin entered the clerk's office for the license. Deputy County Clerk Ira Altschul said that Chaplin's hand shook so much as he was filling out the paperwork that "he could hardly hold the pen. He kept looking around him all the time, and even forgot to take off his hat."[43] From there, they drove to the seaside town of Carpinteria, where seventy-eight-year-old Justice of the Peace Clinton P. Moore married them in his living room in less than five minutes.[44]

Providing further proof the wedding was spur of the moment, Oona wore an unflattering dark wraparound dress with ruffles along the front, hem, and sleeves rather than a pretty white frock. O'Neill had bought the dress at Klein's-on-the-Square, a cut-rate department store on Fourteenth Street in New York City, where she and her mother shopped when they lived hand-to-mouth.[45] Chaplin looked more festive than his bride in a light-brown double-breasted suit with a white boutonniere, a homburg, and wingtip shoes.[46] Afterward, while Chaplin waited in the car, Crocker ducked into a drugstore to buy a bottle of champagne to put the patina of celebration on the event.[47]

Everyone was caught off guard. The day before the marriage, *Daily Variety* reported that Chaplin was planning to elope with Joan, a fantasy to which she and her mother were still clinging.[48] It was the ubiquitous Muir who broke the bad news. After hearing it, Joan became hysterical.[49] She slipped away from the hotel where she was staying with her mother and went to the American Airlines office to book a flight to Mexico because she "couldn't breathe the same air that Chaplin and Oona would breathe." But with no money to pay for a ticket, she dejectedly returned to the hotel. She told Muir that her plan had been to jump out of the airplane.[50] Finally, Joan was carted off to a sanitarium.[51] Joan's mother covered up her daughter's breakdown by telling reporters her daughter was placed in a sanitarium because of the wartime housing shortage.[52]

The marriage would seal O'Neill's fate with her father, who never spoke to her again.[53] The playwright attributed his daughter's decision to marry Chaplin to the silent star's wealth and to her intoxication with publicity.[54] It apparently never occurred to Eugene O'Neill, who won a Nobel Prize after fictionalizing his dysfunctional family of origin, that his teenage daughter might be seeking love from the fifty-four-year-old Chaplin that she couldn't get from her father, who was only a year older.

The bride and groom honeymooned at a secluded estate at 119 Middle Road in Montecito, outside Santa Barbara. There, only the sometimes-loyal butler Chaney stood between them and intrepid members of the press who tracked them down. Chaney turned all the reporters away.[55]

But on his honeymoon, Chaplin became deeply depressed.[56] He wrote in his autobiography that he and O'Neill hid away in Montecito for two months, but it was really only a matter of weeks. By the first weekend of July, he and his new bride got gussied up in evening wear to enjoy champagne at the Mocambo, where Chaplin used to escort Joan. When photographers snapped away, Chaplin threatened to leave unless the management ejected them.[57]

Still hoping for a wedding of his own was the Texas soldier who told his army chaplain he was responsible for Joan's pregnancy. Without alerting his superiors, Pvt. Fredrick John Steinhauser, a twenty-one-year-old machinist from New Jersey, went AWOL from Camp Hulen and hitchhiked twelve hundred miles to Los Angeles to get down on one knee before Joan. But first, on Wednesday, June 23, he stopped at the CBS radio station in Hollywood to announce to the world his intention to marry her.[58]

Once again, Jack Irwin leaped into action, this time enlisting the help of Muir and a pair of private investigators. Muir contacted Steinhauser by phone, and they arranged to meet at the Hollywood Canteen, the entertainment venue for the military that operated at 1451 Cahuenga Boulevard during the war. Muir posed as Gertrude Berry, and a female investigator pretended to be Joan. The actual Joan was still reeling in an Orange County sanitarium where she'd been placed after Chaplin's wedding.[59]

"You remember me, don't you Joan?" the hapless Steinhauser, dressed in army fatigues, asked the young investigator. Muir, showing appropriate motherly concern, inquired as to whether he had the financial means to take care of her daughter. Steinhauser assured her that he did and that Joan would be able to wait out her pregnancy at his sister's house in New Jersey. Irwin, having had enough, told Steinhauser he was a fraud and delivered him to the waiting military police, who hauled him back to Texas.[60] Then there was a lull. "All was finally quiet yesterday on the Charlie Chaplin-Oona O'Neill-Joan Berry marital and legal fronts," reported the *Los Angeles Times*.[61]

But Chaplin wasn't home free yet. Three thousand miles away, in Washington, DC, FBI Director J. Edgar Hoover received a memo from one of his favorite G-men, Los Angeles Special-Agent-in-Charge Richard B. Hood, about Charlie and Joan. Hood had been with the bureau since 1934 and held degrees from Dartmouth and the University of Pittsburgh School of Law.[62] Since local law enforcement authorities had decided against indicting Chaplin for state crimes, Hood and Hoover had talked on August 17 to brainstorm about possible federal crimes Chaplin may have committed involving Oona and Joan.[63]

Aghast at what he heard from Hood, as well as what he'd been reading in the newspapers all summer, Hoover jotted a note on an agency memo with his familiar thick blue pen: "Shouldn't we run this down? If a White Slave violation we ought to go after it vigorously."[64] On August 27, 1943, Hoover answered his own question. "Expedite Investigation and Submission of Report," he ordered.[65] The federal investigation of Charlie Chaplin and Joan Barry had begun.

TEN

"WE NEVER CLOSE A CASE"

Chaplin's celebrity and moral laxity with women gave Hoover the excuse to pick up where Fred Howser left off. Joining him in the effort was Charles Hardy Carr Jr., the ambitious new U.S. attorney in Los Angeles, just appointed to his $8,000-a-year job by President Roosevelt on May 20, 1943.[1] Prosecuting Chaplin would land Carr on the front pages of newspapers all over America—and even some parts of the world—and would prove that federal prosecutors and the FBI would not be intimidated by anyone, no matter how famous.

There was also the matter of manpower. Whereas Howser's investigation had rested entirely on the shoulders of Grossman and Tower, Hoover had nearly 5,000 FBI agents in field offices around the country.[2] The FBI's Chaplin investigation was led by Special-Agent-in-Charge Richard B. Hood, who had about 140 agents working for him in the bureau's Los Angeles field office.[3] G-men in New York, Chicago, Detroit, Richmond, New Haven, Tulsa, Kansas City, Omaha, Oklahoma City, Grand Rapids, and Miami pitched in.[4] The FBI interviewed more than 130 suspects or sources and generated some 1,250 pages of official reports. The FBI's motto, "We never close a case," would make life miserable for Chaplin for at least the next year and arguably for the rest of his life.[5]

Chaplin was doomed in Hoover's eyes not only by his moral failings but also by his radical political ideas. As early as 1922 Chaplin had an FBI file with his name on it, labeled "Charlie Chaplin, et al., Los Angeles, Cal., COMMUNIST ACTIVITIES." His sin back then was to host a reception for socialist labor organizer and future Communist Party candidate for president William Z. Foster.[6] Of late, Chaplin had attacked American capitalism in his movie *Modern Times* and had been calling for the Allies to open a Second Front. Hoover had no tolerance for any political opinion left of center; he couldn't stand FDR or Eleanor Roosevelt, Henry Wallace, Harry Hopkins, or the New Deal.[7]

The Federal Bureau of Investigation began as the Bureau of Investigation in 1908 and became an independent agency within the Department of Justice eight years before the Chaplin Mann Act investigation began.[8] John Edgar Hoover, a forty-eight-year-old bachelor who'd lived with his mother up until she died five years earlier, was "The Director." The bureau would be held in high esteem for many years for its modern crime-solving techniques. Because of Hoover's dedication and cunning, as well as the potentially embarrassing dossiers he amassed on Washington's political elite, he became the most powerful and feared man in America. Cowed U.S. presidents, afraid of what Hoover's files contained about their own misdeeds, reluctantly left him at the helm of the bureau until his death of a heart attack in May 1972.[9]

From his fifth-floor corner sanctuary at the Department of Justice overlooking Pennsylvania Avenue and Ninth Street NW in Washington, DC, Hoover micromanaged the bureau with an iron fist and his thick blue pen.[10] Agents quaked when receiving letters, memos, or teletypes with his hand-scribbled markings in the margins. Nothing was too petty for the attention of The Director. When Agent Hood was diagnosed with athlete's foot and failed to take care of it, an exasperated Hoover wrote: "It was suggested that the necessary action be taken by you to remedy the infection of your feet and the Bureau be advised. To date, no reply has been received from you and it is requested that you immediately advise the Bureau."[11]

FBI agents were mostly accountants and lawyers, which meant they were smart and knew how to dig deep to solve crime. They were lean, white men who had to dress conservatively, retain their hair (The Director thought baldness made a bad impression), keep their feet off the top of the desk, and drive a clean car.[12]

Renowned during the Depression for capturing bandits George "Machine Gun" Kelly, John Dillinger (whose death mask became a popular feature on the FBI Headquarters tour), and Charles "Pretty Boy" Floyd, the FBI had a golden image that would become tarnished after Hoover's death with revelations about agents who broke into homes and offices, tapped telephones, and opened private mail to obtain incriminating information about suspects. Hoover saw Communists around every corner and forced agents to waste endless hours spying on harmless political activities.[13]

Hoover was also obsessed with "White Slave" rings, using the specter of their existence to squeeze larger FBI budgets out of Congress. The White Slave Traffic Act, also known as the Mann Act, was named for its author, Illinois Republican congressman James Robert Mann, and signed into law in 1910.[14] It made it a federal crime to knowingly transport a woman across state lines "for the purpose of prostitution or debauchery or for any other, immoral purpose."[15]

The law was broadly applied to even consensual sex. In *Caminetti v. United States*, the United States Supreme Court held that it was illegal to transport a mistress across state lines for sexual purposes even if she wanted to go.[16] Before Chaplin, the most famous Mann Act case involved Black heavyweight champ Jack Johnson, who in 1912 was indicted for bringing a willing white prostitute from Chicago to Pittsburgh. Regardless of her consent, a judge determined "if money had changed hands, if the woman had crossed state lines, and if a sexual act had occurred, the law had been violated." Johnson was convicted, sentenced to a year in jail, and fined $1,000.[17]

Joan had gone from California to New York in the fall of 1942 with a train ticket paid for by Chaplin and allegedly had sex with him in a hotel there. If that had been Chaplin's intent in buying her ticket, he violated the Mann Act. The first official report of an investigation into Chaplin's relationship with Joan came from the New York FBI office looking into Joan's childhood and summarizing public information about their affair. It was dated September 2, 1943, and labeled "CHARLES SPENCER CHAPLIN; MARY LOUISE GRIBBLE, with aliases Joan Berry, Joan Barry, VICTIM; WHITE SLAVE TRAFFIC ACT."[18] By October, a longer list of Joan's aliases would be added—Mary Louise Berry, Joan Barratt, Mary L. Barratt, Joanne Berry, and Joan Barry. Joan said her legal name was Joan Berry.[19]

The FBI moved quickly but so quietly that not even Joan was aware Hoover had become interested in her case.[20] The fact that she did not approach the bureau demanding that Chaplin be prosecuted undercuts his supporters who were determined to paint her as a crazy, vengeful woman hell-bent on destroying him. Although Joan and her mother were after Chaplin's money, there is no evidence they wanted him thrown in jail. The Chaplin investigation was fueled by what Hoover read in the newspapers.

Early on, the bureau wanted to speak to Joan and Chaplin's butler, Edward Chaney, who accompanied him on the New York trip. Both were off-limits because Joan was eight months pregnant and Chaney was recovering from bladder surgery and a possible nervous breakdown.[21] Until they could be interviewed, agents filled their time and their file pages by surreptitiously poking around the Waldorf Astoria in New York, hoping to find employees who recalled seeing Chaplin and Joan there in October 1942.[22]

Meanwhile, at ten thirty on Saturday night, October 2, Joan gave birth to a six-pound, five-ounce baby girl, whom she named Carol Ann, at South Van Ness Hospital in Hollywood, where she had been admitted under Chaplin's middle name, Spencer.[23] Her doctor was there—as was Chaplin's—although the putative father was absent. Jack Irwin, Gertrude Berry, and a private detective working for Chaplin, Joseph E. Dunne, paced the corridor outside the delivery room prior to the baby's birth. As soon as Carol Ann was born, Dunne watched carefully as the baby's foot was pressed into an inkpad to take a little print.[24]

Joan proudly showed off her newborn to reporters who squeezed into her hospital room. "She's just what I wanted—a girl," Joan beamed.[25] After reporters got their peek at the child, chief nurse Cora Sherman snatched the baby away, put her in the nursery, padlocked the door, and secured the key in the pocket of her starched white uniform. "I'm not taking any chances on any possible hocus-pocus," she told the press.[26]

Recovering elsewhere from surgery, Chaney, who remained friendly to Joan despite all the hell she'd put the Chaplin household through, was believed by the FBI to be a fountain of anti-Chaplin information. But Chaney would turn out to be nothing but a headache for the government, switching his loyalties back and forth between his employer and Joan. Finally meeting with agents on October 30, he admitted he had lied to the district attorney's investigators in June when he told them Oona O'Neill never lived at Chaplin's before they were married.[27] He promised the FBI agents he wouldn't breathe a word to Chaplin about his meeting with them, but then on October 31 he told Tim Durant and on November 1 he sat down with Chaplin's lawyers for a debriefing.[28]

By the end of October, Hoover was antsy for the Los Angeles field office to meet with Joan, but her doctor kept postponing.[29] On November 5, Joan finally walked into the FBI's office with Irwin at her side and gave agents the full Joan experience. "In talking with her it was noted that it is difficult to maintain a logical conversation because she branches off on some other subject which comes into her mind," wrote an FBI agent in a report to Carr about the meeting. With difficulty, the agent extracted the basic story from her about her visit to New York in October 1942. But he also learned to his dismay that Joan was addicted to sleeping pills, "which served to intoxicate her rather than cause her to sleep."[30]

Within a week of Joan's first interview, Hood met with U.S. Attorney Carr to discuss the case. Carr was skeptical about a Mann Act prosecution because he thought it lacked a "commercial angle" and he was uneasy with Joan's "reputation." [31] Most troubling for Carr and the FBI was Joan's relationship with Getty. Despite Joan's (and Getty's) denials, the agents were highly suspicious about the claims that their relationship was platonic.[32]

Carr preferred to prosecute a conspiracy case against Chaplin, his surrogates, the Beverly Hills police, and local public officials for Joan's vagrancy arrest and subsequent ejection from the city. Carr believed the conspirators had violated Joan's civil rights, and he was ready to present the evidence to a federal grand jury on November 24, 1943. But that date came and went without his doing so, which suggests his superiors in Washington might have worried about the strength of his legal theory.[33] Still, Hoover wanted his agents to move the matter forward. "GIVE PREFERRED AND EXPEDITE ATTENTION THIS CASE," he telexed to agents around the country.[34]

By November, news of the FBI investigation was leaking out, yet the bureau foolishly thought it could keep a lid on the story. Hood wrote to Hoover, "Carr and myself have received inquiries from local newspapers for a story on investigation of Chaplin." But he promised the director that "No information has been furnished them to date and it is expected the story can be kept from breaking."[35]

Now it was Chaplin who was antsy. Hood's deputy, Agent James C. Ellsworth, who learned it from a "confidential source," said that Chaplin sent a telegram to Supreme Court Justice Frank Murphy, a pro-labor Roosevelt appointee, asking why the FBI was investigating him. It is unclear how Chaplin knew Murphy well enough to contact him except that Chaplin, who rarely wrote to anybody, had previously sent him a handwritten note (which included a sketch he drew of himself as the Little Tramp) in 1936 (before Murphy was on the Supreme Court) expressing admiration for

Murphy's sense of justice.[36] Murphy phoned Chaplin in response to his telegram, explaining he had no idea why the FBI was sniffing around but that he'd heard from reporters in Washington that Chaplin was under investigation. Perhaps flattered by communication from a man of Chaplin's stature, the justice supposedly promised to try to find out what the FBI was up to, but Chaplin would find out for himself soon enough.[37]

Ellsworth's source also said that Chaplin had even reached out to ex-wife Paulette Goddard for help. Appalled by the FBI's actions, Goddard considered Joan "ghastly" and was surprised her ex had been attracted to her in the first place. Moreover, Goddard had no patience for women who were not savvy enough to stay off the casting couch. Years later, Goddard recalled to Andy Warhol, who interviewed her for a biography he never wrote, that powerful men in Hollywood came on to young actresses all the time but that the smart ones—like her—waited to see the contract and the money before believing their promises.[38] Goddard suggested to Chaplin that he boost his reputation by cracking open his bank account, purchasing a $1 million war bond, and telling the press about it. And feisty Paulette had yet another idea—go straight to Hoover and ask why those "bastards" were asking questions about him.[39]

Chaplin, who had already given up on *Shadow and Substance,* focused on what would become the controversial *Monsieur Verdoux.* One bright spot was that Oona gave up her dreams of a movie career and began her lifetime of devotion to him.[40] Dutifully, Oona typed up his *Monsieur Verdoux* script and lined her dressing room mirror with her husband's photographs.[41] But domestic bliss and engrossing work couldn't keep Chaplin from crumbling once he realized he couldn't stop the investigation. "Even in moments of minor stress, my father could never keep his head," Charles Jr. wrote in his book, *My Father, Charlie Chaplin.*[42] Soon defense lawyer Jerry Giesler became a fixture on one of the rattan chairs at Chaplin's house.[43] Giesler believed the case against Chaplin was far weaker than Errol Flynn's statutory rape case that he'd successfully defended the year before.[44] But that did little to calm Chaplin, who paced back and forth anxiously and endlessly. Giesler would sit calmly in his chair and tell him to stop worrying.[45]

The person who might have been able to truly keep Chaplin calm was gone. Powerful New York lawyer and Tammany Hall fixer Nathan Burkan had represented Chaplin for years, negotiating his million-dollar movie deals and extricating him from disastrous marriages while protecting his fortune. Burkan knew the movers and shakers in Washington, and they knew him. He might have been able to place a few phone calls to the congressmen who controlled Hoover's FBI budget and close down the investigation before evidence was presented to a grand jury. But Burkan had died of a heart attack in 1936 at age fifty-seven.[46]

While Chaplin was wearing out the carpet pacing in front of Giesler, U.S. Attorney Carr was in Washington, doing his own nervous walk in front of his friend, Assistant Attorney General Tom Clark, and their boss, Attorney General Francis Biddle.[47] Carr knew Hoover was hot on a White Slave prosecution, but the young U.S. attorney still clung to his belief that Chaplin and friends had conspired to deprive Joan of her rights and wanted to sell the attorney general on that case. After Carr's pitch, Biddle and Clark agreed, stating they thought the chances for conviction were "good."[48]

And then the lid blew off the Mann Act investigation. In his broadcast on December 26, 1943, Walter Winchell revealed—without mentioning Joan's name—that Chaplin was being looked at by the FBI for a Mann Act violation.[49] The United Press ran the story over the wires on January 5, 1944, and it was published in newspapers around the country.[50] The next day, the *Los Angeles Times* chimed in: "F.B.I. Queries Justice in Chaplin-Berry Case."[51]

Carr could hardly delay the grand jury presentation much longer. He sat down with Joan for two full days, going over her testimony and testing whether she could withstand the rigors of cross-examination. On December 31, 1943, in his office in the Federal Building at 312 North Spring Street, he made sure she understood that she would be "expected to tell the full truth of this matter on the witness stand in the presence of Chaplin."[52] Soon enough, melodramatic Joan was publicly referring to Carr as her "father confessor."[53]

Carr had impaneled a grand jury for the Chaplin case on September 15, 1943, which allowed him to legally issue subpoenas for evidence or witnesses. But it wasn't until mid-January 1944 that Carr started calling witnesses.[54] The grand jury is as old as the reign of England's King Henry II in 1166, when a system was established by which local informers would advise the Crown about suspected criminals so the king could get a cut of the fines and forfeitures assessed against the wrongdoers. The proceedings were secret in order to give the sheriff a chance to arrest the accused before they could flee.[55] The right to indictment by a grand jury for a serious violation of federal law was ensconced in the Fifth Amendment to the U.S. Constitution, ratified in 1791.

A grand jury consists of sixteen to twenty-three persons to whom the U.S. attorney presents evidence to obtain an indictment, which is the vehicle by which a defendant is brought to trial. The role of the U.S. attorney is to advise and assist; he or she has no right to be in the jury chamber during deliberations, and ideally the jurors should be "totally independent" in their decision-making.[56] The secrecy imposed on the grand jury nearly nine hundred years ago remains. The rationale today, besides to prevent tipping off suspects, is to prevent the destruction of evidence and witness tampering. Secrecy also preserves the reputations of the innocent and encourages witnesses to come forward.[57]

As a potential defendant, Chaplin could not be forced to testify, and Giesler informed Carr that he wouldn't.[58] "This whole thing is absurd," Giesler fumed to reporters. Chaplin "has had no connection with any act that would deprive anyone of any rights, and he does not see why he should appear for any private questioning" or testify before the grand jury.[59] Giesler's posturing hid a carefully thought-out strategy. If Carr didn't have the goods on his client, Giesler didn't want to run the risk that Chaplin might blurt out something that would incriminate him. And if an indictment was a fait accompli, he didn't want to lock Chaplin into a version of events that could be used against him during cross-examination at trial.

Chaplin had more troubles than just Carr's investigation. United Artists, the company he co-owned, had been losing money for years. Chaplin's wildly popular movies were the result of meticulous, pokey filmmaking, which did not help profits. In 1941, UA had loaned David Selznick, who had joined the company as a managing partner, $300,000 to make three movies to help lift it out of its financial slump. But Selznick turned around and sold the rights to those movies to another company, leaving UA with nothing for its investment. Livid, Chaplin sued Selznick and threatened to sue UA and Mary Pickford because they wouldn't join him in the lawsuit. Pickford wanted to settle what promised to be an expensive legal battle.[60] But Chaplin was distracted, to say the least. On January 27, 1944, Chaplin's attorney Loyd Wright telegrammed UA President Edward C. Raftery: "Little man indicated recently in view of his situation he did not desire me to approach him on any United Artists matters."[61]

On January 12, 1944, Carr began his grand jury presentation by calling the FBI agents who interviewed Arden, Durant, and the Beverly Hills police officers involved in Joan's arrest.[62] Hearsay is admissible in federal grand jury presentations, allowing prosecutors to call FBI agents as witnesses to summarize statements made to them and thereby help shape the narrative.[63]

Unlike Chaplin, who maintained his right to silence, Judge Charles J. Griffin, who'd ordered Joan out of Beverly Hills, testified for nearly two hours.[64] Muir and Hopper also testified.[65] Mayor Arthur H. Erb told reporters that he and Judge Griffin were cooperating with the prosecution to "see that justice is done."[66] Mayor Erb had no involvement in the case, other than being dragged into it by Judge Griffin and the fact that he'd hired Chief Anderson, who was in hot water because his subordinate, Captain White, had escorted Joan to the train when she was ordered to leave Beverly Hills. Carr lived in Beverly Hills, and the case was ripping apart that wealthy community. Muir reported that Carr was "getting the support of the mayor's political enemies and there is a prospect of a political upheaval in the city of millionaires before the Chaplin-Barry case is finished."[67]

Although they'd given Carr the okay on the civil rights case involving Joan, officials at the Department of Justice in Washington had second thoughts. Coaching Carr from three thousand miles away, department lawyers advised him that the law on that part of the case was "close" and suggested that he "take his time in his presentation." In light of these concerns, Carr now looked more favorably on the Mann Act case, which previously hadn't interested him as much as the civil rights conspiracy.[68]

Los Angeles was in the middle of an unusual winter heat wave the week of Joan's grand jury testimony. On Wednesday, January 19, 1944, the temperature topped out at 88 degrees. The next day, when Joan showed up to testify, it had cooled slightly to 77 degrees, but she still must have been roasting in her demure, high-collared white blouse and dark winter suit.[69] Noticeably heavier than she was when under contract to Chaplin by about twenty pounds, the new mother described herself to reporters as "nervous as a cat." [70] While waiting outside the jury room with Carr, Joan smiled for photographers and chatted with journalists.[71] Once inside, after about an hour testifying in the brown leather witness chair, she asked for a break. As she emerged, flashbulbs exploded. She copped a cigarette from a court employee, saying, "I'm still shaking."[72]

At least one newspaper, the *New York Journal-American*, reported that before the break "her answers to questions were becoming incoherent."[73] It is a crime for prosecutors or grand jurors to reveal what goes on inside the jury chamber, but nothing prevents witnesses from discussing their own testimony. Unless Joan commented on the quality of her answers, the reporter must have had a mole in the chamber. She returned to continue her testimony, and after another two hours, the jury was down for lunch. Reappearing in the hallway "red-eyed and visibly shaken," Joan left on the arms of two FBI men.[74] Returning in the afternoon, Joan completed her testimony, posed for more newspaper pictures, and reconnoitered with lawyers in Carr's office for a postmortem.[75] The next morning Joan showed up drunk at a local supermarket and told any shoppers who cared to listen—and there were several—that she was out celebrating the completion of her grand jury testimony.[76]

Although Joan's bender didn't make the papers, other articles about the grand jury proceedings infuriated Hoover. Eager not to get into hot water with The Director, Special Agent Hood blamed Carr. "I am sure that he has furnished information to the press from time to time, with the understanding that he would not be quoted directly," Hood wrote to Hoover on January 15, 1944. "[C]are must be taken in the future in important cases so that they are not discussed with him until the investigation has been fully completed, so there will be no premature publicity," he added.[77]

The Chaplin case was turning into a hot potato with lawyers at the Department of Justice. Carr told reporters he was holding off asking the grand jury to vote an indictment until he received instructions from Washington about what charges to bring. There was concern Carr's statement might encourage the defense to move to quash any future indictments due to illegal interference with the grand jury from Washington. Carr's friend, Tom C. Clark, who would succeed Biddle as attorney general, just shook his head, knowing that Carr had a tendency to "pop off" at times. Nonetheless, Clark called Carr on the carpet for being indiscreet.[78]

For Carr, it just seemed to be getting worse. Jack Irwin confided to him that Joan's behavior had deteriorated since her grand jury appearance. Specifically, she had gone on a "drinking spree," leading to fights with her mother. Irwin's solution was to have the FBI guard Joan 24/7 to be sure she didn't get arrested and jeopardize the case. Hoover put his foot down. Babysitting Joan was "beyond the purview of our jurisdiction." His advice for Carr: get an indictment and move the case to trial—fast.[79] With the FBI refusing to watch over her, Irwin enlisted Muir to do it. Muir had successfully talked Joan out of a cockamamie idea to run off to Mexico and scolded her for being drunk in public while the case was pending. Joan promised to behave.[80]

On the eve of the grand jury vote, the feet of the Department of Justice officials were growing ever colder. An attorney sent from Washington to Los Angeles to assist with the case told Carr he did not think the government would prevail. But after almost six months of nonstop work, Carr was not about to give up. In his job for less than a year, Carr knew that if he stopped the investigation he'd look weak at best, and at worst, it would look as if he were kowtowing to Chaplin's celebrity.[81]

On February 10, the grand jury returned four indictments. One was against Chaplin for violating the Mann Act by sending Joan from Los Angeles to New York and back to engage in sex. Another charged Chaplin, Durant, Arden, Judge Griffin (whose grand jury testimony obviously did not help him), and police officials White, Marple, and Reno for conspiring to violate Joan's civil rights by running her out of Beverly Hills. A third indictment charged Chaplin, Arden, and White with conspiring to convince Judge Griffin to float Joan out of town. The fourth charged the same trio with conspiracy but added Griffin to the indictment for going along with it.[82] Carr had considered seeking indictments against Minna Wallis, for her role in the conspiracy, and another against her alone or with Durant for perjury for lying to the FBI. But in the end, Wallis remained in the clear and nobody was charged with perjury.[83]

Florabel Muir and Agness Underwood of the Los Angeles *Herald-Express* broke the indictment story, even though reporters were fed it simultaneously. The women, experienced in covering crime, knew how to skip the legalese and jump to the meat of it. Muir bragged in her autobiography, *Headline Happy*, that she'd had the story out before other reporters had even made their way through the opening legalese.[84] Beating the wire services by half an hour was a feat to be proud of, but it took more than Muir's ability to read an indictment. It also involved a little trickery; phone calls were hard to put through in wartime, and Muir, knowing the indictment or indictments were about to be unsealed, called her bosses at the *Daily News* in New York and hogged the line by yakking about irrelevant matters to keep the line open.[85] Once Muir's story got out, the news splashed across papers around the world, knocking World War II right off the front pages. Joan's dream had at last come true; Charlie Chaplin had made her a star.

ELEVEN

THE MAGNIFICENT MOUTHPIECE

The federal courthouse was packed on Valentine's Day 1944 with report-ers, photographers, and gawkers jostling for a glimpse of the Little Tramp getting his comeuppance. After the arrest formalities were completed, Chaplin and his codefendants were ordered to return a week later at 9:30 a.m. sharp to be arraigned by Judge James Francis Thaddeus O'Connor, known as "J. F. T. O'Connor," or "Jefty" to his friends.[1] At the arraignment the judge would determine whether they would remain at liberty or be jailed until trial as flight risks.

The FBI feared that once Chaplin was aware he was under investigation he would flee.[2] But Chaplin wasn't going anywhere. America was his home; he'd spent his entire adulthood in California enjoying a charmed life. The only place Chaplin longed to flee was the courthouse, where Giesler would recall that in the hallways at Chaplin's initial court appearance the mob made "the snakelike sound of hissing, which, of all massed human sounds, is the most frightening."[3] After suffering the humiliation of being arrested, heckled, fingerprinted, and photographed, Chaplin retreated to Summit Drive. Despite the turmoil outside, inside the household there was the promise of some stability and joy. Eighteen-year-old Oona was three months pregnant with Geraldine Chaplin, the first of their eight children together.[4]

But for the moment, a different pregnancy and birth overshadowed that one. Now that Joan's daughter, Carol Ann, was four months old, the baby, Joan, and Charlie were scheduled to take the blood tests that would prove whether the child was a Chaplin. The morning after he was finger-printed, Chaplin walked into a lab at 657 South Westlake Avenue in Los Angeles, rolled up his sleeve, and offered his arm to give a thimble-sized vial of blood to Dr. V. L. Andrews, a physician he'd personally selected. An hour later, Joan and Carol Ann went to the same facility, and each provided blood to a physician of Joan's choosing, Dr. Roy Hammack. The two doctors selected Dr. Newton Evans as a neutral expert and observer.[5]

By the end of the day the results were in: Chaplin's blood type was O, Joan's was A, and Carol Ann's was B.[6] Much to the surprise of many—maybe even Chaplin—it was biologically impossible for him to be Carol Ann's father. The three doctors reviewed the tests and agreed. The news was splashed across front pages everywhere, sharing space with articles about heavy Allied bombing overseas.[7]

Joan collapsed when she heard the results, her mother told reporters.[8] Jack Irwin probably felt like passing out too. When Father Lee had talked him into taking the case, Joan's personal reputation was at stake; now Irwin's professional reputation was on the line. Surely, he wouldn't have taken the case had he not believed Chaplin was responsible for her pregnancy. Now Irwin was saddled with a woman who at best was so promiscuous by 1940s standards that she had no idea who had fathered her child. At worst, she was a conniving liar out to take Chaplin to the cleaners. Either way, it was time for Irwin to make a quick exit.

The legal agreement called for the case to be dropped if testing proved Chaplin was not the father. Initially, Joan and her mother intended to live up to it.[9] Although they could keep the money Chaplin had already paid, his support would now end, and Joan would have to stick to a budget and get a job. A few newspaper articles, most notably one by Muir, insinuated that Chaplin might have gamed the test results. Muir's piece included assertions by unnamed "prominent medical men" that drugs existed that could temporarily change one's blood type.[10] But Morris Fishbein, editor of the *Journal of the American Medical Association*, shot down the Muir article, insisting that blood tests to determine paternity were "conclusive" and that no drug existed that could change a person's blood type.[11]

Irwin wrote to Joan's mother, begging to be relieved as counsel.[12] But no matter what kind of mess Joan had gotten him into, Irwin was a gentleman. He told her mother that the conclusion from the blood test results "in no way disturbs my confidence in Joan's sincerity."[13]

The age-old expression "no good deed goes unpunished" seemed appropriate for the man who stepped up as a favor to his priest. Complicating matters further, once lawyers have entered an appearance in a court case, they cannot walk away from it without a judge's permission. In an affidavit he filed with Los Angeles Superior Court Judge Stanley Mosk, now assigned to oversee the matter, Irwin stated, "In view of my agreement [the stipulation he had signed with Chaplin's lawyers] I certainly could not ethically or properly attack it. Further, your affiant saith not."[14] And then, with the judge's approval, Irwin was gone. He didn't walk away empty-handed; he earned $1,600, or about $23,500 in today's dollars, for his trouble. It was his share of the $5,000 in attorneys' fees Chaplin paid under the stipulation. The rest of the money went to cover legal expenses and to pay the first two lawyers who got involved, Judge Holland and Barry Woodmansee.[15]

The blood test results had no impact on U.S. Attorney Charles Carr. He issued a statement: "The opinions reported by the press concerning the parentage of Miss Berry's child, even if conclusive, are matters concerning civil action and not involved in a criminal prosecution by the government."[16] And with that he returned to the inner sanctum of his office and provided no further comment. Although usually garrulous with reporters, he complained that as far as the Joan Barry case was concerned, he had been misquoted once too often.[17]

Consequently, Chaplin was forced to get down to business with Giesler. The legendary criminal defense lawyer came at the suggestion of Chaplin's friends and his longtime civil attorney, Loyd Wright. Chaplin would later say that he regretted hiring the renowned lawyer because by hiring Giesler it made him look like he was "in serious trouble."[18] Except he *was* in serious trouble, perhaps the worst trouble of his life. Chaplin's regrets about Giesler could have been the result of sticker shock once he saw the lawyer's astronomical bill—$60,000, or $882,000 today.[19] But when Chaplin was under indictment, everyone knew that Giesler was his best chance at avoiding decades behind bars.

While Giesler and Wright prepped witnesses at the bungalow that served as Chaplin's office on his studio property, Giesler sent investigators to dive into every aspect of Joan's romantic past. His planned trial strategy was to tar Joan the way he'd sullied the teenagers who accused Errol Flynn of rape—by convincing the jury that Joan was promiscuous and was the sexual aggressor in her affair with Chaplin. This was a trick he perfected back in 1931 when he convinced a jury in the retrial of fifty-four-year-old movie impresario Alexander Pantages, accused of raping a seventeen-year-old, that Pantages was the victim of a sexually experienced young girl.[20] It is a strategy forbidden by the rules of evidence today.[21] Modern courts consider it irrelevant: an unchaste woman can be the victim of a sex crime just as easily as a virginal one; even then it was irrelevant as far as a Mann Act prosecution was concerned.

Harold Lee "Jerry" Giesler was to California's courtrooms what Chaplin was to the world's movie screens—a maestro. The wealthy in hot water were known to yell, "Get me Giesler!" Just as moviegoers knew Chaplin as "The Little Tramp," the legal community knew Giesler as "The Magnificent Mouthpiece."[22] His wins for the Hollywood community were legendary; besides Flynn and Pantages, he'd successfully represented Busby Berkeley after he killed two people while drunk driving in the wrong direction and Edward G. Robinson Jr. following accusations he was sticking up cab drivers.[23] Only Giesler's mentor, the flamboyant Earl Rogers, who died in 1922, was more revered among the state's trial lawyers.

Two portraits hung on the wall behind Giesler's desk in his office at 215 West Fifth Street in downtown Los Angeles. One was of Rogers in his prime, and the other was of legendary criminal defense lawyer Clarence Darrow.[24] Giesler was a novice in Rogers's office in 1912 when he helped him successfully defend Darrow, accused of bribing jurors in the murder trial of the McNamara brothers who had bombed the *Los Angeles Times* building in a labor dispute. Had Rogers lost, Darrow would have gone to jail for years, lost his law license, and never become one of the world's most famous trial lawyers able to represent clients and causes like he did in the Scopes Monkey trial.[25]

Born in 1886 to a moderately prosperous banker and his wife in the small town of Wilton Junction, Iowa, Giesler attended law school at the University of Iowa without first having gone to college. Unable to pass the required first-year contracts course and sick of the Iowa winters, Giesler moved to Los Angeles and tried law school again at the University of Southern California while supporting himself as a bill collector. One of his marks for collection was Earl Rogers, already famous not only for his courtroom prowess but also for his carousing and inability to hang on to a dollar. Rogers owed several hundred dollars to a law book company, which sent Giesler to collect on the debt, which he never accomplished, despite his best efforts. Instead, Rogers offered him a job as his office boy at twenty-five dollars a month, which Giesler rarely collected on either.

Giesler carried Rogers's briefcase, cleaned his wastepaper baskets, and, as an added bonus, interviewed witnesses and helped investigate murder cases.[26] Often joining him was Rogers's young daughter, the future "sob sister" journalist Adela Rogers St. Johns, on whom Giesler developed a tremendous, unrequited crush.[27]

In 1907, Giesler passed the California bar exam, and Rogers had the young man's name painted on the firm's window. Young Giesler hero-worshiped Rogers, who was movie-star handsome in his elegant suits, silk shirts, custom-made shoes, gardenia boutonnieres, and ever-present lorgnette as he outsmarted prosecutors and unmasked lying witnesses.[28] His courtroom theatrics were so infamous John Barrymore visited Rogers's trials for acting tips.[29] Rogers represented defendants in seventy-seven murder cases during his twenty-five-year career—some with Giesler's assistance—and lost only three.[30] After the notoriety of the Darrow trial, Rogers earned what today would be about $2.8 million a year. But he frittered it away on alcohol, which led to his downfall and early death.[31]

Although given to the same high-end haberdashery, Giesler, unlike Rogers, was no matinee idol. *Chicago Daily Tribune* reporter Marcia Winn, who covered the Chaplin trial, wrote that if Giesler had worn a wig he would have been mistaken for Benjamin Franklin.[32] He was portly, he relied on reading glasses, which he chewed on constantly, and by the 1940s his once sandy-colored hair was thin and gray. Still, the soft-spoken Giesler had learned much from Rogers. He had the same mesmerizing effect on jurors, judges, and trial watchers. He owned the courtroom from his opening statement to his client's (usual) acquittal, thanks to his tireless preparation, engaging storytelling skills, calm demeanor, and virtuoso cross-examination style.[33]

In his youth, Giesler also struggled with alcohol and blamed it for the failure of his first marriage.[34] But unlike Rogers, Giesler overcame the addiction. He worshiped his second wife, the former Ruth Stevens, whom he called "Mrs. Giesler," and was the proud father of three children. Like Chaplin, he was a perfectionist and a workaholic. He took only one vacation with Mrs. Giesler—to Palm Springs—and it was a disaster. Within a week, during which he would not stop taking phone calls from the office, he was bored and miserable and fled back to the delights of his law practice.[35]

In preparation for his Mann Act trial, Chaplin was obliged to spend what he called "long dreary evenings" clutching his nervous, aching stomach and pacing the floor at Giesler's house, where they went over "every depressing detail" of *l'affaire Joan*.[36] Chaplin's nerves were shattered over the prospect of years in prison and the knowledge that he wasn't in control. Here, Giesler was the director and Chaplin merely called upon to deliver well-rehearsed lines. Giesler's motto was "Don't let your client be the lawyer."[37] It was a role reversal for Chaplin, who had written, directed, and acted in his own movies since 1914.[38]

While Chaplin stewed, Carr moved with rocket speed to advance the indictments to trial. On February 21, the six defendants returned to face Carr in court, all with counsel except for Reno, who didn't want a lawyer.[39] For now, the defendants were aligned, but that could change. In fact, Arden was already on the outs with Chaplin. He told FBI agents that after sticking his neck out, Chaplin had shown him "no consideration for his past friendship and loyalty" and, therefore, he was "through with him." The translation may have been that Chaplin wouldn't pay Arden's legal fees. As Arden's allegiances shifted, so did his stories; after initially covering up for his coconspirators, he now sang like the proverbial canary: he said that hiring Judge Holland to represent Joan *had* been Durant's idea, and Chaplin gave him the go-ahead to offer Joan $5,000 to leave the state after her arrest the previous May.[40] After Chaplin eloped with Oona without telling him, Arden placed a sarcastic ad in *Variety*: "FOR SALE: Would like to dispose, cheaply, of slightly used empty bag which I am still loyally holding."[41]

The defendants' lawyers were among the best in the city, and it must have cost a pretty penny to hire them. Durant, the wealthiest among them after Chaplin, retained the most politically connected one, Frank P. Doherty, who had successfully represented Los Angeles Mayor Fletcher Bowron against charges of official misconduct in 1942.[42]

Sammy Hahn, a diminutive Russian émigré known for his celebrity divorce practice, represented Captain White and Sergeant Marple, two of the three police defendants.[43] He was the attorney Muir had had in mind for Joan. In the event that White's and Marple's defenses became incompatible, Eugene Marcus also appeared on Marple's behalf. Marcus had represented silent film star Mary Miles Minter, who had been under suspicion since 1922 for the unsolved murder of movie director William Desmond Taylor because she had been one of the last people to see him alive.[44]

Julian Hazard represented Judge Griffin. Hazard had been the youngest trial judge in Florida but had retired early and relocated to California to practice law.[45] Custom dictated that Hazard still be referred to by the honorific "Judge." His title was a distinct reminder that he, his client, and Judge O'Connor were part of the same elite club. Hazard argued that Judge Griffin had acted in his official capacity in handling Joan's case, had not broken any laws, and should never have been prosecuted. Bates Booth, who had been a Los Angeles prosecutor in the 1930s and whose name had been bandied about in 1940 as a possible candidate for Los Angeles County district attorney, appeared as Arden's lawyer. Like Carr, he had also been a special assistant to the attorney general in Washington, DC.[46]

Once they were arraigned, the defendants were released. The three conspiracy cases—which included Chaplin on the indictments—were adjourned until March 9, but Chaplin and Giesler were directed to return four days later to enter a plea in the Mann Act case, signaling that case would be tried first. In his report to Hoover about the arraignments, Hood wrote, "Photographers had another field day in photographing subjects, particularly Chaplin."[47]

Four days later, on Friday, February 25, instead of entering a not-guilty plea for Chaplin, Giesler moved to have the Mann Act case dismissed, arguing that his client's rights were violated because there were no women on the grand jury that voted to indict him. Had women been present, Giesler asserted, they would have been better judges of Joan's credibility, insinuating that they would not have believed her story. Giesler also argued that the Mann Act was never intended by Congress to criminalize noncommercial, consensual sexual conduct.[48] After listening to Carr's response, Judge O'Connor took the unusual step of adjourning the matter until 9:30 a.m. the next morning—a Saturday—for his ruling, at which time he made short work of Giesler's arguments in a six-page written decision.

O'Connor ruled that federal juries are configured according to the laws of the states where they are located. Under California law, the accused was not guaranteed jurors of any particular gender, but only "a fair and impartial jury" of either sex. As to Giesler's Hail Mary pass about the lack of a commercial angle to the Mann Act accusations, the judge reminded him that the United States Supreme Court's *Caminetti* decision had settled the issue twenty-seven years earlier.[49] Following O'Connor's rejection of Giesler's motion, Chaplin pleaded not guilty—in a loud and clear voice—to both counts of the Mann Act indictment.[50] Carr said he could be ready for trial within ten days, but Giesler needed more time, so the case was adjourned for trial on March 21, 1944, at 9:30 a.m.[51]

With that, Giesler let Carr know he planned to subpoena fifty to sixty witnesses. The first unhappy recipients of Giesler's subpoenas were Getty and his Tulsa lawyer, Claude H. Rosenstein, who'd made good on Joan's outstanding hotel and store debts, presumably at the behest of his client. Joan had visited Tulsa in January 1943, where Getty was then living. Carol Ann was born on October 2, 1943, and Giesler, perfectly able to count to nine, was preparing to muddy the waters by pointing the finger of fatherhood at Getty, even though it had no direct bearing on the Mann Act case.[52]

In a message to Hoover, FBI Agent Hood wrote, "Carr states this indicates Giesler plans to present evidence showing Berrys [sic] activities and alleged immorality over past five or six years."[53] Although Carr did not see the relevance of Joan's past sexual adventures, he recognized that Judge O'Connor might disagree, so he asked Hood to have G-men dig into Joan's past relationships with other men.[54] The FBI was also worried about a March 12, 1944, article published in the Tulsa Daily World reporting that Joan had told an unnamed woman that the reason she left Hollywood was to be with the man she loved in Tulsa. Joan allegedly said, "He's very wealthy, but it isn't his money I'm after."[55] This undercut the government's theory that it was Chaplin who sent her out of California so they could have sex in New York, in violation of the law.

While rummaging through Joan's past, Giesler's investigators located one Melville M. S. Fagan, a British newspaperman staying at the Hotel Great Northern at 118 West Fifty-Seventh Street in New York. Fagan claimed to have information about Joan's other lovers, including Hans Ruesch. FBI agents suspected Giesler was trying to get his hands on Ruesch's diary, which might contradict Joan's version of what happened in December 1942. Ruesch had mentioned the diary to the FBI during an interview but had steadfastly refused to turn it over to bureau agents.[56]

Being sent to trial within a month of arraignment would be unheard of today. Under current law, a felony trial in federal court cannot begin less than thirty days or more than seventy days after a defendant's first appearance before a judge.[57] But the seventy-day speedy trial clock is tolled by motion practice, discovery delays, and plea negotiations, which means a complex case involving a prominent figure could take a year or more to go to trial. Carr may have wanted to move with lightning speed out of fear Joan would fall apart before too long.

On March 2, 1944, just three weeks before the trial was to start, Joan and her mother—after both having had too much to drink—got into a violent argument. As a result, Joan threw Gertrude out of their apartment at 10382 Mississippi Avenue in Los Angeles with just the clothes on her back and $100 in her pocket.[58] To teach Joan a lesson, Gertrude stayed away two nights, which made her daughter frantic.[59] Gertrude resented being stuck at home taking care of Carol Ann while Joan gallivanted around town shopping. But Joan loved being out and about where she could savor her notoriety. At a department store while cashing a check, she told one of the clerks, "Oh you know me; I'm the girl in the Chaplin case."[60]

But shopping sprees and fleeting moments of fame were not enough to calm Joan's nerves. On March 13, Joan's mother called the local FBI office to report that her daughter had driven off, too terrified to testify. "Who am I to think that I can get the best of anybody in this case, with Chaplin's money against me," Joan told her mother before bolting out the door.[61] When FBI agents tracked her down, Joan screamed that she hated her mother and was not going to testify. The agents delivered her in that condition to Carr, who told her to grow up. She would tell her story in court, whether she wanted to or not.[62] As a federal prosecutor, Carr had many tools in his arsenal to ensure witness compliance. He could subpoena Joan, ask a court to hold her in contempt if she refused to honor it, or seek a warrant for her arrest as a material witness and have her tossed in jail if she failed to cooperate.

Carr had other troubles. He had to prepare for the biggest trial of his career against the toughest opponent he would ever be likely to face, under the watchful eyes of his bosses in Washington. The Department of Justice had authorized the prosecution of one of the most famous men in the world for crimes that were hard to prove under the best of circumstances. To prevail, the government was prepared to dip into a bottomless well of resources. At Carr's request, Hoover authorized the entire Los Angeles FBI field office to undertake an investigation of the Chaplin petit jury panel.[63] Within two weeks, agents had combed through the names of 145 potential jurors and prepared an eighty-one-page confidential dossier on their backgrounds for Carr.[64]

The Department of Justice also sent an attorney from Washington, Sylvester Myers, to Los Angeles to help Carr respond to the pile of pretrial motions filed by the defense.[65] Together the defendants had filed eighty-four motions, amounting to about two thousand pages of legal writing, all of which demanded a response from the government.[66] Although Giesler's focus was on the upcoming Mann Act trial, he had to participate in drafting the motions on the other three cases involving Chaplin. The defense lawyers knew their arguments were likely to be rejected by Judge O'Connor, but smothering the government in paper to interfere with Carr's ability to prepare for trial was part of their twofold strategy. They also needed to preserve their appellate rights in the event their clients were convicted.

The lead prosecutor, however, was up to the task. Charles Hardy Carr was just forty years old when he was appointed U.S. attorney for the Southern District of California by FDR in May 1943, besting Jack Irwin, who was on the short list for the prestigious post.[67] Born in Mississippi in 1903, Carr was a graduate of Vanderbilt University and earned his law degree at Yale in 1926. In adulthood, he was tall with flaming-red hair and the soft lilt of a southern drawl that he never lost, even years after moving out West. After a brief stint in private practice in Memphis, he settled in Los Angeles, where at age twenty-nine he was hired as an assistant prosecutor by U.S. Attorney Peirson Hall, where Irwin was one of his colleagues.[68] Carr stood apart from his fellow prosecutors; he was called to Washington to be a special assistant to Attorney General Frank Murphy, who put him in charge of a headline-grabbing investigation into labor racketeering in the movie industry.[69] At the time of the Chaplin trial, Carr was living a comfortable life at 621 North Foothill Road in Beverly Hills, less than a six-minute drive from Chaplin's secluded estate. He was married to forty-three-year-old Margaret Applewhite Cole, a homemaker, and was a young stepfather to her two sons by a former marriage.[70]

Due to the high stakes involved, both Carr and Giesler courted the media. Giesler was a press favorite. His home phone number was in the directory, and writers on deadline knew they could always reach him for a quote or a patient explanation of a thorny legal concept.[71] He even tried to schedule his courtroom examinations of witnesses around reporters' deadlines.[72] This was unfamiliar territory for Chaplin, who unless he had a new picture coming out and wanted good reviews couldn't care less about buttering up the press. Even then he had a knack for annoying reporters; he saved critics the worst seats in the house for the premiere of *City Lights*.[73] Most writers believed that Chaplin was deliberately hostile to the press, but Adela Rogers St. Johns was more understanding: "I think he was always afraid of us."[74]

Reporters from around the world would be in the courtroom, and Loyd Wright, Chaplin's personal attorney who'd represented him for years, warned Giesler that he'd need a press secretary. Giesler agreed and looked to his friend Casey Shawhan.[75] Ralph Fleming "Casey" Shawhan had been a local sports hero in his youth as a member of the 1926 University of Southern California national championship track team.[76] In his twenty-three years as a journalist, Shawhan had worked for every major Los Angeles paper—the *Herald-Express*, the *Examiner*, and the *Times*. By the spring of 1944, Shawhan was doing publicity for Twentieth-Century Fox, and Wright hired him to handle the press for the trial.[77]

The FBI took a dim view of Shawhan's role. Special Agent Hood sniffed that Shawhan's primary purpose was to keep the pressroom at the federal courthouse flooded with a "goodly supply of liquor."[78] Shawhan acknowledged that libations went along with the territory. "It was war time, and liquor and cigarettes were hard to come by," he wrote in an unpublished autobiography. So, before the trial, Shawhan explained to Wright what he'd need to keep the (mostly) boys in the pressroom happy. "I needed cash for lunches, dinners, and booze; and for sandwiches in between, when many busy reporters did not have time to go to lunch."[79] Shawhan also understood what reporters wanted to see from the man on trial. "I also explained that Mr. Chaplin should 'loosen up.'" Shawhan would do his best to humanize the taciturn Chaplin, even if it meant something as simple as convincing the great man to smile for the cameras or sign an autograph.[80]

While Giesler, Wright, and Shawhan were plotting their strategy as if they were the Allies planning the D-Day invasion, Chaplin was bombarded with other bad news from the courts. On March 8, Judge Stanley Mosk in the Los Angeles Superior Court refused to dismiss the paternity case in spite of the blood test results. Mosk ruled that "the ends of justice will best be served by a full and fair trial of the issues" and determined that the stipulation that had been so carefully negotiated between Irwin and Chaplin's attorneys was not in the child's best interest and, therefore, not enforceable.[81]

And as if she weren't full of enough surprises, Joan had another bit of startling news to share with the FBI. J. F. T. (Jefty) O'Connor, the presiding judge, was a good friend of Paul Getty—who Carr knew would be subpoenaed by Giesler as a trial witness—and was a friend of Joan's.[82] Getty often spoke to "Jefty" on the phone. They socialized at one another's apartments, shared dinners, and went to the beach together. On the day Pearl Harbor was attacked, December 7, 1941, they were at the beach, hardly an outing either of them would forget. Getty and Jefty even had dinner together with Joan.[83]

More startling was the fact that Jefty seemed to have had a little crush on Joan. While Joan and her mother were dining at a Los Angeles restaurant, they bumped into the bachelor Judge O'Connor, and he invited Joan up to his apartment. On September 2, 1942, she took him up on the offer—without her mother—but she told the FBI, apparently with a straight face, that she insisted he leave the front door open while they were inside.[84] Whatever happened during the visit, Jefty gave Joan a parting gift: an inscribed copy of his book, *The Banking Crisis and Recovery under the Roosevelt Administration*. He inscribed it: "To Joan Barry with kindest regards from her friend, the author, J.F.T. O'Connor, Los Angeles, September 2, 1942."[85]

The revelation set off alarm bells. Under Carr's grilling, Joan denied she ever had sex with the judge. Hood sent agents scurrying to her old apartment at 9921 Robbins Drive in Beverly Hills to retrieve a suitcase she'd left there with O'Connor's inscribed book inside. In a March 17, 1944, letter to Hoover explaining the situation, Hood wrote, "Carr has expressed wonderment over the fact that Judge O'Connor apparently intends to hear at least the White Slave case against Chaplin when not only does he know Joan Berry, but also Berry has advised that he is a good friend of J. Paul Getty."[86]

Hoover smelled trouble. He promptly reported O'Connor's conflict to Attorney General Biddle.[87] Whether a federal judge must recuse himself is left up to the judge. Nonetheless, there are guidelines on recusal that are nearly as old as the country. In 1792 Congress passed a law requiring a federal district judge to recuse himself if he had an interest in the outcome of the litigation or had been counsel to either party.[88] The basis for recusal was expanded in 1911, which was the rule in effect at the time of the Chaplin trial. The amended law called for a judge to recuse himself if he had "a personal bias or prejudice" for or against any party to the action.[89]

O'Connor's friendship with Getty and Joan, such as it was, did not require that he step aside. He had no deep personal relationship with the litigants and seemingly no bias or prejudice for or against either side. But given that he had socialized with Getty and Joan, his decision to remain on such a high-profile case raises eyebrows. The fact that it *was* such a high-profile case may have been precisely the reason O'Connor wanted to keep it.

Once he learned of O'Connor's connection to Getty and Joan, Carr could have filed a motion asking O'Connor to transfer the case to another judge. But Carr may have feared that if he did, it would delay the trial to the point where Joan, fragile and already terrified of testifying, would fall apart as a witness. Giesler did not ask for the judge to step aside either. Despite Giesler's reputation for thorough pretrial preparation, there were no codified rules of disclosure in criminal cases in those days, and he may not have known about Getty's and Joan's relationship to the judge.[90] Jefty would seriously curtail Giesler's ability to live up to his reputation and destroy Joan on cross-examination once she took the stand. Perhaps it was the right legal call, or perhaps the judge wanted to protect Joan's reputation—and his own.

TWELVE

"THERE CAN'T BE TOO MANY WOMEN ON A JURY FOR ME"

When the Chaplin trial began on Tuesday, March 21, 1944, the world was occupied by war. The Nazis had overrun Hungary and were roaring toward Bulgaria and Rumania.[1] Due in court by 10:00 a.m. each day, Chaplin had no choice but to forgo his routine of a leisurely breakfast in one of the twin beds in his room while perusing the *Los Angeles Times* or *True Detective*.[2] Rush-hour traffic meant he had to be up and out in time to allow at least an hour for the twelve-mile drive downtown.

On the eve of trial, there was no end of editorial comment seeking to place it in some larger social, historical, or political context. *Newsweek* ran a full-page spread acknowledging that Chaplin had placed the movie industry in a "quandary." It felt "no personal love" for him due to his ornery nature, his egotism, his cheapness, and his unwillingness to entertain the troops in wartime, yet Hollywood worried that the scandal would reflect poorly on the movie colony.[3] It raised the specter of another Roscoe "Fatty" Arbuckle scandal from the 1920s. Once the silent screen's biggest star—literally and figuratively—Arbuckle was charged with the murder of actress Virginia Rappe following a booze-filled weekend party in a San Francisco hotel room. Although acquitted after multiple sensational trials, he died destitute, and the scandal resulted in the studio heads hiring Will Hays to clamp down on sex in the movies and the bad behavior of stars off-screen.[4]

Not even the promise of a sunny, mild spring day with the temperatures in the 70s could ease Chaplin's gnawing depression and anxiety.[5] He feared that the public hated him and worried that his career was over.[6] The stress was making him a little crazy; he posted guards around his property and took his home phone off the hook.[7] To distract himself, he tinkered with the script for *Monsieur Verdoux*.[8]

Known for his elegant attire, Chaplin chose his wardrobe carefully for his first day of trial. He selected a navy double-breasted suit and a white shirt, a pale-blue polka-dot tie, a white pocket square, and a gray homburg. His black shoes were as polished as a mirror.[9] His thick mop of white hair contrasted handsomely with his dark suit and the deep tan he'd acquired on his tennis court. The diminutive comic had put on a few pounds since his silent film days, but regular matches with tennis great Big Bill Tilden and others on Chaplin's asphalt, professional-quality backyard court kept him in decent shape for a fifty-four-year-old man. "Tennis is the only thing that keeps me going," he would tell reporters during the trial.[10]

Meanwhile, from his house less than a mile from Chaplin's, Jerry Giesler had his own sleepless nights, with his adoring wife sitting up with him. His mind never rested while he was on trial. He kept a pen and pad at his bedside in case an idea popped into his head.[11] Mrs. Giesler helped however she could, down to selecting his wardrobe, which rivaled Chaplin's for elegance and style. For opening day, his wife chose a gray pinstripe from one of his many bespoke suits, paired with a white shirt, a patterned tie, and a collar bar. She laid everything out neatly in one of the six bedrooms of their spacious home on the corner of 1021 North Ridgedale Drive in Beverly Hills. "The truth is, she takes care of me like a baby," Giesler boasted.[12]

The interstate highway system that would bring the I-10 freeway to Los Angeles did not exist until the late 1950s.[13] In separate cars, Chaplin and Giesler drove along local streets to the massive white granite federal courthouse at 312 North Spring Street. Oona, who had rushed her marriage to Chaplin so she could be at his side during his time of trouble, would not go near the courthouse for the entire trial. Later, she told Charles Jr. that she had wanted to go but her husband had forbidden it.[14] That may have been true, but it's more likely Giesler feared that newspaper photos of the aging Chaplin at the courthouse holding hands with another teenage bride—one who was pregnant no less—would not go over well with the public when his client was accused of sexual shenanigans involving a different young woman only a year and a half earlier.

Knowing it was never a good idea to keep a judge waiting, Chaplin and

Giesler arrived an hour early, parked their cars in a nearby lot, walked to the courthouse, and entered the building through one of the five sets of massive bronze double doors with carved eagles over them. The trial drew an army of newspaper reporters and photographers.[15] Chaplin, surly with them in the past, greeted them with a pleasant "good morning."[16]

Inside the spanking new and stunning Art Deco Federal Building, just completed in 1940 and today a National Historic Landmark, Chaplin and his attorney blew past the murals of early California history, skipped the ten elevator banks, and headed straight to the escalator to go up one flight to the courtroom. By 9:15 a.m., Chaplin and his attorney were solemnly pacing the beige and black terrazzo floor while the public (mostly middle-aged women) lined the hallway hoping for a coveted seat inside.[17] Chaplin's trial had attracted the biggest crowd at the new courthouse to date, which added to his anxiety.[18] When the red leather, aluminum-studded doors to Judge O'Connor's Courtroom No. 7 opened at 9:30 a.m., some spectators spilled in while others hung back, hoping for a glimpse of "the girl." A few were bold enough to stop young females, with or without red hair, to ask if they were Joan.[19]

Turns out Joan *was* in the building, but FBI agents had her stashed away in U.S. Attorney Carr's office in case jury selection ended early and she was needed as a witness. She posed for news photographers, and in the presence of her FBI handlers she limited her comments to pleasantries about the health of Carol Ann, soon to be six months old.[20] Marcia Winn of the *Chicago Daily Tribune*, who observed closely and wrote with exacting and colorful prose, thought Joan looked "nervous and on the verge of tears."[21]

Downstairs, as they pushed through the crowd to get into the courtroom at 9:40 a.m., Chaplin murmured to Giesler, "Well, let's get it over with."[22] Chaplin took his seat in a red leather chair at the defense table looking, according to Winn, "glum and nervous."[23] From that moment until the trial ended ten days later, Chaplin could hardly say a word or make a move without it being recorded by the press. When asked, after the second day of trial, how he could remain serene under such close press surveillance, Chaplin replied, "Doesn't bother me. I paid attention to the proceedings."[24]

At 10:05 a.m., the door behind the judge's raised wooden bench opened and Judge O'Connor, with his gray eyes and gray hair, emerged from his chambers. Winn described him as "a squat, almost square little man."[25] The clerk, Francis E. Cross, who sat directly in front of the judge at a desk below the bench, called the court to order. With that, the long-anticipated case of *United States of America v. Charles Spencer Chaplin*, Indictment 16617, had begun. Other than the whirring of the air-conditioning system, nothing could be heard in the high-ceilinged, windowless room encased in foot-thick concrete walls except the judge softly reading the charges against Chaplin.[26]

Long wooden counsel tables ran perpendicular to O'Connor's bench in the well of the court. The jury box ran alongside the prosecutor's table, which is customary because the government bears the burden of proof in a criminal trial. The area in front of the judge was reserved for lawyers and litigants and was separated from the general public by a thigh-high wooden rail. Carr, Assistant U.S. Attorney Gerald Desmond, and at least two FBI agents sat at the prosecutor's table. They plopped down brief-cases, notepads, files, and grand jury transcripts to signal to the jury how much evidence they had against Chaplin.[27] Giesler and Chaplin occupied the defense side with only each other—a pair of Davids battling the government Goliath.[28] Giesler on trial was like Chaplin behind the camera: singularly focused and completely in control.

Having watched Giesler on trial for years, Florabel Muir said the secret to his success was that he knew the prosecutors' cases better than they did.[29] Giesler thought the Chaplin trial was his toughest.[30] And while he would use his formidable legal skills to zealously represent Chaplin, he was no fan of his client's behavior. "He certainly never should have taken up with Miss Berry," Giesler wrote years later. "His conduct was morally reprehensible. . . ."[31]

The reporters sat parallel to the jury and the lawyers' tables. Beyond the rail were several rows of seats for spectators, although O'Connor was more lenient than most judges and allowed the overflow crowd to stand along the wall. Still, there were plenty of disappointed people who didn't get in. Judge O'Connor also was liberal about allowing cameras into the courtroom. Press cameras had been a regular part of trial proceedings until the 1935 Lindbergh baby kidnapping trial in Flemington, New Jersey. During the Lindbergh case, hundreds of reporters and photographers descended on the rural Hunterdon County Courthouse, turning the trial into an unruly, cringeworthy circus and trampling on the rights of the accused, Bruno Richard Hauptmann.[32]

In 1937, a committee of lawyers and powerful publishers, horrified by the indignity of the Lindbergh trial, called it "the most spectacular and depressing example of improper publicity and professional misconduct ever presented to the people of the United States in a criminal trial."[33] Consequently, the influential American Bar Association adopted Canon 35 of the Canons of Judicial Ethics, which called for a ban on courtroom photography. Nearly every state banned courtroom cameras as a result. And just months after the Chaplin trial ended, cameras were banned in federal courts, where they are barred to this day.[34]

Jefty O'Connor was at heart a politician and a publicity hound. When he was comptroller of the currency, he used to send copies of his speeches to Hedda Hopper.[35] He allowed press photographers to take pictures at the Chaplin trial—including of the participants—before and after every day's session and during recesses. He forbade photos during testimony. To remedy that prohibition, photographers pressured Casey Shawhan to convince Chaplin and Giesler to reenact the trial's great moments in an empty courtroom where they could take pictures.[36] Chaplin, on orders from his counsel, complied. Still, he refused to allow himself to be photographed in his eyeglasses. "I look bad enough without them," he grumbled.[37]

O'Connor took a winding path to the bench. Born in 1886, he was a Catholic farm boy—one of seven brothers—from Grand Forks, North Dakota. He learned to read and write in a one-room schoolhouse, yet in 1909 he graduated from Yale with a law degree. The judge wrote an unpublished autobiography where his description of his family, including his "faithful shepherd dog, 'Shep,'" made it seem as if the O'Connors belonged on the MGM back lot with the celluloid Judge Hardy and his son, Andy. On lazy days during his boyhood, O'Connor wrote in his book, he had "no watch but such a luxury was neither necessary nor convenient. My time piece was eternal, and the modern split second did not belong to that age."[38] He considered himself an industrious youth, milking cows, selling newspapers, shining shoes, and making ice cream sodas at the local fountain for spending money. His idea of fun was waiting for the circus to come to town, attending a square dance, having Sunday supper at his mother's table with the farmhands, and saying his prayers. He worked his way through undergraduate school at the University of North Dakota as a reporter for a local newspaper, getting paid by the inch for his stories.[39]

After graduating with his law degree from Yale, O'Connor returned home to Grand Forks to practice law and dive into local politics. He was a fixture in the Democratic Party for decades but had a hard time winning elections. The exception was when he won a seat in the North Dakota

House of Representatives, where he served from 1915 to 1919. In 1920 he was the Democratic candidate for governor of North Dakota but lost to Republican incumbent Lynn Joseph Frazier.[40] Two years later he ran unsuccessfully for the United States Senate.[41]

With his political career having hit a dead end in North Dakota, O'Connor relocated to Los Angeles in 1925. Before long, he was back in the political game, serving as the Southern California campaign manager for Franklin Roosevelt's 1932 presidential run. FDR rewarded him by naming him comptroller of the currency, placing him in charge of regulating the national banks, a daunting job during the Depression.[42] O'Connor resigned in 1938 to run for governor of California, but he lost again. FDR appreciated his public service and said: "He kept the banks and your money safe." Those words were etched on Jefty's tombstone when he died a little more than five years after the Chaplin trial ended.[43] In 1940 FDR took the sting out of O'Connor's gubernatorial defeat by granting him a lifetime appointment to the prestigious federal bench.

Given the insatiable public interest in the Chaplin trial, the press played an outsized role in the proceedings. A core group of about thirty reporters and photographers covered the trial every day, along with a few famous columnists like Hopper, Adela Rogers St. Johns, and Sheilah Graham, who drifted in and out. Margaret Buell Wilder, author of the then popular novel *Since You Went Away*, wrote front-page columns for the *Los Angeles Examiner* and angled for an exclusive interview with Carr and Joan, which Carr refused. Reporters came from as far away as London, and *Newsweek, Time*, and the wire services—United Press, International News Service, the Associated Press, Reuters, and Western Union—all had reporters assigned.[44]

Three women journalists stood out: Muir, Agness Underwood of Hearst's *Los Angeles Herald-Express*, and Katherine Marcia Winn of the *Chicago Daily Tribune*, who wrote under the byline "Marcia Winn." Their experience, wit, and strong writing skills set them apart. Muir, age fifty-four, had begun her journalism career while still a student at the University of Washington. She'd been through two years of law school at the University of Utah, understood the trial process, and sometimes beat the police to a crime scene. At the scene of one of the first murder stories she'd ever covered, she climbed in the window of a house where a man had killed his wife so she could filch family photos of the deceased before the cops got there. She left with the pictures and blood on her shoes. Underwood, age forty-three, a former foster child who was once homeless, would rise to become the first woman city editor of a major newspaper, the *Herald-Express*. Her editor once said that Underwood's "favorite occupation is following a good murder. Favorite story, a good murder. Favorite photograph, a good murder."[45]

In contrast to Muir and Underwood, Winn focused on the atmosphere of the trial and the foibles of its participants. Single and only thirty-two years old when she was sent to Los Angeles to cover the trial, the slender, five-foot-five Winn was more Joan's contemporary than Chaplin's and understood what made her tick—or at least tried to. She shared the same conservative political views as her newspaper, the *Chicago Daily Tribune*, owned by Colonel Robert McCormick, a Republican isolationist, who gave her away at her wedding.[46] Winn portrayed Joan as a creature deserving of pity, and she was disgusted with Chaplin's cavalier treatment of his former protégé. In reading her stories more than eighty years later, her eye for detail, her plucky sense of humor, her insight, and her ability to weave those qualities into her information-packed pieces make the courtroom drama come to life.

Still, male reporters assigned to cover the Chaplin story outnumbered the women, not only because there were more of them on major newspapers but also because the men who served as editors thought Chaplin's celebrity too important to leave to the "sob sisters." Underwood bristled at being called a "sob sister." "To hell with that," she said.[47] "I've never sobbed a story in my life," she stated proudly in her autobiography.[48] "I'd rather have a fistful—an armload—of good solid facts . . . then the story writes itself."[49] In an age where women were considered inferior professional colleagues, Underwood's managing editor paid her what passed for a compliment, telling her that she "should have been a man."[50]

Day one of the trial was occupied by jury selection, a process about as exciting as watching grass grow but crucial to the litigants. A panel of fifty-six prospective jurors trooped into the courtroom. Judge O'Connor told them he wanted their minds to be as "blank as this sheet of white paper, across which you should write the story of the evidence."[51] Chaplin drummed his fingers on counsel table and every now and then blew his nose.[52] Winn noticed he also did a little tap dance under the table with his dainty feet while seated.[53] Unbeknownst to Winn, Giesler had convinced the bailiff to raise Chaplin's chair a few inches higher so that he would seem even smaller than he was.[54] "He looked helpless, friendless and wistful" Giesler wrote years later.[55]

Good lawyers know a trial is won or lost in jury selection. Assembling a jury filled with people receptive to one's case based on their ages, professions, cultural backgrounds, and life experiences is a delicate art that takes years of practice. Twenty-eight of the potential jurors were women, which thrilled Giesler. "There can't be too many women on a jury for me" was his motto. He found them "more attentive" and "tougher minded" than male jurors. The only women he had no use for on juries were older unmarried ones, whom he derisively called "spinsters." He feared they were bitter.[56]

There was no getting away from Hollywood connections. Louis J. Odets, the father of Chaplin's friend Clifford Odets, who had written *The Golden Boy*, along with a seamstress from MGM's wardrobe department and a minor actress were among the potential jurors.[57] There were other connections in what was still small-town Los Angeles. Carr's barber was on the panel. After he announced he'd cut the hair of most of the best-known lawyers in town, he was released for cause.[58] The first day was not terribly taxing; after only seventy-five minutes, the judge called a recess, returned at 11:30 a.m., and then broke at about noon for a two-hour lunch. There was another fifteen-minute recess called at 3:16 p.m.[59]

In federal court, the judge questions potential jurors and invites the lawyers to suggest questions for the judge to either ask or reject. Judge O'Connor asked if anyone on the jury panel held a bias against movie people and if they understood that being under indictment did not mean Chaplin was guilty. Jurors were also asked if they'd read anything about the case in the newspapers. Most said they had but denied they had formed any opinion about it.[60]

Giesler wanted to know whether anyone knew Hedda Hopper or read her column.[61] Given the vitriol she'd shown Chaplin in print, he didn't want her fans on the jury. Judge O'Connor asked a perfectly appropriate question that, if answering it himself, would have disqualified him as a juror and should have disqualified him from presiding over the case—did anyone know Joan?[62]

By the end of the first day, two jurors were excused after expressing prejudice against Chaplin because he was a British citizen.[63] In addition to dismissing jurors for cause, the lawyers could dismiss jurors for no reason whatsoever. The prosecution was entitled to six of these "peremptory" challenges and the defense ten, with each side alternating until their challenges were used up. At the end of the day's session, Chaplin returned home, ate dinner with Oona, and collapsed into bed, only to get up and repeat the entire sequence again every day for the next two weeks.[64]

Chaplin seemed in good spirits on day two. His outfit was a gray flannel suit, white shirt, and gray patterned tie with brown shoes and, strangely, red socks. Giesler wore a tan suit, and Carr wore a loud, eye-catching brown plaid with cuffs.[65] On that day, which was as warm and sunny as the one before, both sides got down to the serious business of selecting the jury they wanted. Carr made a desperate attempt to alter the pattern of jury selection. He made a motion asking the judge to rule that for each peremptory challenge made by the government, Giesler would have to use up two of his in succession. It may have seemed an arcane legal point, but had the judge gone along with it, Giesler would have lost an important strategic advantage that allowed him to have the last word on the composition of the jury. The judge shot down Carr's proposal and ruled they would follow the law that called for one-to-one challenges.[66]

With that out of the way, Carr used his challenges to get rid of Odets's father, the MGM wardrobe mistress, and the B-movie actress. Giesler used a challenge to eliminate one of his dreaded spinsters.[67] The slow, grinding process continued until 4:30 p.m., when the jury of seven women and five men was selected. The jurors were long in the tooth, which was part of Giesler's game plan. At least one was pushing seventy; others were retired or married to retirees, and several had gray hair. Giesler had used his challenges to knock off those who were too young to have appreciated Chaplin's days as the Little Tramp. Winn described the jurors as looking "like a cross section of the elderly persons who come to California to die in a nice climate."[68]

Besides wanting the jurors to be old enough to remember Chaplin back in the day, Giesler also wanted jurors too old to identify with twenty-three-year-old Joan and her life as an adventurous, sexually active, single woman. Giesler did get stuck with two elderly, unmarried women, one of whom was described by Winn as "an ex-piano teacher with hair dyed a pale blue."[69] But it was some consolation for Giesler that she and the other unmarried female juror—an unemployed bookbinder—were old enough to have sat through a silent movie matinee in their youth. In the end, Giesler and his client appeared happy with the jury.[70] Carr, on the other hand, was not. He told FBI Agent Richard Hood, without explanation, that the jury panel from which he had had to choose was "very poor."[71]

In a policy that would be unheard of today for safety reasons, the newspapers published the full names and home addresses of the Chaplin jurors. The jury foreman, Roscoe Reeder, an oil company advertising executive, was one of the younger jurors at age forty-two. Chaplin's fate was now in his hands, as well as those of sixty-nine-year-old Grant Ritchie, a retired farmer born in a rural town eighty miles outside Chicago;[72] Beatrice Allan, the gray-haired wife of a construction engineer; and Vera Danis, the wife of a Beverly Hills real estate speculator.

Most of the jurors were salt-of-the-earth types, supporting themselves and their families with respectable, if not dull, jobs. The fiftyish Pearl Adams, the unmarried bookbinder who was a registered Republican, was selected along with Lydia Hussey, old enough to have a thirty-six-year-old daughter (twice as old as Oona Chaplin) and the wife of the retired chemist who invented Clorox. Bernard Davis of Van Nuys was the only juror who had any link to the movie industry. He was the caretaker on the estate of Jack Moss, the associate producer on Orson Welles's *The Magnificent Ambersons* in 1942.[73] Juror Edyth Lewis was married to a canned goods salesman; Hazel Gill was the wife of a steamfitter and the mother of five; Rowan Segner was a Pasadena bank clerk; Loretta Easley was Winn's blue-haired piano teacher who had previously lived with her elderly mother; and Claude Millsap worked for a shirt company.[74] Two alternate jurors were selected in the event that one of the seated jurors became ill or unable to continue on the case: Charles E. Kells, an accountant, and Margaret Ingram, the widow of a pharmacist.[75]

Egged on by Shawhan, or perhaps becoming more relaxed as jury selection was going his way, Chaplin worked on improving his taciturn image. He chatted with reporters during recesses and signed an autograph on an envelope shoved into his hand by a fourteen-year-old girl outside the courthouse.[76] Not that it was likely to do him much good; he had slighted too many Hollywood reporters over the years. As Underwood remarked, "The attitude of the comedian, while polite, was not of the kind to make us break our necks to pull his chestnuts out of the fire."[77]

During the seemingly interminable, daylong voir dire of the jurors, Chaplin quietly doodled on yellow paper. He drew one of his favorite childhood drawings, a bridge with a train crossing over it, and a pair of the Little Tramp's oversized shoes.[78] Chaplin wrote in his autobiography that Giesler tore up his handiwork, fearful the press would seize on the drawings to analyze his mental state.[79] But Shawhan actually slipped the

Chaplin drawings into the hands of Gene Sherman of the *Los Angeles Times* and to writers from the Associated Press, Reuters, and the United Press. "Each had their own 'exclusive' Chaplin doodle," Shawhan later wrote in his unpublished autobiography, "about as hard to get in those days as a Picasso." Their publication was part of Shawhan's campaign to humanize Chaplin.[80]

Despite the publicity, Judge O'Connor did not sequester the jurors. Instead, he allowed them to go home with the admonishment they not read or discuss anything about the case outside of court.[81] When the trial resumed on Thursday, March 23, counsel agreed outside the presence of the jury that all witnesses should be barred from the courtroom except when testifying, so as not to influence each other.[82] That directive would end up keeping J. Paul Getty, subpoenaed by Giesler, stewing in a witness room in the courthouse for days. The trial had already consumed nearly a week of Getty's busy life. Getty was terrified of flying and did all his U.S. travel by train.[83] He boarded the Super Chief from Tulsa on Sunday, March 19, and arrived at Los Angeles's Union Station at eleven thirty in the morning on March 21, in time to run to the Federal Building and catch some of the jury selection before he was banished from the courtroom.[84]

Given how much was at stake, the lawyers kept their opening statements surprisingly brief. Carr, with the burden of proof, was required by law to go first. He spoke quietly with a gentle southern drawl for no more than fifteen minutes. He presented a bare-bones outline of what he intended to prove, that Joan and Chaplin were introduced in 1941 by Durant, that the silent film king placed her under contract, and that during that first summer "they began to see each other constantly."[85]

He told jurors that Joan terminated her contract in June 1942 but that Chaplin kept her on the payroll, implying an ulterior motive. Because Chaplin was taking too long to write a script for her screen debut, Joan wanted to return home to New York with her mother and forget about an acting career. Chaplin resisted letting her go, relenting only when he planned to go there himself and wanted her company. Carr told jurors that Chaplin invited Joan to be at his Second Front speech in Carnegie Hall and paid for her and her mother to travel to New York by train. In New York, Carr continued, Chaplin had sexual relations with Joan in his hotel room and gave her $300 to return to California to continue their intimate relationship—thus covering the two Mann Act counts of the indictment.[86] By 10:20 a.m., Carr sat down.[87]

Although the defense had no obligation to make an opening statement, Giesler did, in equally hushed tones. As the soft-spoken, confident Giesler stood to deliver his remarks, few in the audience would have guessed he suffered such terrible stage fright that his knees shook and his heart pounded—often for the first ten minutes he was on his feet.[88] Giesler's job was to cast doubt on the government's version of events and suggest an alternate narrative. He said that Chaplin spent a lot of money to make Joan a star by getting her teeth straightened and enrolling her in acting lessons. Implying that Joan was ungrateful, he said that she became tired of waiting for Chaplin to get down to business and focus on adapting *Shadow and Substance* for the screen, which was the movie in which she was to star. As a result, she broke her contract and nagged Chaplin to let her return to New York[89]

Although Chaplin and Joan found themselves in New York at the same time, Giesler denied they ever had sex there. Painting a picture of Joan as a loose woman, Giesler said, "Any time Mr. Chaplin wished to have intimacies with this young lady, either in Los Angeles, Beverly Hills, or anywhere, she would do so willingly and gratuitously without the necessity of taking her to New York for any such act."[90] At 10:58 a.m., after no more than thirty-eight minutes, Giesler sat down. The court recessed until 11:15 a.m.[91]

When court reconvened, Carr called his first witness. The night before, at an informal press conference, the U.S. attorney had tantalized reporters with the possibility that Joan would be that witness. "You boys will all be here," he smiled. "If she's called you'll see her."[92] Instead, his first witness was Lois Runser Watt, the bookkeeper for the Chaplin Studio and the widow of Max Watt, the night watchman who had had the thankless task of guarding the Chaplin estate on New Year's Eve 1942, when Joan made her unannounced and unwelcome visit to Summit Drive through a broken window.[93]

Watt's testimony was perfunctory, merely a way to get into evidence the contracts, letters, and checks that would establish that Joan worked for the Chaplin organization, then left it, and—most importantly—that Chaplin paid her cross-country train fare. Through Watt, Carr introduced the June 23, 1941, six-month contract between Chaplin's studio and "Miss Joanne Berry" at a salary of $75 a week and the December 22, 1941, written extension of that contract for another six months at $100 a week. Carr also introduced two letters between Joan and Alfred Reeves, general manager of the Chaplin Studio, both dated May 22, 1942. In the first, Joan explained that she wanted to break her contract. In the other, Reeves accepted her termination request, agreeing to pay her until the contract's original expiration date of June 23. Yet Joan's checks continued until September 26, 1942, when she received the last one for $92.[94]

The jury was shown an invoice submitted to the Chaplin Studio, dated October 1, 1942, from a travel service for $263.48 and a check for that amount to cover the one-way train fare for Joan and her mother from Los Angeles to New York. During cross-examination, Giesler turned the tables by asking Watt about every cent Chaplin spent to launch Joan's career: nearly $9,000 in salary and perks; a $1,000 Christmas bonus in December 1941; $1,186.29 to cover her bills at a local department store; $439 for dental work; and $195 for acting lessons.[95] Giesler's probing about these expenditures was designed to demonstrate that Chaplin was serious about wanting to make Joan a star.

At 11:56 a.m., Watt finished her testimony and Judge O'Connor broke for his usual two-hour lunch. Chaplin, Giesler, and Shawhan headed to a private dining room at a downtown café, trying to avoid photographers as best they could. When court reconvened at 2:02 p.m., spectators were standing three-deep along the back wall of the courtroom. There was a momentary hush as a beautiful young woman emerged from a back door and approached the witness stand. Scattered audience members murmured about her stunning good looks. As she raised her blue-gloved right hand and swore to tell the truth, soft auburn curls flowed over the navy blue velvet collar of her lighter blue spring coat. She had large brown eyes and a smooth, flawless complexion. Her full, expressive mouth was covered in deep red lipstick. Chaplin put on his black horn-rimmed glasses to get a better look.[96] Even he could see that Joan Barry was ready for her close-up.

THIRTEEN

JOAN FINALLY IN THE SPOTLIGHT

Pulling her blue leather gloves off and on and answering questions in a voice so soft that Judge O'Connor had to admonish her to speak up, Joan Berry recounted the lurid saga of her troubled two-year relationship with Charlie Chaplin. Although visibly nervous, she didn't ramble like she had in interviews with Carr and the FBI. Spectators were riveted— not one whisper could be heard in the courtroom. If Chaplin's tutelage "was responsible for her performance" on the witness stand, wrote Marcia Winn, "she did him credit."[1]

"Your name, please, your full name," Carr began.

"Mary Louise Berry," she answered, revealing her unglamorous real name.

"Have you ever met the defendant, Chaplin?"

"I have," she replied, without looking at her former mentor and lover, although he sat a mere twenty-five feet away and stared at her intently. She described how Durant introduced them in May 1941 and how within days she and the famous funnyman were seeing each other "pretty constantly."

She clarified, "[F]ive or six times each week." With her eyes demurely lowered, she confessed that within weeks of their meeting, she and Chaplin were having sex.[2]

Although the spotlight Joan had longed for was finally shining on her, this performance must have been agonizing. In the 1940s women were supposed to be chaste before marriage, and if they weren't, they couldn't admit it. Newspapers would publish stories the next day telling the world she was what then was called "damaged goods." The Associated Press wire service described Joan as the "24-year-old unwed mother."[3]

Forgotten in the frenzy that swallowed up Joan and Charlie after he was indicted was that she did not seek to have Chaplin charged for any crimes. That was Carr's goal; she was the vehicle that allowed the ambitious U.S. attorney to meet it. Joan wanted Chaplin's money. She needed it to support her newborn and her fancy taste in clothes, hotels, and restaurants. And as he stared at her, Chaplin had to have been silently kicking himself with those dainty feet for not having thrown some of his ample supply of money at her. Durant had urged him to do so when Joan first told Chaplin she was having his baby. Had he listened, she might have refused to cooperate with the prosecutor and he might not be sitting in the dock, contemplating the nightmare of years behind bars and eventual deportation to England.

While Chaplin and the crowd, which included at least 40 spectators hugging the rear walls of the courtroom, hung on Joan's every word, Giesler hardly seemed to be listening. He was fishing through one of three large briefcases filled to the brim with papers and notes. It was pure theater; Giesler wanted to look befuddled to lull Carr—and Joan—into complacency.

In the corridor, 150 or so court watchers who couldn't fit inside rubbernecked for a glimpse of the show each time the courtroom's doors opened.[4] Some of them claimed—falsely and futilely—to be related to Judge O'Connor in an attempt to get a seat. Giesler was as big a draw as Chaplin and Joan. "That guy's a smoothie, he fascinates me," said one courthouse regular about the famed lawyer.[5]

Scholars have observed that people's reactions to newsworthy criminal trials "tell us something about ourselves."[6] Holding the mirror up to those obsessed with the Chaplin case, Gene Sherman of the *Los Angeles Times* compared them to tacky tourists, "for whom The Trial is something like riding the glass-bottom boats at Santa Catalina Island."[7] Visitors from as far away as Louisville, Kentucky, and New York City came so they could brag to the folks back home that they had been there. One elderly woman said she chose the trial over a movie because she was sick of war pictures. A Pullman porter said he had hurried over from Union Station—an eight-minute walk—while his train was stopped for a layover.[8] Judging from the age of those hoping to get in, Giesler had been smart in putting together an older jury. "The bobby-sox brigade was conspicuous by its absence," wrote Hedda Hopper after her own visit.[9]

People with connections found seats. Carr's attractive and adoring wife was in the audience every day, watching what would be her husband's most famous trial as U.S. attorney.[10] Former Montana congressman Washington J. McCormick, who in 1910 had seen Chaplin on American tour in *A Night in an English Music Hall*, came to court to wish Charlie the best.[11] Another spectator who managed to get in every day and under Chaplin's skin was Hollywood ne'er-do-well Tippy Gray. A gold medalist in bobsledding at the 1932 Winter Olympics, Clifford Barton "Tippy" Gray was a little-known musical theater and film actor of the silent era. Chaplin wrote in his autobiography that he'd seen Gray at Hollywood parties since 1918 and considered him a no-talent playboy.[12] It wasn't clear why Chaplin was so irked by Gray's presence, other than that he suspected Gray was in cahoots with the government after spotting him dining with J. Edgar Hoover at Chasen's shortly after his indictment was unsealed.[13]

On this third day of trial, Chaplin wore a light tan suit in the double-breasted style he favored and a white shirt. Joan's matching coat and glove outfit made her look more schoolgirl than femme fatale, so Carr had probably offered sartorial coaching along with tips on testifying. Tom Caton of the *Los Angeles Times* had the bad form to write that Joan had packed on twenty pounds in recent months.[14] Style was front and center at the trial. The female jurors were dressed to the nines. Easter was three weeks away, but they broke out their colorful spring bonnets all the same. And a few kept their hands inside chic white gloves all day long while listening to the testimony.[15]

Carr's direct examination of Joan held few surprises. He led her chronologically through signing her contract with Chaplin in June 1941. He got her to reveal that their hot sexual relationship had cooled by January 1942. By April, Joan told Chaplin she was "a little bit annoyed" because he was dubbing *The Gold Rush* for redistribution in the sound era rather than working on *Shadow and Substance* for her.[16] She nagged him to let her break her contract and go back home to New York, which he refused to do after having spent $20,000 on the script and much more on improving her appearance and training her for a role in the film.

Joan testified that finally, in September 1942 after they fought about it for months, Chaplin changed his mind and agreed to let her go home to New York. At this point in her story, Joan was speaking so rapidly the judge had to instruct her to slow down. He also leaned over from the bench and coached her, "Don't be nervous."[17]

Joan explained that Chaplin did an abrupt about-face, telling her, "I am letting you go, because I'm going, too, to make a speech on the Second Front."[18] He bought a pair of train tickets for her and her mother to travel from Los Angeles to New York and suggested that once she arrived she either stay at her aunt's house or come to the Waldorf Astoria, where he would be registered.[19]

Consequently, Joan and her mother left for New York on October 2. She stated that after she got to New York and spent four days with her aunt and one night at the Waldorf, she abruptly moved to The Pierre, where she remained another three weeks. She never told Carr who paid the bill. And despite Chaplin's desire to have her in New York for sex, their first face-to-face encounter wasn't until the night of Chaplin's Second Front speech on October 16, when she drifted past him on the dance floor at the Stork Club in the arms of a "young man," who was David Hecht.[20] Jurors must have wondered why Chaplin waited so long to get what he'd paid for.

Joan testified that she sauntered over to Chaplin's table, where he was sitting with Durant and others, and he asked her if she liked his speech and said he was "under the impression" they were going to meet up later.[21] Nonetheless, it wasn't until three days later that they did so, when she, Chaplin, and Durant had dinner at the 21 Club, followed by drinks at El Morocco. Afterward, all three of them went to the suite Chaplin was sharing with Durant at the Waldorf—at Chaplin's behest because there were a few things he wanted to "talk over" with her.[22]

At the Waldorf, Durant excused himself and went to his bedroom while Joan and Chaplin remained in the main sitting area where they made small talk "about the Russian people, how fine they were."[23] Then in trying to explain what happened next, she faltered and, after a pause, blurted: "He said: Joan, will you come into the bedroom with me?" She agreed and they had sex there. An hour and a half later, at about three o'clock in the morning, Chaplin escorted her back to The Pierre in a cab.[24]

In the cab, she said, Chaplin invited her back to California and offered her $300 for the return trip. The next afternoon, at Chaplin's request, she returned to the Waldorf, where he gave her three $100 bills. Joan returned to California—without her mother—and on November 2, she checked into the Beverly Hills Hotel. Once she was back in California, their relationship sputtered along, she said, with them having sex just three more times at his house in December.[25]

While Joan testified, a tall, distinguished older man with thick white hair watched her intensely. He had a nest of heavy black eyebrows hovering over each eye, "fully an inch, an umbrella sufficient for any rainstorm," wrote Winn.[26] The man was Joseph Scott, the attorney who replaced Jack Irwin as Joan's daughter's lawyer in the paternity case. He was sizing up his star witness and making notes to use for the upcoming paternity trial. When Joan spotted him from the witness stand, she broke into a huge smile that lit up her face.[27]

To prove the second count of the indictment and to take the sting out of what he knew would be a devastating cross-examination, Carr asked Joan about the night she came to Chaplin's home armed with a pistol. There was some confusion about the date—Joan thought it was either December 19 or 21.[28] But Mrs. Lyle Corcoran, who worked at the Hollywood gun store where Joan purchased the weapon, testified and produced a bill of sale showing that Joan didn't buy it until December 22, so it had to have been later.[29]

"State whether or not you had a gun?" Carr directed.

"I did," she replied, admitting she'd purchased it.

"Did you threaten to shoot him?" Carr asked.

"No," Joan said.

"How long were you in his house?" Carr asked.

"I stayed all night."

After a few more questions, Carr asked, "When you first arrived, how did you get in?"

"I broke a window." [30]

Once inside, having overheard him flirting with someone on the other end of his phone, she burst into his bedroom and pointed the gun at him. Although it would have been a logical question, Joan claimed that Chaplin did not ask if she intended to kill him. Instead, he supposedly asked if she planned to kill herself, which she denied. He taunted her by suggesting that committing suicide in front of him would be "very dramatic" and that the newspapers would "eat it up."[31]

They had sex that night with the weapon resting a few feet away on a nightstand, she said. Both fell into a sound sleep until his snoring woke her at about three o'clock in the morning, and she moved to the Paulette Goddard Room across the hall, bringing the gun with her. When she left around noon the next day—without the gun—Chaplin, she said, had offered to pay her twenty-five dollars a week so he could "rehabilitate" her. To get this allowance she had to promise not to bother Chaplin and only see him when he wanted to see her.[32] She also testified they had sex on two other occasions in December, once earlier in the month and again on December 30.

Carr motored through her direct examination in under ninety minutes. After he ended abruptly at 3:28 p.m., the court took a seventeen-minute recess.[33] Carr needed to quit before Joan became emotional and unfocused, a state he knew only too well. The evidence presented was bare-bones, but if believed by the jury, it was sufficient to support Chaplin's conviction on two counts of violating the Mann Act. The sordid details about Joan's abortions, the daughter she claimed was Chaplin's, her past suicide attempts, or her subsequent arrests and banishment by the Beverly Hills authorities were not relevant to the Mann Act prosecution.

During recesses throughout the trial, Chaplin stretched his legs by pacing in the twenty feet of space alongside counsel table in the well of the court. With his hands clasped behind his back he occasionally smiled for newspaper photographers who used the recess to snap as many pictures as they could. He teased them by placing a triangular paper drinking cup from the courtroom's glass water fountain on his head and yanking it off before the photographers could snap his picture. When they expressed their disappointment, he laughed.[34]

When the trial resumed at 3:45 p.m., it was time for Joan to face Chaplin's lawyer.[35] Giesler began his cross-examination gently, but anyone who knew his style understood it would not be long before he moved in for the kill. With no burden of proof, Giesler merely had to sow enough seeds of doubt in the minds of the jurors to win a not-guilty verdict. It was a task that sounded easier than it was. Feature writer Margaret Buell Wilder observed, "[I]n the box, diffident and quiet against the paneled background of the court, Miss Barry made a pretty picture. Even to a layman it is obvious that she might be photogenic."[36] Early press reports portrayed her as a sympathetic figure and another in a string of Chaplin's young conquests. Although jurors knew she was no innocent maiden, Giesler still had to be careful not to bully her or he risked having the jurors turn against him.

"You had just returned from Mexico City when you met Mr. Chaplin, hadn't you?" Giesler began.

"You were interested in getting into motion pictures?" he asked.

"Yes," she replied.

"At that time you were keeping company with another gentleman?"

"Yes," Joan answered.

"And it was this other gentleman you had been seeing in Mexico City?" Giesler asked, opening the door to her relationship with the married oil-man Jean Paul Getty. She admitted that too.

"How soon after you met Chaplin were you intimate with him?" Giesler continued.

"The best I can remember was about two weeks after. It was after I had signed my contract."

"You'll pardon me," Giesler said politely before pouncing, "but your consent to have relations with him was voluntary?"

"Yes," Joan replied, quietly.

Immediately thereafter, Giesler dropped his first bomb, "You had had relations with other men?"

In a whisper, Joan answered, "Yes."[37]

This was not exactly what she had told FBI agents who had been grilling her about her private life for months. And none of her male companions ever admitted having sex with her either. To hear Joan's admirers tell it, they had no sexual interest in this single, strikingly pretty, sexually adventurous young woman. A moment too late, with the cat out of the bag, Carr jumped to his feet. "I object. This has no bearing on the case," he said, and then foolishly added, "Even if you put a common prostitute on the stand, it could have no bearing on the issues in this case." It is inexplicable why Carr would breathe the word "prostitute" before a jury of mostly women of a certain age for whom Joan's sexual encounters with Chaplin must have already been difficult to accept.[38]

Point made, Giesler moved on.

The most dangerous weapon in Giesler's trial arsenal was his ability to tarnish the reputations of women who cried sexual abuse by his clients. In 1929, theater magnate Alexander Pantages was convicted of raping a seventeen-year-old girl and sentenced to fifty years in prison. In a twelve-hundred-page legal brief, Giesler convinced an appellate court that the trial judge was wrong to prohibit questions about the girl's prior sexual history. Giesler argued that such evidence was relevant to show that the victim was engaged in possible blackmail, entrapment, or an effort to obtain favors from a powerful man.[39]

In Pantages's retrial in 1931, with Giesler allowed to inquire into the accuser's sexual past, Pantages was acquitted. Giesler's technique worked again in the Errol Flynn trial. The jury acquitted the thirty-three-year-old

Hollywood womanizer after Giesler was allowed to present evidence that a pair of starstruck teenagers cried rape because they feared they would be prosecuted for their own sexual misdeeds.[40]

Giesler asked Joan point-blank. "Did Mr. Chaplin say he wanted you to go to New York to have sexual intercourse with him?"

Joan looked horrified. "He never said that in those words!"[41]

Giesler was off and running, wanting to know who picked up her hotel tab in New York, which prompted an immediate objection from Carr, sustained by the judge. So Giesler wisely narrowed his question to make it relevant: "Did Mr. Chaplin?"

"No," Joan replied, and Giesler cut her off before she could explain.[42]

Giesler pounded away at poor Joan until the judge called it a day. It was 4:30 p.m. when she stepped off the stand with the unhappy prospect of having to do it all over again the next day.[43] In reporting back to Hoover on Joan's performance, Hood wrote: "Carr confidentially advises he is well pleased with Berrys [sic] appearance on stand today." But Carr did not share the compliment with Joan because she was in the middle of cross-examination, and communication between the prosecutor and his witness was unethical once cross-examination had begun.[44]

By Friday, March 24, the weather was slowly warming and the crowds at the courthouse were rapidly growing.[45] When he arrived at court that morning, Chaplin fumbled through his pockets for change to pump into the meter where he parked his car. He strolled in the sunshine toward the entrance of the Federal Building with fans following close behind.[46]

Joan returned to the witness stand wearing three shades of purple—an amethyst blazer, a dark fuchsia blouse, and a darker purple skirt.[47] Inexplicably, she also wore a gold wedding band on her right hand.[48] Chaplin, in a gray suit, broke out his black-and-white spring spectator shoes.[49] Because Joan could barely be heard the day before, the judge had ordered the overnight installation of a public address system. But it didn't work, leaving reporters and jurors still straining to hear as best they could.[50]

Giesler continued his cross-examination by reviewing Joan's contract and skipped to the heart of the case, the October 1942 trips to and from New York. Every question was designed to show that Chaplin's train tickets came with no strings attached.

"Now, when you left here for New York, your mother accompanied you?" Giesler asked.

"Yes," Joan replied.

"Mr. Chaplin was not on that train, was he?"

"No," she said.

He got her to admit that she and Chaplin did not travel back to California together at the end of the month either.[51] As to the alleged New York hotel tryst, Giesler forced Joan to admit that it was *she* who phoned Chaplin once he got to the city and not the other way around. Most important, when she did call, he didn't want to speak with her.

"I want to ask you whether you had been told [by Chaney, the butler] Mr. Chaplin would not talk with you?" Giesler asked.

"Yes," Joan replied, "but may I explain?" The judge stepped in, telling Joan: "That will not be necessary."[52]

Joan was adamant that Chaplin invited her to the hotel at the end of their evening together. Giesler pressed her to reveal intimate details, which she did in a whisper. Yes, she confessed, Chaplin undressed completely and then put his clothes back on after sex at the Waldorf.[53]

Giesler had two goals in attacking Joan's testimony about what happened when she returned to California. Joan said Chaplin wanted her back to resume their relationship and gave her $300 to pay for the trip. Giesler had to show that wasn't the reason Chaplin gave her the money and that she was lying when she said they had sex in California. It was a serious blow to the government's case when Joan admitted that on November 6, four days after she returned to California, Chaplin told her he never wanted to see her again.[54]

Giesler asked about the November 1942 trip to Oklahoma that Joan took after Chaplin told her their relationship was over. Once Giesler established that Joan went to Tulsa, he had more ammunition with which he hoped to blow up the government's case—a series of letters Joan had written to Chaplin from a hotel there, which Chaplin had presciently saved for a rainy day and given to his lawyer. It was about to pour all over Joan. Giesler had marked for identification Defense Exhibit B, a two-page letter from Joan to "Charles" and an envelope to "Charles Chaplin" dated November 22, 1942. He also had marked as Defense Exhibit C a one-page letter, also to "Charles," and an attached envelope postmarked November 18, 1942.[55]

"Do you remember writing letters to Mr. Chaplin from Tulsa?" Giesler asked, tiptoeing into his subject.

"Yes, I do."[56]

He showed her Exhibit B and asked if that was her handwriting. As soon as Joan acknowledged that it was, Carr asked to see it. After reading it carefully, he leaped to his feet, sputtering an objection about its relevance. Judge O'Connor took the letter, turned his swivel chair around so that his back was to the courtroom, and read it in silence. When he was finished, he faced forward and ruled that Giesler could not reveal the first page of the letter or the first six lines of the second page. The rest, he determined, was fair game.[57]

Giesler was now ready to fire. He slowly and clearly read the permissible parts of the letter in open court. In it, Joan had resorted to her old trick to instill jealousy—pretending she was about to marry someone else. "I'm leaving tomorrow on the 12:15 plane and will probably stay with mother over Thanksgiving," she wrote. "Then, the 'fatal plunge.' He wants to get married Saturday. By the way, I've had a lot of explaining to do as to the reason I'm in Tulsa and not in New York. Luckily the 'best girl friend and I must see her' still works."[58]

Giesler picked up Defense Exhibit C, but the judge again insisted on reviewing it first. This one, Judge O'Connor ruled, was admissible in its entirety. It was an agonizingly humiliating letter, written four days before the previous one. It was filled with regret and self-pity over how she'd behaved and how she'd foolishly let her unrequited love for Chaplin interfere with her golden opportunity to become a star. While revealing it may have been necessary to save Giesler's client, there was an element of cruelty in exposing Joan's degradation to the world.

The letter began: "Charles: I'm so sorry for the unbalanced and undisciplined way I have acted—sorry because it's caused you annoyance and embarrassment. I can't ask you to forgive me because I know what I've done is past forgiving."[59] Although breaking into Chaplin's home on multiple occasions and threatening him with a gun were beyond the pale, Chaplin had behaved like a cad toward Joan. Yet nowhere in the letter did Joan display righteous anger over the mixed signals he had sent her regarding their romance or complain about the pressure Chaplin had put on her to abort two pregnancies or the pain and danger she had endured in having them.

The pathetic letter revealed her intense disappointment over losing the role of Brigid (which she repeatedly misspelled "Bridget") in *Shadow and Substance*. "I never doubted—for one second—that I was to be Bridget. That knowledge compensated for the pain I felt when I knew that I was never really close to you. I thought loving you, and knowing that you never wanted, or would never allow me to become a part of your life was torture, but now that I know I am not to be Bridget, my cup is full." After thanking him for buying the play for her, she fed his ego by further thanking him for "letting me know you—you the greatest genius and artist living."[60] Reporters smelled a hot story, and during Giesler's reading of the letters, they slipped in and out of the courtroom to file their copy for late editions on the East Coast and for afternoon papers in California.[61]

Joan seemed stunned that Giesler intended to reveal her private letters to Chaplin. As he read aloud, she buried her face in her hands. Even Chaplin became uncomfortable. For the first time during Joan's testimony, he stopped staring at her and nervously tapped his toe.[62] Eventually, he too had had enough, and he covered his face with one of his hands.[63] But still, Giesler kept twisting the knife. "I know you're not interested in my plans, but I'd like to tell you anyway," he continued reading. "I'm going back to New York to get married. (There really is a boy who wants to marry me.) I'm going back to New York just as I left it. No clothes, no car, no money." She told "Charles" in closing, "Forget all those mean things I've done if you can and remember instead that stupid girl who ruined the greatest chance the motion pictures have ever offered."[64]

Unable to tolerate it any longer, Joan began to weep. She turned her tear-stained, mascara-streaked face to O'Connor, perhaps hoping that their secret, unspoken friendship might cause him to take pity on her. For whatever reason, he rescued her from further torture. The judge looked at the clock, saw that it read 11:50 a.m., which was ten minutes earlier than the usual lunch break, but said, "The court will recess until 2 p.m."[65]

Joan left the court for the elevator bank, clutching a linen handkerchief as she sobbed. She was surrounded by an escort of FBI men who "formed a determined wedge around her and nudged through the screaming, squealing, running, pawing crowd," wrote Gene Sherman of the *Los Angeles Times*.[66] Sherman gave Chaplin credit for Joan's painful yet moving performance on the stand. "The girl he had taught to act had stolen the scene," he wrote.[67] Back at their desks, the FBI agents guarding Joan immediately reported to Hood about Joan's breakdown on the stand. And, of course, Hood immediately told Hoover. But, in keeping with agents' fear about sharing bad news with Washington, Hood painted a rosy picture. "Berry regained her composure over the noon hour."[68]

Joan's letters, written after Chaplin had rejected her and she was lonely and financially desperate, seriously undercut the government's theory of the case. If Chaplin had given her $300 to return to California to be at his sexual beck and call, then why had he dumped her so quickly and what was she doing fourteen hundred miles away claiming she was about to marry someone else? There was no man waiting to marry her in New York over Thanksgiving in 1942, and her willingness to lie to Chaplin suggests she was making a last-ditch effort to win him back by making him jealous. After her letter-writing sojourn in Tulsa, she came back to California with money that she'd obtained there, so even if she and Chaplin had sex once she got back, it had nothing to do with his having given her money in New York in October.

After lunch, FBI men blocked the crowd as Joan returned to court. The afternoon was a letdown. Giesler tried to keep the drama going by hinting that Joan went to Tulsa to get money from a wealthy man there, and he asked about a conversation she'd allegedly had with Hans Ruesch in which she admitted as much. Carr objected, and the lawyers huddled in a fifty-eight-minute bench conference in which they fought about it in whispers. Carr argued that Joan's past romances were irrelevant, while Giesler howled that the evidence was crucial to his defense. The judge sided with Carr: relationships with other men were off-limits.[69]

Stopping Giesler's attack was probably the right legal call, but the judge's relationship to Joan and Getty—the man he must have known she was talking about—put him in an ethical quandary. Getty considered O'Connor a "close friend."[70] The judge had met Joan through Getty, who had described her as "one of my girlfriends for a brief (and I must confess, quite hectic) period."[71] Perhaps the judge barred Giesler from this line of questioning because it was the correct legal decision, or maybe he did it to protect his "close friend" Getty, a married man, from public embarrassment. Or his ruling may have been intended to keep his own relationship with Joan—brief and chaste as it probably was—from surfacing.

When the trial resumed after the court's midafternoon recess, Giesler proved himself as good an actor as his client. He gave no sign that the judge had destroyed his defense. Instead, he made a little bow in the direction of the bench and politely announced that his cross-examination was over. Never in his many years in the trenches had Giesler fought with a judge who ruled against him. He simply accepted defeat and kept going.[72]

Before the judge's devastating ruling, however, Giesler tried to plant a few other seeds of doubt in the minds of jurors about Joan's December encounters with Chaplin. In asking about the gun incident, Giesler insinuated that Joan had never let go of the gun, making it impossible for them to have had sex. Giesler had also tried to undercut Joan's claims that she had had sex with Chaplin on two other occasions in December. Joan claimed she showed up unannounced to Chaplin's home at one o'clock in the morning on a night in early December, probably the tenth or the eleventh, and they had sex.[73] But Joan stumbled when Giesler asked whether they'd had sex again on December 30.

"I was supposed to go up that night for my $25," she said.

"He gave you $25 at the door?" Giesler asked.

"We went inside," she replied. "He gave it to me."

"Was there an additional act of intimacy?" Giesler asked.

"I don't know—I guess there was. I don't remember where it was. . . . Yes, there was one."

"Are you sure?" Giesler prodded.

"Yes."[74]

On redirect, Carr returned to the gun episode by asking where Joan had placed the gun during sex. "Sometimes it was in my hand, but most of the time on the table beside me." Clearly, he was trying to show that at least for some part of the time, the gun was set aside, allowing them to have engaged in sexual intercourse.[75]

On recross-examination, Giesler asked one pointed question: "In May 1943, did you ask Mr. Chaplin for any money?" Joan said that she had not, an answer which would come back to haunt her.[76] When she finally stepped off the stand, she was smiling, relieved that she had been spared any serious questioning about her sexual past.[77]

For the remainder of the afternoon, Carr raced through a half dozen witnesses to establish how Chaplin facilitated his goal of moving Joan across state lines. The testimony was necessary but dull.[78] Among the quick witnesses were a travel agent who verified that Joan's train tickets had been paid for by the Chaplin Studio; a hotel employee who established that Joan, Chaplin, Durant, and Chaney had been at the Waldorf on the night of October 16 into October 17; and an FBI agent who identified a photo of Chaplin and Durant in New York.[79]

Providing the only drama for the afternoon, Carr called Frederick James Cannon, the elevator operator at the Waldorf the night Chaplin and Durant rode up with a woman whose hair he described as "really beautiful, a kind of auburn color, and a long bob." To prove that the woman Cannon was talking about was Joan, Carr called her back into the courtroom so Cannon could identify her. Cannon took a long look and at first hesitantly said she was the woman he had seen, and then after looking at her longer, he more boldly stated, "I'm sure she's the one."[80] Court wrapped up for the week at 4:35 p.m. on Friday afternoon.[81]

Joan, Charlie, the lawyers, the judge, the jurors—and the public—would have a much-needed three-day break. Each Monday, Judge O'Connor presided over a calendar filled with pretrial applications in other pending cases, so the Chaplin trial would not resume until Tuesday.[82]

The world weathered another weekend of war news. The Red Army was shelling the Nazis in Rumania.[83] American bombers were pummeling the northern French-Netherlands coast.[84] A mass invasion of Europe by Allied ground troops was in the works, which should have been a bright spot for Chaplin, who had been making Second Front speeches for two years urging the Allies to invade Europe.[85]

Closer to home, it had been a rough week for Joan and a delight for the standing-room-only crowd that had been lucky enough to see and hear her in person. While trial fans eagerly awaited next week's installment, when Chaplin was expected to be the star attraction, Joan went to the Mississippi Avenue apartment in Los Angeles that she shared with her mother and daughter to recuperate.[86]

Getty, meanwhile, who had been cooling his heels in a tiny witness room since the trial opened, left the courthouse late Friday afternoon and headed to his office to salvage some of the workweek. Hotel-loving Getty stayed at the luxurious Beverly Wilshire, even though he had a mansion in Santa Monica at 270 Ocean Front, today the Pacific Coast Highway, next door to Marion Davies's colossal spread.[87]

He had good reason for hiding out in a hotel: he didn't want Teddy to know he was in town to testify at the Chaplin trial as one of Joan's "other men." On Friday night, Lynch sang on *Hollywood Showcase*, Hopper's coast-to-coast radio program that was broadcast from Los Angeles.[88] Getty listened in his hotel room, ate dinner alone, read part of a book, and went to bed. But before falling asleep, he phoned his wife to compliment her on her singing, which he told her he heard while listening over his car radio in Tulsa, which was a lie.[89]

Getty was just postponing the inevitable. Sooner or later, his wife would learn he would be testifying at the trial. To keep the unpleasant thought at bay, he spent all day Saturday, March 25, inspecting his California oil wells. On Sunday and Monday, probably having told Lynch he'd just arrived, he left his hotel and went home, spending time with her at the beach.[90] Getty remained under Giesler's subpoena and couldn't leave town until he either testified or was told by the court he was no longer needed.

Despite the serious setback handed to him by Judge O'Connor, Chaplin seemed nonplussed as he walked alone to his car on Friday afternoon, one hand in his pocket and the other holding a long-stemmed pink carnation that an elderly woman had given him as thanks for signing an autograph. He walked "briskly, gaily, with almost a dancing step, twirling the carnation with the casual flickering motion he once made famous with a cane."[91] He would tell reporters the following Tuesday that he spent most of the three-day recess playing tennis. "[A] little tennis—that's what keeps you fit."[92]

But Chaplin's insouciance would shatter as the weekend wore on. Chaplin paced and fretted in his study. Giesler used the time more productively; he reviewed trial transcripts in which he had stuck hundreds of little yellow paper strips to remind himself of important points that he didn't want to forget. In between, Giesler sat in Chaplin's study to go over the next week's trial strategy with his nervous client. Whether or not he believed it himself, Giesler calmly reassured his client: "We'll get through it fine."[93] Giesler still had one ace up his sleeve, assuming the judge would let him play his hand.

FOURTEEN

THE BIG THAW

Spectators lined up by six o'clock in the morning outside the Federal Building to snare a seat in court as the Chaplin trial entered its second week on the warm, sunny Tuesday of March 28. Four hours later, once everyone who could fit—about 250 people—had squeezed inside Courtroom No. 7, Giesler ignited fireworks by asking the judge for permission to recall Joan.[1] He had a few more questions. Carr was on his feet in a second, begging the judge not to allow it. It was a blatant attempt to skirt O'Connor's prior ruling that had stopped Giesler from prying into Joan's relationships with other men, Carr argued.[2] Which, of course, it was.

Although O'Connor had pulled the plug on that line of questioning the previous Friday, Giesler wasn't about to give up. Instead, he burned the midnight oil all weekend to come up with a new rationale—beyond destroying Joan's reputation—to justify delving into her prior sexual relationships.

Lawyers ask judges to reconsider a ruling when they think they have a new and improved argument. Giesler's latest pitch was that he only wanted to ask about Joan's sexual activities at a time relevant to the indictment. He asked for an opportunity to show Joan had had sexual encounters with others during the relevant time period—November and December 1942.[3] "It is only fair that the background of the young lady (Miss Berry) should be brought to light so that truth may be brought to its proper level."[4] Carr was having none of it. Whether a woman was pure or not was irrelevant as to whether the statute was violated.[5]

Giesler's argument was a stretch, to be sure. But Chaplin claimed he gave Joan $300 in New York because she told him she was broke. If she traveled elsewhere to meet and squeeze money from other men, it tended to support Chaplin's defense. Further, Giesler asserted that some of his questions would explore Joan's motive for making these allegations, which is always relevant in a criminal case. During this back-and-forth between the lawyers and the judge, which took place in heated whispers at the bench while the jury was out of the room, Chaplin, with little else to do, turned his chair toward the elbow-to-elbow crowd and gave it a stern once-over.[6]

Airing the dirty laundry of a woman claiming to be a victim of sexual misconduct is offensive. But presenting it as Giesler did, to counter the government's allegations and to show a sinister motive on the part of its star witness, was a closer legal call for the judge. O'Connor now waffled. Giesler's stellar reputation surely had something to do with the judge's indecision. O'Connor worried that if Chaplin were convicted, the judge's exclusion of every scintilla of evidence about Joan's sexual history would give Giesler a winning appellate argument. No judge enjoys getting reversed, but to get reversed in a trial that was front-page news would make O'Connor a national laughingstock. The judge was in such a quandary that he called a half-hour recess to retreat to his chambers.[7]

When the judge returned to the bench at 11:15 a.m., Giesler asked that Defense Exhibit E, a list of forty-one questions for Joan, be marked for identification. The judge ordered the exhibit be placed under seal—off-limits to the press and public—to be reserved for a higher court to review in the event of Chaplin's conviction. The jurors were called back at 11:52 a.m., and O'Connor immediately sent them out for lunch until 2:00 p.m. Whatever was going on, they were never going to know about it.[8]

After lunch, the judge announced a ruling that amounted to an uneven, un-Solomon-like splitting of the baby. He denied most of Giesler's request—whittling his forty-one proposed questions to just five that focused on Joan's relevant past relationships and her motive for testifying. Giesler claimed in his autobiography, *The Jerry Giesler Story*, that he was permitted to ask "only ten or twelve" questions.[9] Regardless of the number of questions he was able to ask, it was fewer than he'd wanted. Giesler looked pale and seemed upset, but it may have been another one of his acts.[10] He could not have thought the judge would let him ask forty-one questions about Joan's past, but by asking for so much he was using an old lawyer's trick in the hope he'd get the judge to agree to let him ask at least a few of them. The judge played right into the hands of the wily defense attorney, giving him just enough fodder for cross-examination and summation.

Joan reappeared after lunch but wasn't on the stand long. She wore her purple coat, this time with a yellow sweater underneath, and clutched a large handbag while she testified.[11] Giesler sided up to the witness box, as close as he could get without being told to step back by O'Connor, and read the few questions the judge allowed from long sheets of legal paper. Giesler usually memorized the questions he asked witnesses and knew these like the back of his hand, so this too was part of his performance art.

The lawyer obeyed the judge's ruling—sort of. Years later, when chortling over his Chaplin trial strategy, Giesler wrote: "I'd ask a question, . . . the witness would answer, then I'd say, 'That was question number one. Now, your honor, in accordance with your ruling I will skip other questions you have ruled that I am not permitted to ask. . . .'"[12] And so on. Giesler hoped the jury would wonder why he was barred from asking those questions and would conclude the government was hiding something. Giesler's gamble worked. As soon as he started requestioning Joan, a sea change came over the jury—and the spectators too. "The frozen hatred for my client thawed until, at the end of the trial, the audience was more pro-Chaplin than anti-Chaplin."[13]

The questions Giesler had asked during his cross-examination the week before had been designed to shatter Joan's story about the events of late 1942. These new ones were designed to shatter Joan. Giesler forced her to concede that before going to New York in October 1942, she had told Edward Chaney that she hated Chaplin because he wouldn't let her go back home.

"'My boyfriend's in New York and I want to see him.' Did you or did you not say that?" Giesler asked.

"I did." This was the first hint there was another man in the picture, and it provided a reason for her to go to New York that had nothing to do with Chaplin. It was a blow to the government's allegations.

Yanking off his reading glasses, Giesler looked Joan in the eye and asked about a conversation with Chaplin's secretary, Catherine Hunter, on or around May 7, 1943, in which Joan asked her to tell Chaplin she was back in Beverly Hills so she could goad him into getting her arrested. Did she warn Hunter, Giesler asked, that she would "'put his name in headlines from one end of the country to another,' and did she [Hunter] not say, 'That sounds like blackmail?' And didn't you then say, 'How dare you accuse me of blackmail?' And didn't she say, 'I think you are acting very foolishly Joan!'?"

"I did not!" Joan said angrily.[14]

Giesler moved in for the kill: Did Joan demand money from Chaplin after she told him she was pregnant? "On or about June 1, 1943, in the yard of the home of Mr. Chaplin, you and he being alone, did you not for the first time accuse him of being the father of your unborn child and demand that he give you $75,000 for you and your mother and put $75,000 in trust for the child, that you had the press on your side, and when you got thru [sic], they would blast him out of the country?"[15]

Carr leaped to his feet. Objection—it was a collateral matter. But the judge disagreed and allowed it. Gleefully, Giesler took aim at what he hoped the jury would see as Joan's hustle and repeated the question. "Yes or no, did that conversation take place?"[16]

"It did not take place," Joan said, but her attempt to explain was cut off by O'Connor, who admonished her. "That's enough." He said, "The prosecutor can ask you more if he wishes in good time."[17] Despite Joan's adamant denial on the witness stand, her former lawyer, Judge Holland, had told the FBI otherwise.

Chaplin couldn't keep his eyes off Joan and the show his lawyer was putting on. Giesler kept going. Was Joan acquainted with "J. Paul Getty of Los Angeles, New York, and Tulsa?"[18] Little did billionaire Getty know—as he twiddled his thumbs a fifth day in the witness room of the Federal Building—that his name was being bandied about in Courtroom No. 7 and that the lid would soon blow off whatever he was trying to keep from his wife about Joan.

"I am," Joan admitted, generating a buzz from the courtroom crowd.[19]

Giesler asked Joan about her visit to Tulsa—now that the jury knew Getty lived there—between November 17 and 23, 1942, forcing her to admit that while in Tulsa she had purchased a ticket to return to New York but had cashed it in and used the money to go to California instead.

"The money that you used . . . to bring you back to California was not money advanced to you by Mr. Chaplin?" Giesler said.

"That is true," she agreed.

"It was money you obtained elsewhere?" he asked.

"Yes," she replied.[20]

Giesler sat down with a broad smile, confident that Joan's honest answer had just torpedoed the government's case, at least as far as the second count of the indictment was concerned. If Joan returned to California with money given to her by someone else, then Chaplin didn't violate the Mann Act. If she and Charlie happened to have sex once she got back, it was simply two consenting adults engaged in intimacy.

During Carr's brief redirect examination, he asked Joan if her version of the poolside conversation differed from Giesler's. When she said, "Yes, that's right," Carr sat down. Her ordeal over, Joan ran out of the courtroom.[21]

Shortly before the afternoon recess, the government called its final witness, Chaplin's butler of three years, Edward Charley Chaney. Winn described him as "a tall, slender man with blond hair pressed eternally into place."[22] Chaney was supposed to be the icing on the cake, providing corroboration that Chaplin had had sex with Joan in New York in October and in California in December. Instead, Chaney melted on the witness stand under the pressure of being under oath yet sitting only a few feet away from his boss. He tried to have it both ways by damning Chaplin in the most neutral manner he could. Carr could barely keep from blowing his stack.

By 1942, Chaplin was at the mercy of a new, inexperienced, and not terribly loyal household staff. For eighteen years, until Goddard moved into Summit Drive in the early 1930s, Chaplin had been well served by Toraichi Kono, his Japanese chauffeur whose role expanded into chief of staff and special confidant. Because he was so impressed with Kono, Chaplin favored Japanese servants.[23] But Goddard wanted to be the lady—and boss—of the house. Kono quit in disgust.[24] After Pearl Harbor, Chaplin lost the rest of his Japanese staff because they were among the eleven thousand Japanese interned by the U.S. government during the war at Manzanar, about 225 miles northeast of Los Angeles.[25] Their non-Asian replacements were less discrete and not as loyal.[26] Chaplin hired the fifty-one-year-old British-born Chaney in December 1941 as a $175-a-month butler. Chaney's Austrian wife served as Chaplin's cook.[27]

Chaney was a nervous wreck while he testified, and Chaplin was a nervous wreck while he listened.[28] The butler kept looking at Chaplin for approval from the witness stand while Chaplin avoided his glance.[29] Chaney had been a thorn in everyone's side from the minute he started singing to government investigators. He liked Joan, visited her while she was pregnant, and was disgusted by Chaplin's treatment of her. Although he corroborated key parts of Joan's story in early interviews with the FBI, he also squealed to Chaplin's lawyers about what agents had asked him.

The FBI knew that Chaney was playing both ends against the middle, and Carr should have been wary in relying on him as a key witness. Lawyer Jack Irwin had warned FBI agents that in contrast to what Chaney had told them, he had said in a deposition for Joan's paternity suit that he had not overheard Chaplin make admissions to his lawyers about having had sex with Joan.[30]

"State whether you heard Mr. Chaplin make a statement about having sexual intercourse with Miss Berry in New York," Carr asked in his direct examination.

"The word 'sex' was never used sir," replied the proper Chaney.

"What did Mr. Chaplin say?" asked Carr.

"He admitted being with Miss Berry," Chaney answered. Even the judge stepped in to tell him to repeat what he'd heard—exactly.[31] Still, Chaney did not say the magic words "sex," "intercourse," "affair," or any number of synonyms for the acts that Carr had to prove.

With his face turning as red as his hair, Carr rummaged through the pile of papers on counsel table, pulled a document from the stack, had it marked for identification, and shoved it into Chaney's hand. It was a copy of the signed statement Chaney gave to the FBI on October 30, 1943.[32] On that date, Chaney said that when Chaplin was talking to his lawyers Loyd Wright and Pat Millikan in June 1943, he'd overheard his boss "tell them that he had had an affair with Joan Berry in New York City in October, '42." Chaney further told FBI agents that Chaplin "also told his attorneys that he had been intimate with Joan Berry in his house in December, '42. This was the time when she came up there with a gun."[33]

The prosecutor asked if the copy of the statement refreshed Chaney's memory.

"Yes, it does a little," the butler sheepishly replied.

"Well, let's have that little, Mr. Chaney," snapped Carr. [34]

Chaney stammered, blaming his inability to recount what Chaplin said on the fact that his boss had been swearing, which he was uncomfortable repeating in court.

"Well, omit the swearing," the judge, now as impatient as Carr, told him.

"He said, 'Sure, he'd been with her. He'd been with her many times.'" That was as far as Chaney would go.[35]

"Do you recall being in my office this morning?" an exasperated Carr asked.

"Yes."

"Well, give us what you remember then," Carr asked. Chaney reluctantly revealed that he had told the prosecutor that morning that Chaplin had admitted he'd been intimate with Joan. With that, Carr sat down.[36]

Fearful of what Chaney might sputter next, Giesler kept his cross-examination brief. Afterward, Carr asked one final question of the reticent butler. "You're still working for Mr. Chaplin, aren't you?" And after Chaney said he was, Carr excused the witness, and the government rested its case. It was 3:15 p.m.[37]

For the next hour Giesler argued vigorously outside the presence of the jury for a directed verdict of "not guilty," which, if granted, would mean that the judge would decide there was not sufficient evidence from which the jury could determine that Chaplin committed the crimes with which he was charged. During his argument, Giesler's gentlemanly veneer fell away. Pounding counsel table with his fist, Giesler scoffed at Joan's story as "peculiar, absurd and asinine."[38] For O'Connor, it had been a long, trying day; he sent the jury home shortly after 4:30 p.m. and said he would wait until the next morning to hear Carr's response. It took a long time to clear the crowded courtroom; the trial fans lined up near the exit, clamoring for Chaplin's autograph, and he patiently accommodated them.[39]

Day six of the trial on Wednesday, March 29, was shaping up weather-wise to be a warm and sunny carbon copy of the day before. Chaplin arrived in a gray flannel suit with a blue polka-dot tie that sharp-eyed reporters thought looked suspiciously like the one his butler had worn the day before.[40] The first hour was taken up with Carr's objection to Giesler's motion. Afterward, the judge adjourned for fifteen minutes to consider the arguments.[41] When he returned at 11:16 a.m., O'Connor denied Giesler's motion on the first count of the indictment, which covered the trip to New York, but left open the door for a possible dismissal later on the second count.[42] The ruling was a bad sign for Carr. By winning the fight to reopen Joan's cross-examination, even for just those few questions, Giesler had scored an important victory. Joan's testimony about her November visit to Tulsa to see Getty and her admission that her return trip to California had not been paid for by Chaplin were probably fatal blows to the second charge in the indictment.

After the jury entered the courtroom, it was Giesler's turn to present a case. His first witness was Getty's Tulsa attorney, Claude H. Rosenstein. On the stand, Rosenstein authenticated checks written from his law firm's account. Admitted into evidence were Defense Exhibit G, a check for $93.80 made out to the Santa Fe Railway Co. and earmarked for "Joan Barry's transportation (from Tulsa to New York by way of Chicago, the witness said)"; Defense Exhibit H, a check dated November 23, 1942, and made out to the Beverly Hills Hotel for $249 (for Joan Barry's bill); and Defense Exhibit J-5, a check for $110 to the Mayo Hotel in Tulsa (for another Joan bill).[43]

Other checks to cover Joan's expenses were marked for identification but never admitted into evidence. Giesler wanted the jury to see how much Joan depended on the financial kindness of men besides Chaplin, but the judge thought those checks were irrelevant. So the jurors never learned about the $800 that Getty's lawyer paid to Harry Cooper for Joan's clothes; the $37 to Elizabeth Arden for her facials; the $35 to Joan's doctor; and the $350 check that went directly into Joan's pocket. A one-page document signed by Joan and dated April 16, 1943, which was an IOU to Getty for $700, never saw the light of day in court either.[44] The judge allowed only three checks into evidence directly relating to Joan's return to California in October 1942.[45] Before Rosenstein was excused, Giesler was able to establish one critical fact—that Rosenstein was *not* Chaplin's lawyer, nor did he undertake any of those expenses on Chaplin's behalf.

"You weren't acting as attorney for Charles Chaplin?" Giesler prompted.

"No," Rosenstein replied.

"It was not Mr. Chaplin's money nor did he have any interest in it?" Giesler asked.

"None whatsoever," Rosenstein said.[46]

In the afternoon, Giesler called Rosenstein's real client, Jean Paul Getty, to the stand. The mere mention of Getty's name created an audible stir. Even Chaplin adjusted his black-rimmed glasses to get a better look as Getty marched in, raised his right hand, swore to tell the truth, and sat down. Marcia Winn's description said it all: Getty looked like "a pained Tibetan monk."

"He has a thatch of gray hair, a cold, dour face, and a mouth curved down like a thin, perfect segment drawn by a compass," Winn wrote, adding that the billionaire spoke in "hollow, funereal tones."[47] No matter, because Getty did not speak for long. Giesler first established that Getty knew Joan. And, of course, neither Getty nor O'Connor revealed that they knew one another.

"In the year prior to 1941, did you see her frequently?" Giesler asked Getty in reference to Joan. The question brought an objection by Carr. Giesler tried again.

"Did you see her in Tulsa during the month of November, 1942?" Giesler continued. Getty replied that he had, and that was the end of his testimony.[48]

Had Giesler asked more about Joan's Tulsa visit, Getty would have said that when she arrived on a bus in November 1942 she was desperate, flat broke, and appeared to be on the brink of a nervous breakdown. A calculating cross-examiner, Giesler knew when to leave well enough alone. This information might have created sympathy for Joan. Instead, Giesler accomplished exactly what was needed: the jury knew that Joan knew Getty, and it was likely that he paid for her return trip to California after having seen her in Tulsa in November. Giesler would connect the dots during summation. There was no need to antagonize the powerful oilman, who was already upset about having wasted a week of his busy life cooped up in a federal courthouse and who may have ended up in the doghouse at home because of it.

The Magnificent Mouthpiece disappointed the press by letting the billionaire off so lightly, however. "And there went Getty," tsked-tsked Winn, "the backbone of the defense."[49] That evening, Getty grumbled in his diary too. "Testified for about 3 minutes."[50]

After Getty's departure, Giesler ran through his roster of witnesses. The most important was Hans Ruesch, who was presented by Giesler as Chaplin's so-called alibi witness. Joan had recalled for jurors the details about the night she went to Chaplin's with her gun, but she never had a command of the details about the other two nights in December on which she claimed to have had sex with Chaplin. For the first night, which was either the tenth or the twelfth, it was her word against his; she said it happened, and Chaplin said it didn't. But on December 30, the other night that she testified they had been intimate, a cast of characters claimed to have spent time with Joan when she was supposedly with Chaplin.

Hans Ruesch saw Joan often in November and December 1942 during the brief time he lived in California. Tall, dark, and handsome, Ruesch was a Swiss bachelor who was born in 1913 in Naples to a wealthy family that owned a textile mill, a hospital, and a printing business.[51] Before the war, Ruesch drove Alfa Romeos and Maseratis in Grand Prix racing events across Europe.[52] He arrived in the United States as part of a prewar immigration quota in October 1939.[53] By March 1944, Ruesch was living in New York City to pursue a career as a writer. It was at Ruesch's Sulgrave Manor apartment in Beverly Hills that Joan had faked her New Year's Eve 1942 suicide attempt. The following day, after her arrest for vagrancy, Joan was wearing Ruesch's pajamas under her silver fox coat in jail.

Giesler kept his questions simple. Had Ruesch been with Joan on December 30, 1942? Ruesch confirmed he had, testifying that they were together in the late afternoon at his apartment and then went to the Players Restaurant at about seven or eight o'clock in the evening, where they remained for all of thirty minutes. Later, they saw each other again for about five minutes at the apartment of their friend Lionel Bonini. The next time Ruesch saw Joan was at about two or three o'clock on the morning of December 31st when she returned to his apartment, escorted by the police.

Giesler asked what Joan's condition was "with regard to sobriety?" The question prompted a fierce objection from Carr. O'Connor overruled it.

"She was in one of her states," Ruesch answered, resulting in courtroom laughter and a scolding from the judge. He rapped his gavel for order. Later, Ruesch made it clear: Joan "definitely was not sober."[54]

Ruesch described Joan's sorry state when he saw her. "[H]er dress was quite disorderly. It was dirty as though she had been lying in the dirt. There was blood on her head. Her stockings were torn. She was bleeding at both knees. The heel of one shoe was missing."[55]

On cross-examination Carr desperately tried to shake Ruesch's memory. "Isn't it a fact that the occasion you refer to about Miss Berry's bloody condition was on December 13?" Carr asked.

"I think it was rather the 30th," Ruesch replied.[56]

Like he did with Chaney, Carr waved around Ruesch's prior inconsistent statement that he had made to an FBI agent in New York in which he said that the incident took place in early December. But Ruesch blamed his discrepancy with the dates on not having had the chance to check his diary before he spoke to the agent. "I went through the diary and recollected lots I didn't before, even today I remember things I didn't yesterday," he said.[57] Ruesch had steadfastly refused to share his diary with the FBI once agents learned he kept one, so the extent to which he was telling the truth couldn't be evaluated.

He was also certain the incident took place on December 30–31 because that was the last time he ever saw Joan. Carr tried to insinuate that Giesler had bought and paid for Ruesch's altered testimony.[58] When Carr asked Ruesch if he were currently living in a bungalow at the luxury Huntington Hotel in Pasadena, Ruesch admitted he was.

"Who pays for it?" Carr asked.

With Ruesch looking befuddled and a little guilty, Giesler rescued him by muttering, "Why I guess we do." The Chaplin team had put Ruesch up there since March 21 in preparation for trial.[59]

Following the afternoon recess, during which Chaplin was spied snoozing by at least one reporter, Giesler quickly paraded several Chaplin employees before the jury.[60] Their perfunctory testimony was offered to show that it was Joan's idea to go to New York in the fall of 1942, not Chaplin's. Studio manager Alfred Reeves testified that he'd spoken with Joan on September 26, 1942. "Did she tell you she was going to New York for good," Giesler asked, "that she had . . . given up the idea of a screen career, and that Mr. Chaplin had agreed to pay her fare and that of her mother?"

"Yes," Reeves replied.

"Did she tell you she was thru [sic] with picture work?"

"Yes, sir."[61]

Next, Chaplin's devoted cameraman, Roland H. Totheroh, who had shot every Chaplin movie since 1916 and had filmed Joan Barry's screen test for *Shadow and Substance*, testified that Joan also told him she wanted to go to New York. Totheroh testified that he had warned her that she was "throwing away" a wonderful opportunity in motion pictures.[62]

Chaplin's bookkeeper, Lois Watt, returned to the stand. She testified that Joan left her car at the studio with instructions to sell it, implying that Joan never intended to come back to California to drive it again. Catherine Hunter, Chaplin's secretary, disputed Joan's denial that she'd threatened Chaplin with blackmail in a phone call in the spring of 1943.[63] As his employees came through for him, one by one, Chaplin appeared bored by it all.[64] Chaplin saw all the witnesses leading up to his testimony as the coming attractions. Tomorrow the public would hear from the star of the show.

FIFTEEN

"OH, I THINK I KISSED HER BEFORE THAT"

"Call Mr. Chaplin, Your Honor."[1] It was late afternoon on March 30 when Giesler summoned his client to the stand after forcing the impatient audience to fidget through the testimony of obscure witnesses.[2]

Chaplin rose from his seat. As he stood, he pulled the cuffs of his navy suit jacket to his wrists with his fingertips and walked quickly to the stand. Every eye was locked on him. He raised his right hand, swore to tell the truth, settled into the witness chair, and shifted his shoulders to get comfortable.[3] Those who hadn't seen *The Great Dictator*, or who didn't know him personally, had never heard his voice. He spoke with a proper British accent, thirty-two years and fifty-five hundred miles from the Lambeth slums of his youth, where nobody spoke the King's English. One sentence out of his mouth showed why his signature character could never speak on-screen. Charlie's voice belonged to a gentleman, not a tramp.

Before court opened, there had been a contretemps between Chaplin and the photographers. Knowing Chaplin would testify, they wanted him to pose on the witness stand so his picture could accompany their stories. He balked. Agness Underwood complained to Giesler, who had enough to worry about, so he dumped the problem on Casey Shawhan. The PR man convinced Chaplin that the court of public opinion was as important as the court in which he currently found himself, so Chaplin trudged to a vacant courtroom, where he pantomimed testifying while the photographers snapped away.[4] Every photo of Chaplin on the witness stand that appeared in newspapers the next day was a fake.

Once he really took the stand, Chaplin's performance rivaled Joan's, as it should have. Besides the thirty years he'd spent in front of the camera, he'd paced around his house all morning in his bathrobe, rehearsing his testimony to himself in a monotone.[5] Beyond his carefully scripted lines, Chaplin also fell back on his peerless skills as a mime. Not since the Tramp planted a loving kiss on the mouth of little Jackie Coogan after rescuing him in *The Kid* had Chaplin used body language so beautifully. He punctuated his words with gestures and, when overcome with emotion, cradled his head in his hands. At key moments, he summoned tears. Years later, Giesler would rave that Chaplin was "the best witness" he'd ever seen in court.[6]

Marcia Winn agreed, although she seemed to suspect it was all one big act. "If this were acting today, it was superb. It was pantomimic. It was verbal. It was shadow, substance, wry gentle smiles and unstanchable tears," she wrote.[7] Chaplin would be on the stand for two days.[8]

"Kindly state your full name," Giesler asked his client.[9] Scene 1, Take 1.

"Charles Spencer Chaplin." There was no trouble hearing him; having first stepped on a stage when he was still in short pants, Chaplin knew how to project all the way to the rafters of the cavernous courtroom.[10]

But when Giesler asked him his address, Chaplin stumbled. "I don't . . . 1185."

Giesler rescued his nervous client. "If I told you it was 1085 Summit Drive, would that be correct?"

"Yes."[11]

Chaplin found his footing. From then on he spoke confidently, looking directly into the eyes of the jury of seven women and five men—just as he used to look directly into the eyes of the audience in his early silent films, as if he and they were sharing a secret.[12] After a few more preliminaries— his age, the address of his movie studio, the length of time he'd lived in Los Angeles—Giesler dived in. "Are you acquainted with Joan Berry?"[13]

Every inch of the courtroom was packed with people, sitting and standing. Chaplin's butler and chauffeur, barred from coming inside because they were witnesses, had their noses to the crack in the door of Courtroom No. 7 to see and hear what their boss had to say. An FBI agent came over and told them to knock it off.[14]

Chaplin rattled off the story of his relationship with Joan, the romantic aspect of which he downplayed. But he complimented her acting potential. He described the screen tests he'd directed, which proved what he had already suspected: Joan "photographed very appealingly." He added,

"I thought she had histrionic ability."[15] He talked about how he had bought *Shadow and Substance* to give her a leading part and had paid for her straightened teeth and acting lessons. But despite the time and money Chaplin put into grooming Joan for stardom, she quickly lost interest.

"Did she develop for motion pictures?" Giesler asked.

"I don't think so. . . . I don't think she concentrated. . . ." he replied.[16]

Chaplin testified that Joan broke her contract with him to test for Sam Marx at MGM, only to beg to return when it failed to pan out. Chaplin agreed to take her back but refused to give her another written contract; he wanted to see if she would knuckle down and do the hard work needed for success. She didn't.

Continuing, Chaplin testified that Joan grew impatient because she thought he was dawdling with the *Shadow and Substance* script and begged him to let her go back to New York. Chaplin resisted, still hoping to salvage his significant investment—$20,000 for the rights to the play alone, not counting the costs of Joan's self-improvement. But when her nagging became intolerable, he relented.[17]

Before she went, she asked him to pay train fare for her and her mother and for her outstanding bills. "I said I would."[18] He bought train tickets and tossed in an extra $500.[19]

"Did you go to New York for any purpose other than making a talk at Carnegie Hall on Oct. 16, 1942, after your acceptance there?" Giesler asked.

"I did not," Chaplin responded.[20]

Once in New York, their first contact was coincidental, he insisted. Following his speech, he dined at the 21 Club with Paulette Goddard and actress Constance Collier. Later, Chaplin, Durant, and Arthur Kelly, an executive with United Artists (and the brother of Chaplin's first love, the late Hetty Kelly), visited the Stork Club, where they bumped into Joan.

"Did you ask her to get together later on?" Giesler asked.

"No," Chaplin replied.

"Did you at that time ask to see her anywhere in New York City?" Giesler followed up.

"I did not," Chaplin said.[21]

The next time Joan's name came up was when "Edward told me that she had called and I told him I didn't want to see her," Chaplin testified.[22]

Durant convinced Chaplin to "give her one night, otherwise she would come to the hotel and cause trouble." Durant arranged a dinner for the three of them at the 21 Club, which took place several days later. The date lasted until the wee hours, and when the three of them were in a taxi, Joan suggested she return with them to the Waldorf. "She said she would like to look over our suite," Chaplin testified.[23]

Joan had checked into and out of the Waldorf just days before Chaplin arrived in New York. It is preposterous that she would have suggested a middle-of-the-night hotel suite inspection except as a ruse to rekindle their romance. So, either Chaplin invited her up, or he took her up on her request to visit because he figured he would score. Chaplin denied there was any sex once they were back at the hotel; there was only small talk.

Afterward, Chaplin escorted her to The Pierre in a cab, at which time she told him she was "very hard up." He found that statement incredible, given she was staying at the luxury hotel. "[S]he said that was on Mr. Getty," Chaplin said, so he agreed to give her money. He told her to come back to the Waldorf the next day, at which time he gave her $300. He denied it was to pay her transportation back to California.[24]

In response to Giesler's question about whether Joan had asked Chaplin for money in the past "other than her salary," Chaplin replied that she did so frequently and that he'd given it to her.

"What amounts did you advance?"

"Two hundred dollars, $300, $1000," Chaplin answered.[25]

Chaplin returned to California at the end of October 1942. Joan arrived a few days later and in short order started phoning him. He said that after he initially refused to talk to her, she wore him down, and in the middle of November he invited her to dinner at Romanoff's. Chaplin said he picked her up at the Beverly Hills Hotel but "she was not in a condition to go," implying she was drunk. Joan begged him to put her under contract again, but he refused because "she was too unreliable." The couple bickered, the evening quickly fell apart, and Chaplin drove her back to her hotel, confirming what Joan had testified to earlier: "I left her and said I did not want to see her again."[26]

With Chaplin out of the picture, Joan took off for Tulsa, which Chaplin said he knew about because he got Joan's two letters that Giesler had placed into evidence earlier. The mention of Tulsa allowed Giesler to suggest that Joan was turning her gaze to Getty and was determined to bilk any rich man she could. Besides undermining the government's theory of the case and impugning Joan's credibility, this testimony also insinuated she was loose, Giesler's signature method of destroying women who dared to accuse his clients of sexual misdeeds.

The next time Chaplin saw Joan, she was standing in his bedroom, pointing a loaded gun at him. Recounting that night brought Chaplin to tears.[27] "Well, I had just come in, it was rather late, possibly past 12:00, and I was about to retire," Chaplin recalled. "I was speaking over the telephone. Suddenly, I heard a disturbance and I looked to where my bathroom door is on my right here (indicating), and from the doorway Joan came in, pointing a gun, and she made a half circle. . . . I remember that very distinctly," he said. "She came to me and she said, 'I'm going to kill you.'"[28]

"Although it was rather melodramatic and absurd, I was scared," he said.[29] "I went through and tried to reason with her why she should treat me so, why she should embarrass me to my help down at the studio and create scenes and go into tantrums and all—oh so much. However, I went all through that, practically the whole of my association with her. I told her that I had done everything I possibly could. . . ."[30]

After listening to Chaplin's lengthy monologue, Joan changed her mind and decided to kill herself instead. "[W]hen I got through she said, 'Well . . . I don't think you are worth it.'"[31]

While Chaplin was staring down the barrel of Joan's gun, his sons arrived home from a Christmas party. The memory of their entrance into this bizarre tableau made him cry. After a long pause, Chaplin covered his mouth with his hand and composed himself.[32] Watching this testimony from the gallery, FBI Agent Hood described Chaplin as being "near collapse."[33] Winn was sarcastic in her description to her readers. "Ah, the sorrow of it! And the tragic mold of Mr. Chaplin's face as he told it. . . ."[34]

Chaplin continued. "I heard a disturbance in the hall, and my children were downstairs." They had discovered signs of a break-in and were worried. Chaplin left his bedroom and went out into the hallway to reassure them. "I said, 'There is a little trouble, sons; you had better go back to your mother and stay there the night.'"[35]

Charles Jr. and Sydney were teenagers in 1942, living with their mother, Lita Grey, but they had their own bedroom at Chaplin's house. Going to their mother's was impossible because they had no car and it was too late to summon a cab. Realizing they were stuck there, Chaplin insisted they go to their room. They obeyed and he returned to Joan and her gun. "Look here, my two children are here. You must go home," he told her.[36]

Joan wasn't as obedient as his sons and refused to budge. Instead, she complained—once again—of being destitute. Given that she wasn't working, traveled all over the country, and treated herself to fine hotels in the cities she visited, it wasn't hard to understand why she was always broke. "You can't stay here, you won't stay here. I'll throw you out," Chaplin threatened.[37]

Unable to end this standoff, which had a whiff of slapstick despite being so dangerous, Chaplin said he allowed her to take her gun and sleep in the Paulette Goddard Room, which was connected to his by a bathroom with doors on each side. Chaplin locked the bathroom door that opened into his bedroom. After successfully containing her, Chaplin said, he went to sleep.

"That night in your home, did you have intimate relations in your bedroom with Miss Berry, before which she laid the gun down and afterward picked it up again?" Giesler asked.

"I did not."[38]

Chaplin's eyebrow-raising reply had no more ring of truth than his Waldorf story. Joan came to the house waving a gun. She was mentally unstable. His children were in the house. Why in the world would he leave her unattended all night in a room adjoining his—locked or not—with a firearm in her hand? Even if she were no longer a threat to him, she was still a threat to herself. Had Joan committed suicide in Chaplin's home in the dead of night, beyond the personal tragedy, the scandal would have been catastrophic. It is more likely that Chaplin used his formidable skills as a lover to distract and calm his disturbed ex-girlfriend. Afterward, with both of them exhausted from the trauma and the sex, they fell into a sound sleep. Chaplin could have admitted to having been intimate with Joan that night if he were confident that the jury believed him when he claimed he did not give Joan $300 in New York so she could return to California to be his lover. But he and Giesler were taking no chances.

The next morning, Chaplin went down to breakfast. It is equally absurd that Chaplin would calmly eat his toast while Joan remained upstairs—on the same floor as his sons—still clutching her gun, unless he was sure their lovemaking had neutralized her anger and despair. Still, he needed to get Joan out of the house because he had already begun courting Oona and couldn't run the risk she might drop by. He couldn't admit that, however, because in December 1942 Oona was only seventeen. Chaplin said he went upstairs to wake Joan. He said he tried again to relieve her of the weapon. "Give me that gun. Don't be absurd," he told her.[39]

Before Joan left that morning, Chaplin bent her ear with another ponderous lecture. "I went through the whole thing. I said that was the wrong way to get help, coming up to the house with a gun." Joan cried during this speech, he said, which may have made Chaplin feel guilty enough to dig into his pocket and hand her the last $60 that was in it. He told her if she needed more to come back the next morning and see Edward, and at last she gave up the gun.[40]

By this time, Chaplin had been testifying for about two hours before a mesmerized audience. One of the elderly jurors had a hand cupped behind an ear so as not to miss one syllable.[41] At 4:30 p.m., the judge adjourned for the day.[42] Outside, after being cooped up in a windowless courtroom, the trial goers found themselves in glorious sunshine with the temperature in the 80s.[43]

On Friday, March 31, Chaplin was back in the hot seat, bright and early. Dressed in a gray suit with a matching vest, he resembled a prosperous middle-aged banker. With one elbow on the judge's bench to support his head, he looked as if he'd gotten little sleep the night before. After establishing that Chaplin did not pay Joan's New York hotel bills or her bill at the Beverly Hills Hotel in November, Giesler directed Chaplin's focus to the night of December 30, 1942, leading into New Year's Eve. The size of the trial audience had grown since the day before.[44]

"I believe I was playing solitaire in my front room. I suddenly heard bells ringing in my kitchen," Chaplin testified. "I opened the door. I saw lying on the mat outside Miss Joan Berry . . ." he said, his voice trailing off.[45]

"Just go ahead," Giesler coached.[46] Chaplin's description of Joan curled up on his doorstep was the same position in which Marx had seen Joan a year and a half earlier on the sidewalk in front of his house when she wanted him to arrange a screen test for her at MGM.

Winn was less impressed with Chaplin the longer he talked. Too young to have spent her Saturday afternoons at the silent movies, she was not in awe of his celebrity or his cinematic genius. Nor did she share the cynicism about Joan's story shared by the older, tougher news gals who had cut their teeth on the police beat. She saw Joan as a human being—albeit a flawed one—rather than a "type," either the desperate starlet or the manipulative gold digger. "Certainly Chaplin did not help his cause too much today," she wrote. She scoffed at his "King Lear sorrow at a frustrated and besmirched faith (his own)]," as well as "the casual manner in which he threw all the blame for intimacy and associating upon a young girl."[47]

Chaplin continued talking about December 30. "I looked at her. She paid no attention. I left the door, and went down to the basement where the help sleep. I began ringing bells, the inter-room communication, so everybody would be up. I knew we were going to have a lot of trouble."[48]

Carr jumped up as soon as the words "a lot of trouble" left Chaplin's mouth; it was an inadmissible conclusion of the witness. "I move to strike his statement." The motion was granted. The judge gave Chaplin a little lecture about sticking to the facts.

"I see. I beg your pardon," Chaplin replied. He explained that he rang the bells to wake the servants because he was afraid of Joan, who had come to his house armed with a pistol only the week before. But the only help he roused was a new employee he didn't know well, so he took care of the "trouble" himself. [49]

"I opened the door and tried to arouse her, but she couldn't make much sense. Finally she did say, 'I am destitute. I have nowhere to go.'"[50]

Chaplin said he told her, "Destitute or not, you are not going to stay here," and when she told him she had no car, he said he would take her where she wanted to go. Initially, that was to Olympic Boulevard, but as they got closer to the destination she repeated she had no place to sleep and said she would sleep at the police station.

"Did she enter your house at all on the occasion just related?" Giesler asked.

"She did not," Chaplin replied. "I wanted to get her out of there," he said.[51]

Chaplin's direct testimony finished shortly after lunch.[52] Before turning Chaplin over to Carr for cross-examination, Giesler asked Chaplin if Joan tried to extort $150,000 from him for herself, her mother, and her unborn child. Chaplin said she had. By the time Giesler said, "Take the witness," he'd done all he could do, which was to raise doubt in the minds of the jurors about the government's case and make his client appear sincere and sympathetic.[53]

Carr's cross-examination of Chaplin, like Giesler's direct exam, began at the beginning. Although Chaplin reluctantly admitted he and Joan had been sexually intimate, he refused to admit that he felt any romantic feelings for her—even in the early days of their affair. She often told him she loved him, but he said he never responded in kind. He denied calling her for a date after their first dinner meeting at Perino's in May 1941.

"Well, how did you get together?" Carr asked, with a hint of exasperation in his voice.

"I think we met at Mr. Durant's home," he replied.

"Mr. Durant left you and Miss Berry alone for quite some time that evening, didn't he?"

"I think so."

"At that time you told her you were more or less enchanted by her?"

"No, I did nothing of the kind."

"You told her she was a very pretty girl and very interesting?"

"I told her she was interesting. I . . . may have said something about her having personality," Chaplin responded.[54]

They saw each other again a day or two later. "Do you remember telling her she was a very pretty girl and that particular night trying to kiss her?" Carr asked.

Chaplin smiled. "O, I think I kissed her before that!" The courtroom erupted in laughter, evoking a stern admonition from the judge. "This is a court of justice, not a place of amusement," O'Connor barked.[55]

"About July 1, you began to tell her you were in love with her?" Carr asked.

"Not at any time!" Chaplin retorted. Nor did he ever bother to telephone her. "I never call anyone. I hate telephones!" But he did admit taking her yachting, having her sleep over at his home—"sporadically"—and reading Shakespeare to her.[56]

"And quite often she would spend the night?" Carr asked.

"No," Chaplin replied curtly.

"Well, how often?" Carr followed up.

"I don't know," Chaplin said, adding that the romantic relationship existed only until December 1941.[57]

"During August, 1942, you were having sexual relations with Miss Berry?" Carr asked.

Chaplin waited a long while before answering, "No, I was not."

"During July, 1942?"

"No."

"June, 1942?" Carr asked.

"No."

"May, 1942?"

"I haven't any fixed date, but it was quite a long, long time," Chaplin said.

"Did you see her in May, 1942?" Carr asked.

"I don't recall."

Carr would not let go. "In April?" he asked.

"Maybe."[58]

"Sex isn't very important in my life," Chaplin said dismissively—and unbelievably.[59]

Chaplin made a strange and surprising admission during cross-examination, vaguely alluding to Joan's abortion in January 1942, without ever calling it such or taking responsibility for getting her pregnant. Chaplin claimed he learned of this unspecified "operation" when Joan arrived at his home accompanied by a nurse, after Joan had disappeared from his life for several months—although he had just told Carr their romantic relationship had only ended a month earlier, apparently a slip-up.[60]

"I was suddenly confronted with the nurse, and that was the first I knew of it," he explained. "That's why I have been suffering ever since! That's why she has been doing what she has ever since!" he added, again summoning tears.[61] The judge struck his statement from the record and told Chaplin to calm down. [62] Obviously referring to Joan's second abortion, Chaplin sought to plead ignorance about her condition and signal that he couldn't have been responsible because he hadn't seen her in months, which wasn't true. The newspapers provided no context about the delicate topic, nor did Carr delve into it further, perhaps fearing it could generate hostility toward Joan. The elderly jury—probably already reeling over two weeks of testimony about Joan's casual attitude toward sex—would not look kindly on news she had had three out-of-wedlock pregnancies and had terminated two of them.

"Does Miss Berry have a key to your home?" Carr asked.

"Yes, she stole keys," Chaplin replied.

Moving on to the night Joan appeared in his bedroom with her gun, Carr asked Chaplin how long she was there. "I don't know," he replied. "I was so excited, so upset, so bewildered. It seemed hours, maybe two hours," he said.[63]

"You didn't call the police?"

"No," Chaplin replied.

"You had cars available to take Miss Berry away, didn't you?" This would have been the logical and safer solution to getting rid of Joan and her weapon that night.

"Yes," Chaplin admitted.[64]

Carr spared no effort sullying Chaplin. "Do you recall slapping Miss Berry on Dec. 12, 1942?"

"I have never slapped any woman in my life," Chaplin shouted.[65]

Before he was through, Carr also pressed Chaplin about his claim that Joan tried to extort $150,000 from him during their long poolside parley in June 1943 when they discussed Joan's pregnancy. But it was Joan's version that Carr posited, which he brought her back on redirect to repeat, namely, that she proposed to Chaplin and he refused, telling her he was "not marrying anyone" and threatening to "blacken" her name if she went public. He denied it all.[66]

And then, shortly after lunch, Chaplin's ordeal was over.[67] Carr announced that his cross-examination was through, and the defendant stepped off the stand. To the extent that Carr seemed to be browbeating Chaplin without objection, it was purposeful, Shawhan wrote later. "Giesler . . . often let the red haired, fiery, belligerent prosecutor berate and bully Chaplin without protest. Giesler's motive was part of his plan—part of his staging of the drama—to make that gray haired defendant be the bedeviled, scared, harrassed [sic] bewildered little man—the little man he so often portrayed in his pictures."[68]

Tying up loose ends, Giesler called Chaplin's civil attorney Charles "Pat" Millikan to refute the butler's claim that Chaplin admitted to his lawyers that he had slept with Joan in New York and California in the fall and early winter of 1942. Millikan denied it happened. And then at 2:57 p.m. the defense rested. The court took a half-hour recess.[69]

Afterward, Carr presented a rebuttal case, recalling Joan to the stand—her fourth appearance—to counter Chaplin's characterization of their poolside meeting as a $150,000 shakedown. There was nothing new to add; rather, it was just another opportunity for Carr to have her repeat her version for the jury, which made Chaplin out to be heartless. She said that when she told Chaplin she was pregnant, he suggested she go to New York to have the baby—in other words, to get lost.[70] When she asked him why he wouldn't marry her, she testified that he told her, "'I'm not marrying anyone,'" although he married Oona only weeks later.[71]

Before calling Joan again, Carr had tried to close the door on Giesler's insinuation that Joan was a money-grubbing con artist. He summoned FBI Agent Frank Angell, who testified that Joan didn't initiate the Mann Act prosecution but that the FBI sought her out to be a witness in its case. Carr called FBI Agent Percy J. Landry, who testified that he was never shown the diary that Ruesch claimed supported his "alibi" for Chaplin, even though he'd asked to see it.[72]

At 3:52 p.m., with the testimony over, the judge sent the jurors home.[73] The public would have juicy reading material to enjoy over the weekend. By this time in this long-running soap opera, Chaplin's mistress was so well known that she no longer needed a last name in the headlines. "Joan Tells of Life with Chaplin," wrote the *Los Angeles Times*. "Joan Tells Chaplin Threat; Asserts Actor Said He Would Blacken Name," wrote the *Chicago Daily Tribune*. The lawyers would spend the weekend preparing to take center stage with their closing arguments.

SIXTEEN

"HERE LIES THE BODY
OF JOAN BERRY"

Chaplin could not understand what Giesler and Carr would find to talk about for two and a half hours, the time allotted by the judge for each of their summations.[1] If he felt any anxiety as he left the courthouse on Friday, March 31, after two grueling days on the witness stand, he didn't show it. He was overheard saying matter-of-factly, "I am interested to see what happens now."[2]

Chaplin's blasé attitude may have been rooted in his actor's sixth sense that he had performed well on the court stage. Smug and self-satisfied with his testimony, Chaplin thought it was obvious that anyone could see that Joan's story was nonsense. The prospect of being found guilty was the furthest thing from his mind, or at least that's the way he saw it in hindsight when he was rewriting history in his autobiography.[3]

After both sides rested, Giesler renewed a motion for a directed verdict of not guilty, which Judge O'Connor promptly denied. Not surprisingly, Judge O'Connor ruled there was sufficient evidence to let the jury decide Chaplin's fate; after two weeks on trial in such a high-profile case, the judge wasn't about to risk national condemnation by snatching it from the jury and deciding in Chaplin's favor.[4]

Even so, climbing into the car for the rush-hour drive home, Chaplin could relax somewhat: his work was done. The heavy lifting now fell to Giesler, whose job it was to tie up the loose ends, present a logical counternarrative to the government's theory of the case, and bring it home by getting his client acquitted. The veteran lawyer had an uncanny knack for reading jurors and knew how to educate and entertain them. "He was as knowledgeable about the value of the 'gimmick' and surprise twist as any $2,500-a-week Warner Brothers scriptwriter," wrote Giesler's biographer, John Roeburt.[5] He'd once delivered a closing argument with such emotion that he broke both his wrists while pounding on the jury box. The judge, the jury, and his adversary were none the wiser until he showed up in court the next day with his hands in casts.[6]

In another case, Giesler had represented a cuckolded husband who faced the death penalty for shooting his wife and her lover while they embraced on a piano bench. Giesler had *the* piano bench brought to court, sat on it during summation to show how the couple was positioned before the crime, and threw himself on the floor to demonstrate where their bodies landed after the shooting. While lying there, Giesler delivered the rest of his closing argument; his client was convicted of manslaughter but was spared the gas chamber.[7]

The judge expected the lawyers to be prepared to sum up first thing Monday morning, April 3. By 9:08 a.m. on that cool, cloudy day when the United States Supreme Court would rule eight to one that Texas Democrats could not prevent Blacks from voting in party primaries, American bombers would blast Budapest, and President Roosevelt was recovering from bronchitis, Carr was on his feet, addressing the jury.[8]

For the first ninety minutes, standing behind his lectern like a professor and wearing a dark blue suit, Carr methodically reviewed the evidence and explained why it supported Chaplin's conviction, reserving a final hour to attack whatever arguments Giesler would make. Carr had his work cut out for him.[9] No matter how much sympathy the jury felt for Joan—and even if she was telling the truth about having had sex with Chaplin in New York and California—the evidence that he transported her across state lines for that "immoral purpose" was weak.

Admittedly, there were facts in Carr's favor: Chaplin funded Joan's trip to New York, was with her in his hotel room in the middle of the night, and gave her a significant amount of money before she returned to California. Carr asked the jury to dismiss as far-fetched Chaplin's assertions that he never had sex with Joan at the Waldorf or in California in December. Carr spoke in calm, measured tones steeped in the soft drawl of his native Mississippi. But deep down, even before the case was over, he realized his mission might be futile. "All the government asks," he said, "is a verdict unaffected by bias or personal prejudice."[10]

Joan carried a lot of baggage—her sexual history, her crazy behavior, her hunger for money. The weight of it fell on Carr's shoulders, forcing him to spend valuable summation capital fending off Giesler's anticipated arguments. The judge had shielded Joan from her sexual past, but hints of it had seeped out all over the trial. Getty, the man from Tulsa, who probably paid her New York hotel bills and her fare back to California, was the elephant in the middle of the courtroom. Joan's sketchy relationship with him put Carr in the uncomfortable position of arguing in that buttoned-up age that a victim's chastity or lack of it was irrelevant to a Mann Act charge. Knowing that Giesler would argue that Joan's testimony was a polished performance, Carr told the jury, "Now I will leave it up to you to determine which of them was the better actor."[11]

Carr was further bogged down by the alibi testimony of Ruesch, who claimed he saw Joan on December 30, at or near the time she was supposedly having sex with Chaplin. The most damning statement he could come up with to attack Ruesch's credibility was to "beware of a man who keeps a diary."[12] Carr finished the first part of his summation at 10:44 a.m., the court recessed for fifteen minutes, and then it was Giesler's turn.[13] Reporters were laying odds on a hung jury.[14]

Like Carr, Giesler asked the jurors to look dispassionately at the facts, set aside emotion, and to "use common sense." [15] But Giesler needed to do more than that; he had to convince the jury that this was a he-said-she-said, and that what she said couldn't be trusted. To destroy Joan's credibility, Giesler had to turn a young, attractive, tragic woman—albeit one saddled with the Scarlet Letter of single motherhood—into a liar and immoral opportunist. He was effective; after Giesler was through, Carr stood up and said: "Here lies the body of Joan Berry."[16]

Today, Giesler's strategy of attacking a fragile woman would look like bullying. Back then it worked wonders against women who dared defy societal expectations that they be unmarried virgins or dutiful wives. Speaking without notes, Giesler warmed to his subject. He paced back and forth before the jury box like a hungry cat as he ripped Joan apart. He waved around an imaginary gun.[17] He called her a criminal, reminding the jury that she'd admitted to burglary, assault with intent to kill, and possibly robbery and kidnapping the night she showed up at Chaplin's with her loaded pistol. "Lots of poor devils are in San Quentin for less," he shouted.[18]

He raised questions he wanted the jurors to raise among themselves in the jury room: Why did Chaplin pay to send Joan's mother to New York if the trip was for his sexual pleasure? Why was the ticket only one way if he'd wanted to keep her around in California for the same purpose? And why hadn't Chaplin paid Joan's New York hotel bills and phoned her in the city the minute he got there if he wanted her as his sexual plaything?

But even Giesler didn't seem to buy Chaplin's claim that he and Joan never had sex at the Waldorf. If Chaplin and Joan had had sex there, Giesler said, it wasn't because Chaplin intended it. Instead, opportunity knocked when they bumped into each other at the Stork Club. As further proof there was no intent on Chaplin's part, Giesler recalled that Joan admitted she'd phoned Chaplin's butler at the hotel and asked, "'Do you think he would talk to me?'"[19] Giesler thundered: "There is no more evidence of [a] Mann Act violation here than there is evidence of murder."[20]

After lunch, Giesler kept going another two hours, until a quarter to four.[21] From the press table, Chaplin appeared thinner than he had on the trial's first day. He sat slumped in his chair as the lawyers talked away the afternoon.[22] Of all the moments of the trial, it was this one where Chaplin was the most powerless, sitting on the periphery like a mere extra player as the lawyers hogged center stage.

Giesler continued. Joan had hoodwinked Uncle Sam into pursuing a baseless prosecution, he insisted. "I tell you, this girl has victimized the Government and she has victimized this defendant, and I ask you to judge him as if you were in the same circumstances and conditions," he fumed. "[T]he girl had private vengeance in her heart since June,1942, to say the things which have led up to this prosecution. I doubt that she ever dreamed it would arrive at this stage," Giesler raged.[23] But there was no evidence Joan angled to get Chaplin indicted; in fact, it was the FBI that came to Joan to make the case that J. Edgar Hoover wanted to "expedite."

It wasn't just Joan who supposedly had it out for Chaplin. In a story published in the *Los Angeles Examiner* the day after summations, it was revealed that the House Committee on Un-American Activities planned to include Chaplin's Second Front address at Carnegie Hall, which had been sponsored by the Artists Front to Win the War in October 1942, in a report it was drafting about Communist front activities in the United States.[24]

The trial left Chaplin "scorched and burned far beyond recall by worldwide publicity," Giesler cried. Any commensurate bad publicity Joan endured was her own fault, he said. With a straight face, he contended that Chaplin never "blanched" Joan's good name in defending himself.

"[H]er predicament was of her own making," Giesler insisted. "If only she had gone along, who knows what a great star she may have become under the tutelage of her mentor."[25]

Giesler painted Joan as a loose woman willing to give her body to Chaplin at "any time, any place, without having been taken 3,000 miles for such an act."[26] Overcome by his own voice, Giesler committed a titanic Freudian slip by calling Chaplin "Mr. Pantages" during his emotional summation, which got a hearty laugh.[27] Pantages was the alleged rapist Giesler saved from fifty years behind bars by convincing a jury in 1931 that it was a precocious teenage girl who seduced *him*.[28]

"That was another case, Your Honor," Giesler said contritely.[29]

When Carr stood to make his final fifty-minute pitch to the jury, he sternly reminded jurors: "She is not on trial here."[30] Before sitting down for the last time, Carr quoted from a poem from an unnamed author, "The Woman Divine." He read in part: "They scorned the woman—but forgave the man; it was ever thus, since the world began. . . ."[31] There was a spirited debate among the cynical reporters in the gallery about whether the poem was corny, but it moved some spectators to tears.[32] Novelist Margaret Buell Wilder loved it. "During those last minutes of his final rebuttal he out-Giesler-ed Giesler," she wrote of Carr's poetic reading. "It was a wow-finish. . . ."[33]

It was a long day for Chaplin, who, exploding with the tension of the past two weeks, vented to reporters outside the courtroom, claiming he was a "victim of war hysteria." He was being prosecuted for his political views, he asserted. "I have never been interested in politics, but I know now I put my foot in it when I gave that speech for the second front," he said.[34] It is a position Chaplin and his supporters would hold for the rest of their lives, and there was some truth in it.

Judge O'Connor waited until the next day to begin his fifty-five-hundred-word legal instruction to the jury.[35] Chaplin wore a double-breasted gray suit for the occasion and listened respectfully as the judge spoke.[36] For fifty minutes O'Connor droned on with his legal guidance for jurors' deliberations, but he probably sedated and confused them.[37] Although the most important part of a criminal trial, jury instructions are deadly boring because each arcane nuance of the law must be carefully explained to laypeople. The Chaplin jury instructions had been parsed over—word for word—between the lawyers and the judge in his chambers the prior Friday afternoon.[38] While the instructions were supposed to give the jurors a neutral lesson in the law, the lawyers did the utmost to shape them to favor their side.

Besides the jurors receiving standard instructions for the prosecutor's burden of proof beyond a reasonable doubt and the legal definition of the Mann Act, Carr asked the judge to remind them: "Even if it could be proved that the woman was of unchaste character it would still be a violation of the statute if her transportation was for the purpose of sexual immorality."[39] The judge made sure the jurors did not vote to convict Chaplin because they didn't like the way he lived. "You are instructed that the defendant is not on trial before you for any matter or thing of which you may have heard or read as relates to the matters of his citizenship, the question of the paternity of any child, or as to any matters of his private or professional life."[40]

The jury began deliberations at 11:02 a.m. Chaplin's hope for a twenty-minute acquittal was dashed when the jury was still holed up in a room one flight up from the courtroom at 11:58 a.m., at which time Judge O'Connor ordered the jurors to stop. They were treated by the court to lunch at a downtown hotel restaurant, where they went as a group, guarded by three bailiffs.[41] Because they were outside the sanctuary of the jury room, their conversations were limited to small talk while they ate. After finishing lunch at 1:40 p.m., they walked back to the courthouse to continue debating Chaplin's fate.[42]

While the jury was eating, Chaplin, Giesler, and Shawhan dined at a restaurant near the courthouse too. Chaplin barely touched a bite, while Giesler scarfed down his meal so they could beat the jury back to the courthouse. The lawyer had a fixation against keeping jurors waiting in the event they sent out a note asking for a clarification of the judge's instructions or requested read-back of the testimony. They made it back ten minutes before the jury and spent the afternoon watching the clock.[43]

At 3:15 p.m., about two hours into their deliberations, jury foreman Roscoe Reeder sent a note asking for a read-back of Joan's testimony about how she and Chaplin got together in New York, focusing on the phone conversation in which Durant invited her to dinner.[44] The question boded well for Chaplin. It meant the jury was struggling with whether Joan's visit to his hotel suite was part of a plan Chaplin hatched back in California. The judge read back the relevant testimony from the transcript.[45]

From the start of the deliberations, the jury leaned toward acquittal. In an informal straw poll on the first count of the indictment, five jurors voted guilty and six voted not guilty, with one juror taking no position. The discussion and secret balloting continued. The second time the jurors took a poll, the guilty votes were down to three, with eight jurors voting not guilty and one still not voting.

By the third secret vote only two women—Vera Danis, a housewife, and Loretta Easley, the piano teacher—thought Chaplin was guilty of the first count. Finally, on the fourth straw vote, the jury reached a unanimous verdict of not guilty on that count, which involved the trip to New York. The jurors had a much easier time with the second count. On the first ballot, only one juror believed Chaplin gave Joan $300 so she could return to California to engage in sex with him. By the second ballot the jury had reached a consensus of not guilty.[46]

While the jurors discussed the evidence, Giesler, an old hand at waiting for a verdict, spent the afternoon kibitzing with his pals in the press. His stomach was doing "flip-flops"—although he hid it well.[47] It fell to Shawhan to babysit Chaplin. The two paced the second floor of the courthouse. As the minutes turned to hours with no word, Chaplin sank into one of his dark depressions. Shawhan encouraged him to look on the bright side—perhaps there was a holdout or two, which would mean, at worst, a hung jury and a retrial. "I pointed out to him that Giesler always learned a great deal about the prosecution's case during the first trial," Shawhan recalled later. Chaplin shuddered at the thought. "I knew in a way that Chaplin was thinking of the expense of a second trial, as well as the trouble, because Giesler did not come cheap," Shawhan wrote.[48]

The waiting took its toll on some of the reporters too. Writing for the New York *Daily News*, Muir had to work around the three-hour time difference and arrange with Western Union to run a wire from the federal courthouse so she could meet her early deadline once the verdict came in. To prevent other reporters from glomming on to it, Muir filed frivolous stories every half hour. Most of them had nothing to do with the case and would never see print. It cost the *Daily News* a bundle, but it was worth it once there was a verdict because it allowed Muir to use the open line to scoop her colleagues.[49] Agness Underwood wasn't so lucky. Judge O'Connor let her stake out a phone in his chambers to use when the verdict came in. A competitor cut the line.[50]

When 5:30 p.m. came and went without a verdict, Chaplin bummed a nickel from a newsman and called Oona from a pay phone in the second-floor corridor. "I don't think I will be home for dinner," he told her and continued pacing with Shawhan.[51] Shortly before 6:00 p.m., a bailiff shouted, "It's a verdict!"[52] The waiting crowd stampeded into the courtroom, but Shawhan and Chaplin hung back. "I wish to this day I could have had a motion picture of Chaplin's face at that moment," Shawhan wrote later. "He was not acting, and was the picture of a confused, fearful, anxious old man."[53]

Carr and his minions blew past Shawhan and Chaplin. Once again, Chaplin's nemesis, Tippy Gray, was right behind.[54] Inside, the room was packed and the tension palpable. Chaplin could barely swallow as he and Shawhan headed in. The clerk banged the gavel three times, and as O'Connor emerged from his chambers, everyone stood. After another bang of the gavel, the audience was quietly seated. At 6:08 p.m., the jury filed back into the courtroom. The judge asked: "Ladies and gentlemen of the jury, you have reached a verdict?"[55]

Foreman Roscoe Reeder stood. "We have."[56] Chaplin's lips trembled, and he nervously fiddled with the knot of his tie.[57]

The clerk handed the written verdict sheet to O'Connor, who examined it silently and handed it back. Special Agent Hood reported to Hoover that when the judge reviewed it, he turned his head to the side ever so slightly and smiled.[58] Margaret Buell Wilder thought the judge looked relieved.[59] The jurors' faces were solemn. Carr tapped his fingers on counsel table. Giesler, his face puffy and pasty, looked every day of his fifty-eight years.[60] Eyes closed, the lawyer gripped the defense table tightly with both hands. Chaplin stared blankly into space, his body rigid but his left hand trembling so rapidly that Giesler grabbed it and held on tightly.[61]

Deputy Clerk Francis E. Cross read the thirty-seven words that ended Chaplin's nightmare. "We, the Jury in the above-entitled cause, find the defendant, Charles Spencer Chaplin, Not Guilty as charged in the first count of the Indictment; and Not Guilty as charged in the second count of the Indictment."[62] Before he could finish, women screamed and men whistled and clapped. The judge banged his gavel to restore order, and Cross was able to get out the rest of the words. Chaplin clutched Giesler's hand even harder, and the lawyer whispered something to him, lost in the shouts of "Hooray, Charlie!"[63]

Chaplin looked at the jury and whispered, "God bless them! God bless them!"[64] Giesler, his face dripping with sweat, turned to Chaplin and grabbed both his hands. Like the Little Tramp and the once blind flower girl in the last scene of *City Lights*, lawyer and client stared at one another, tears blurring their vision, for what seemed to observers like a very long time.[65]

And then their bond broke. "No courtroom epic, hatched in the warm typewriter of a hack scenarist, possibly could have outdone the real-life Charlie Chaplin denouement in the Federal court of Judge J.F.T. O'Connor—complete with spontaneous cheering above the frenetic rapping of the bailiff's gavel," wrote Gene Sherman of the *Los Angeles Times*.[66] Try though he did, O'Connor could not restore order once the verdict was announced.[67]

Carr was a gentleman in defeat. "He's been tried according to the American system and was acquitted," said Carr afterward.[68] And then he shook Chaplin's hand.[69] But Carr had more important things to worry about; his mother, Maibelle Landers Carr, was near death in a Memphis hospital after having suffered a stroke.[70] By six thirty the next morning Carr would be on an American Airlines flight to be at her side.[71]

Once the judge and the prosecutor disappeared, the courtroom audience burst through the rail leading into the well like fans pouring onto the ballfield after the final game of the World Series. They mobbed Chaplin as flashbulbs popped, and reporters shoved notebooks under his nose. "I always had faith in the American people and American justice," Chaplin told the reporters clamoring for a quote. "This verdict confirms my faith."[72]

Years later, Chaplin would write in his autobiography that while home alone, four months pregnant Oona was outside on the lawn when she heard news of the verdict from a distant radio and fainted dead away.[73] That made for dramatic reading, but at the time, journalists reported that Chaplin had instructed George Woods, Giesler's private eye, to telephone Oona with the good news. She told the *Los Angeles Times* shortly thereafter, "Oh, I'm so happy I can hardly speak!"[74]

In her autobiography, Muir wrote that she was pleased with the verdict, despite having been largely responsible for setting the prosecution in motion. She believed that the Mann Act should have been limited to protecting women from being forced into commercialized prostitution.[75]

When asked later about the jury's deliberations, juror Rowan T. Segner, a Pasadena banker, said the jury thought Chaplin was motivated by "kindness" when he paid the train fare for Joan and her mother to return to New York and later gave her $300.[76] Lydia Hussey, the wife of a retired chemist, changed her vote to not guilty on the second ballot. "I discounted both testimonies to a certain extent." Hussey told reporters that despite feeling sorry for Joan, she believed the failed starlet was making "a cheap bid for notoriety." Housewife Beatrice Allan said she never believed Joan, and shirtmaker Claude Millsap did not think Chaplin went to New York intending to have sex with her. Foreman Reeder, an oil company executive, did not believe Chaplin's denial about having sex with Joan in New York but did not think that was why he sent her there and voted against conviction on each straw ballot.[77]

Giesler, always mindful of his manners in a court of law, whispered instructions to Chaplin to shake hands with the jury. Chaplin dutifully bestowed his "God bless you" wishes on each of them.[78] As the courtroom crowd thinned, juror Beatrice Allan, dressed for the occasion in a well-tailored suit and elaborate hat, turned to columnist Wilder and asked, "Do you think it was a popular verdict? Does the judge look pleased?"[79]

Outside, Chaplin gave news photographers the large smile they asked for before climbing into the car with an equally happy Giesler and giving a last wave before driving off.[80] That night, back home on Summit Drive, Chaplin and Oona ignored the phone, the servants, the neighbors, and the friends, built a fire in the fireplace, sipped stiff gin and tonics, and contemplated the rest of their lives. After two weeks of living on fear and adrenalin, Chaplin couldn't help but feel an emotional letdown.[81]

Reporters scrambled to find Joseph Scott, who was representing Joan's daughter in the upcoming paternity case. He said that the comic's acquittal was of no moment. And he reminded the press that Chaplin had readily admitted to sexual activity with his client, which was evidence of a sort that he'd fathered her child.[82] Reporters also found Joan. She had no comment but invited a reporter from the *Los Angeles Examiner* up to her apartment to see the baby.[83] By nightfall, when news of Chaplin's acquittal had made it into the extra additions of the papers and more reporters found their way to Joan's door, she posed for pictures with Carol Ann. "He looks happy, doesn't he?" she said about Chaplin.[84]

The Los Angeles newspapers on April 5, 1944, plastered the screaming headlines on their front pages. In the *Los Angeles Times*, the article shared the top of the front page with stories about Tom Dewey's victory in the Wisconsin Republican primary and an Allied air raid that wiped out a Japanese base in New Guinea. "Chaplin Not Guilty" the *Times* headline read.

Elsewhere around the country the verdict was also the top story. The *Washington Post* ran a banner headline above the latest war news, "Chaplin Acquitted of White Slavery Charge." The *New York Herald Tribune* ran its story at the top of the page too, "Chaplin Freed on Both Counts of Indictment under Mann Act." The *New York Times* placed the story above the fold: "Chaplin Acquitted in Mann Act Case." Even small papers in the middle of nowhere recognized their readers were hungry for news about the verdict. In upstate New York, the *Rochester Democrat and Chronicle* ran the story on the front page, "Chaplin Wins Acquittal," as did the Allentown, Pennsylvania, *Morning Call,* "Spectators Cheer Wildly as Jury Acquits Chaplin."

Before leaving the courthouse after the verdict, Casey Shawhan organized a group photo of the reporters and photographers who covered the trial from beginning to end, including Judge O'Connor. Although he didn't stick around for the picture, Chaplin joined the reporters and the judge in later autographing it.

That evening, after the boisterous crowd left the building and peace and quiet had returned, custodian J. L. Corrigan swept clean empty Courtroom No. 7. As he pushed his broom, he heard crunching under his feet. The floor was littered with spent and broken flashbulbs.[85]

FIG 1 Charlie Chaplin as the Little Tramp, circa 1915. Photo: The Lambs Foundation Inc., Lillian Fitzgerald/ John Jay Jaffin Collection

FIG 2 The Little Tramp stealing a kiss from Edna Purviance, his leading lady at the Essanay film studio in 1915. Edna was the first of his many romances with his female leads. Photo: The Lambs Foundation Inc., Lillian Fitzgerald/John Jay Jaffin Collection

FIG 3 Charlie Chaplin at the Hollywood Bowl circa 1941 with actress Paulette Goddard, who may or may not have been his third wife. Everywhere Chaplin went, photographers followed. Chaplin and Goddard were a couple for nearly a decade, breaking up shortly before Charlie met Joan. Photo: The McClain Collection, Gerth Archives and Special Collections, California State University, Dominguez Hills

FIG 4 Joan Barry when she was known as Mary Lou Berry in her 1938 Newtown High School yearbook. After graduation from the Elmhurst, New York, public school she made her first unsuccessful foray to Hollywood. Photo: Courtesy Newtown High School, Elmhurst, New York

FIG 5 Oil billionaire J. Paul Getty circa 1942. He was smitten with Joan; between September 1940 and May 1942 they saw each other at least one hundred times. Chaplin's lawyers were unsuccessful in pinning Joan's pregnancy on him, although they tried. Photo: LeRoy, Institutional Records and Archives, The Getty Research Institute, Los Angeles, CA, IA 20009

FIG 6 Another of Joan's admirers, David Hecht, who was Getty's hotshot young attorney. He lived at The Pierre, a swank Manhattan hotel owned by Getty, and he squired Joan around the city in October 1942. Like Chaplin's, Hecht's blood type was O, so he couldn't have been the father of Joan's baby either. Photo: Courtesy Dave and Tony Hecht

FIG 7 Joan's distant relative by marriage Sam Marx, who became a producer at MGM, with his wife, Marie (a former Ziegfeld girl), at the 1939 New York World's Fair. Marx arranged for a screen test for Joan at his studio. Eventually, he tired of her attention-seeking suicide attempts and her repeated requests for money. Photo: Courtesy Kenneth Marx

FIG 8 Joan spent most of December 1942 in Los Angeles
with the handsome and exotic European race car driver
Hans Ruesch. She was arrested on New Year's Day 1943
while wearing his pajamas following a bogus suicide
attempt. Here Ruesch appears at Chaplin's Mann Act
trial. Later, Chaplin's lawyers tried unsuccessfully
to convince jurors in Joan's paternity case that Ruesch
was the father of Carol Ann. Photo: Herald-Examiner
Collection, Box 1535, Los Angeles Public Library

FIG 9 Chaplin being fingerprinted by U.S. Marshal George Rossini in connection with his Mann Act arrest in federal court as his lawyer Jerry Giesler keeps a watchful eye on the process. Photo: mptvimages.com

FIG 10 A tense day in federal court as U.S. Attorney Charles H. Carr examines his notes at counsel table with a worried-looking Chaplin and Giesler seated behind. In the rear of the courtroom, Chaplin press spokesman Ralph "Casey" Shawhan watches warily over his client. Photo: Courtesy Linda Shawhan Shewak

FIG 11 Casey Shawhan as his fellow reporters knew and loved him. Photo: Courtesy Linda Shawhan Shewak

FIG 12 Joan Barry steps down from the witness stand
after testifying against Chaplin. Photo: Courtesy
University of Southern California on behalf of USC
Libraries Special Collections

FIG 13 Group picture of the reporters and photographers who covered the Chaplin trial posing with Judge J. F. T. O'Connor after the acquittal, taken on the day the jury returned its verdict, April 4, 1944. Even Chaplin, who generally loathed the press, autographed the photo, although he didn't stick around to be in the picture. He inscribed it "To Agness," who was Agness Underwood, who covered the trial and would go on to be the first woman city editor of the *Los Angeles Herald-Express*. Photo: Agness M. Underwood Collection, Special Collections and Archives, University Library, California State University, Northridge.

FIG 14 Chaplin and Giesler are all smiles as they drive away from the Los Angeles Federal Building after beating the Mann Act charges on April 4, 1944. Photo: mptvimages.com

FIG 15 Joan and her mother, Gertrude, meet the press after filing paternity charges against Chaplin. There is no love lost between mother and daughter. Photo: Courtesy University of Southern California on behalf of USC Libraries Special Collections

FIG 16 Little Carol Ann Berry ready for her close-up at the Chaplin paternity trial in California Superior Court. Photo: Courtesy University of Southern California on behalf of USC Libraries Special Collections

FIG 17 Carol Ann at about age ten with her attorney and bene-factor, lawyer Joseph Scott, aka "Mr. Los Angeles." Photo: Courtesy Carol Ann Berry

FIG 18 Joan Berry on the grounds of the state mental hospital where she lived for a decade. This photo was taken on the only day her daughter ever came to visit. Photo: Courtesy Carol Ann Berry

FIG 19 An aged Charlie Chaplin receiving love, admiration, and the longest standing ovation in Oscar history from his Hollywood peers at the annual Academy Awards ceremony on April 10, 1972, at the Dorothy Chandler Pavilion. Photo: Margaret Herrick Library

FIG 20 Joan Barry in popular culture, the 2012 Broadway play *Chaplin: The Musical*. Emilee Dupre plays a very pregnant Joan while Jenn Colella, in a large hat, plays a solicitous Hedda Hopper. The play ran for four months before closing in early 2013. Photo: © Joan Marcus

SEVENTEEN

"WE HOPE CHARLIE CHAPLIN
NOW DISAPPEARS"

Charles H. Carr's seventy-three-year-old mother succumbed to her stroke three days after the trial ended. After her funeral in Tunica, Mississippi, Carr made his way to Washington to get his marching orders about the remaining Chaplin indictments.[1]

Back in California, after two weeks of being under a media microscope, Chaplin desperately wanted peace. Shortly after their marriage, Oona had revealed that, unlike his prior wives, she had no interest in an acting career. The ordeal of the trial made him painfully aware how much he needed a woman who catered to his needs. For once, he basked in the joy of marriage to a woman who didn't want to be a movie star.[2]

With that devoted wife and her black kitten at his side, Chaplin boarded a train to New York and rented an old stone farmhouse in Nyack, about thirty miles north of the city.[3] The plan was to spend months in seclusion while Chaplin finished his latest movie script and Oona gave birth to their first child, due in August.[4] But the couple had to wait and see what the government would do about the remaining open indictments.

After the verdict, lawyers for Chaplin's codefendants called on Carr to dismiss those cases. Sammy Hahn, who represented Captain White and newly promoted Lt. Marple, said that dismissing them was the "only sportsmanlike thing for Carr to do."[5] But Carr dug in his heels and made it clear he thought the conspiracy cases were stronger.[6]

The conventional wisdom among Chaplin fans to this day has been that the government was hell-bent on destroying him for his political views.[7]

The Communist Party, like Chaplin and many on the left, saw the indictments as punishment for his speaking out in favor of a Second Front.[8] No doubt Chaplin's progressive ideology and sympathy for socialism put him on the government's radar and that Hoover and Hopper wanted to see him held accountable. That being said, high-ranking, respected lawyers at the Department of Justice—all the way up to the attorney general—had been lukewarm from the beginning about prosecuting Chaplin for his shenanigans involving Joan Barry. But the investigation seemed to take on a life of its own. Notwithstanding, these same lawyers now saw no percentage in continuing to prosecute him and wanted to put an end to it, if for no other reason than to protect their own careers.

The federal government was subject to significant criticism over Chaplin's Mann Act prosecution and not just from the left. "Mr. Chaplin's transgressions against the moral code did not warrant invoking the stern provisions of the Mann Act against him," wrote the editors of the *Washington Post*. They chastised the government for the "unutterable stupidity" of using the Mann Act against a pair of consenting adults.[9] Even the editors of the conservative *Chicago Daily Tribune* thought the indictment was a mistake. "The Mann act was intended to stamp out the white slave trade. Chaplin is no Galahad, but he's no white slaver. . . ."[10]

Reactionary columnist Westbrook Pegler took the government to task too. Although he considered Chaplin "not nice," "stingy," and an associate of "the Communist enemies of the country in which he took refuge from two wars," Pegler still thought the prosecution was misguided. "The Federal Government . . . . . . , especially in these times, could better use its manpower and money than to flog a man, however mean, for taking a guest on a trip."[11] The press sensed that even the scandal-loving public was through with it. The small-town *Petaluma (CA) Argus-Courier* wrote: "We hope Charlie Chaplin now disappears from the headlines completely."[12]

Hopper was among the last of the holdouts in favor of prosecuting Chaplin, and although readers in Los Angeles didn't know it, she claimed the *Los Angeles Times* had censored her about the subject. A portion of her April 27, 1944, column that Hopper said was purposefully excised took Carr's boss, Attorney General Francis Biddle, to task. The edited phrase was "If Biddle was influenced by that cheering mob around Chaplin in the courtroom, it's too bad. Public reaction doesn't agree with their actions. I've always thought the civil rights suit more important than the first one."[13]

On April 11, a week after the verdict, Giesler and lawyers for the code-fendants were back before Judge O'Connor to discuss pretrial motions in the remaining cases with U. S. Attorney Carr's assistant, James M. Carter. Chaplin was home sick with the flu. Carr was still in Washington, so the government lawyers requested a continuance. The judge adjourned until April 26.[14]

To prevail on the remaining conspiracy indictments, Carr would have to prove, beyond a reasonable doubt, that Chaplin and company had agreed to violate Joan's civil rights (to live freely wherever she wanted) and had committed one or more overt acts to further that agreement.[15] The indictments were rooted in the sordid saga that had resulted in Joan's arrest for vagrancy, her guilty plea without counsel, and her getting "vagged" out of town.

The consensus in Washington was that the complex conspiracy to run Joan out of Beverly Hills didn't have the same public appeal as the juicy "White Slave" allegations. Even FBI Director Hoover joined the chorus of naysayers who wanted to pull the plug. He told Assistant Attorney General Tom Clark, chief of the criminal division at the Department of Justice, "[T] his case would be an anti-climax after the previous trial, inasmuch as the general public would probably not understand the issues involved here." Hoover warned there was also a risk that Chaplin would become a "martyr, and the less publicity attracted to the case, the better."[16]

Carr, who had staked so much of his reputation on the indictments, voiced his own doubts. Before leaving for his dying mother's bedside, Carr had complained to FBI Supervisor Richard Hood in Los Angeles—who, of course, told Hoover—that Joan had turned out to be a lousy witness and that the facts of the Mann Act case turned out to be flimsier than Carr had initially believed.[17] But whether to continue with the rest of the cases wasn't solely Carr's decision. U.S. attorneys are appointed by the president to four-year terms and confirmed by the Senate. They serve in each of the federal judicial districts as the area's top law enforcement officers, responsible for prosecuting crimes against the United States. These are prestigious posts, reserved for highly educated, respected lawyers who have a professional or political relationship with either the president or the U.S. senator from the state where they serve. They enjoy broad discretion in bringing charges.[18] Although U.S. attorneys are under the supervision of the attorney general and other officials in the Department of Justice, it is unusual for the bosses in Washington to interfere in their cases. But a high-profile prosecution of a defendant of the magnitude of a man like Chaplin would be the rare exception.

While Carr and the Department of Justice were exploring options, Judge O'Connor made their decision easier by dismissing the indictments against Beverly Hills City Court Judge Charles Griffin. Griffin asserted he was immune from federal prosecution when acting in his judicial capacity. On April 14, Judge O'Connor agreed and in a twenty-page decision granted Griffin's motion to dismiss.[19] O'Connor's decision infuriated Carr and his staff, but Attorney General Francis Biddle saw it as a gift. Even before the decision, Biddle had instructed Carr to dismiss the rest of the Chaplin cases and be done with the matter. But once Biddle learned about O'Connor's decision, he told Carr he was "glad" because "dismissal of remaining charges would be a natural event." Some part of Carr still chafed at Biddle's suggestion to drop the rest of the cases. Carr groused privately to FBI agents that Biddle was overly sensitive to the negative publicity equating the prosecution of Chaplin with "persecution."[20]

In his decision dismissing the Griffin indictments, Judge O'Connor reached back to 1792 for historical context, acknowledging that judges had long had immunity for decisions they made on the bench. To rule otherwise, he wrote, "would mark the beginning of the end of an independent and fearless judiciary."[21] But this wasn't an apt analogy. This was not a situation where a disgruntled litigant, unhappy with a decision, filed suit against a judge, which if entertained *would* have a chilling effect on judicial independence. Here, a judge was under indictment for the crime of violating the legal rights of a defendant as a favor to a Beverly Hills celebrity.

Griffin should have thanked his lucky stars that he was walking away scot-free from serious charges that he had betrayed his oath of office. Instead, he fumed at Carr for having indicted him in the first place. "[B]ecause of the prominence of one of the defendants," Griffin complained in open court, "my name and picture has drawn the headlines I presume of every newspaper in the United States, and not only the United States, but the world." And now that he had been exonerated, Judge Griffin was livid that the courtroom wasn't swarming with reporters to record that fact. "It is good for some space on the back page of the paper, perhaps," Griffin moaned.[22] But the angry judge didn't even get the satisfaction of lashing out at Carr to his face; the U.S. attorney was still huddled with his bosses back in Washington.[23]

Carr returned to O'Connor's courtroom on April 26—but still couldn't bring himself to dismiss the pending cases. He said he needed more time to conference with the attorney general, even though Biddle had already told him what to do. The cases were adjourned until May 9.[24] On that day, the steady chipping away at the remaining indictments continued. Carr moved to dismiss the indictments against Marple and Reno, conceding that they, too, had acted within their official capacity when they interacted with Joan at the Beverly Hills police station. Judge O'Connor granted the application, signaling that he also wanted the case to go away. But Carr let it be known in court that he had wanted to appeal O'Connor's decision in Judge Griffin's case and was not on board with dismissing the remaining indictments. In a sign he was livid at Biddle for cutting him off at the knees, Carr said he would not move to dismiss the cases without written instructions from the attorney general. O'Connor put the matter over until May 16.[25]

While lawyers in Washington were telling Carr to cut his losses, FBI agents in Los Angeles were pressuring him to be more aggressive. The agents wanted him to indict Minna Wallis, Hans Ruesch, and Lionel Bonini for perjury. But Carr stood firm against the FBI; indicating that going after the trio would appear vindictive and lead the public to conclude that he was doing it because he had failed to convict Chaplin.[26] Notwithstanding his bickering with local agents, Carr sent a letter to Hoover graciously praising the local FBI. "Throughout the entire period the case was under investigation, both the work and cooperation of your office here was excellent," Carr wrote.[27]

In Washington, the standoff continued, with Biddle trying to bulldoze Carr into dismissing the cases on his own—and presumably taking whatever heat came with it—and Carr holding out for a written order to do so. Finally, the Department of Justice blinked. With a letter in hand from Washington signed by Tom Clark directing Carr to dismiss the cases, Carr marched into Judge O'Connor's courtroom on Monday, May 15, 1944, and did so. With no fanfare, on motion of U.S. Attorney Carr, all the remaining cases were dismissed.[28] Chaplin wasn't there to hear the good news; he'd slipped away to Palm Springs with Oona on May 4 and was joined there by Durant a few days later.[29]

Once the threat of further prosecution of his client was over, Giesler lost no time mending fences. Smart defense attorneys know that keeping on the good side of the local FBI can inure to the benefit of their clients; there would be other indictments of other clients down the road. On May

18, he sent a letter to the Los Angeles FBI field office with compliments for the "fair and courteous manner" in which the agents had treated him and his client.[30]

Giesler lost even less time heaping praise on Judge O'Connor. On May 16, the day after the cases against Chaplin were dismissed, Giesler wrote to the judge thanking him for "the very fair and courteous manner" in which he conducted the trial. He called it "a great pleasure" to appear before him. He also gave O'Connor a thumbs-up for his decision dismissing the indictment against Judge Griffin. Giesler praised it as a lesson in "common sense and justice" and suggested that had it been appealed by the government—which, in the end, it wasn't—it would have been upheld.[31]

For Carr, the loss of the most important trial of his career, followed by the death of his mother and his tussle with Washington over his professional autonomy, must have been devastating. Perhaps recognizing that Carr had lost face and political strength, Biddle made a show of public support for him. On a five-day visit to Southern California in August 1944, Biddle praised Carr at a local Democratic Club meeting as "one of our ablest and most loyal United States Attorneys."[32]

Carr was now adrift in a sea of mundane cases that were the bread and butter of wartime federal prosecutors. He indicted food market and restaurant owners for using counterfeit ration coupons to satisfy steak-loving customers while housewives couldn't get meat to feed their families.[33] He went after people who wrote fake chain letters on USO stationery;[34] wives and girlfriends who were illegally pocketing deductions from servicemen's checks;[35] and a black-market gasoline sale ring.[36]

Washington higher-ups also rejected the one prosecution that could have been another front-page blockbuster for Carr—indicting Tokyo Rose. Born Iva Ikuke Toguri in Los Angeles, the former UCLA student became known as "Tokyo Rose," after she broadcast anti-American propaganda to American soldiers stationed in the South Pacific.[37] Clark, having succeeded Biddle as attorney general, threw cold water on Carr's idea of indicting her for treason. There were several women who filled the airwaves under the nom de guerre "Tokyo Rose," and Clark expressed doubt that Carr would be able to prove that Toguri was one of them.[38]

Chaplin remained in touch with Durant. He and Oona attended a dinner party on April 18 at Durant's home—none too wisely given that they were still under indictment as coconspirators—in honor of Katherine Dunham, the Black ballet dancer with whom Durant was rumored to have been having what then was considered a scandalous interracial love affair. At the table were Mikhail Kalatozov, a Soviet film director, and his wife. During the war, Kalatozov was the cultural attaché at the Soviet embassy in the United States and also directed several Soviet propaganda films.[39] The FBI snooped on this event, keeping Hoover fully informed and adding fuel to the fire that Chaplin was a Communist sympathizer[40]

Not long after Carr dismissed all remaining charges, Chaplin and Oona made their cross-country trip. They left California by train on May 30 and arrived in New York on June 2 for their planned extended stay.[41] They lasted less than four weeks in their rustic paradise. As often happened, Chaplin's short attention span kicked in and he grew restless. He complained that the setting was not conducive to work.[42]

Although she was nearly nine months pregnant with her first child and barely out of childhood herself, Oona boarded the train back to California alone on June 26, arriving in Beverly Hills three days later. Chaplin stayed in New York, not returning to California until July 15, two weeks before the birth of Geraldine Leigh on July 31, 1944.[43]

After having fathered three sons, Chaplin was happy to finally have a daughter. But it was a different little girl who would command his attention for the next year. Her first name was Carol Ann and her lawyer, a seventy-seven-year-old warhorse of the California bar named Joseph Scott, was determined that she be given a last name. And Scott wanted that last name to be "Chaplin."

EIGHTEEN
"LIKE AN OCEAN BREEZE
IN A MUSTY ROOM"

In 1911, the same year that twenty-two-year-old Charlie Chaplin was criss-crossing America with Karno as the star of *A Night in an English Music Hall*, forty-four-year-old Joseph Scott was solidifying his reputation alongside Clarence Darrow by defending the McNamara brothers, who were accused of blowing up the *Los Angeles Times* building and killing twenty-one people in a violent labor dispute.[1]

When Chaplin and Scott met face-to-face in a California courtroom thirty-three years later, Chaplin was one of the most famous men in the world and Scott was revered as "Mr. Los Angeles." Scott was a founder of the Los Angeles Chamber of Commerce, had served as president of the Los Angeles Board of Education, had raised millions for the community chest, was a tireless volunteer for the Boy Scouts, and was recognized by popes for his service to the Catholic Church.[2] This pair of icons would lock horns in an epic battle over the fate of Joan's red-haired daughter, Carol Ann.

None of this was supposed to happen. In June 1943, the parties agreed that Chaplin would pay Joan's birthing expenses, and if it turned out her child was not his, Joan would keep the money and he'd walk away. The court signed off on their written agreement. By the 1940s, there could be no serious challenge to the science of ABO blood typing that was used in the Chaplin case. Karl Landsteiner, an Austrian American doctor and researcher, discovered and named blood types at the dawn of the twentieth century, winning the Nobel Prize in 1930.[3] With blood types being hereditary, they quickly became a tool in determining paternity. Four months after the child's birth, that same test showed that Chaplin's blood was type O, Joan's type A, and Carol Ann's type B; Chaplin was not Carol Ann's father.

Loyd Wright was gleeful. "This vindicates Mr. Chaplin," he gloated.[4] Sticking by the agreement, Joan's lawyer John Irwin agreed that Wright should ask presiding judge William Baird to dismiss the paternity suit.[5] Wright got his own surprise when instead of dismissing the case pro forma, Judge Baird told him to have the case placed on the court's calendar.[6] As directed, Wright filed a formal motion to dismiss and asked that it be calendared on February 23. Nonetheless, Gertrude Berry did not intend to pursue the matter further. "The case is over as far as I'm concerned," she told reporters. She admitted that with Chaplin's money gone, she or Joan might have to go out and get a job.[7]

Just when the paternity suit seemed dead in the water, attorney Joe Scott dived in. On February 21, two days before Judge Baird was scheduled to hear the case, Gertrude suddenly retained Scott.[8] It was a win-win for Joan and her mother. Scott took the case on a contingency basis, so it cost the Berrys nothing, and if they won, he'd get paid and Carol Ann would be a little millionaire. Scott promptly announced that he would attack the validity of the stipulation that called for the case to be dismissed based on the blood test results.[9]

Scott probably came to Gertrude the way Irwin did, through the local Catholic archdiocese. Scott was the city's leading Roman Catholic lawyer, whose deep religious faith permeated everything he did. He started every day of his adult life at Mass, usually at the Old Plaza Church in downtown Los Angeles. He carried a replica of the baby Jesus through the streets of the city every Christmas for the Las Posadas festival, which commemorated the biblical story about there being no room at the inn for the Christ child.[10]

Liquor never touched Scott's lips. He and his wife, the former Bertha Roth, whom he met in the church choir and married in 1898, were the parents of either nine or eleven children—accounts varied. Two of the Scott sons joined the priesthood; one became a monsignor. He sent his daughters and granddaughters to the Ramona Convent School in Alhambra to be educated by the Sisters of the Holy Names of Jesus and Mary. Between 1929 and 1933 he had been the dean of the Loyola University School of Law, a Jesuit institution in downtown Los Angeles.[11]

216

Scott could not bear to see the granddaughter of a pious Catholic woman like Gertrude left without a proper surname or financial support. The case would also bring mountains of free publicity to Scott, a man who loved the spotlight. Throughout his professional life and well into old age, Scott was out most nights on the speaking circuit.[12] Yet each and every Sunday, always dressed in a suit, Scott made time to visit his daughter Josephine and her children. While visiting, he introduced his grandchildren to bubblegum.[13]

Scott was born to a Scottish father and an Irish mother on July 17, 1867, in the picturesque village of Penrith, England, about three hundred miles northwest of London. In childhood he wanted to be a priest. He attended a seminary, but somewhere along the way he changed his mind about a life in the church. He graduated from the University of London before coming to America in 1889. Scott taught English literature at St. Bonaventure College, a Franciscan school in upstate New York. Restless, he and a priest friend traveled west by train. Once there, Scott became an attorney the way many young men did in those days, by apprenticing in an established legal office. He was admitted to the California bar in 1894, and by 1900 he and Bertha were living in Los Angeles with their nine-month-old son.[14]

Tall, jaunty, and physically fit with a square jaw, Scott faintly resembled the actor Boris Karloff, without the hideous *Frankenstein* movie makeup. In his youth, Joe Scott was dark and good looking with signature thick, bushy black eyebrows that stayed that way long after his hair turned snowy white. He knew everyone and everyone knew him. He gave the nominating speech for Herbert Hoover at the 1932 Republican National Convention in Chicago.[15] He counted Irish Prime Minister Eamon de Valera and Richard Nixon as friends.[16]

Although Scott was often referred to as Joan's lawyer, he actually represented her child. The case was brought in the name of Gertrude E. Berry, as guardian ad litem for the unborn child. A guardian ad litem stands in the legal shoes of a person who, for whatever reason—usually infancy or a mental defect—cannot protect his or her own interests. Once Joan's daughter was born, the case name was amended to read *Carol Ann Berry, an infant v. Charles Spencer Chaplin*. After Scott's law firm took over from Irwin, it was Scott's partner, Aloysius H. Risse, known as "A.H." or "Al," who became Carol Ann's guardian ad litem.

Only a handful of lawyers in California had the gravitas to stand up to Scott as an equal in a court of law; one of them was Jerry Giesler, but he never got the chance in Chaplin's paternity case. Perhaps Chaplin thought it would be an easy win because the blood test results exonerated him. Or maybe it was his distaste for parting with a dollar—he'd already spent $60,000 on Giesler, or $882,000 today.[17] Instead, Chaplin left the case in the hands of his longtime civil attorneys, Wright and Millikan. Even Chaplin's own son thought that was a grave mistake.

Charles Chaplin Jr. believed his father needed Giesler's "adroit showmanship" more than ever in the paternity case to protect "not only his interests but his reputation as well."[18] Nonetheless, Wright and Millikan, in their own way, were lions of the bar. Loyd Wright had been on retainer for Chaplin for years, and he represented United Artists.[19] The Wright and Millikan client roster included Mary Pickford, Howard Hughes, Mae West, W. C. Fields, Gloria Swanson, Shirley Temple's parents, and the Marx Brothers.[20] Wright was so embedded with the Hollywood elite that Joe DiMaggio and Marilyn Monroe borrowed his weekend cabin in Idyllwild, California, in the San Jacinto Mountains for their honeymoon.[21] Wright would go on to become the president of the American Bar Association and to serve as Vice President Nixon's chair of a commission to study the laws and regulations surrounding the government's controversial security and loyalty programs.[22]

Millikan handled the day-to-day courtroom appearances, and he and Wright wrote motions and plotted strategy. Notwithstanding the fact that he was not Giesler, Charles English "Pat" Millikan would hold his own against "Mr. Los Angeles." Millikan's political views were the polar opposite of his client's. Born in Kentucky and a lieutenant in the army in World War I, Millikan was a straight-arrow conservative who believed that "patriotism must be made popular."[23] He stood a little over five foot ten, weighed 185 pounds, and had thinning gray hair, pale blue eyes, and a ruddy complexion. He lived in Glendale with his wife, Gertrude, and their four children.[24]

The fact that Judge Baird didn't dismiss the paternity case should not have been surprising. A judge is free to reject stipulations that are against public policy. In California, the law had not caught up to the science. Scott was adamant that his client deserved her day in court.[25] He insisted that the lawyers could not stipulate to allowing the paternity decision to be decided by three doctors when it was a legal matter.[26] Luckily for Scott and unfortunately for Chaplin, the case was transferred to Judge Stanley Mosk, who was months away from a hotly contested retention election, and the notoriety of the case promised to be valuable during his campaign.[27]

Stanley M. Mosk was just thirty-one years old in 1942 when the governor appointed him to the California Superior Court, making him the state's youngest judge. To retain his position, Mosk was required to run for election in 1944 to a full six-year term. Slender and boyish looking with brown hair and wire-framed glasses, Mosk was considered a bright up-and-comer.

Born Morey Stanley Mosk (he reversed the names for his campaign literature) in 1912 in San Antonio, Texas, he and his brother, Edward, were raised in a secular Jewish household by parents who struggled in the clothing business. The family set up retail stores in Boston, Los Angeles, San Antonio, and Rockford, Illinois, moving wherever they could eke out a living. Mosk graduated from the University of Chicago and began law school there, but the Depression forced him to follow his family to Los Angeles, where he graduated from Southwestern Law School, a comedown from Chicago.[28]

The liberal Mosk would enjoy a stellar career. In 1958, he would be elected attorney general of California after Edmund G. "Pat" Brown Sr. left the post to become governor. In 1964, Governor Brown appointed Mosk to the California Supreme Court, where he would remain for thirty-seven years, the longest tenure in the court's history. As it turned out, Chaplin and Mosk would have something in common besides the paternity case—lengthy FBI files.[29]

Like Chaplin, Mosk initially was on the FBI's radar for political causes that he had championed during the Depression—his abhorrence of police brutality, antilabor violence, and municipal corruption—which Hoover's FBI would perceive as Communist inspired. Later, the FBI learned that the judge's staid family life was a fiction; he was involved for years with a married woman whose husband was in jail for narcotics peddling.[30]

Beyond the taboo sexual transgression, the affair would call into question the judge's ethics and judgment. Mosk would use his government position to pressure Los Angeles authorities into awarding his mistress a liquor license for a Hollywood nightclub frequented by prostitutes and their pimps. Mosk brought her on a business trip to Mexico, paid the down payment on her sports car, and allowed her to use credit cards in the name "Mrs. Stanley Mosk." Governor Brown probably used this knowledge to blackmail Mosk into staying out of the 1964 U.S. Senate race.[31]

On March 1, 1944, while a steady late winter rain pelted the windows of Judge Mosk's courtroom in City Hall Tower in downtown Los Angeles, the hearing on the Chaplin-Berry case went on for a grueling five hours, with a break here and there for lunch and for other calendar matters.[32] Neither Chaplin nor Joan attended; both were busy preparing for the Mann Act trial that was then due to start in federal court.[33] While Mosk took notes, the lawyers launched a furious battle. Scott's face was red and his voice boomed as he aimed his verbal arrows directly below the belt of the absent Chaplin and provided a preview of what was to come. "I want a group of wholesome men and women with no alien principles to decide whether this child should have its day in court," Scott thundered, clearly referring to Chaplin's sexual prowess and lack of American citizenship.[34]

Demonstrating a remarkable ignorance about the science of blood typing or perhaps banking on Mosk's knowing nothing about it, Scott called the test "a cockeyed theory."[35] Scott preferred the unscientific method of having the jury compare Chaplin's blue eyes with the baby's eyes to decide whether he was the girl's father.[36]

Millikan scoffed at Scott's stupidity, real or feigned. "The whole trouble with Mr. Scott's cockeyed theory is that he is too cockeyed far behind," Millikan said about the old man. He accused Scott of refusing "to believe in anything modern insofar as law is concerned."[37] Prepared for the battle, he came armed with 26 citations from other jurisdictions in which blood test stipulations between parties were considered binding and legal.[38] Millikan emphasized that Joan and Gertrude had consulted with multiple lawyers before signing it and that Judge Baird had "read every word carefully" before approving it.[39]

Scott was having none of it. He told the judge that if the blood test were the sole determining factor in the case, it would "say in effect, 'You little tramp, get out of here' and to let the rich father do as he pleases."[40] Millikan shot back that if Scott would use "as much effort finding the real father of this child as he does attempting to persecute Mr. Chaplin, this baby would be cared for."[41]

By three o'clock in the afternoon, Mosk had heard enough. He admitted he was no Solomon and would not split the baby from the bench.[42] For a full week the judge wrestled with the case. On March 8, in a seven-page decision, he denied the motion to dismiss and ordered Chaplin to file an answer to Joan's complaint within ten days. Scott hailed the decision; it was "like an ocean breeze in a musty room."[43]

Judge Mosk was no fool. He knew that the blood evidence was valid but focused instead on whether the stipulation was fair to the child. "[T] here is no reason to deny, and every sound reason to accept blood tests as a scientific advance of importance," he wrote. This left the judge in a tight spot. Chaplin couldn't be Carol Ann's father, but her circumstances would be greatly diminished—and Mosk might be roundly criticized—if he dismissed the case. "[T]he ends of justice will best be served by a full and fair trial of the issues," he wrote.[44] In other words, give the headache to another judge and jury.

The judge skirted around Judge Baird's approval of the stipulation by determining that his colleague had merely sanctioned the parties' agreement that blood tests would be conducted.[45] It was a blatant misreading of Judge Baird's order, signed on June 10, 1943, directing that the parties "perform the terms thereof as set forth therein."[46] The "terms," which everyone knew, included ending the litigation if the blood tests showed Chaplin wasn't the father. Chaplin would never have agreed to it otherwise, and Irwin wouldn't have felt the ethical need to resign from the case once the test results were in.

The progressive Mosk missed the opportunity to put California in sync with forward-thinking jurisdictions on this issue. But there was precedent for Mosk's decision. In 1937, in *Arais v. Kalensnikoff*, the California Supreme Court refused to hold blood test evidence as definitive proof of paternity, but there were factual distinctions between that case and Chaplin's. In *Arais*, a man had supported a child and the mother and was considered by family and neighbors to be the father, only to abandon them after blood tests showed he was not. The Arais court determined: "Parentage is not exclusively a subject for expert evidence."[47] But Chaplin had never held himself out as Carol Ann's father; he steadfastly insisted he was not.

Gerald Uelmen, former dean of the Santa Clara School of Law and Mosk's biographer, speculated that the judge was not willing to go out on a legal limb "for Charlie Chaplin's wallet."[48] Professor Andrea Roth of the University of California at Berkeley School of Law, who has researched the use of scientific evidence in court, said judges are hesitant to accept new scientific gadgets or tests as dispositive evidence at trial. "There is a fear they will replace the jury," she said.[49]

Judge Mosk could have rendered a decision in Chaplin's favor based on the parties' intentions when they entered into the stipulation. This had been Millikan's strongest argument; it was what everyone wanted. Unfortunately for his client, this was not the Mann Act case, where the U.S. government was taking aim at a grown man whose lifestyle, politics, and morals diverged from the mainstream. This was a battle between an arrogant, aging multimillionaire and an adorable curly-haired, chubby-cheeked toddler who would have nothing without his money.

Mosk's political problems hovered in the background. He had been on the bench less than two years, and his first retention election was scheduled for two months after the Chaplin decision. As Mosk explained to his brother, Edward, who was serving overseas during World War II, "I did not discount the value of the blood test, but held simply that the experts must be subject to cross-examination, and that, under the state of our law at present, no test is deemed to be conclusive, but rather merely evidentiary." It was "a popular decision," he bragged, noting he'd received "fan mail from all parts of the country."[50]

Mosk's campaign literature touted the decision: "He is widely and favorably known for his decision in the Chaplin paternity case, and for being an able, experienced and energetic jurist."[51] Mosk won the retention election with the most votes ever amassed by a judge in Los Angeles County up until that time.[52]

Joan was thrilled by the decision. "It's about time I was getting a break," she told Muir.[53] Millikan lost no time running to the intermediate appellate court to ask that it be reversed. On March 9, Millikan filed a writ of mandamus, alleging that Judge Mosk had exceeded his authority by invalidating the settlement.[54] The district court of appeals denied the writ without comment.[55]

Chaplin had thirty days to take his arguments to the California Supreme Court, which he did.[56] On May 15, the same day that the federal government dropped all remaining criminal charges against Chaplin and his alleged coconspirators, the California Supreme Court ruled against him in the paternity action.[57] Two of the seven justices on the supreme court wanted to hear the case, but four votes were needed.[58] Perhaps the two dissenters were interested in revisiting the *Arais* decision and moving the state's courts in line with jurisdictions that accepted the established blood science as the final word.

Chaplin filed his answer to the paternity uit on May 25, denying he was the father of Joan's child and claiming that Joan knew it and only sued him because he was "reputed to be wealthy." It was extortion, pure and simple, he said. "[T]hey believed that defendant would make a cash settlement rather than be compelled to stand a trial on the allegations. . . ."[59] Joan's financial demands were not insignificant. She wanted $2,500 a month in child support, which would be a whopping $43,000 today, and she wanted Chaplin to pay her legal fees.[60]

Once Scott chose to fight the stipulation, and the blood tests showed Chaplin was not Carol Ann's father, the comic closed his checkbook. He had made a final payment to Joan of $1,100 on February 17, 1944. Additionally, when it became apparent that another trial loomed, Chaplin stalled. His lawyers said they couldn't try the case before October. But Scott was not without tools in his legal arsenal. He pulled out his next one—a cry of poverty. He claimed that Chaplin's cheapness had made Carol Ann destitute and that an early trial was crucial to her survival.[61] And Chaplin was not without his own weapons. He demanded an accounting of the $11,700 he'd already paid to Joan and her mother.[62]

For once, the state court agreed with Chaplin and ordered Gertrude Berry to appear on June 14 before Myron Westover, the supervising judge of the Los Angeles Superior Court, to explain where Chaplin's money had gone. Scott avoided having to put Gertrude on the stand, however, by offering to stop pressing for a fast trial if Chaplin would resume making payments, a request to which Chaplin consented. The lawyers agreed that the amount Chaplin would pay while the trial was pending would remain secret.[63]

With that, the trial was scheduled for December 13, 1944.[64] Once again, the saga of Charlie and Joan—and now added to the drama, little Carol Ann—would compete with World War II for space on the front pages of newspapers nationwide.

NINETEEN

"I HAVE COMMITTED NO CRIME"

As the paternity trial loomed, Joe Scott told reporters—no more adjourn-
ments.[1] Both sides claimed to be ready to go, but on December 12, the day
before trial, there was no judge free to hear it in the busy Los Angeles civil
court.[2] Delay was what Chaplin's lawyer, Pat Millikan, had been hoping for.
Millikan begged Presiding Judge Ruben Schmidt, the most recent judge
overseeing the case, for an eleventh-hour postponement to summon his
missing star witness, Hans Ruesch. Now living in New York, Ruesch was
dodging Millikan's subpoenas. He wanted no part of Millikan's accusing
him of being Carol Ann's father in a crowded Los Angeles courtroom.[3]

Before seeking more time from the court, Millikan had tried to get
Scott to consent to a delay of forty-five to sixty days, but Scott had refused,
telling Millikan he'd be happy to extend *him* every professional courtesy
but "had no desire to extend any courtesies at all to the defendant."[4] His
refusal had nothing to do with his visceral dislike of Chaplin; rather, handsome Ruesch was the last person Scott wanted to see on the witness stand.
He knew his client had been alone with Ruesch on too many evenings in
December 1942. Millikan threatened Scott that if he didn't consent, he'd
file a motion for an adjournment along with an affidavit loaded with spicy
details about Joan's sex life. But Scott was not cowed.

Millikan made good on his threat. His seven-page affidavit was stuffed
with titillating revelations about Joan. Careful newspaper readers who
had followed the Mann Act trial knew that Joan had engineered a fake
suicide attempt at Ruesch's place on New Year's Eve in 1942 and ended up

behind bars the next day in his pajamas. But the public had no idea that she'd been with Ruesch—unchaperoned—on multiple occasions in his one-and-a-half-room apartment at a time she could have conceived or that she'd left him passionate love notes.[5] Millikan's affidavit painted Joan as a gold digger and a blackmailer. She allegedly told Ruesch that she was broke but could "get money any time from J. Paul Getty because he had made a trip with her to Mexico and that there is a law against that in the United States."[6]

The Millikan affidavit, a sworn statement of facts to support his motion that became part of the public court record, was a wake-up call for Joan; fighting Chaplin for child support was going to be dirty business. The state court judge would not protect her like Judge O'Connor had. In the paternity case, Joan's sexual encounters approximately nine months before Carol Ann's birth were fair game.

Just as Millikan had predicted, the *Los Angeles Times* ran with the racy details, but whatever their humiliation value, they didn't help Millikan get what he wanted—time. "Motion denied," Schmidt ruled after reading it. But the affidavit opened the judge's eyes too; the case was going to be an endless headache unless he could transfer it to a trial judge. Suddenly, a judge materialized who could handle it, Scott's contemporary—seventy-three-year-old, balding, bespectacled Henry Montague Willis. To facilitate the trial, Judge Schmidt switched his large chambers and courtroom on the eighth floor of the Hall of Records with Willis's smaller quarters.[7]

Chaplin didn't show up for the preliminaries. In a civil case, a litigant is not required to come to court unless he is representing himself or is needed as a witness. Joan wasn't there either. She was supposedly home nursing a cold. Sitting front and center, however, were Gertrude Berry and her now fourteen-month-old, adorable, carrot-topped grandchild.[8]

Once the case reached Judge Willis, Millikan again asked for it to be dismissed because of the stipulation. It was blatant judge shopping—Judge Mosk in the superior court, the three judges of the intermediate appellate court, and five of the seven members of the California Supreme Court had all ruled against him, and there was nothing new. Millikan had Chaplin waiting in the wings ready to testify on the merits of the motion. Judge Willis did not reject it outright but agreed to hear arguments the next morning. With that, Carol Ann let out a wail and had to be carried out.[9]

On December 14 Chaplin appeared in court wearing a somber expression and a polka-dot tie, but he no sooner took the stand and gave his name and address than Scott spewed a string of objections.[10] Scott called the stipulation "lopsided and inequitable."[11] Seeing Chaplin for the first time in months at the hearing, *Chicago Tribune* reporter Marcia Winn thought that he still looked "decidedly debonair" but had aged; the court process had taken a heavy toll on the fifty-five-year-old comedian.[12]

Judge Willis agreed with Scott, saying that while he loathed disagreeing with a colleague, Judge Baird's prior stamp of approval on the stipulation "did not add one iota of value" to it.[13] Carol Ann deserved her day in court.

Millikan had one final card to play—he wanted the judge to decide the case without a jury. Scott demanded that his client's case be tried to a jury.[14] Seeking a bench trial in front of old Judge Willis was a smart strategy. Millikan knew the danger Chaplin faced once jurors laid their eyes on Carol Ann. Judge Willis was an experienced jurist who would be swayed by fact, not emotion. A member of the bar since 1894, Willis had worked in private practice and as a prosecutor. He was elected to the California Senate and served there from 1907 until 1911. He was appointed to the municipal court in 1926 and was elevated to the superior court in 1931.[15]

The Willis family had been in California since the gold rush. Born on his father's farm in San Bernardino in 1871, he had been a skilled pole-vaulter, horseback rider, and marksman in his youth. Willis's father, after whom he was named, had also been a judge.[16] By 1944 Judge Willis was old and looked it—pale skin, thinning white hair, round owlish eyeglasses—but in his day, Willis had been a progressive thinker. When he was a state senator he'd drafted a bill to abolish capital punishment and was an early proponent of women serving on juries.[17]

Judge Willis denied Millikan's request.[18] The law was clear; both sides had to agree to waive a jury, and Scott wouldn't.[19] Jury selection began on the mild, partly cloudy afternoon of December 14.[20] It was a grueling process that would last three days, with each of the lawyers seeking to blunt the bad facts sure to emerge. Scott worried that jurors would see Joan as a fallen woman once they heard she was no wide-eyed virgin, and Millikan feared that Carol Ann would steal jurors' hearts. Millikan probed each potential juror with the same question: "Because the child is innocent, beautiful and lovely, would you be inclined to favor her?"[21] Chaplin did not stick around once it was clear his testimony would not be needed, and Joan never showed up at all while the lawyers vetted the jurors.[22]

By this time, editors had lost interest in the Chaplin-Berry soap opera. There was still a war on. The hometown *Los Angeles Times* had consigned the Chaplin paternity story to the inside pages. The primary incentive for editors to run it at all was the photogenic baby at the center of the dispute. During the boring process of jury selection, newspapers published pictures of Carol Ann in her West Los Angeles home playing with her kiddie car or snuggling with "Boots," her stuffed bear.[23] The editors may have been sick of the spectacle, but the public continued to pack the courtroom.[24]

Wright and Millikan drove many a hard bargain in the conference rooms of their business clients. Millikan looked like the patrician corporate lawyer he was, impeccably dressed in his three-piece suit. But he was not a courtroom natural like the state's legendary trial lawyers: Earl Rogers, Jerry Giesler, and his client's tormentor, Joe Scott. One of Millikan's convoluted questions to a potential juror ended, "[I]f you find from the evidence that has been introduced that Miss Barry had sexual relations with some man or men other than Mr. Chaplin at or near the time that she claims she became pregnant, and if you find from this evidence, or should the court instruct you that if you find from that evidence, that it is impossible for Miss Barry to say who is the father of the child, and in such event you would be required to find a verdict in favor of the defendant, would you be perfectly willing to follow the instructions?"

"Huh?" responded the juror.[25]

As in the criminal trial, the lawyers packed the jury with older, married folks. There were six gray-haired, elderly ladies, some in dowdy hats; one young woman; and five old men. All the jurors had children except for the only bachelor.[26] The jury included a retired navy serviceman, a Beverly Hills property manager, an interior decorator, a retired Western Union employee, and the wives of a floor finisher and a stamp collector.[27] Judge Willis, concerned about the trial's glacial pace as the Christmas holiday approached, lengthened each court day by a half hour so they could finish in less than two weeks. That would turn out to be wishful thinking.[28]

The testimony began on Tuesday, December 19. Scott had the burden of proving by a preponderance of the evidence—in other words, that it was more likely than not—that Chaplin was Carol Ann's father. His first witness was Dr. Russell Starr, who brought the baby into the world at 10:30 p.m. on October 2, 1943, at South Van Ness Hospital in midtown Los Angeles.[29] Dr. Starr's purpose was to educate the jury on the length of a human pregnancy (about 270 days, give or take a couple of weeks) and to identify Carol Ann as the child he had delivered, which he did while bouncing her on his lap and laughing with her during his testimony.[30] Millikan shuddered.

Scott's next witness was Chaplin, who took the stand at 3:00 p.m. In a civil case, a litigant can call an adverse party, although the lawyer may treat the questioning as if it is cross-examination and is not bound by the testimony.[31] Scott hoped for a scene straight out of Hollywood by asking the judge to allow Carol Ann to be seated in a high chair next to Chaplin while he testified so the jury could compare their features. Willis wisely refused.[32]

Scott needed to make three crucial points. First, that Chaplin and Joan had had sexual contact in December 1942. Then, he had to shatter Chaplin's image as the loveable Little Tramp by revealing him to be a selfish lover who would turn his back on a destitute woman, pregnant with his child. Finally, he had the Sisyphean task of debunking the science that proved without a doubt that Carol Ann's father was another man.

Wearing a beautifully tailored, double-breasted navy suit with a white shirt and patterned tie when Scott called him to the stand, Chaplin flatly denied he saw Joan on December 10. Scott pivoted to the night of the gun incident. When testifying, Chaplin focused on his most important audience—the jurors. He waved his hands expressively like the great silent star he once was, as if acting out the scene, and like any great director, he knew how he wanted it to play.[33]

"I looked and I saw Miss Berry there," Chaplin said. "She had a gun. She circled around and came towards me," he explained. "She said she was going to kill herself and she said she was going to kill herself in my house, in order to create a scandal," he said.[34] Unfortunately, at his federal trial, Chaplin had claimed that the first words out of Joan's mouth were that she intended to kill *him*.[35] The next day on the stand, Chaplin corrected his story—probably with the help of a little overnight coaching by counsel. His explanation for the discrepancy was that he'd forgotten that she first threatened to kill him.[36] His excuse wasn't credible; nobody forgets being threatened with death at the point of a loaded gun.

As in *The Great Dictator*, where Chaplin expounded about war and peace in the movie's last minutes, on the witness stand Chaplin talked—and talked—adding asides where he thought necessary. "And I said to her, 'Why have you treated me this way? Why this attitude, when I have tried everything in the world to build you up, not only materially but spiritually to give you a reputation—to give you a profession—to teach you—to teach you to act, because I believed in you.' I believed in that girl. I said, 'Why do you do this? Why do you want to conspire against me? This is not the first time you have broken into my house. You have broken in several times. You know that.' I said, 'Why do you do this? I have tried to be your friend.' I said, 'There has never been any misunderstanding about our relationship.'"[37]

Finally Scott had enough. "Just a minute," he interrupted. "Was this a one-sided conversation?"

"Yes," Chaplin responded. "I lectured her."[38]

"What did she say?" Scott asked eventually.[39]

Chaplin admitted he didn't "know in exact detail." But the substance of it, he said, was "that she had no place to sleep and she intended to sleep in that house [his] that night."[40] Either Chaplin hadn't listened to a word Joan said, the sight of the gun was more traumatizing than he'd let on, or the great actor had only rehearsed his own lines, not Joan's. "This happened a long time ago and this is something I would want to forget."

"I don't doubt that," Scott said snidely.[41]

Chaplin used Scott's remark as an invitation to gripe about his treatment since Joan brought her lawsuit. "I have been pilloried and verbally lynched."

Scott cut him off. "I move to strike that as not responsive to any question." The judge agreed and told the jury to disregard Chaplin's lament.[42]

Later, Scott got caught in a trap of his own making by asking Chaplin about Joan's familiarity with 1085 Summit Drive, obviously trying to show they'd had many opportunities for sex. "She has been in that house a lot?" Scott asked.

"Yes," Chaplin replied.

"Many nights?" Scott continued.

"She has broken in many times," Chaplin answered.

"She has been in that house many times?" Scott repeated.

"Usually through breaking in," Chaplin insisted.[43] So much for Joan being fragile and helpless.

As in the Mann Act trial, the gun incident was the key dramatic moment and, had Chaplin truly been Carol Ann's father, the night Joan probably would have conceived. Yet nothing about Chaplin's reaction to Joan in his bedroom with a pistol made any sense. He had a working telephone within reach but never called the police. Joan and Chaney had a rapport, but Chaplin never asked for the butler to come in to help him calm her down. While still in her distraught state, Chaplin allowed her to occupy a room adjoining his with a loaded gun in her hand, but he supposedly slept like a baby. The only rational explanation for what happened is that Chaplin seduced her, gun and all, and after a satisfying sexual encounter they both nodded off.

When Scott asked Chaplin what Joan said to him the next morning while supposedly *still* holding her gun, he said their conversation mirrored the one they'd had the night before. "She had no place to go and she was destitute."

"What did you say?" asked Scott.

"I said, 'Well, whatever you are, or whatever your condition is, you have brought it on yourself.'"

Incredulous, Scott asked, "She was responsible and you were not responsible, is that it?"[44]

"Yes," was Chaplin's cold-hearted response.[45]

As the lawyer for the sweet, gurgling baby, Scott must have jumped for joy. Chaplin, a man who lived in a mansion, just admitted he'd had no sympathy for a woman who was a step away from living in the street.[46]

Realizing his mistake, Chaplin tried to explain, but Scott cut him off. Chaplin shouted, "Just a moment, please. Let me finish, will you please? I told her that I had tried—I have committed no crime!" Scott had lit Chaplin's short fuse. In a rage, the Little Fellow pounded his fists on the edge of the witness stand. Chaplin's use of the word "crime" may have been carefully rehearsed with his lawyers to remind the jurors that eight months earlier he'd been acquitted of the criminal charges against him involving Joan.[47]

Scott sought the judge's help in shutting up his own witness. "Just a minute, if your Honor, please," Scott said. "We don't want any dramatics."[48]

But in Chaplin's mind, the camera was rolling. "Your honor, I'm human. And this man is trying to make inferences as though I am a monster."[49]

Judge Willis had enough. "I don't want any dramatics or exuberance or vehemence on either side, from counsel or witness." He instructed Chaplin to answer the questions put to him "and keep control of your own spirit and temper so that we can proceed calmly."[50]

Chaplin quieted down. He was on the witness stand for about an hour when the court recessed at 4:00 p.m.[51] Back in the hot seat at 9:45 a.m. the next day, Scott returned to the conversation between Chaplin and Joan in June 1943 that took place at the swimming pool, where Joan finally told him face to face that he had made her pregnant. "That is impossible," he replied.[52]

Chaplin launched into another monologue. "I said, 'Why are you doing this to me?' I said, 'Why, why have you tried to conspire, knowing full well that I am not the father of that child. Why have you done this?' I said, 'I have been your very best friend. I have tried to help you.'" He was particularly irked that she had blabbed to reporters. "You have given a lot of interviews to papers, bitterest lies," he told her.[53]

Did he promise Joan that he would support the child? No, Chaplin said.[54] Scott pushed ahead asking if Joan said, "I don't want you to care for the baby. I want you to marry me."[55]

"Yes, she said that," Chaplin admitted. But he denied that he had told her that he had no intention of marrying anyone again.[56] Chaplin was on his fourth wife and could hardly admit to the jurors that he had told such a lie to Joan. Instead, the man who'd supposedly had two thousand sexual conquests told Joan he wouldn't marry her because she had an unsavory reputation. Marriage between them was impossible, "knowing the kind of life you have been leading. That is what I said to her." And then Chaplin threatened to say more. He asked Scott: "Do you want me to go further?"[57]

Scott did not, but he couldn't resist highlighting Chaplin's hypocrisy. "Oh, and I understand that you know all you have been doing is entirely reputable and moral, is that it?"

"Yes," Chaplin responded. Millikan objected, which was sustained by the judge.[58]

Scott asked, "Haven't you tried since this case has started to find men that would go on the witness stand and say they had intimate relations with Joan Berry?"

Chaplin said he hadn't done that. "[N]aturally my lawyers have," he added.[59]

Joan was Scott's final witness. Unlike in his criminal trial, where Chaplin was forced to sit in court and face Joan when she took the stand, at this trial Chaplin was long gone by the time she testified.[60]

She still had the look of a schoolgirl in her pale blue coat over a yellow sweater with a minimum of makeup save for a little lipstick. She fiddled with a piece of paper while talking, and her fingernails were free of polish.[61] As soon as Scott asked who fathered her baby, Millikan leaped to his feet and angrily objected, but the judge overruled him. Joan replied, "Charles Chaplin."[62] It was Millikan's view that Joan was qualified to testify about when she had had sexual intercourse with Chaplin or that she hadn't had sex with anyone else during the time she could have conceived.

But given that the purpose of the trial was for the *jury* to decide if Chaplin was the father, Joan's opinion was irrelevant.

Scott was not above resorting to hocus-pocus to establish paternity. After Joan said Chaplin was left-handed, Scott asked her which hand was Carol Ann's dominant one, but the judge stopped him. He also attempted to introduce childhood pictures of Chaplin's two sons so the jury could decide whether they looked like Carol Ann, but the judge refused to allow that either.[63]

Joan's testimony, punctuated by tears when necessary, recapped what she had said in federal court, minus mention of her New York City trip in October 1942. Given that the New York trip predated when she could have become pregnant, it was irrelevant. Joan said she'd brought the gun to Chaplin's because she was in extremis over the demise of their relationship, not because she intended to kill anyone: apparently, the gun was a prop for dramatic effect.[64] She said she told him: "I am almost out of my mind. I have waited and waited. You haven't called me. I don't know what to do."[65]

In tears, Joan looked to Judge Willis and said, "This is very embarrassing to me." But the judge was icy. "It shouldn't be embarrassing. You had many months of preparation for this case," Judge Willis remarked dryly.[66]

Joan's version of their poolside talk was starkly different from Chaplin's. She said Chaplin accepted her claim that he was the father of her unborn child. "If you say so, I believe you," he supposedly said. He also allegedly told her to keep the baby if she wanted to, go to New York, and train for the stage, promising to support them.[67] Their parley ended abruptly after Joan went inside his house, where she discovered women's clothes in a bedroom closet and became irate, which is why they were all sitting in a courtroom now.[68]

Millikan's goal was to show that Joan was a liar and a con artist. But he had to approach her gingerly, and he did. Marcia Winn, who also covered the paternity trial, reported that the press had nicknamed Millikan "Gentleman Pat" because of his "courteous, warm and gentle cross-examination of Miss Berry."[69] Millikan recognized that despite the rigid societal standards against unmarried women having sex in the 1940s, Joan was now a mother in need of financial support and her innocent child needed a name. The jury was filled with mothers, and the lawyer could not risk alienating them. Asking about her extortion attempt against Chaplin was one way he'd hoped to reduce sympathy for her, but she denied ever demanding $150,000 from Chaplin during their poolside talk.[70]

As expected, he harped on her relationships with Getty, Ruesch, and Bonini but never asked point-blank if she'd had sex with any of them, knowing she would deny it. Instead, he planted the seed that any one of them could be Carol Ann's father. Joan said she'd visited Bonini and Ruesch in their apartments and that she had slept at Ruesch's the night before her fake suicide attempt. She denied that she had told the detective and the prosecutor in Tulsa that she was in love with Getty and said she'd never stayed overnight with the oilman at the Mayo Hotel there.[71]

Once again, Joan's cloying letters to Chaplin from Tulsa were the subject of cross-examination. During questioning about them, Joan ran crying from the stand and into the arms of Joe Scott. "I've got to go, I've got to get out of here! What are they trying to do to me?" she cried dramatically. Rising to his role as protector, Scott asked Millikan, "How much more of this stuff have you got?" Millikan offered to take a little break so Joan could compose herself, but it was not necessary.[72] She calmed down so quickly it was hard to believe the jury wasn't witnessing some of her Max Reinhardt training. Later, when asked about the love notes she'd written to Ruesch, Joan began weeping again. She tearfully denied that the notes she left at Ruesch's were meant for him. "You know," she said, "I was in love with Charles."[73] It boded poorly for Millikan and his client that a juror slipped her a handkerchief.[74] It seemed a good time to take a four-day break for Christmas, the judge decided.[75]

When court resumed after the holiday, Scott ended his direct case on Tuesday, December 26, with a dramatic finish: an in-court identification procedure. Joan stepped off the witness stand while an unknown woman raced into the courtroom carrying Carol Ann and placed her in Joan's arms. Joan and Carol Ann faced the jury. Chaplin, who had been ordered to court for the demonstration, rose from counsel table and stood about four feet away from Joan and the baby, also facing the jury. As Carol Ann charmed the courtroom by laughing and cooing, Chaplin stood deathly still. The judge let the show go on for about two minutes. "That's sufficient," he said.[76] Immediately afterward, Chaplin returned to the witness stand, called by his own lawyer to rebut Joan's testimony. He was on the stand less than a half hour, mainly to deny ever having had sex with Joan in December 1942.[77]

Millikan presented four other witnesses: former Chaplin chauffeur Harvey Holahan; Elizabeth Hanni, who was Ruesch's former landlady; O. C. Lassiter, a former assistant county attorney in Tulsa; and Tulsa police detective Riley Stuart.

Holahan debunked Joan's story that she had sex with Chaplin on December 30 leading into December 31. If Holahan were to be believed, there wasn't time. He testified that he'd heard the sound of a visitor on the property that night but that shortly after the person arrived, Chaplin drove the visitor away. Holahan said he never saw who was in the car, but the circumstantial evidence was that it had been Chaplin and Joan.[78]

Ruesch landlady Elizabeth Hanni explained the Joan Berry–Hans Ruesch relationship as best she could now that Ruesch was outside the reach of a California subpoena. She again told her story about admitting Joan to his apartment. She said that Joan casually climbed into Ruesch's pajamas. Hanni also undercut Joan's claim that she only had eyes for Chaplin by telling the jurors that Joan had told her she was in love with Ruesch.[79]

Lassiter and Stuart, the prosecutor and detective from Tulsa, supported the defense suggestion that Getty might be Carol Ann's father. In January 1943 in Tulsa, Detective Stuart arrested Joan for skipping out on a hotel bill. To get out from under that arrest, Joan told them that she had stayed at the hotel with Getty and that his lawyer would cover the bill. Joan also supposedly told them she had "gone overboard" for Getty.[80]

Finally, to avoid calling him as a witness, Scott and Millikan stipulated that if he were to testify, Getty's attorney, Thomas A. Dockweiler, would say under oath that Getty had bailed Joan out of debt. On November 23, 1942, Getty advanced Joan $1,374.80 at 6 percent interest and took a chattel mortgage on her silver fox coat and her car as collateral. He also advanced her another $300.[81]

Millikan saved his strongest evidence for his own dramatic finish: the blood test results. Scott fought tooth and nail to keep the damning evidence out of the case. "This child is due her day in court, but she couldn't have it if three men (physicians) come in here and say she couldn't possibly be the child of Charles Chaplin," Scott asserted. Judge Willis disagreed, noting that blood typing evidence is "some proof of parentage," and allowed the testimony.[82] Two of the doctors who participated in the blood testing, Newton Evans and Roy W. Hammack, explained to the jurors—in a manner that wasn't easy to understand—the established science of blood typing and why it meant Chaplin was not Carol Ann's father.[83] In a word, it was "impossible."[84]

After eleven long days of testimony, the jurors listened to summations, which began on Friday, December 29. First up was Scott, who used all his theatrical flourish to brand Chaplin a menace to womanhood, going well beyond where he should have been permitted to go by the judge. The question was whether Chaplin was Carol Ann's father, not whether he treated Joan like dirt. But Scott, shouting so loudly that his voice thundered throughout the Hall of Records, hurled blatant ad hominem attacks at Chaplin purely to poison the jurors. Neither Chaplin nor Joan was present for Scott's tirade.[85]

Despite his snow-white hair and seventy-seven-year-old wizened frame, Scott saw himself as the knight in shining armor for Carol Ann and, by extension, for her mother. Old enough to be Chaplin's father, Joan's grandfather, and Carol Ann's great-grandfather when the paternity trial began, Scott aimed to figuratively wipe the courtroom floor with the Little Tramp. In Scott's oratorio, Chaplin was a "gray-headed old buzzard," "cheap cockney cad," and "master mechanic in the art of seduction."[86] He was "a runt of a Svengali with the instincts of a young bull."[87] The insults continued—for hours. Scott called Chaplin a "pestiferous, lecherous hound" and worse.[88] He didn't spare his own client either. He called Joan "a girl of limited intelligence," and a "wretched girl, aflame with the glamor of Hollywood," too stupid to have made up her story against the world-famous movie man.[89]

Scott's performance was itself "aflame." He paced back and forth, shouted, and invoked literature, the Bible, and his own devout Catholic brand of fire and brimstone. Although Scott admitted his client "fell by the wayside," Chaplin was "old enough to be the father of Joan and at that time should have had something else on his mind besides prowling around with young girls."[90] Clearly, Scott thought the price for Chaplin's sin should have been a shotgun marriage to Joan. He called the poolside chat Joan's "five-hour bout of pleading" for Chaplin to marry her and give her baby a name as opposed to a $150,000 shakedown.[91] Scott also proffered irrelevant insults and insinuations about Chaplin's loyalty to America, none of which should have been allowed. "What good has Chaplin, with his two English butlers and a swimming pool, ever done this country?" Scott asked. "That's what makes for Communism."[92] In one of its few front-page stories about the paternity trial, the Los Angeles Times observed that Chaplin "got second billing at his paternity trial yesterday. The star of the proceedings was Joseph Scott. . . ."[93]

Even hearing Scott drag his name through the mud through secondhand accounts was enough to unnerve Chaplin. On Saturday night, December 30, having forgotten his house keys after going out, Chaplin angrily kicked in the glass door of his home to get back in, severing the muscles in his left ankle. The impulsive action landed him first in the Beverly Hills Hospital Emergency Room and then, when the seriousness of his injury became apparent, in Cedars of Lebanon Hospital, now Cedars Sinai, for several days.[94] His injury kept him out of court for Millikan's closing argument the following Tuesday after the holiday recess and in a wheelchair for the remainder of the week.[95]

While Chaplin was recuperating in his hospital bed on January 2, Millikan urged Judge Willis to throw water on the flames fanned by Scott in his summation. Millikan made seventeen motions to strike portions of Scott's inflammatory speech. The judge granted eight of them.[96] Willis directed the jury to disregard the terrible names Scott had gleefully hurled at Chaplin as "unjustified vituperation."[97] Although jurors are presumed to obey a judge's instructions to disregard a particular statement or argument, the reality is that, once heard, it is hard to un-ring a bell.

Millikan behaved like a gentleman during his summation and wisely avoided insulting Joan and, by extension, offending the women on the jury. One can only imagine what a Giesler summation would have sounded like after Scott's over-the-top performance; Giesler's roaring would have made Scott's outbursts seem like mewing from a kitten. Millikan focused on his most powerful evidence, the uncontroverted science that proved that Carol Ann was not Chaplin's daughter—although not before remarking that Scott had "crucified" his client the Friday before. As to the blood tests: they are "unrefuted and irrevocable," Millikan told the jurors, leaving Scott "in a hell of a fix."[98]

Although he tried to take the high road, Millikan would have been remiss not to argue that there were other candidates for fatherhood of Carol Ann. He referenced Joan's many visits to Ruesch's apartment. Tossing Scott's words back in his face, Millikan referred to Ruesch as the "tall and handsome man in the case" and reminded jurors that his own client was just "the runt of a Svengali."[99] Millikan asked the jurors to ponder a question that was never adequately answered. "Why doesn't the young woman put the label of fatherhood on the real father of this child?"[100]

It wasn't easy to answer. When Joan became pregnant she was desperate. With her professional connection to Chaplin severed, she had no income. Joan may not have known who the father was, but of the possibilities, Chaplin was the most promising. It is hard to believe she would have considered accusing Chaplin if he hadn't been at least a *possible* candidate, leading to the logical conclusion that they'd had sex at least once in December 1942. After the shame Chaplin endured during the Lita Grey divorce scandal, Joan might have thought Chaplin would do anything to avoid similar bad press, including marry her. She couldn't turn to Ruesch because he had left California and was not in Chaplin's financial league. Further, Joan had no leverage to force Ruesch to marry her because at that time he had no professional reputation to protect. Getty was already married for the fifth time and showed no signs of leaving his wife. Marx and Hecht had stopped taking her phone calls.

The blood test results may have been as much of a surprise to Joan as they were to everyone else. But by time they were in—February 15, 1944— it was too late to turn back; she had already told investigators for the Los Angeles County District Attorney's Office and FBI agents that she hadn't slept with those other men. She had testified against Chaplin in the grand jury, and the U.S. attorney was on the verge of making Joan his star trial witness in federal court. Scott and the regressive evidentiary rules in California allowed the charade to keep going, which held out the hope for a nice life for Joan and her daughter.

Because he had the burden of proof, albeit a slight one, Scott got the last word at the trial. He apologized for his venom against Chaplin, but his words rang hollow. "I perhaps owe an apology to the jury because of my limited vocabulary in trying to picture the kind of man Chaplin is," the renowned speaker claimed. He then hit back at the scientific evidence by playing on the jury's sympathy. "Where would we get the money for doctors to refute this testimony?"[101] He taunted the defense for not putting Ruesch or Getty on the stand, although he knew that Ruesch was hiding from Millikan's subpoenas in New York and that Getty would deny sexual contact with Joan.[102]

After the lawyers finished, Judge Willis instructed the jurors on the law within about thirty-five minutes. The question for them was simple: Was Charlie Chaplin the father of Carol Ann? If they had doubts, then they must rule in his favor, Willis said.[103] Despite the scientifically unassailable blood test evidence, Willis was constrained to tell the jurors that under California law that evidence was not considered "conclusive or unanswerable—therefor [sic]you are not bound by an opinion based on such tests." However, he reminded the seven women and five men that the burden of proof was on the plaintiff and that if they found that Joan had slept with other men during the relevant time and didn't know which one was the father, then "your verdict must be in favor of Chaplin."[104]

The jury began deliberating at 10:20 a.m. on January 3, 1945, and continued for six hours over two days. Nine jurors had to vote against Chaplin for him to be deemed the father of Carol Ann. In the first straw poll, the jurors voted seven to five in favor of Chaplin, and they never budged, even after six straw polls.[105] By the middle of the second day, the foreman, property manager Ferdinand J. Gay, told the judge it was impossible for the jurors to reach a verdict. At noon on Thursday, January 4, the judge declared a mistrial. In doing so, he said the jurors had showed "an independent sort of intelligence," the meaning of which was unclear.[106]

Some of the jurors did not accept the validity of the blood tests, reporters learned after speaking with them. And none of them believed Chaplin when he testified that he never had sex with Joan in December 1942. The barrier to reaching a verdict was the belief that Joan had been sexually intimate with Getty and Ruesch during the time she conceived.[107]

Chaplin always had a way with women, and this trial was no exception. Only one of the seven women voted against him, while all the men but one thought the evidence showed he was Carol Ann's father. Scott's disgust with the women on the jury was palpable. "The outcome is just as I thought it might be, with the women throwing the rocks at Carol Ann," he groused.[108] This was sour grapes from Scott, who was an experienced trial lawyer and had been selecting jurors for more than thirty years. He chose them as much as Millikan did. Neither Chaplin nor Joan was in court to hear the news, and both refused to speak to reporters afterward.[109]

Before the sun set the next day, January 5, the indefatigable Scott was back in court filing motions to set a quick date for the retrial.[110] "I have just begun to fight," a fired-up Joe Scott told reporters.[111]

TWENTY
"ALL UNHAPPY IN CHAPLIN CASE"

Still not vindicated in the courts after a year, Chaplin took his revenge on-screen and threw himself into preparing the script for his next movie, an updated story of history's murderous French husband Henri Landru, which would become *Monsieur Verdoux*. In the three months between paternity trials, Chaplin worked nonstop on the screenplay, spewing venom onto the pages against capitalism, the church, the legal system, and especially women.[1] He killed off multiple wives left and right in the film without remorse.

Meanwhile, Joan still harbored dreams of a movie career. Louella Parsons revealed in the *Los Angeles Examiner* that Joan signed a contract with Monogram Pictures in February 1945 to be a featured player in an untitled, and as yet unmade, murder mystery.[2] Monogram was hardly the Chaplin Studio. It pumped out forty to fifty B movies a year on the cheap to fill the bottom half of a Saturday matinee double bill, like other studios on so-called Poverty Row. The small Monogram studio near Gower Street in Hollywood was the place some stars got their big break on the way up—Randolph Scott and Alan Ladd—and others got their small paycheck on the way down—Kay Francis and Bela Lugosi.[3] Monogram productions were "cheap, vulgar, inept, and ultimately forgettable."[4] Even there, Joan's screen career was short lived. Two novice producers tried to raise money to make a film with Joan and pitched it to Monogram.[5] Once Louella leaked the story, however, Monogram backed off, and no film was ever made at the studio either with or about Joan.[6]

The paternity case was back on the trial calendar. In Los Angeles County the protocol was to send cases for retrial to a different judge who might be able to broker a settlement. Presiding Judge Samuel R. Blake summoned the lawyers for a conference just a week after the jury deadlocked. Given the animosity between the parties, fueled by Scott's scathing treatment of Chaplin in court and Chaplin's sense of invincibility after beating the Mann Act case and almost winning the paternity trial, there was no chance for a settlement. Scott angled for a fast retrial, pleading that his client was destitute. "That's not true, and you know it, Mr. Scott," Millikan shot back; Chaplin had been paying Joan $75 a week for two years, or about $1,120 a week in today's dollars.[7] The judge fixed May 2, 1945, as the new trial date to accommodate Millikan's busy court schedule and to give the parties one last chance to settle.[8] A month later, with Millikan's workload easing and no settlement in sight, the lawyers advanced the trial to April 4.[9]

Meanwhile, Chaplin's troubles moved from the courts to Congress. Sen. William "Wild Bill" Langer, a North Dakota Republican, introduced legislation, Senate Bill 536, on February 15, 1945, to start deportation proceedings against him "to protect the morals and the girls of the country."[10] In 1934, while he was governor of North Dakota, Langer had been convicted of a conspiracy to defraud the federal government and removed from office, but he refused to leave, barricading himself in the governor's mansion. Six years later, when elected to the U.S. Senate his colleagues tried to prevent him from being seated because of the contretemps caused by his conviction, citing "moral turpitude," ironically, similar to the reason he gave for wanting Chaplin ousted.[11]

Chaplin came out swinging. "It's been going on for four years—ever since I made an anti-Nazi film, *The Great Dictator*." Chaplin claimed that because he "dared to speak on behalf of Russia, urging the allies to open a second front." He also placed the blame on certain journalists: "Reactionary columnists called me a Communist and an ingrate."[12] The press lost interest in Langer's bill, and Congress never had any. It was referred to the Committee on Immigration, where it quietly died.[13] The bill was a distant warning bell to Chaplin that trouble was brewing in postwar America, but he didn't seem to hear it.

The quiet scene at the Los Angeles County Hall of Records on the warm, clear Wednesday morning of April 4, 1945, was a far cry from the hoopla surrounding the Mann Act case the year before or Chaplin's first paternity trial. As the lawyers made routine pretrial motions before the

242

newly assigned judge, Clarence Kincaid, only a handful of reporters and one spectator—an old man—watched. Charlie and Joan were nowhere in sight.[14]

As soon as the potential jurors shuffled into court, Millikan tried—yet again!—to get the case dismissed. This time, he argued that the signed, court-approved stipulation was an affirmative defense to Carol Ann's lawsuit. An affirmative defense prevents the case from going forward, regardless of its merits, because of some fact or applicable law. If so, judgment must be entered in favor of the defense.[15] Judge Kincaid sent the jury to an early lunch while he listened to Millikan's arguments. It took him only a few minutes to figure out that Chaplin's lawyer had dressed up his old argument in a new legal theory, and he denied the motion.[16]

Once the jury panel returned, it was Scott's turn to upset the applecart. Now *he* wanted the case tried without a jury. Scott's about-face was prompted by a cold, hard look at the numbers. He'd been unable to convince more than five jurors of the merits of Carol Ann's case in the prior trial, and he needed at least nine to prevail. If he left it up to the judge, he only had to persuade one person. The proposal was so unexpected that Millikan hadn't bothered to broach it with Chaplin, so he asked for an adjournment to talk to his client. The judge sent the jurors home with instructions to return the following morning.[17]

There wasn't much in Clarence Leslie Kincaid's background to provide a clue as to how he might rule if he, instead of a jury, were to judge the facts. At forty-seven, Kincaid was far younger and less experienced than Judge Willis, but he had a reputation for a keen intellect and strong work ethic. A 1920 graduate of the University of Southern California's law school, Kincaid had been appointed to the municipal court in 1931 and elevated to the superior court three years later.[18] With his wavy brown hair and blue eyes, the five foot ten, 175-pound Kincaid made a commanding presence in court.[19]

Given his successful track record with juries, Chaplin was reluctant to place his fate in the hands of a judge.[20] The next day Millikan announced that his client wanted his case heard by a jury. Eleven women and one man were chosen, which was another hopeful sign for Chaplin, given that the women on his previous juries had been staunchly in his corner.[21] The jurors chosen by the lawyers were an unsophisticated, salt-of-the-earth bunch. Retired Cecil Croxen, the only man, was chosen by his fellow jurors to be the foreman.[22] He was married without children. Eight of the eleven female jurors were married, most of them housewives. A divorced juror who lived with her janitor-father worked in a bakery. One of the married women was an executive secretary. The daughter of one of the women jurors was a nun. Her presence must have been a comfort to Scott, the devout Catholic.[23]

Opening statements and testimony were set to begin on the chilly, drizzly morning of Monday, April 9, but as soon as the court convened, there was another surprise.[24] Chaplin was a no-show. Millikan told the court that Chaplin was still recuperating from the injuries he had sustained after kicking in the door to his house over the New Year's weekend.[25] But that had happened more than three months earlier, and it sounded like malingering.

Scott had issued a trial subpoena to Chaplin and gave it to his investigator to serve. The investigator trekked up the hill to Summit Drive, where he found the supposedly ailing Chaplin on the tennis court, looking none the worse for wear. When Chaplin saw the process server "he ran like a scared jack rabbit up to the house," Scott told Judge Kincaid. The investigator rang the bell on the front porch of Chaplin's home, but Oona opened the door and told him her husband wasn't there.[26]

"Your Honor won't be very long in this case before your Honor realizes there is a lot of mendacity . . ." huffed Scott.[27] As a sanction for Chaplin's ducking the subpoena, Scott asked the judge to let him read a transcript of Chaplin's testimony from the first paternity trial to the jury.[28]

Not eager to have Chaplin tarred as a liar, Millikan said Chaplin wouldn't come to court because his feelings had been hurt by Scott at the last trial. Millikan told the judge that Chaplin "did not take it that he owed Mr. Scott any courtesy whatsoever because Mr. Scott had been so extremely discourteous to him and called him many names in his argument to the jury, names that were wholly unjustified and constituted misconduct."[29] Millikan was savvy enough, however, to realize that Chaplin's disappearing act reflected poorly on him with the court and would not play well with the jury either. He asked that after Scott's first witness—Joan's obstetrician, Dr. Starr—the court take an early recess so he could try to talk sense into his client. The no-nonsense judge refused.[30]

As soon as Dr. Starr finished, the judge told the jury that instead of Chaplin testifying in person as Scott's adverse witness, his testimony from a prior trial would be read in court, with no further explanation.[31] Scott stood and read verbatim from the transcript. "Direct examination of Charles Chaplin by myself," Scott began, dealing a serious blow to the defense.[32] Scott's cheap shots against Chaplin in the previous trial and Chaplin's responses didn't pack the same punch when presented in the lawyer's singsong reading voice. When Scott had hurled his insults at Chaplin in December, the experienced actor had been able to modulate his voice, alter his facial expressions, and use his unparalleled pantomime skills to express shock and hurt. Now the jury only heard Chaplin's cold, harsh words as read by Scott—words that reeked of smugness and a lack of compassion for Joan's plight.

Chaplin's nonappearance may have cost him the trial. To the jurors it must have seemed as if the millionaire movie star considered himself too important to waste his time answering for his behavior in a court of law. His absence signaled contempt for the legal system and disregard for them. Worst of all, the still handsome Charlie Chaplin lost his chance to charm the eleven women on the jury his legal team had wanted there so badly in the first place.

After Scott droned on for a full day reading Chaplin's words into the record, his next witness was Chaney, who again changed his story about the night Joan broke in with her gun. Now Chaney added the damning observation that the morning after, he saw water inside the bathtub where Joan had bathed "and a douchebag in it."[33] The sight of the once popular—and not terribly effective—method of birth control tended to corroborate Joan's claim that Chaplin and Joan had engaged in sexual intercourse.[34]

The next day, April 10, "Gentleman Pat" Millikan took off the gloves to attack Chaplin's former butler. "Mr. Chaney, the testimony that you gave yesterday afternoon in which you stated in the bathroom . . . you observed water in the bathtub and a douche bag, you made no statement concerning that at your former appearance as a witness in the case, did you?"

"I was never asked that question, sir," Chaney replied.

"I say you made no statement about it," Millikan repeated.

"No, sir," Chaney admitted.[35]

Perhaps Chaney was telling the truth when he intimated he would have dropped this bombshell previously if only he'd been asked. But Chaney's loyalties shifted constantly. Chaplin's antics involving Joan had caused Chaney nothing but headaches. He endured hundreds of weepy phone calls from her and was given the unpleasant task of blocking her access to Chaplin once the boss grew tired of her. He suffered through hours of interrogation by the FBI and by lawyers in depositions for Joan's paternity suit. He was subpoenaed to testify before the grand jury and at multiple trials. When Chaney made a mistake on the witness stand about the years he'd worked for Chaplin (he said from 1941 to '43 instead of 1942 to '44) and Millikan corrected him, Chaney blurted: "To tell you the truth, I am trying to forget it."[36]

Joan was Scott's next and final witness. She took the stand late on the morning of April 10 and was still there the next afternoon. The drama and the crying were over. Not even Millikan's reading of her pathetic letters to Chaplin from Tulsa rattled her. This time Joan's story changed too. Joan testified that she had had sex with Chaplin a total of four times in December 1942: on December 10; on December 23, when she broke into his house with her gun and again on the morning of December 24; and on his living room rug on December 30.[37]

Millikan pounced. The awkwardness he'd displayed during jury selection in the first trial vanished by the time he had Joan on the ropes on the afternoon of April 10. His cross-examination, while respectful, hammered at the inconsistencies in her story. Millikan referred to Joan's September 14, 1943, deposition taken with her lawyer, Jack Irwin, at her side, where she said she visited Chaplin's home three times in December 1942. In that deposition Irwin had asked: "On any of those occasions did you have any intimate relations with Mr. Chaplin?"

"Yes," Joan had replied.

"On how many of those three visits that you particularly remember?"

"Two," she had answered.[38] Joan had no choice but to admit to the discrepancy on the witness stand once Millikan had confronted her with her prior conflicting deposition testimony.

In that same deposition, Irwin had asked Joan whether she'd been intimate with Chaplin on December 10. Joan had responded, "I don't believe so—no, I know I wasn't."[39] Another important detail changed.

Millikan also confronted her with what she had told FBI Agent H. Frank Angell on January 7, 1944. "[I]t is a fact, isn't it, that you did not say anything to Mr. Angell about any alleged act of sexual intercourse with Mr. Chaplin in the yellow room [Paulette Goddard's bedroom] on the morning of the 24th of December, 1942 did you?" Millikan pressed.

"I remember, yes, I am quite certain that I did tell him about the 24th. . . . I told him as best I could all the intimacies we had had," Joan said.

Millikan pushed and Joan stumbled. "I think I did. I don't see why I would omit that."[40]

Millikan pushed harder. "You didn't give any testimony in this case in the Federal Court in which you stated that you had intercourse with Mr. Chaplin the morning of the 24th, did you?"

"I don't know," Joan responded.[41]

On redirect examination, Scott tried to rehabilitate Joan by showing she was in an addled state when she was deposed by Irwin. "What was your condition physically or mentally at the time that deposition was taken?" Scott asked.[42]

After Joan and her mother filed the lawsuit in June 1943 and Chaplin had gotten married, Joan fell apart. She blamed her contradictory deposition testimony on the fact she'd had "a complete nervous breakdown and I had to go to a sanitarium."[43] Three months later, when she was two weeks away from giving birth, the deposition was taken. Joan said she was "still very, very distraught, very, very upset and I supposed I was nervous."[44] Millikan stood up on recross and reminded her (and the jury) that it was her own attorney who was leading her through the deposition and that he had prepared her for it, so she should have had nothing to be nervous about.[45]

Although Millikan had no burden of proof, he had to do more than show that Joan might have been exaggerating the number of sex acts she'd engaged in with Chaplin; he had to suggest an alternative father for Carol Ann. He got Joan to admit that she'd seen Getty in Tulsa in November 1942 and that he'd supported her after she blew through the $300 Chaplin gave her in New York in October 1942. "With the exception of that $300 you had not received any money from Mr. Chaplin from October 2nd down to December 24th, when Mr. Chaplin gave you $60, is that right?" Millikan asked. Joan conceded that was correct.[46]

Then Millikan turned his focus to Hans Ruesch, showing they were romantically involved from November until New Year's Eve of that year. "Isn't it a fact, Miss Berry, that Mr. Ruesch visited you at your bungalow at the Ambassador Hotel on several occasions while you were there?" he asked.

"No, not on several occasions."

"How many occasions?" he asked.

"One occasion when he came and called for me and read poetry to me and that is all, he read Omar Khayyam," she replied.

Millikan replied, "He read poetry to you a long time?"

Al Risse, Carol Ann's guardian and Scott's co-counsel, interjected, "She said Omar Khayyam."

"Well, that would be a long time too, then," Millikan quipped.[47]

Millikan harped on her multiple contacts with Ruesch in December 1942, asking Joan if they went out for cocktails or dinner at the Mocambo (December 4 and 20), The Prime Rib (December 14), The Players (December 7, 10, 20, 27, and 30), Victor's (December 20 and 28), The Copper Room (December 9), A Bit of England (December 19), Simon's Drive-In Restaurant (December 24), and the Villa Nova (December 30). He asked Joan whether she'd visited Ruesch at his apartment on Olympia Boulevard on at least seven occasions (December 14, 19, 20, 21, 24, 30, and 31) and whether they'd gone apartment hunting together (December 6). Did Ruesch send her flowers (December 15), take her to the Palladium (December 17), take her to the movies (December 28), and invite her to a party at his apartment (December 27)?[48]

On and on it went. When Millikan asked if, after having dinner on Christmas Eve with Ruesch and Bonini, Joan had then gone to Ruesch's apartment, Joan replied, "Well, you see, as I say, I can't remember, but if you say I was with Mr. Bonini and Mr.—it is possible. . . ."[49]

Sensing trouble, Scott jumped up. "I object to any statement of that kind. I am representing a baby here."

"You put the witness on the stand," Millikan taunted.[50]

"But she doesn't have to make an observation to you, she can answer the question. I have a baby to look out for," Scott insisted, reminding the jury every chance he could that he represented a helpless infant.

The objection made no sense to anyone, including the judge. "I don't know what that has to do with Mr. Millikan's right to cross examination this witness," Judge Kincaid said as he overruled Scott's objection.[51]

In deciding whether Chaplin was the father, the jury could consider whether Joan had the opportunity to have sexual intercourse with someone else around the time she conceived. Unfortunately for Millikan, both the question and the answer equal evidence at a trial, so he was stuck with Joan's evasions and denials. It would be up to the jury to decide whether she sounded truthful. If Millikan had succeed in subpoenaing Ruesch on his client's behalf, the young writer would have testified that Joan was a frequent—but often uninvited—guest in his apartment and had, on occasion, stayed overnight. He also would have said that she became such a pest that he sometimes left her alone at his place and rented a hotel room for himself.[52]

When it was the defense's turn, Chaplin showed up to testify, which must have left the jurors wondering why they'd had to endure listening to Scott read his prior testimony earlier in the trial. Like Joan, Chaplin had mellowed, at least insofar as his sniping with Scott. His direct testimony began on the cool, partly cloudy morning of Thursday, April 12, and was finished before the midmorning recess.[53] Again, he denied having sex with Joan in December 1942.[54]

On cross-examination, Chaplin made Joan sound unhinged. Describing the gun incident, he told Scott that he'd told her, "I know you are trying to create a scandal. I put nothing by you. That is absolute blackmail."[55]

Scott countered, "You didn't believe her when she said she was going to kill herself?"[56]

"Yes, I did, she had a loaded gun in her hand. . . . She is capable of anything, she was completely crazy," Chaplin replied.[57]

During this second trial, Scott censored himself when cross-examining Chaplin and Chaplin in turn held his temper. But they could not disguise their mutual contempt. "I have a distinguished witness on the stand and I am trying to be deferential," Scott said during his cross-examination.

"So different from the last time," Chaplin snapped.

"Thank you. You remember—" Scott replied.

"It is like a love match," Chaplin interjected sarcastically.

"Not with me," Scott answered.[58]

And, later, Scott instructed Chaplin to put on his glasses to review a document. "[P]ut on your glasses again. I am sorry to disturb your equanimity—"

"Poor Joe, you are just too solicitous," interrupted Millikan.

"I am very solicitous. I don't want to misquote him, or particularly, misunderstand him," Scott replied.

"I think you have misunderstood me a great deal and you have misunderstood this trial," Chaplin said.[59]

Once again, Scott asked about the poolside sit-down with Joan. She made threats "and I threatened back," Chaplin snapped.[60]

The fact that Chaplin engaged at all with Joan by the pool in June 1943 was a tacit admission that they'd had sex in December 1942, which Scott picked up on and used in his summation. If Chaplin hadn't slept with Joan since February 1942, he would have told her to get lost within five minutes of her pregnancy announcement. But by engaging with her, he demonstrated his consciousness of guilt and his fear he might be a father again.

Following the short afternoon recess, the trial came to a grinding halt.

When court reconvened, Judge Kincaid made a startling announcement: President Franklin D. Roosevelt was dead! He had succumbed to a stroke in Warm Springs, Georgia, earlier in the day. In deference, the judge sent everyone home.[61]

The next day, to accommodate the schedules of the doctors who were to testify about the blood tests, the remainder of Chaplin's cross-examination was postponed and the doctors were taken out of turn. What they had to say came as no surprise: under the accepted rules of science, Chaplin could not be Carol Ann's father.[62] When they were finished, Chaplin returned to the witness stand for a few final questions.

Scott had a surprise rebuttal witness waiting in the wings: J. Paul Getty. In his testimony, Getty said he saw Joan at the Mayo Hotel in Tulsa on November 17, 1942, and took her to dinner at a restaurant nearby, followed by a movie.[63] Over the next few days, they met again for dinner and they saw a few more movies before Getty dropped Joan off at the railway station on November 23. His appearance in court served primarily as an opportunity for Scott to have him adamantly deny having had sex with Joan while she was in Tulsa.[64] The newspapers showed little interest in Getty's appearance this time around. Getty kept his diary entry about his court appearance vague and self-serving. "On stand at 1:35 for about 5 minutes," he wrote. "Hope it cleared the air. I answered briefly and truthfully."[65]

On cross-examination, Millikan suggested that Getty could be lying. Getty admitted that while he was squiring Joan around Tulsa in November 1942, his wife Teddy was in California, so he had the opportunity to sleep with Joan had he wanted to, and Mrs. Getty would have been none the wiser.[66] Getty also conceded on cross-examination that he'd spent a lot of money on Joan, planting the seed in the jurors' minds that the pair was romantically involved. And despite Getty's assertions that the money he gave Joan was a loan, she'd never repaid a cent.[67]

Summations began first thing Monday morning, April 16, 1945, Chaplin's fifty-sixth birthday. Millikan's turn took up a little more than two hours.[68] He focused, as he should have, on the strength of the blood tests and the fact that Getty, Ruesch, and Bonini had access to Joan during the crucial months of December 1944 and January 1945.[69] He repeated Chaplin's claim that he'd never had sex with Joan in December 1942 and that the blood evidence didn't lie. In trying to convince the jurors that they should accept the test results, he posited a logical question—if there was disagreement in the medical community about the validity of the tests, why hadn't Scott brought in any experts to say they were not reliable?[70]

"What a question to ask this baby!" Scott exclaimed. "What money has she [Carol Ann] got? Her mother is broke, and the money that I have had has gone into my little bank account, if I have any left, do I have to get somebody up here on that?" [71] It was an improper and disingenuous argument. Scott's professed personal money woes were irrelevant. And, if there had been a scientist on earth with a contrasting view about the validity of blood tests, Scott would have found him and gladly paid his expert witness fees. Rather than addressing the test's validity, he reminded the jury of the prevailing law at the time. "[Y]ou are not bound by the testimony of the doctors. . . ."[72]

Scott told the jury he called Getty as a witness so the jurors could scrutinize his appearance. "[W]e wanted you to look at the man and the baby, and I ask you can you see anything in the face of this little girl that looks like Getty, a man with a face like Getty here?"[73] But Scott was taking a big chance with that argument. Getty, with his graying but once reddish blond hair and pale complexion, looked far more like Carol Ann than Chaplin did. And the child he would have with his wife, Teddy, in 1946, Timothy Ware Getty, who died tragically at age twelve from a brain tumor, was a red-haired boy with fair freckled skin who resembled Carol Ann.[74]

Scott astutely picked up on the deeper significance of Chaplin's poolside parley with Joan. "Why did he take all the time down at the pool if this girl was simply a gold digger. . . . unless his conscience was hurting him?"[75] The pious Scott seemed to equate Joan with a late-day Hester Prynne, and he branded her with a figurative scarlet A. "[T]he girl is ashamed of herself, and the one thing I will say about the poor, wretched girl . . . she is conscious of what she has done, she has degraded her sex and womanhood. . . ." And, unable to stop himself from insulting Chaplin one last time, Scott said that Chaplin "throws that little chest of his out, and that four feet two inches of his body . . . and he has the effrontery . . . to say the reason why this is being done is because he made a speech in New York about the second front."[76]

The judge began instructing the jury on the applicable law on the afternoon of April 16 and didn't finish until the next day.[77] On April 17, at 5:20 p.m., after just under three hours of deliberation, the jury voted eleven to one in favor of Carol Ann. "We, the jury in the above entitled action, find that the defendant Charles Spencer Chaplin is the father of the plaintiff

Carol Ann Berry. This 17 day of April, 1945." The foreman, Cecil A. Croxen, signed the verdict.[78] With those words Charlie Chaplin was deemed Carol Ann's legal father, and the lives of the litigants were impacted forever. A faint round of applause broke out among the small group of about thirty spectators scattered around the courtroom. Neither Charlie Chaplin nor Joan Berry was among them. After two weeks of being relegated to the back pages, the verdict brought the story back to page 1 of the *Los Angeles Times*, complete with a file photo of a miserable-looking Chaplin holding his head in his hand.[79]

The jury's lone holdout was sixty-five-year-old Mary James, a Welsh housewife. "I have to live with my conscience," she said.[80] Other jurors told reporters they were unimpressed with Chaplin. Some thought he was "acting" and "evasive" in his testimony.[81] "His account was fishy," said one juror.[82] Joan, on the other hand, was perceived as "honest." And none of them were persuaded by Millikan's effort to pin the pregnancy on either Ruesch or Getty. Yet it was the presence of these men in Joan's life that prevented the first jury from being able to decide if Chaplin was Carol Ann's father.[83] Obviously, the jurors ignored the blood evidence.

Every jury has its own dynamic, and the difference in the verdicts between the two trials may have been as simple as different personalities looking at the same evidence. But by twenty-first-century standards, where forensic evidence has become the gold standard at trials, it is shocking that the law permitted the jury to ignore what by 1945 was the accepted science of blood typing.

The fact that Chaplin dodged Scott's subpoena and stayed away from most of the trial was devastating. As the defendant, he should have been sitting at counsel table, drinking at the water fountain during court recesses, and whispering with his lawyers throughout the testimony. His presence would have made the jurors think that he was taking the matter seriously and that he was invested in the outcome. Further, his celebrity would have awed the jury, and for that reason alone the vote might have ended in his favor.

Judge Kincaid wasted no time setting a hearing to determine what Chaplin would have to pay his daughter. He ordered the lawyers to be prepared to present evidence at a hearing before him, with no jury, the very next afternoon.[84] The fireworks began immediately. Scott wanted between $1,000 and $1,500 a month for his client, or about $21,000 in today's dollars.[85] "He is a millionaire, and no man today with a couple of

English butlers and a swimming pool and all the appurtenances that go with it could pose as not being able to support this baby in affluent circumstances," Scott told the judge.[86]

Millikan fought hard. "Certainly the first thing to be determined in this matter is not what Mr. Chaplin's resources are, as Mr. Scott suggests. . . ." he argued. "[T]he whole question is what the necessities of the plaintiff are, and the only way in which the resources of the defendant are in any way material is to determine whether or not the defendant has the ability to meet the necessities shown by the evidence of the plaintiff."[87]

Scott contended that the $75 a week that Chaplin had been voluntarily paying Carol Ann throughout the proceedings was hardly sufficient. He called it "a pauper's program for this child." He told the court that the rent on the small bungalow in Los Angeles shared by Joan, her own mother, Gertrude, and Carol Ann cost $150 a month.[88]

"We are not obliged to support the mother or grandmother of this child," Millikan retorted.[89] He fought tooth and nail against putting Chaplin on the stand so Scott could give him the third degree about his net worth, which all of Hollywood knew was astronomical. "[T]here is no logic or reason . . . for the Court to hear evidence upon the wealth of the defendant when I concede and offer to stipulate that he has the financial ability to respond to a reasonable order. . . ."[90] For all the Monday morning quarterbacking by Chaplin's own son, Charles Jr., about why his father should have hired Giesler for the paternity trials, it was here that the firm of Wright and Millikan proved its worth; it knew how to protect the wealth of its elite clients.

Scott called his law partner and Carol Ann's guardian, Al Risse, to the stand. Risse testified that every effort to get Joan a job in show business had failed, without indicating whether she'd tried to fall back on her once formidable typing skills. "I can't understand why that is material here," Millikan interjected, "this is not an action in which support is sought for Miss Berry."[91]

"No," retorted Scott, "but counsel has said the burden is not to be borne by the father if the mother is able to support her."

"Not at all; I am willing to concede that you are dense today," Millikan chided. Normally a judge would step in and stop lawyers from insulting one another in open court, but Kincaid remained silent.[92] Perhaps like the press, the public, and the litigants, he'd had enough of the Chaplin-Berry-Scott-Millikan soap opera.

On cross-examination of Scott's legal colleague, Millikan laced into Risse about Joan's extravagant spending, asking if he was aware of purchases she'd made at luxury department stores like Saks Fifth Avenue and I. Magnin. "Do you have any knowledge as to whether or not those purchases were made for clothing for this child?" Millikan asked.[93]

"I have not," Risse replied.

"That is all," Millikan said and sat down.[94]

Surprisingly, Scott and his firm failed to have an itemized list of expenses for the baby and relied on the opinion testimony of Risse. Additionally, Scott sought $50,000, equal to $719,000 today, in legal fees and yet had no hourly breakdown, bills, or invoices to establish the cost of his services either.[95] Instead, Risse described anecdotally the many nights and weekends the lawyers spent on the case, forcing them to ignore other matters pending at the firm.[96]

Millikan was adamant. Scott wasn't entitled to a penny more than the $5,000 already agreed to under the long-disputed stipulation between the parties. Millikan argued that the stipulation was only found void as to the rights of the child. Because Scott took over from Irwin, who had agreed to the fee amount, Scott was stuck with it, Millikan argued.[97]

Throughout, Judge Kincaid said little. But after both sides finished their arguments, he ruled from the bench, without so much as a five-minute recess to think about it.[98] Chaplin would continue to pay what he had been paying Joan's daughter: $75 a week. Scott would get the previously agreed upon legal fee of $5,000. It was a stunning victory for Chaplin, after his huge loss the day before.[99] It was Kincaid's way of saying he didn't think much of the jury's verdict. But it was devastating news for Joe Scott, who was uncharacteristically unable to speak when he heard the judge's decision. His eyes filled with tears. "I can't believe it," he muttered.[100] Outside the courthouse, still smarting, Scott told reporters, "I'm not satisfied—I will say that."[101] And when Joan learned the news, she gasped: "I can't work and take care of the baby, too. I don't know what I'll do."[102]

But no one on the other side was happy either. Chaplin was on the hook for two decades of support for a child who was not his. The lawyers at the firm of Wright and Millikan were faced with years of filing appeals to higher courts. The headline of a local newspaper in a tiny town two and a half hours north of San Francisco captured the mood best: "All Unhappy in Chaplin Case."[103]

TWENTY-ONE

"THE BIGGEST ROLE OF MY LIFE"

After the bitter disappointment of losing the paternity suit, Chaplin and his wife repaired for five days to Palm Springs on April 22.[1] Meanwhile, his lawyers immediately set to work filing a motion for a new trial. Hedda Hopper used the verdict to encourage her fans in government to deport him. After claiming she talked with some powerful politicians, she wrote in her column that they told her that the Joan Barry scandal "constituted moral turpitude—and bigger people than Chaplin have been deported on those grounds."[2]

Judge Kincaid quickly denied Chaplin's motion, refusing to substitute his judgment for the jury's.[3] Millikan filed a notice of appeal to the district court of appeal.[4] The next move belonged to Scott. He ran to the superior court in July for a subpoena to force Chaplin to show cause why he shouldn't be compelled to continue supporting Carol Ann while his appeal was pending. Chaplin hadn't sent Joan a dime since a week before the jury found against him.[5]

Judge William S. Baird, who had signed off on the infamous stipulation, ordered Chaplin to appear in court on July 16 with his "books and accounts reflecting the nature and extent of all real and personal property owned by you and the amount of your annual income from all sources."[6] Having no interest in touching this hot potato again, Baird promptly transferred the case back to Judge Kincaid for him to resolve. Chaplin showed up in court looking like a French banker, sporting a long, thin continental mous-tache for his upcoming role as Monsieur Verdoux. Although it was in his best interest to appear financially strapped, Chaplin looked prosperous in a finely tailored, gray three-piece suit.

First, Joan took the stand to say that she had no money, no job, and no prospects for finding one—at least in the movies—now that the Monogram Pictures project had fizzled. She said that she was four months in arrears on her $150-a-month rent for the bungalow she shared with her mother and child and that the only thing between her and skid row was a $400 loan from Scott.[7]

Millikan did what he could to keep Chaplin—who had brought no records with him, despite the judge's order—from having to testify about his wealth. Millikan offered to stipulate that his client had more than $1 million. Scott wouldn't stand for it. "Why doesn't this man comply with the court order and bring in his books and records?" Scott bellowed.[8] The reason, Millikan explained, was that the studio bookkeeper was on vacation and she was the only Chaplin employee capable of deciphering his accounts. The idea that one person had the key to the books of a major motion picture company would have been laughable at any other Hollywood studio, but the Chaplin organization consisted of the star and a handful of loyal underlings.

Ultimately, Chaplin took the stand. Within minutes, he and Scott locked horns. Chaplin seemed "nervous and fidgety."[9] It wasn't long before Chaplin was shouting that Scott was "abusing" him and "blackening" his character.[10]

"What is your income?" Scott demanded.

"It varies," snapped Chaplin.

"Don't you know what you're worth?" Scott asked, incredulous that a man of Chaplin's station wouldn't know.

"No," Chaplin replied petulantly.

"When you pass out of this world one of these days, how much of an estate will you leave?" Scott asked.

"I have no idea," Chaplin replied.

"Are you worth a million dollars?" Scott continued.

"Yes. And more." Chaplin countered.[11]

Eventually, Scott squeezed out of Chaplin that he was worth around $3 million, or a little over $43 million today[12]—but not before the star was caught off guard when Scott asked if he'd withdrawn $290,000 from his account at the Hollywood State Bank two days after the paternity verdict, the implication being he was trying to hide assets. As Chaplin started to explain, the judge stopped him. The question required only a "yes" or "no," Kincaid instructed.[13] Walking back to his seat, a shaken Chaplin muttered, "I'd like to answer that one." He continued to grumble after he sat down. "They won't let me talk."[14]

Nonetheless, Scott didn't fare much better this second time around. Judge Kincaid ordered Chaplin to resume payments to Joan at the same $75-a-week rate he'd been paying—retroactive to April 18. He also made Chaplin pay Scott $500 to cover the cost of the day's hearing and another $2,750 to fight the pending appeal.[15] Now there could be little doubt that Kincaid thought little of the verdict. The bare minimum that Kincaid ordered would allow Carol Ann to be decently cared for, but it wasn't a windfall.

Joan had to face the reality that it was past time to get a job. Suddenly, she had a stroke of good luck—a show business opportunity seemed to fall from the sky into her mailbox. A Pittsburgh booking agent, Don D'Carlo (occasionally spelled "DeCarlo" in the press), sent her a letter offering to launch her career as a nightclub singer. D'Carlo had been on the periphery of showbiz for years. In the 1930s, he'd represented Pittsburgh native Gene Kelly before the actor was famous, getting him booked in regional nightclubs.[16] Since 1939, D'Carlo had been the sponsor of the Miss Pennsylvania competition, through which he fed contestants to the Miss America pageant in Atlantic City.[17]

Joan signed a two-year, exclusive contract with D'Carlo in the summer of 1945 and relocated to Pittsburgh to prepare for her new stage career.[18] It was a smart move on Joan's—and D'Carlo's—part. With the trial still fresh in the public mind, her notoriety was sure to draw an audience. By the fall, she was reportedly landing singing gigs for $1,250 a week (an eye-popping $18,000 today) while her daughter—now legally Chaplin's too—was left in Grandmother Gertrude's care back in Los Angeles.[19] The news stories about the size of Joan's earnings were most likely planted—and exaggerated—by D'Carlo to entice nightclub owners to book her at top dollar. Consorting with rich fellows who would pay her hotel bills and buy her clothes was now a thing of the past. "I haven't any time for men," Joan announced to a local newspaper reporter when she arrived in western Pennsylvania in 1945 to begin her singing career.[20]

The singing tour was a sad reminder of what might have been. Four years earlier, Joan had been under contract to one of the most famous directors in film history, who might have made her the next Paulette Goddard. Instead, D'Carlo, a small-time agent from the boondocks, could do no more than book Joan into third-rate nightclubs in one-horse towns like Aspinwall, Pennsylvania. For her first professional outing at the Riviera, a venue on a highway twenty minutes outside of Pittsburgh, she was advertised as the "Vivacious and Dynamic Former Protégé of Charlie Chaplin."[21] One New York columnist mused that Chaplin should sue Joan for using her association with him to advertise her new career.[22]

Surprisingly, Joan snagged a four-week holiday engagement in New York City beginning December 5, 1945, at the Greenwich Village Inn at 5 Sheridan Square in the heart of the bohemian area of the same name. The inn's golden years were in the 1920s, when its owner chose to ignore Prohibition and run a popular speakeasy.[23] There was a time when Pearl Bailey and Cab Calloway were headliners there.[24] By the mid-forties, the club was on its last legs.[25]

Joan's nine-minute New York show was panned in *Variety*. She sang three 1940s standards, "No Can Do," "That Old Feeling," and "I'll Be Yours," and then "appeared to be relieved to get off the floor," wrote an unnamed reviewer. The same writer said that her hairdo needed "redesigning" (without specifying how), her voice was "naturally thin," and she didn't know how to "put over a number." The reviewer described Joan as being so anxious on stage that she could barely be heard above the din of patrons talking and clinking their cocktail glasses. The reviewer also observed that there had never been "a more nervous performance exhibited in this town than Barry on her opening night."[26] *Newsweek*'s reviewer agreed; Joan suffered from "a bad case of stage fright" that left her hands and face "quivering" so obviously that she apologized to her audience.[27] In fairness, she had arrived at the Greenwich Village Inn straight from the dressmaker with forty-five minutes to spare until her first show and with nothing in her stomach. For dinner she made do with a warm Coke.[28]

Outside of New York, the reviews didn't improve. At the Brown Derby in Chicago in February, the *Variety* critic called her show "passable" and described Joan as "completely flustered by nervousness and stage-fright." Although she calmed down as the evening wore on, her performance didn't improve. The best the critic could muster was, "Not much of a voice here, and presentation is at times amateurish."[29] On another night, Joan was forced to endure hecklers. "Have they no reverence for motherhood?" a reporter for *Downbeat* magazine asked snidely.[30]

Meanwhile, back in California, lawyers were hard at work cranking out appellate briefs.[31] Chaplin's arguments to the higher court were nothing new: the judge should have dismissed the case pursuant to the stipulation, Joan was not credible, and the blood test proved Chaplin was not Carol Ann's father.[32] Counsel for Carol Ann argued that her $75-a-week support award was inadequate and that Scott deserved far more than $5,000.[33] But by this time, the newspaper-reading public had moved on. Although juicy revelations about the extent of Chaplin's wealth appeared on some front pages, articles about the parties' appeals did not. Charlie and Joan had become yesterday's news.

In the spring of 1946, the three-judge appellate panel finally heard oral arguments.[34] A month later, the court unanimously upheld the trial court's verdict, although one justice, Marshall F. McComb, held his nose while doing it. "In the case at bar a widely accepted scientific method of determining parentage was applied. Its results were definite. To reject the new and certain for the old and uncertain does not tend to promote improvement in the administration of justice," wrote the fifty-two-year-old McComb in a concurring opinion.[35] But his hands, like those of the rest of his colleagues, were tied. Until the legislature amended the law or the California Supreme Court reinterpreted it, the lower court was powerless to do anything.

Justice Emmet H. Wilson, age seventy, who had been on the appellate bench only a year, wrote the majority opinion and was joined by McComb and Presiding Appellate Division Justice Minor Lee Moore.[36] "A minor who must by necessity appear by his guardian, is not bound by the admissions of the guardian which mean the sacrifice or giving away of the ward's property," Wilson wrote.[37] This made sense; otherwise, unscrupulous guardians could swindle helpless infants and the courts would be powerless to protect them. To that point, the appellate panel criticized Judge Baird for signing off on the stipulation without at least holding a hearing to determine if it was fair to the child.[38] Had he done so, and determined after listening to the parties that it *was* fair, the Chaplin/Berry paternity litigation might have been avoided.

Unfortunately, for modern science and fundamental fairness, the justices were constrained by the 1937 decision of *Arais v. Kalensnikoff*, in which the California Supreme Court held that blood test evidence was not conclusive proof of paternity. Lower courts cannot overrule higher ones. As Justice Wilson acknowledged: "The decision in the Arais case has been the subject of discussion and criticism in law reviews and other legal periodicals, but not by other courts . . . and it remains the law of this state until modified or overruled by the court that rendered the opinion."[39]

Given the scientific evidence pointed to a man other than Chaplin, the other relevant legal question was whether Joan's testimony was sufficient to support a finding that Chaplin was Carol Ann's father. The appellate court, like Judge Kincaid, refused to substitute its judgment for the jury's. "A witness is presumed to speak the truth. Whether Miss Berry was entitled to full credit was for the jury and the trial judge to determine," Justice Wilson wrote.[40]

Finally, the court scoffed at Millikan's assertion that by requiring Chaplin to stand alongside Joan and Carol Ann so the jury could compare their resemblance, the court unfairly left the jury with images of "the ancient masterpieces of 'Madonna and Child.'" Hardly, said the court. Given the scandalous evidence presented at the trial, "the minds of the jurors [were] fixed on the unspiritual and terrestrial affairs of the mother and defendant."[41]

But Carol Ann and her mother didn't do so well on appeal either. The justices affirmed the $75-a-week support award and criticized Scott for failing to provide evidence pertaining to the financial status and needs of the litigants. "The record is devoid of facts pertinent to this material feature of the case," the court admonished.[42] It is unclear why Scott failed to present evidence on this critical point; he may have thought that Chaplin's fame would carry the day. But the appellate justices refused to "indulge a presumption as to the style of living of defendant," by taking judicial notice of "night club gossip and stories appearing in newspapers and magazines within the domain of proof of wealth. . . ."[43]

Given Chaplin's immense wealth, it is hard not to wonder whether the appellate court—like Judge Kincaid—was expressing displeasure with a verdict that saddled a man with twenty-one years of financial responsibility for a child they all knew wasn't his. Notwithstanding, the court invited the child's guardian to return to court "at any time and from time to time, for an increased award," as long as there was "more extensive evidence."[44]

The only winner was Joe Scott; the appellate court held that the stipulation's $5,000 cap on the lawyer's fees was void.[45] The matter was returned to the trial court for a hearing on an adequate fee award.[46] It must have stuck in Chaplin's craw to know that he would have to open his wallet wider for Scott, given how much he loathed him.

Wright and Millikan filed a thirty-six-page petition to the California

Supreme Court on July 2, 1946, asking it to hear the case, hoping it might overrule *Arais*.[47] Ten days later, Scott urged the court to reject the appeal, reminding the justices that Chaplin had made the same losing argument no less than seven times to the lower courts. Scott further argued that the intermediate appellate court ruling was consistent with settled California law.[48] Less than two weeks later, the California Supreme Court issued a one-line order: "Appellant's petition for hearing DENIED."[49] Two justices, Roger Traynor and B. Rey Schauer, both from the liberal wing of the court, voted to hear the case, but that was insufficient for the seven-member court to review it.[50]

The last unfinished business between Charlie and Joan concerned Scott's fees. Shortly before Christmas 1946, Chaplin's lawyers offered to settle with a $25,000 check for Scott and his colleagues, but Scott wanted $75,000.[51] The matter landed back in court. Carol Ann's lawyers presented three legal experts who testified that a fair fee ranged from $60,000 to $75,000.[52] The judge awarded Scott $28,000 for his work and directed that his three associates be paid at a rate of $8 an hour. The final award for Scott and the firm came to $42,706, or about $566,000 today.[53]

With years of nerve-racking criminal investigations, expensive litigation, and bad publicity finally behind him, Chaplin focused on shooting the final reels of *Monsieur Verdoux*. He was less than two months away from wrapping up filming and soon after would begin the editing and production process for the April 1947 premiere.[54] And there was another mouth to feed on Summit Drive; Oona had given birth to their second child, Michael, on March 7, 1946.[55]

Joan tried to concentrate on her career, too, but as usual it was a bumpy ride. Joan's relationship with D'Carlo deteriorated, landing them in court.[56] D'Carlo tried to garnish her $1,250 salary from a Detroit nightspot where Joan had performed in January 1946. He claimed she hadn't paid him a dime since they signed their contract despite the fact that he gave her a $1,000 cash advance, gave her $2,000 for her new wardrobe, and hired her voice and dramatics teachers. He also claimed to have covered a $450 food and liquor bill that she ran up while performing at the Riviera.[57]

She accused D'Carlo of demanding half her wages in violation of union rules. Joan also claimed to have suffered his improper sexual advances as well as his jealous wife's reaction to them, which interfered with her ability to concentrate on her singing. Siding with Joan, Detroit Circuit Court

Judge Theodore J. Richter ruled that she was entitled to 60 percent of her earnings, with the rest going to D'Carlo.[58]

The backstory of the dispute was that Joan's Greenwich Village Inn booking had been arranged by a different agent in violation of her exclusive contract with D'Carlo. But the American Guild of Variety Artists (AGVA), the performers' union, voided Joan's contract with D'Carlo because it called for a fifty-fifty split of her earnings, which exceeded the 10 percent cap on commissions for licensed booking agents.[59] D'Carlo was ordered by the union to return her gowns and musical arrangements, which he'd seized after Joan had signed with the other agent behind his back. Joan, meanwhile, was ordered by AGVA to pay D'Carlo $2,500 of her earnings to cover the cost of her clothes and singing lessons.[60]

The agent who booked Joan into the Greenwich Village nightspot was Charles Yates of the Joe Glaser agency in New York City.[61] Glaser, a former Chicago prizefight fixer, founded his talent agency with Louis Armstrong, whom he also represented. One of Armstrong's biographers, Ricky Riccardi, described Glaser as "crude, foul-mouthed [and] racist," personality traits that "didn't endear him to many."[62] Presumably, his clients tolerated his odious personality because he did well by them. The Glaser agency, renamed Associated Booking Corporation and still in business, was the real deal, representing such famous performers as Billie Holiday, Duke Ellington, and Benny Goodman.[63]

Yates opened doors for Joan in better venues in bigger cities. In February 1946 Joan was booked at the Brown Derby in Chicago.[64] In March 1946, she earned $1,000 a week at the Little Rathskeller in Philadelphia, and in April she was booked at $1,250 a week at a nightclub in Boston. But Joan and D'Carlo continued their legal warfare. D'Carlo filed suit in Philadelphia, seeking $50,000 in damages for breaching their contract. He claimed that Joan came to him "without a dollar in her pocket." The amount of money he spent on her budding career had grown in the latest round of legal papers, now reaching $7,000 for Joan's costumes, voice lessons, and other expenses.[65]

Joan told reporters that she'd offered D'Carlo $300 a week "to keep him happy," but that didn't satisfy him. "Now it looks as though he wants a heap of money all at once," she told a reporter. "Of course, I haven't got it."[66] D'Carlo came off in the dispute as an unscrupulous agent trying to take advantage of a naive client. Joan again seemed to be running up bills that she'd hoped a man would pay.[67]

But no matter who was managing Joan, her singing career took some familiar turns. A two-week engagement in Detroit in January 1946 ended a week early after she stormed off the stage because the audience heckled her about Chaplin. It was also rumored she wasn't getting along with her fellow performers.[68] During a four-day engagement at the Pines Night Club in Youngstown in May 1946, Joan slammed her dressing room door on the club manager's hand, smashing his fingers, because he wanted her to grant an interview to a local newspaper reporter. She finally met with the reporter, only to throw a temper tantrum during which she tossed her sheet music into a corner of her dressing room with such force that she knocked over a lamp, ending the interview.[69] Two months later she was suspended from AGVA for "conduct unbecoming a member"; she had backed out of an appearance at the Greystone Club in Mansfield, Ohio, at the last minute, leaving the venue high and dry. The union ordered her to pay $150 to the club to cover the cost of advertising her appearance.[70]

And then as quickly as it began, Joan's singing career was over. She quietly married a divorced brakeman for the Pittsburgh & Lake Erie Railroad, thirty-six-year-old Russell Seck. The press didn't catch wind of it until several months after the fact. In January, Joan told the *Los Angeles Times* that she and Seck had eloped on November 16, 1946, about six months after they met.[71] But when Russell Jr. was born in Pittsburgh on July 20, 1947, just eight months later, Seck told the *Times* that he and Joan had gotten married on October 16, 1946.[72] In her complaint for a divorce years later, Joan would claim they married on September 1, 1946.[73]

After the marriage—whenever it was—Joan, her husband, and her two children lived in a modest apartment at 275 North Craig Street in Pittsburgh's East End, a far cry from the splendor of Chaplin's six-acre spread in Beverly Hills. "Being a housewife is really wonderful," Joan chirped to the *Pittsburgh Post-Gazette*. "This is the biggest role of my life—that of the happy wife and mother."[74]

Unfortunately, Joan would not live happily ever after. And neither, for that matter, would Chaplin.

TWENTY-TWO

"PROCEED WITH THE BUTCHERY"

Monday, April 14, 1947, was a chilly spring day in New York City, where the daytime high never got above 51 degrees.[1] Nonetheless, Charlie Chaplin was sweltering in the center of the Grand Ballroom of the Gotham Hotel at Fifth Avenue and Fifty-Fifth Street as he faced a hundred or so reporters. Dressed in a light-gray, three-piece suit, with the reading glasses he loathed in one vest pocket and a pen in the other, the still handsome film maestro hooked his thumbs into his waistband and tried to muster a look of confidence. Besides the eyeglasses, only a smattering of age spots on his hands revealed that he was two days shy of his fifty-eighth birthday.[2]

United Artists had arranged the news conference so Chaplin could promote *Monsieur Verdoux*, which had opened at the Broadway Theatre to poor reviews the previous Friday night. Chaplin hadn't faced a large press contingent since the paternity trials had ended, and he had no illusions as to how he'd be received. "[P]roceed with the butchery," he thundered.[3]

Years of wrangling with Joan Berry had cast a long shadow over Chaplin's life and work. In dollars and cents, he would pay nearly $150,000 in child support for twenty-one years, negligible to a man of his wealth, but given he was not Carol Ann's father, it would be a constant thorn in his side. His bitterness toward Joan and the American legal system would seep into *Verdoux*, his first flop.[4]

Orson Welles gave Chaplin the idea for a documentary based on the life of the infamous French serial killer. Chaplin paid Welles $5,000 for the rights and began work on a fictionalized script.[5] As Henri Verdoux,

Chaplin plays a debonair bank teller who loses his job during the Depression and turns to bigamy and murder to support his invalid wife and their son, marrying women and killing them for their money. There is no hiding Chaplin's bitterness toward women in the film. First, there is the not-so-subtle irony of killing the women he seduces for *their* money, whereas Joan, in his view, tried to destroy him for *his* money. Verdoux is eventually apprehended and executed. As he goes bravely to the gallows—a sacrificial white-haired angel in a white flowing shirt—Chaplin expands his targets beyond women and pontificates about the evils of capitalism, organized religion, and war.

The Chaplins and Mary Pickford attended the premiere together. "Scattered hissing" broke out in the audience, wrote David Robinson in his biography of Chaplin.[6] Unable to tolerate it for the film's entire two hours and four minutes, Chaplin snuck into the lobby, leaving Oona and Mary to suffer the audience's disdain.[7] The early reviews were dreadful. "It is slow—tediously slow," wrote Bosley Crowther in the *New York Times*.[8] The film demonstrated "a woeful lack of humor, melodrama or dramatic taste," groaned Howard Barnes in the *New York Herald Tribune*.[9]

The Gotham Hotel news conference showed how much the press had turned against Chaplin. The hostile questions barely focused on the movie. "Could you define your present political beliefs, sir?" asked one reporter.[10]

Chaplin sneered, "[I]f you step off the curb with your left foot, they accuse you of being a Communist." He continued, "I've never belonged to any political party in my life and I have never voted in my life!" And, after a brief pause, Chaplin asked, "Does that answer your question?"[11]

"Not precisely," the reporter responded. "Could you answer a direct question? Are you a Communist?"[12]

"I am not a Communist!" he shouted. But then, in typical Chaplin fashion, he muddied the waters. He rambled about how much he had admired the Russians during the war and incomprehensibly got bollixed up, equating voting with dividing people, which he said "leads to fascism."[13]

The news conference debacle, the film's bad reviews, and poor box office sales led Chaplin to yank the movie from theaters after its five-week New York run. For all of 1947, it would take in only $162,000 despite a reported cost of $2 million.[14]

Weakened by the Joan Barry scandal and his unpopular movie, Chaplin was like a boxer on the ropes when the government moved in for the knockout punch. As the Cold War heated up, Chaplin's years of idolizing the Soviet Union, refusing to apply for U.S. citizenship, and associating with far-left thinkers, Communists, and fellow travelers caught up to him. Sen. William Langer, having failed to get Chaplin deported two years earlier, still had the comic in his crosshairs. A month before *Monsieur Verdoux* opened, Langer had referred to Chaplin on the floor of the U.S. Senate as "one of the darlings of the Communist Party," who had "an unsavory record of law-breaking, of rape, or the betrayal of American girls 16 and 17. . . ."[15] A month after Langer's tirade, the House Committee on Un-American Activities (HUAC) was given an extra $50,000 to boost its staff to investigate Communist infiltration in Hollywood.[16] Chaplin was about to be one of the committee's targets.

In *Naming Names*, his book about the history of the Red Scare, Victor Navasky writes that HUAC came gunning for Hollywood because the Communist Party had sought to raise money there in the 1930s and to proselytize through motion picture content. In reality, while a number of young artists joined the party during the lean Depression years, movies were a collective endeavor, and a lone Communist screenwriter or director had a limited ability to slip subliminal messages from Moscow into the final product. But by magnifying the threat of Communists in Hollywood, HUAC could garner widespread press and public attention, Navasky explains.[17]

The major Hollywood studios panicked and colluded to blacklist those who were or had been Communists, as well as those who refused to cooperate with HUAC. As one unnamed producer told the *Hollywood Reporter* about suspected Communists and uncooperative witnesses, "We'll fire them and let 'em sue."[18] Under the old studio system, actors, writers, and even directors were bound to multiyear contracts, which legally indentured them to big-name operations like Paramount, MGM, Columbia, and Warner Brothers. But Chaplin had run his own studio for years, so no matter what he said to Congress—or refused to say—he couldn't be fired. Nonetheless, these were perilous times, and Chaplin needed to be careful; ticket-buying fans and theater owners could turn their backs on him at any time.

As an uneducated man whose fame was built on slapstick, the intellectually insecure Chaplin routinely showed off his acquired wisdom and waxed eloquent about his unconventional solutions to world problems. In his autobiography, Chaplin proudly recounted friendships with lefties like Salka Viertel, Clifford Odets, Hanns Eisler, and Leon Feuchtwanger that blossomed during the trials when he felt ostracized from his movie star pals[19] He was so close to this crowd that John Howard Lawson, head of the Hollywood branch of the Communist Party, conscripted Chaplin to be a pallbearer at Theodore Dreiser's funeral on January 3, 1945.[20]

Through the newspapers, Chaplin first caught wind that Rep. John Parnell Thomas, the New Jersey Republican who chaired HUAC, planned to subpoena him.[21] The *Hollywood Reporter* revealed that Chaplin and his émigré pal Hanns Eisler, a German-Austrian composer who worked on the music for *Monsieur Verdoux* (and would later write the East German national anthem), were to be the first industry witnesses hauled before the committee in Washington, DC, on September 23, 1947.[22]

By July 15, Eisler had been summoned to appear, but Chaplin had not.[23] Chaplin hired former Hearst reporter turned public relations man to the stars Russell Birdwell and went on the offensive.[24] Birdwell had directed the *Gone with the Wind* publicity campaign and counted Howard Hughes, Carole Lombard, and Marlene Dietrich among his clients.[25] Birdwell was likely behind the telegram that Chaplin dashed off to HUAC and later leaked to newspapers: "From your publicity I note that I am to be 'quizzed' by the House Un-American Activities Committee in September. . . . Forgive me for this premature acceptance of your headlined newspaper invitation."[26] It was a gutsy but perhaps ill-advised move; while it showed that Chaplin would not be cowed by the Washington witch hunt for Communists in Hollywood, it signaled to legislators and policymakers that he was arrogant and unrepentant.

"While you are preparing your engraved subpoena," Chaplin wrote, "I will give you a hint on where I stand. I am not a Communist. I am a peacemonger."[27] Chaplin invited Chairman Thomas to phone him "collect"—to save the committee's time and the taxpayers' money—and ask him pointblank about his politics.[28]

Congressman Thomas ignored the challenge, but on September 19, 1947, in a HUAC press release, Chaplin was listed as one of forty-three actors, writers, and directors—some Communists, some rabid antiCommunists, and others in between—whom the committee intended to summon to Washington.[29] Chaplin was in famous company: Gary Cooper, Walt Disney, Sam Goldwyn, Berthold Brecht, Robert Montgomery, Larry Parks, Ronald Reagan, Dore Schary, Robert Taylor, Dalton Trumbo, and Jack Warner.[30]

Chaplin stuck his thumb further into the eye of the committee by opening *Monsieur Verdoux* in Washington on September 26, just days after Eisler's scheduled appearance. He invited HUAC members to the premiere, but none accepted.[31] But by October, Chairman Thomas backed down. Thomas told reporters, without providing an explanation, "We may complete this case without Charlie Chaplin."[32] HUAC never pursued Chaplin further.

Charles J. Maland, author of *Chaplin and American Culture*, suggests that the Little Tramp's star power remained strong enough that HUAC did not want to give him a spotlight.[33] Much later, right-wing newspaper columnist Westbrook Pegler took credit for talking HUAC out of summoning Chaplin. He wrote that he had warned his friend, a member of the committee, that if Chaplin were subpoenaed he "might make monkeys of them by walking onto the set in his low-comedy pants, hat and cane." It caused the committee members to drop the idea.[34]

While Chaplin was battling with HUAC from his perch in California, Joan was on the other side of the country, playing the role of the contented housewife. In Pittsburgh on July 20, 1947, Joan gave birth to her first son, ten-pound, three-ounce Russell Charles Seck Jr.[35] Somebody alerted the press because she and Carol Ann were photographed for the *Chicago Tribune* smiling over the bassinet of the baby. The photo was taken after Joan came home from the hospital and had had the opportunity to groom. Her lush, shoulder-length wavy hair was nicely styled, her long red nails were neatly manicured, and her makeup was freshly applied. Her daughter, in a frilly party dress, stood next to Joan and smiled adoringly at her baby half-brother.[36]

Although Joan was still booked for the occasional stage gig—she sang at the Flatbush Theatre in Brooklyn over the weekend of January 2, 1948— her singing voice was reserved for entertaining her children while doing the dishes, one of her favorite tunes being "I'll Be Seeing You in All the Old Familiar Places."[37] Pittsburgh life was tame compared to Hollywood life, where millionaires in evening clothes had twirled Joan around dance floors at nightclubs. Husband Seck donned his dark uniform every morning and spent his workday punching passengers' tickets on the sixty-four-mile stretch of the Pittsburgh & Lake Erie Railroad. He did not smoke or drink, nor was he college educated, but he had a curious mind and sophisticated tastes. He listened to classical music in the modest family apartment on an elaborate home audio system, read poetry as well as Greek and Roman mythology, and enjoyed the opera and museums. He collected and refurbished antique furniture and Tiffany lamps. Seck's attraction to his wife was her beauty; he appreciated her looks the same way he appreciated fine art, music, and collectibles.[38]

Once Joan settled in Pittsburgh, neither she nor Chaplin nor the lawyers who'd serviced them over the years had the stomach to continue the bitter fight over money. Early in 1948 the parties quietly consented to a $25-a-week increase for Carol Ann, bringing her weekly support to $100, or about $1,070 in today's dollars, which was quickly approved by yet another superior court judge to whom the case had been shuffled.[39]

But a husband, children, and financial security were not enough to keep Joan tied to one place. She fell victim to her wanderlust—or perhaps her mental illness. Sometime after Christmas 1947—perhaps following her stage appearance in Brooklyn—Joan abandoned Pittsburgh forever with four-year-old Carol Ann and her infant son and moved to Mexico.[40] When reporters caught up with her in Mexico City in May 1948, she insisted she was there for a vacation and hadn't decided how long she would stay.[41] Joan's children were too little to understand why they left Pittsburgh or why they were always on the move. But as long as they were with their mother, they felt safe and happy.[42]

By October 18, 1948, Joan was back in California, giving birth at the Inglewood Women's Hospital to her last child, a son she named Stephen Irving Seck. On the birth certificate, she listed her husband as the child's father but gave her permanent address as 824 Calle de Arboles in Redondo Beach, where she said she had been living since June.[43] Two weeks after Stephen's birth, Joan officially separated from her husband, although he visited them in California from time to time.[44]

Once she put down more or less permanent roots in Los Angeles County, Joan chose not to live with her mother. Gertrude Berry was pushing fifty when Joan came back to town. Gertrude had a job in local government and shared a two-bedroom, single-family home at 3039 Chadwick Drive in the El Sereno neighborhood of East Los Angeles with its owner, Elizabeth Baltes, a widow who worked at the county assessor's office.[45] Gertrude never remarried after divorcing Joan's stepfather, John Berry, in 1942.

John Berry, who had been released from Folsom State Prison in 1945 following a forgery conviction, returned to New York to continue his life of crime. Berry used his stepdaughter's stage name, "Barry," when he was arrested at Penn Station in Manhattan on October 21, 1948, carrying a woman's handbag with $206 inside that he stole from a passenger aboard a New York to Washington, DC, sleeper car.[46]

Joan moved with her three children into a small adobe house at 1725 Stanford Avenue in Redondo Beach with Eleanor Dorothy Jericho, an unmarried Pittsburgh artist, and three Siamese cats.[47] A 50" x 150" piece of land in Redondo Beach could go for as little as $1,000 back then, or about $11,600 in today's dollars.[48] Joan probably met her in Pittsburgh, where Eleanor grew up, but the nature of their relationship is unknown.[49] The 1950 federal census lists Joan Seck, age twenty-nine, as the nonworking, married head of the Redondo Beach household. Jericho, age thirty-four, is described as Joan's "partner," whose occupation is listed as a "draftsman" for a building contractor.[50]

While Joan was doing her best to live a quiet, albeit unconventional, life with Eleanor and the children, anti-Communist hysteria eclipsed the common sense of the nation, and the figurative bullet that Chaplin had dodged in 1947 finally struck him. His own studio wouldn't blacklist him, but the federal government could oust him. Chaplin's loyalty to the United States had been suspect as early as April 1922, when "an unidentified informant" told the FBI that at a dinner for Upton Sinclair, Chaplin "was present as one of the representatives of the radical movement in Southern California."[51] A "reliable confidential informant" also told the bureau that Chaplin hosted a reception later that year for Communist Party leader William Z. Foster, attended by what FBI agents called "Parlor Bolsheviki."[52]

The FBI "evidence" that Chaplin was Red was flimsy. It consisted of rumor, old newspaper clippings, and guilt by association. Chaplin's former codefendant Robert Arden, who broke with him after they were indicted, told FBI Special Agent Hood that "Chaplin was both a millionaire and a Communist," without offering any basis for his opinion.[53] Elsewhere in Chaplin's FBI file was an unattributed item from a Hopper column in which she claimed that Chaplin "contributed $25,000 to the Communist cause."[54] Chaplin's friend, the author and magazine publisher Max Eastman, dismissed the idea and said the closest Chaplin came to contributing to the "cause" was when he gave Eastman $1,000 to help subsidize his Socialist magazine, *The Liberator*, after Eastman's bookkeeper absconded with the publication's funds.[55]

There is no doubt Chaplin flirted with the *idea* of Communism, but there is no credible evidence he was a party member. Chaplin loved to spout off at dinner parties; besides boring his guests, his greatest sin may have been that he, too, was a "Parlor Bolsheviki." Before the Red Scare the government never thought he was much of a threat; it spied on him and built files about his alleged subversive activities but never sought to deport him. Chaplin took trips outside the United States three times since he became a permanent resident in 1912, and prior to leaving he dutifully applied for a reentry permit as required of all aliens who leave the country and wish to return. Each time he was allowed back in without any problem.[56]

But that changed in March 1947, when FBI Director Hoover insisted that Chaplin's name be flagged as a security risk.[57] That directive generated a twenty-four-page, single-spaced report that recounted the rumors and poorly sourced claims about Chaplin's Communist connections that had been accumulating dust in his FBI file for twenty-five years and rehashed the sordid details of the Joan Barry case.[58]

On February 26, 1948, hoping to take Oona and their children to Europe for a leisurely four-month vacation, Chaplin began the process of obtaining a reentry permit, which was granted two months later.[59] But suddenly, and without explanation, Chaplin decided against leaving. Perhaps the tone of an interview he had with the Immigration and Nationalization Service spooked him. On Saturday, April 17, 1948, Deputy INS Commissioner John P. Boyd showed up on Summit Drive with a stenographer, placed Chaplin under oath, and grilled him for four hours about his loyalty to the United States, his contacts with Communists, his politics, and his sexual habits.[60] Chaplin's answers were guarded and evasive.[61]

"Have you ever committed adultery?" Boyd asked, well aware Chaplin was sleeping with Joan in 1941 and '42 while he was still legally married to Paulette, assuming, of course, that Chaplin and Goddard ever *were* married.[62]

"I have never been charged with adultery," Chaplin responded.

"That isn't the question, Mr. Chaplin. Have you ever committed adultery?" Boyd asked again.

"How do you define that?" asked Chaplin coyly.[63] After Boyd explained how he defined it—having a sexual relationship with one woman while married to another—Chaplin denied he'd done so.[64] He also denied conspiring to procure an abortion for Joan, even though the INS had good reason to believe otherwise based on information they'd obtained from the nurses who'd assisted Dr. Tweedie with the abortions.[65]

Moving on, Boyd pressed Chaplin to explain a statement he'd made to a journalist in which, when asked if he was a Communist sympathizer, Chaplin had replied, "That has to be qualified."[66] Chaplin's convoluted response meandered around the subject. "During the war, everybody was more or less a Communist sympathizer. . . . I never read a book about Communism. I don't know anything about it. I never read Karl Marx or anything like that. My interpretation of Communist was Russia. It wouldn't naturally be Russia under the old regime, but as they are Communist and they are fighting for what they feel is their cause, I naturally felt they put up a very good cause."[67]

Perhaps the most honest—and logical—statement Chaplin made to Boyd was when he said, "I am sure that I am not a Communist and my name will never be connected with any Communist. I have $30,000,000 worth of business—what am I talking about Communism for?"[68]

Regardless of his tone during the interview, Boyd didn't have a legal leg to stand on to bar Chaplin from the country. The only basis for deporting Chaplin would have been if he'd been convicted of a felony involving moral turpitude. An INS official noted: "The file carries a number of newspaper reports concerning the alien's [Chaplin's] marital difficulties and his affair with the Barry girl but . . . nowhere in the file is there any evidence which would justify the initiation of deportation proceedings at this time because of crime."[69] Similarly, there was no basis to deport Chaplin due to his failure to become a citizen because there is no "obligation upon any alien lawfully admitted for permanent residence to become a citizen. . . ."[70] And, Chaplin's alleged "Communistic leanings" didn't warrant deportation either: "[I]t is required by law that we establish membership or affiliation in a proscribed organization. The file now before us does not contain any proof as to these factors."[71]

But after being put through the ringer, followed by a demand from the IRS for a $1.5 million bond if he left the country to cover a claim for $1 million in unpaid taxes, Chaplin thought better of leaving.[72] For the next four and a half years, he remained in Beverly Hills, warming to the role of family man, which he didn't do the first time around with his sons by Lita Grey. Oona soon gave birth to two more children, Josephine in 1949 and Victoria in 1951, while Chaplin worked on his semiautobiographical movie swansong, *Limelight*.[73] Little did he know the movie also would be his swansong to America.

"A MINOR CASE OF ANXIETY"

Chaplin made the fateful decision to hold the premiere of *Limelight* in his native London. He finished the movie in May 1952 and planned to return home in the fall for the opening, park the children in boarding school, and take Oona on the grand tour of Europe before returning to the United States the following spring. He applied for a reentry permit and in the summer of 1952 was granted one by the U.S. government.[1]

London was the perfect place to showcase *Limelight*, a paean to the bygone days of the British music hall, where Chaplin and his family got their start in show business. Chaplin plays Calvero, the once famous but now washed-up alcoholic music hall star (like his real father) who saves a struggling ballerina from suicide. Afterward, her career thrives while Calvero's continues its decline. A tentative romance blossoms, but the ballet dancer, played by Claire Bloom, falls in love with a younger, more suitable mate played by Chaplin's handsome real-life son, Sydney (a plot perhaps betraying Chaplin's deep-seated fears about losing Oona, who was thirty-six years his junior). The movie ends at a benefit concert for the aged Calvero during which he drops dead of a heart attack backstage.

On September 5, 1952, the night before Chaplin left Beverly Hills for London, Durant hosted a goodbye clambake for him. The next day, which was hot and sticky with temperatures in the low 90s, Durant drove Chaplin and Oona to Union Station in Los Angeles, where the couple boarded the Santa Fe Chief for New York.[2] Arriving in New York three days later, Chaplin kept a low profile at his posh Fifth Avenue hotel, the Sherry-Netherland, because he was ducking yet another subpoena, this one involving a law-suit by a disgruntled ex-employee of United Artists, the company he still owned with Mary Pickford. If he'd been served, it might have kept him from making the trip and changed the course of the rest of his life.[3]

The day before sailing for Europe, Chaplin visited Richard Avedon's photo studio at 640 Madison Avenue between Fifty-Ninth and Sixtieth Streets. Avedon had been angling to take Chaplin's picture for months; the artistic result of their finally getting together was a famous shot of Chaplin smiling wickedly into the camera while placing a finger on each side of his head to resemble the devil.[4]

And then it was time to go. On the late summer day of September 17, 1952, still avoiding the process server, Chaplin snuck aboard the Queen Elizabeth ocean liner in New York Harbor at five o'clock in the morning and hid in his stateroom until the ship left at five o'clock in the evening.[5] Former Hearst reporter Harry Crocker, who'd played Chaplin's rival for Merna Kennedy in *The Circus* and had been a witness at his wedding to Oona, came along as press spokesman.[6] There were 1,432 passengers traveling to Cherbourg, France, with some, like the Chaplin family, going farther to Southampton.[7] Once the liner left the harbor, Chaplin felt relaxed for the first time in years. He and Oona lounged on deck chairs and breathed the fresh sea air while their children played in the care of their ever-present nannies who had escorted them from California to New York by train to join their parents for the European journey.[8]

Two days later it was clear and calm over the Atlantic Ocean.[9] While Chaplin dined on larded beef with Oona, Crocker, pianist Artur Rubinstein, his wife, Nela, and Broadway producer Adolph Green, a white-coated steward rushed to their table and whispered urgently into Crocker's ear. Could he please come to the office of the ship's captain, Commodore G. E. Cove?[10]

There, four transatlantic messages awaited him. The first was a shocker: President Truman's attorney general, James P. McGranery, announced that Chaplin's reentry permit had been revoked. The other three were from reporters who'd already caught wind of the announcement. News traveled fast; the ship-to-shore phone was ringing off the hook. Now it was Crocker's turn to send a note with the steward—tell Chaplin to excuse himself quietly and hurry to Crocker's cabin.[11]

The attorney general's announcement struck Chaplin like a bolt of lightning. Stranded in the middle of the ocean, with his American wife and their four young children, the life he'd known for forty years had been swept away, as if on a wave. Chaplin and Crocker put their emotions aside and their heads together to craft a response that would not antagonize the government if Chaplin harbored any hope to ever return home. The result was a terse statement, probably drafted by Crocker. "Through the proper procedure I applied for a re-entry permit, which I was given in good faith and which I accepted in good faith. Therefore, I assume that the United States government will recognize its validity."[12]

When Chaplin's grown son, Charles Jr., heard the news, he saw things more clearly. "Well, guess I'll never see Pop again," he said.[13]

Although sandbagged by Uncle Sam, Chaplin should not have been surprised. The country was in the middle of the Cold War, the Red Scare, and a political turn to the right regarding what we now call "family values." Chaplin had thumbed his nose at all three. And, as if all that weren't bad enough, he'd stopped making the Little Tramp movies the public loved. Like a guest who stays too long at the party, Chaplin's American hosts finally had enough of him.

Ironically, Chaplin's misfortunes shared the front pages of newspapers with those of vice presidential candidate Richard Nixon, once a member of HUAC and the embodiment of conservative America. Nixon had been the beneficiary of an $18,000 slush fund, and he was about to make his infamous September 23, 1952, "Checkers Speech," which would sway a reluctant Dwight Eisenhower to keep him on the GOP ticket.[14]

The Queen Elizabeth chugged into Cherbourg at 12:56 p.m. on September 22.[15] Reporters stampeded onto the ship and elbowed their way into the buffet room, where they peppered Chaplin with questions.[16] The Hollywood star met the press in a dark three-piece suit, white shirt, and light tie, which he polished off with a carefully folded pocket square.[17] Years later, Chaplin would write in his autobiography that the Cherbourg news conference was "dreary and exhausting."[18]

While in Cherbourg, Chaplin and his family strode the deck of the ship like royalty and pretended they didn't have a care in the world. British Pathé made a newsreel; Chaplin appears relaxed and smiling in it as he holds court with the assembled journalists.[19] The New York Times reported that he was "in a jovial, holiday mood."[20] The six of them—Oona, looking older than twenty-seven with her black hair severely parted in the center and knotted in a bun at the nape of her neck, wearing a boxy, matronly jacket; Chaplin in a dark suit; and their four children in their Sunday best—

leaned against the side of the ship and waved to the press and passengers. Chaplin, the moody introvert, kissed his children for the cameras and cheerfully signed autographs.[21]

The Queen Elizabeth left at 7:28 p.m. for the six-hour journey to Southampton, which turned into one long party.[22] Some thirty reporters who'd hopped on in France joined Chaplin for cocktails and were treated to an impromptu concert when he pulled up a seat at the piano and played tunes from *Limelight*.[23] The ship arrived in Southampton at 1:25 a.m.[24] After disembarking, the family boarded a train for the seventy-mile journey to Waterloo Station in London, where one thousand fans were waiting.[25] Like a visiting head of state, Chaplin stepped off the train in a formal morning suit. He was circumspect with waiting reporters. When asked if he might settle in Europe, Chaplin replied, "I'm still domiciled in the U.S.A."[26] From there, the Chaplins were bundled into a car for the five-minute drive to their suite at the Savoy Hotel.[27]

Back home, reaction to the attorney general's announcement was mixed. Right-wing columnist Westbrook Pegler praised McGranery's action, calling it "the first honest show of initiative against the Red front of Hollywood by the Department of Justice in the entire campaign against the treason."[28] Other writers insinuated that politics were at play. "We have no sympathy for Chaplin," wrote the editors of the Santa Monica *Evening Outlook*. Nonetheless, they questioned the timing of the government's actions against him. The editors continued: "The fact that Chaplin has behaved himself in recent years, and that the Justice Department dropped all charges against him . . . makes the present Department action look like persecution for political purposes."[29] The venerable Bosley Crowther of the *New York Times* wrote: "It is hard to imagine anybody less deserving to be exposed to the suspicion of being an enemy of this country than this famous and accomplished man."[30]

There was no legal basis to deny Chaplin's reentry. But now that the attorney general had done it, immigration officials scrambled to find evidence to back up the boss. INS investigators fanned out to reinterview the usual suspects who had been questioned a decade earlier by the Los Angeles County district attorney and the FBI during the Joan Barry investigation. Their first stop on September 30 was to Joan's home in Redondo Beach. This time, she had no intention of helping the government nail Chaplin; either she feared he'd cut off her child support if he couldn't return to the United States or she still harbored affection for him.[31]

Joan was vague about the details of their decade-old affair. "[A]s a result of these sexual relations you had with Mr. Chaplin, you became pregnant some time in 1941?" the investigator asked.

"As far as I can remember, yes."[32]

"Now Mrs. Seck, do you remember when you first told Mr. Chaplin that you were pregnant?"

"Gentlemen, I can't remember right now. It was such a long time ago," she replied.[33]

When Joan was asked about Chaplin's connections to Communism, she insisted there were none. "[H]e had no real feeling for it [communism] whatsoever except that he was a great humanitarian."[34]

But some things about Joan didn't change. Having had their first exposure to her, INS investigators were taken aback. They described her as "very erratic and unsatisfactory as a witness." In a memo to the file, an unnamed investigator continued, "She cries and paces the floor and it is impossible to get a straight statement from her."[35] Ultimately, it didn't matter how erratic Joan was; she refused to sign the transcript of her statement to the INS and bolted out of California.[36]

Investigators were hitting brick walls with other witnesses too. Dr. Tweedie, who had performed Joan's abortions, had died seven months before the Chaplins left for England.[37] Durant was interviewed on October 3 with Chaplin lawyer Loyd Wright at his side. Durant steadfastly denied any knowledge about—or involvement in—Joan's abortions.[38] Similarly, efforts to find anybody with firsthand knowledge that Chaplin was a Communist proved futile.[39] Chaplin's former chauffeur and confidential secretary, Toraichi Kono, happy to spill the beans about Chaplin's bad behavior with women, claimed to know nothing about Chaplin's political opinions, although one would think he'd heard Chaplin discuss them during the many years he'd worked for him.[40]

Marion Davies was interviewed on November 17, 1952, and proved to be one tough cookie. Try as he might, the INS investigator could not get Davies to admit she and Chaplin were ever intimate. "We are going to ask you questions that might be embarrassing," he warned her. "Any questions that would embarrass me, would only if I were guilty, but I am not," she retorted.[41]

The investigator asked her if she had ever been an overnight guest in Chaplin's home: "I have my own home, why should I stay there?" she replied.[42]

"Miss Davies, our office has information to the effect that during the period from 1924 to 1931, that you, to use the common term, had an affair with Mr. Chaplin, is that correct?"

"That is a lie, but how can they prove it, were they there?"[43]

Nonetheless, the attorney general called Chaplin "an unsavory character" at a news conference on October 2, 1952. "There have been public charges that Chaplin was a member of the Communist Party, grave moral charges, and the making of statements that would indicate a leering, sneering attitude toward a country whose hospitality has enriched him," McGranery said.[44]

The November 1952 presidential election between World War II hero Republican Gen. Dwight D. Eisenhower and the Democratic candidate, Gov. Adlai Stevenson, probably played into McGranery's decision to go after Chaplin. Truman's lame-duck attorney general may have been hoping to boost the Democratic ticket by taking a tough stand against the so-called Communist menace. While Chaplin was meeting with reporters in Cherbourg, Ike held a news conference accusing Stevenson of "faintness of heart" when it came to foreign policy. The Democrats could score big points by flexing their muscles against a Parlor Bolsheviki.[45]

On October 16, 1952, *Limelight* opened at the Odeon in Leicester Square with proceeds going to the Royal London Society for the Blind. Chaplin dressed in white tie and tails; Princess Margaret attended in a white gown with a wide crinoline skirt and over-the-elbow white gloves. Outside, two hundred police officers held back an estimated ten thousand fans.[46] The European love affair with Chaplin continued in France, too, where thousands greeted him at the Paris premiere of the movie. He was made an officer of the French Legion of Honor, the highest distinction available to foreigners.[47] In contrast, back in the states, pressure from the American Legion caused theater owners to cancel showings of *Limelight*.[48]

Chaplin stood a strong chance of winning his bid to reenter the country, but the thought of another expensive legal battle and the nerve-racking media circus that would accompany it may have been too much to bear. On November 17, Oona boarded a plane alone for New York and from there she went to California. She attended a United Artists' board meeting, closed up the house on Summit Drive, sacked the servants, cleaned out the Chaplin bank accounts and safe deposit boxes, and returned to England.[49] Louella Parsons reported that Oona had transferred as much as $5 million in cash to a British bank.[50]

With his fortune safely out of the country, Chaplin marched into the

American Embassy in Geneva on April 10, 1953, and surrendered his reentry permit.[51] He bought a mansion in Switzerland.[52] On June 11, 1953, the INS closed its investigation into Chaplin because it was clear he wasn't coming back.[53] In August 1953, Oona gave birth to their fifth child in Switzerland, a son they named Eugene, after her long-estranged father. The following February, Oona renounced her American citizenship.[54] Chaplin sold his Hollywood film studio in October 1953 for about $700,000 ($6.7 million today).[55] The family's exile was complete.

About a year before Chaplin left America, Joan divorced Russell Seck. In her complaint filed in Los Angeles Superior Court on May 27, 1952, Joan cited "extreme cruelty" as the grounds, without any supporting facts, and asked for custody of their sons. They had no property to split, and they'd lived apart longer than they'd lived together.[56] Joan remained a troubled woman and a lost soul, plus she was on her own again with no job and three young children. Chaplin diligently made his $100-a-week payments, but they were earmarked for Carol Ann.

A week after her interview with the INS, Joan applied for a new passport. On the application, for reasons known only to her, she falsely gave June 1, 1920, as her birthday rather than the real date of May 24, 1920. She told authorities she intended to visit Ireland, England, France, Switzerland, and Italy, planning to leave in December 1952 and stay for a year.[57] Maybe Joan was still obsessed with Chaplin and harbored the delusional idea to follow him to Europe. Or perhaps she was headed elsewhere and wanted to throw the government off her trail.

Before the Chaplin investigation was closed, Joan responded to a subpoena to appear at the INS District Office in Los Angeles on October 28.[58] Shortly afterward, Joan disappeared.[59] The government rightly suspected she and her children would find their way to Mexico City. Mexican authorities kept tabs on her at the U.S. government's request with the skill of the Keystone Cops in an old Mack Sennett movie. First, they were watching the wrong woman, forty-seven-year-old Mary Mathews Griebell from Jersey City.[60] (Joan's birth name was Mary Louise Gribble). And the only picture of Joan that Mexican investigators had to work with was at least eight years old.[61]

While in Mexico, Joan tried to rekindle her acting career and perhaps thought her past association with A. C. Blumenthal would help. It didn't.[62] Seventy years later, Carol Ann recalled little about their Mexican sojourn, other than attending school with Spanish-speaking classmates where she didn't know a word of the language. And for years after her return, she struggled in school because the trip had interrupted her education.[63]

When nothing panned out for Joan in Mexico after months, she showed up at the American Embassy in Mexico City, broke and desperate, to renounce her citizenship, although how becoming a Mexican citizen would have improved her life is unclear. On March 17, 1953, the American attaché E. DeWitt Marshall sent a telegram to the INS district director in Los Angeles: "Joan Barry stranded and attempting to renaunce [sic] USC here are you interested in her return."[64] The reply: "NOT INTERESTED THIS TIME RETURN OF JOAN BARRY."[65] It seems the government had no further use for Joan, so it abandoned her—like most of the men in her life had done when they grew tired of her.[66] Shortly before leaving Mexico in June 1953, Joan wrote to Chaplin's attorney Loyd Wright to tell him that she now accepted the science that determined Chaplin could not be the father of her daughter and wanted to contact the court to ask that he be permitted to discontinue paying her child support.[67] She never got around to it.

Unmoored in Mexico City, Joan somehow found her way back to Los Angeles and was reduced to seeking charity for her children. On Friday, June 26, 1953, with an attorney from Joe Scott's firm accompanying her, Joan checked herself into the psychiatric ward of Harbor General Hospital. Her lawyer, William B. Esterman, blamed Joan's breakdown on her inability to provide equally for her three children. The so-called Chaplin child was well cared for on $100 a week, but Joan's estranged husband didn't have that kind of money to support their two sons.[68] Once reporters caught wind that Joan was in the psych ward, they raced there to interview her, but Scott refused to permit it.[69] After three days of tests, doctors found no evidence Joan was psychotic and released her.[70]

In this crisis, Scott had a conflict of interest. His client was Carol Ann, and in seeking to protect her, he was forced to take a position that might hurt Joan. Gertrude Berry wanted her daughter involuntarily committed because Joan had sought to renounce her American citizenship and suffered unspecified "idiosyncrasies."[71] Whether Joan's mother was acting in her daughter's best interest is questionable. What caring mother would possibly want to subject her daughter to the draconian treatments inflicted on psychiatric patients at the time—including insulin shock therapy or even lobotomies—because of "idiosyncrasies"?[72]

There was no love lost between Gertrude and her daughter. Gertrude was appalled by Joan's sexual behavior and may have seen forced mental health treatment as the behavior modification—or punishment—her daughter needed. Carol Ann remembered that when she became old enough to date, Gertrude would sternly remind her, "Don't be a slut like your mother."[73] It was an ugly, ominous message that contributed to erad-icating any connection that Carol Ann had to her mother. And once Joan was locked away in a psychiatric hospital, Carol Ann's $100 a week would be under Gertrude's control, or so she may have thought.

Esterman, representing Joan, denied there was anything ailing her beyond "a minor case of anxiety" caused by financial pressures and a crash diet on which she had lost seventy pounds in a just few months.[74] But Esterman's assessment may have been as unreliable as Joan's moth-er's. A weight loss that drastic could have meant Joan was suffering from anorexia rather than a "minor case of anxiety." There was a family history of mental illness—her father had shot himself to death, and her paternal grandmother committed suicide by blowing out a gas lamp and taking deep breaths. Joan's litany of mental health symptoms—attention defi-cit disorder; abuse of alcohol and sedatives; violent verbal outbursts; wild mood swings; scattered thinking and speech; suicide attempts; and stalking behavior—pointed to something far more serious. Nonetheless, Esterman said he would fight efforts by Gertrude to commit Joan.[75]

Unfortunately, on a sticky July night, a month after Joan's first visit to the mental ward, police found her wandering shoeless on the street at one thirty in the morning. She was incoherent. They took her to Harbor General Hospital, where doctors said she was fine and released her to the police who had brought her there. They drove her to her home in Redondo Beach. Two hours later, the same officers found Joan again wan-dering barefoot along 190th Street in Torrance, nearly five miles from her house, with blistered feet, talking to herself. The officers returned her to the hospital.[76]

With Seck in Pittsburgh, the tragic fallout of Joan's mental breakdown for her children was that they were placed in juvenile hall—an experi-ence that Carol Ann still considers among the worst of her life. There, she was separated from her brothers while strangers stripped her clothes off and put her in a shower. She had some vague sense that "bad kids" were sent there. The fate of Carol Ann and her brothers—like Jackie Coogan in *The Kid*, Paulette Goddard's siblings in *Modern Times*, and Charlie and Syd Chaplin in real life—was placed in the hands of child welfare officials.[77]

Joan and Gertrude were headed for another one of their showdowns.

Joan refused to voluntarily commit herself and Gertrude had seventy-two hours under California law—the maximum time Joan could be held in a psychiatric facility without a court order—to decide whether to seek to have her daughter involuntarily committed.[78]

Gertrude opted for involuntary commitment. [79]After a brief hearing before Los Angeles Superior Court Judge William P. Haughton, Joan was committed to Patton State Hospital, a mental institution. Psychiatrists determined she suffered from schizophrenia. After the judge made his decision, Joan said, "I realize I need treatment."[80] The karma had come full circle; Joan's and Chaplin's lives were once again entwined, with both of them in forced exile.

EPILOGUE
*"BITTERNESS IS A VERY HARD THING
TO KEEP UP"*

In 1962, a decade after he was banished from America, seventy-three-year-old Charlie Chaplin and U.S. Secretary of State Dean Rusk were awarded honorary doctoral degrees from Oxford University. The Little Tramp was recognized as "a man who sympathizes with the underdog." At a champagne party before the ceremony, Chaplin and Rusk shook hands and exchanged toasts. "There was no bitterness between us, no bitterness at all," remarked Chaplin afterward. "Bitterness is a very hard thing to keep up," he said graciously, and wisely.[1]

But a few years earlier in 1957, Chaplin was still bitter when he made *A King in New York*.[2] In it, he plays deposed King Shahdov, who arrives penniless in New York with grand ideas for peaceful uses of atomic power, only to end up a product pitchman on TV. In scenes ripped from Chaplin's own real-life headlines, the king is photographed being fingerprinted by immigration officials and is hauled before the House Committee on Un-American Activities. Chaplin's son Michael plays an insufferable child who spews Marxist propaganda until the government breaks his spirit by forcing him to denounce his left-leaning parents.

The film was not released in the United States, but the *New York Times*, surveying reviews in European papers, pronounced Chaplin's eighty-first movie a flop. London critics called it "the work of a very bitter man" and "clumsy political satire."[3] When the film was finally distributed in America twenty years later, critics appreciated it as another entry in the Chaplin oeuvre. The movie "sags below the rest of his work" but is "important to see," wrote Nora Sayre in the *New York Times*.[4] A decade later, Chaplin fared even worse with *A Countess from Hong Kong*, a recycled project from the 1930s once intended for Paulette Goddard. It was a tired, miscast farce with Marlon Brando and Sophia Loren in the leads. "So the dismal truth is it is awful," wrote Bosley Crowther in the *New York Times*.[5] Chaplin's moviemaking days were over.

Off-screen, Chaplin lived like "A king in Switzerland." After years of dickering with the IRS, he moved to the tax haven.[6] He, Oona, their eight children born between 1944 and 1962, and the army of servants needed to take care of them lived at the Manoir de Ban, on thirty-seven acres in Corsier-sur-Vevey, overlooking Lake Geneva. Chaplin bought the place in 1953 at a fire-sale price—reportedly about $100,000, or $968,000 today— from an American whose wife had died falling down the stairs there.[7] As if on a movie set, Chaplin and Oona recreated Beverly Hills, adding a built-in swimming pool, tennis court, and barbecue grill.[8] They were as "Californian as two avocados," remarked a profile writer in the *Saturday Evening Post*.[9]

In his autobiography, Chaplin wrote of the joy he'd found in marriage to Oona. Her closest friend, Carol Matthau, who married actor Walter Matthau after divorcing William Saroyan, called Chaplin "the most in-love man I ever saw."[10] Charles Chaplin Jr. believed that his father "felt security at last in a woman's love."[11] Oona's biographer, Jane Scovell, wrote that Oona "wallowed in the sheer joy of being Mrs. Charles Spencer Chaplin."[12] One of the few dissenting voices came from wife number 3, Paulette Goddard, who coincidentally lived near the couple. In her dual biography of Goddard and her then husband Erich Maria Remarque, *Opposite Attraction*, author Julie Gilbert revealed that in a gossipy letter to Remarque, Goddard claimed that Chaplin routinely slipped away to visit a young mistress in a nearby village. "[He] can't stand all those kids at home."[13]

By the mid- to late 1960s, Chaplin's relationship with his children bore the strains of many baby boom–era fathers and their teenagers, except that at Chaplin's advanced age, the generation gap was a two-generation gap. Michael Chaplin called him "a bit of a handful as a father."[14] The title of Michael's memoir, *I Couldn't Smoke the Grass on My Father's Lawn*, published in 1966, said it all. Oona was a loving mother, but her biographer wrote: "Had all the Chaplins been placed on a sinking ship, the cry from Oona's lips surely would have been, 'Charlie First!'"[15]

The French have an expression, *coup de vieux*, which literally means a "slap" or "blow" of old age, an idiom for sudden aging. Chaplin suffered from a *coup de vieux*, having aged markedly between his bit role in 1967 as a ship's steward in *A Countess from Hong Kong* and the 1972 Academy Awards ceremonies when he shuffled on-stage to accept his Oscar. And, on March 4, 1975, when Queen Elizabeth knighted him at Buckingham Palace, tapping him on both shoulders with a sword and pronouncing him "Sir Charles Chaplin," he was in a wheelchair and unable to bow to Her Highness.[16]

Chaplin had been considered for knighthood in 1956, but the behavior that contributed to his ouster from the United States also gave the queen pause. But by 1971, attitudes had changed there too. The British ambassador to the United States told the queen's advisers that "a lot of water has flowed under the bridge since 1956" and that a knighthood "would no longer arouse great indignation or the storm of criticism."[17]

The Little Fellow and his family never fully accepted that he was partly to blame for his fate. Chaplin claimed he was punished for being a "nonconformist."[18] His son Michael blamed his father's troubles on the Red Scare. "America was going through one of its periodical flurries of mass hysteria, and Charlie Chaplin was one of its top whipping boys."[19]

Chaplin died in his sleep on Christmas Day 1977. He was eighty-eight.[20] He had been felled by a stroke in 1976 that left him progressively weaker.[21] The Little Tramp's death inspired well-deserved tributes from around the world.[22] But the headline writer on Chaplin's obituary published in the *New York Times* demonstrated better insight than Chaplin or his son about his troubles: "The Comedian Had Crises with Women, the Talkies, Taxes and Cold War Politics."[23] Three months after his funeral, in a bizarre, almost slapstick turn of events that Chaplin would have appreciated, his coffin was snatched from the cemetery in Vevey in the dead of night and hidden in a nearby wheat field. A pair of bumbling auto mechanics were arrested after demanding a hefty ransom, which Lady Chaplin refused to pay.[24]

Loved and protected by Chaplin for thirty-four years, his fifty-two-year-old widow found that her lifetime of devotion came at a heavy price. As Mrs. Chaplin, Oona had given up her country, her youth, her acting ambitions, and any hope of reconciling with her distant and difficult father. Eugene O'Neill died on November 27, 1953, without having acknowledged his daughter since her wedding a decade earlier.[25] Despite Oona's abandonment by her father, the family curse never left her. The famous playwright had suffered from alcoholism and had been institutionalized.[26] His oldest son and Oona's half-brother, Eugene O'Neill Jr., killed himself by slitting his wrists and ankles with a razor in 1950.[27] Oona's brother Shane was a drug addict who either fell or jumped from the window of his fourth-floor apartment in New York City, less than a year before Chaplin died.[28]

Oona had her own problem with alcohol. Attentive observers noticed that she'd begun drinking even before Chaplin's decline with a not so secret spot of whiskey in her teacup now and again. "[W]hen at last death came to Charles Spencer Chaplin, the era of the teacup ended—Oona stepped out of her protective shelter and emerged as a full-fledged alcoholic," wrote Scovell.[29] Oona's former daughter-in-law, Patrice, who was married to Michael Chaplin from 1965 to 1973, claimed to have caught Oona in the bathroom drinking whiskey that she'd stashed in a liquid soap bottle.[30] Chaplin biographer Kenneth S. Lynn said Oona drank "with a truly O'Neillian compulsion."[31] Lady Oona Chaplin died of pancreatic cancer on September 27, 1991.[32]

Carol Ann Berry, legally Chaplin's daughter, never saw him again after the paternity proceedings ended. Not long after Chaplin was ousted from the country, California adopted a version of the Uniform Act on Blood Tests to Determine Paternity. Had the law been in effect in 1944, the Chaplin case would have ended the day all three doctors determined that blood tests excluded him as Carol Ann's father. The jury and the public may have regarded the paternity verdict as Chaplin's comeuppance, but in legal circles it was considered a miscarriage of justice.

"The *Chaplin* verdict is contrary to science, nature and truth; it bears no relation to fact," wrote New York attorney Sidney B. Schatkin in a law review article.[33] "Of all legal proceedings, the issue in a paternity case is peculiarly within the realm of science, and if truth is to be ascertained and justice achieved, the aid proffered by science must not be rejected by the courts," he added.[34] Five years later, Cornell University law professor Arthur John Keeffe wrote: "It brings discredit upon the legal profession and makes a mockery of a court of justice to permit a jury to accept or reject in accordance with their prejudices a fact capable of exact scientific determination."[35] Continuing in the *Stanford Law Review*, Keeffe wrote, "There is no place in America for unjust decisions of this sort where a defendant is made by judicial decree to support a baby that is not his."[36]

As early as 1935, New York was the first state to admit evidence of blood grouping tests in paternity trials. Under New York law, if there was no dispute as to the test results among the medical experts, then the legal proceedings ended. Between 1935 and 1950, seven states enacted similar laws—California was not one of them. However, even in these states, some judges left the decision in the hands of juries but would grant new trials if they ignored the science and got it wrong. "This overwhelming disregard of *fact* is appalling," wrote another law review author.[37] "In effect, the courts are conceding the reliability of blood grouping tests on the one hand and allowing juries to find against them on the other."[38]

Looking back, Berkeley law professor Andrea Roth called the situation "kind of crazy."[39] In an article about the intersection of science and law, Professor Roth blamed the Chaplin verdict (and others involving less famous fathers) on the exalted view of the jury system in American law. Jurors are considered "uniquely good at determining credibility," and judges are loath to cede jury decision-making to "a futuristic alternative," like a scientific test, she wrote.[40]

This discontent in the legal community had to be addressed. The National Conference of Commissioners on Uniform State Laws was established in 1892 to draft nonpartisan legislation to bring clarity to state laws. Conference members are practicing lawyers, judges, law professors, and legislators.[41] In 1952 the commissioners debated how to address the admissibility of blood typing evidence in paternity trials. They recognized that allowing juries to override the undisputed conclusion of scientists was unfair and urged judges not to "permit juries to hold on the basis of oral testimony, passion or sympathy, that the person charged is the father and is responsible for the support of the child. . . ."[42]

The updated law crafted by the commission was adopted in California as part of the state's Code of Civil Procedure in 1953. It permitted a court to order blood tests in a civil action and read: "If the court finds that the conclusions of all the experts, as disclosed by the evidence based upon the tests, are that the alleged father is not the father of the child, the question of paternity shall be resolved accordingly. If the experts disagree in their findings or conclusions, the question shall be submitted (to the finder of fact) upon all the evidence."[43] By 1958, a majority of courts in the United States treated "unchallenged blood test results as 'conclusive' when they showed non-paternity," which would have ended the Chaplin paternity trial before it started.[44] Today, of course, DNA is the gold standard for paternity testing with its undisputed accuracy rate and is routinely ordered in contested child support cases all over the country.[45]

But it was too late for Chaplin. Because his case was decided before the law changed, the jury's verdict stood. Although Chaplin never missed a support payment, Scott nonetheless filed a motion once Chaplin left the country asking that he be required to set up an account for Carol Ann's care. A judge granted Scott's motion in part and ordered Chaplin to deposit $10,000—$96,300 today—into an account to guarantee that Carol Ann would continue to get her money.[46]

The court order barely dented Chaplin's piggy bank, but his support payments made a big difference in Carol Ann's life. Over the years, they would pay for boarding school, college, a car once she was old enough to drive, nice clothes, and a lump sum of about $30,000 in 1964, when she turned twenty-one, the equivalent of about $250,000 today.[47] But long before that, back in the summer of 1953, with Joan locked away in Patton State Hospital for the foreseeable future, a suitable guardian had to be found for nine-year-old Carol Ann. Both Grandmother Gertrude and Eleanor Jericho, the artist with whom Joan and her children had lived in Redondo Beach, offered to care for her, perhaps out of love or maybe because Carol Ann came with Chaplin's $100 a week. When asked by a judge whom she wanted to live with, Carol Ann chose her grandmother, a woman she barely knew. Carol Ann wanted nothing to do with Eleanor because she had seen her drown the kittens of her adored Siamese cats, a sight that would forever haunt her.[48]

Carol Ann has a distinct memory of being taken at age nine by her grandmother to Union Station in Los Angeles to reconnect with her brothers, five-year-old Stephen and six-year-old Russell, who had been in foster care since their mother's breakdown. She believed they were all going to Pittsburgh to visit the boys' father. Instead, the boys were put on the train to live there permanently and Carol Ann was left behind with Gertrude, waving goodbye. As the train pulled away, Carol Ann cried uncontrollably. The boys never saw their mother again, and Carol Ann was eighteen before she saw either brother again.[49]

Carol Ann and her grandmother shared a bedroom in the house at 3039 Chadwick Drive in Los Angeles.[50] They were never a close-knit family; Joan might as well have been dead. A picture of Joan was locked away in Gertrude's bedroom trunk—which Carol Ann was forbidden to open—and on the rare occasions when the child dared ask her grandmother about Joan, her questions were met with a cold silence.[51]

Each month Gertrude would dress Carol Ann in her Sunday best and take her by the hand to Joe Scott's law firm in downtown Los Angeles. While Gertrude and Scott talked business behind his closed office door, Carol Ann played in the reception area at his secretary's typewriter. Despite the fire and brimstone he'd breathed at Chaplin in court, Scott was gentle and kind with Carol Ann. Over the years he sent her encouraging letters when she achieved good grades, and he gave her little gifts of prayer books, holy cards, and a rosary handmade by Irish nuns that she treasured.[52]

With a trial lawyer's instinct for sizing up a situation, Scott sensed something was amiss between Carol Ann and her grandmother. Carol Ann's education had already suffered because Joan had yanked her out of school to traipse around Mexico in 1948 and again in 1952. With his strong Catholic connections, Scott secured Carol Ann's admission to the prestigious Ramona Convent School in Alhambra, run by the Sisters of the Holy Names of Jesus and Mary, where he had sent his own daughters. Carol Ann thrived there. As one of about one hundred students who lived on campus, Carol Ann loved the nuns and made good friends.[53]

Carol Ann saw her mother only two more times. In the summer of 1961, her aunt Agnes, Joan's sister, brought Carol Ann to Patton State Hospital for a visit. Joan dressed up in a fashionable white shirtwaist and had her fiery red hair styled in a chin-length bob. Aunt Agnes took a picture of Joan smiling on the hospital grounds in the afternoon sun. Carol Ann still remembers that day fondly and has held onto the photo all her life.[54]

The next time Carol Ann saw her mother was at her high school graduation on June 6, 1962. Joan surprised her daughter by showing up at the graduation ceremony—shades of her impromptu visits to Getty and Chaplin. Carol Ann remembered a "feeling of awkwardness" because neither her grandmother nor her aunt had warned her that Joan would be there.[55] In adulthood, Carol Ann regrets not maintaining contact with her mother. "My damned grandmother never said, 'Maybe we should call or visit your Mom,'" Carol Ann now says. "It breaks my heart."[56]

Shortly after her high school graduation, Carol Ann was contacted by officials from the mental hospital and told that after nearly a decade her mother was eligible to be discharged but needed a family member willing to care for her. Would Carol Ann take her? As an eighteen-year-old about to begin her college studies in Oregon who had not had a relationship with her mother for years, she declined. "I remember being bewildered at how I would possibly take care of her," Carol Ann says.[57] It begs the question whether the same request was made by hospital officials to Gertrude or Joan's sister Agnes and whether, they too, refused.

Today, people post the intimate details of their lives on Facebook and a Google search allows personal information to be retrieved in seconds. But in the 1960s it was different. Over the years, Carol had a faint inkling that there was some scandal involving her mother and Charlie Chaplin, but she has no recollection of how she knew that. When she got to college, she decided to investigate. One afternoon she slipped away to the public library in Portland, where she thumbed through biographies of Chaplin and found an old copy of a magazine that told the sordid story. Suddenly Carol Ann understood why there was so much that was hush-hush about her mother's past, and she felt pain for her mother and for herself.[58]

Carol Ann legally could have used the name "Chaplin," but she never did. As a condition of cooperating with this book, she asked that her current surname not be revealed. Once she left home for good, she shunned contact with her grandmother, who died in a Los Angeles nursing home in 1980. She heard again from Eleanor Jericho, or more accurately from Eleanor Jericho's lawyers. Carol Ann was sued twice over a grant deed that Jericho had given to her in 1951 (at Joan's insistence) for the Redondo Beach property where they'd all lived before Joan was debilitated by mental illness. The first time was in 1959 when Jericho filed a complaint alleging she was in possession of the property and wanted clear title to it, but she never pursued the action beyond filing the initial lawsuit and the court dismissed it.[59] After Jericho died, her heirs sued Carol again to get title to the property, claiming that Carol Ann had once told Jericho she would give it back. Carol Ann won that suit in Superior Court in Los Angeles, and said she later sold the property for a little over $25,000.[60]

Following a brief, unhappy marriage when she was twenty-two, Carol Ann divorced and in 1968 married a man she'd known in college. He held a degree in economics and for thirty years worked at various jobs on the railroad; Carol Ann was a social worker. They had two children. Now eighty-one, Carol Ann and her husband have retired to a rural area of the Pacific Northwest. Mental illness continues its journey through the Joan Berry family. Carol Ann has suffered from lifelong depression, and her son, who worked at a university where he counselled students with financial aid issues, committed suicide in 2009 when he was thirty-nine years old.[61]

Carol Ann's half-brother Russell was a Vietnam War veteran who had

post-traumatic stress disorder, and may have also suffered from undiagnosed manic depression. He lived as nomadic a life as his mother once
did, never marrying or setting down roots. He died of an aneurism in 2013
when he was sixty-five.[62] Of the family's struggles with the loss of their
mother, separation from their siblings, and mental health challenges,
Carol Ann's surviving half-brother, Stephen Seck, said, "It's like ripples in
a pond; it affects all of us."[63]

When he wrote his autobiography in 1964, Chaplin portrayed himself
as the victim of Joan Barry, whom he considered a crazy, dangerous con-
niver. Certainly the stress, expense, and embarrassment of the trials, the
unfairness of the paternity verdict, the interference with his career, and
the outsized role the scandal played in his exile from the United States
provided justification for his feelings.

More recently, the seven of what were then Chaplin's eight surviving
children (Josephine died in the summer of 2023), who control the Charlie
Chaplin Archive, which houses his personal and professional papers and
photographs, refused several requests to cooperate with this book and
barred this author from access to the closed Barry case files stored there.
One can only surmise they do not want to participate in any project that
they see as tarnishing their family's legacy, although the scandal has been
part of the conversation about Chaplin for the last eighty years.

In trying to put that scandal into context today, it is clear that Charlie and Joan each placed their own needs and desires first and that neither considered the long-term consequences of their actions. If what goes
around comes around, then one could speculate that years of carelessness
and self-absorption finally caught up with both of them.

Without excusing Joan's gun-toting break-in at Chaplin's house in
December 1942 or the many other times she harassed him, Joan was nonetheless the more vulnerable of the two. Her mental illness and abuse of
alcohol and drugs impaired her judgment and left her unable to focus on
a career, a relationship, or a plan to get what she wanted from life. Her
father's suicide and her fractured relationship with her mother left her
so needy that she mistook fleeting sexual attraction for long-term love.
Chaplin, with his extraordinary wealth and outsized celebrity, could have
had almost any woman he wanted—from the hatcheck girl to the most
popular star in Hollywood. If greater responsibility goes along with greater
power, then he should have thought twice before embarking on a relationship with a woman whose emotional volatility was obvious early on.[64] Even

those closest to him, like Tim Durant and employees at his studio, urged Chaplin to walk away from Joan.

The subtext of the story of Charlie Chaplin and Joan Barry is the way it typifies the experiences of women barely out of girlhood who flock to Hollywood with dreams of stardom. Women always have had to fend off advances from men in the industry. Even the highly respected Frances Marion, a pioneer Hollywood powerhouse who wrote 325 filmscripts, some for Mary Pickford, and the first woman screenwriter to win an Oscar in 1930, felt she had to tolerate a pinch on the rear end from future MGM boss Louis B. Meyer when he first hired her to work on a script.[65]

Almost immediately after signing Joan to a movie contract, Chaplin became sexually involved with her. Was that the implicit price of that contract? Most of Chaplin's relationships with the women who became his leading ladies were transactional: they got movie deals and he got wives or lovers until the next film or until he tired of them. Chaplin's relationship with Oona, who was seventeen when they met and said she was intent on being an actress, might have followed the same trajectory had she not eschewed a career for the privilege of becoming Mrs. Chaplin.

The story of the casting couch could be told about many men besides Chaplin. Actress Joan Collins, once the girlfriend of Chaplin's son Sydney, said that in the early 1960s "studio executives were promising actresses roles if we'd go to bed with them."[66] The most egregious example is Harvey Weinstein, the Oscar-winning founder of Miramax and The Weinstein Group and one of Hollywood's most powerful producers. On October 6, 2017, the *New York Times* blew open the hidden story about how he had been sexually abusing actresses and coworkers with impunity for thirty years.[67] Weinstein was prosecuted and convicted of rape and related sexual offenses in New York and California and sentenced to decades in prison, although the New York case was later overturned by the state's highest court because the trial judge allowed the jury to hear too much about Weinstein's history of bad behavior with women.[68] In the aftermath of the Weinstein revelations, the #MeToo movement was born.[69]

Chaplin's bad behavior pales next to Weinstein's. Weinstein was a bullying sexual predator; Chaplin was a charming womanizer who had a penchant for seducing girls barely out of adolescence. Chaplin skated past any real damage because of his prodigious sexual appetites in 1927 (other than to his wallet and his nervous system) when wife Lita Grey's salacious divorce complaint became public and his extramarital affairs were revealed. His fans forgave, even if they didn't forget. But he wasn't so lucky when he got tangled up with Joan Barry in the 1940s. Then, Chaplin's behavior resulted in his own #MeToo-like moment. As with Weinstein's downfall, it was a pair of journalists—syndicated columnist Hedda Hopper and New York *Daily News* correspondent Florabel Muir—whose reporting shed light on Chaplin's conduct. By calling Chaplin out on the imbalance of power in his relationship with Joan—despite the fact that she was an adult and the sex was consensual—they compelled law enforcement to investigate his behavior.

As misguided as the 1944 Mann Act indictment and subsequent trial turned out to be, it was the beginning of the end for the Little Tramp. The paternity trials kept the story alive, damaging Chaplin's reputation so badly that a jury was willing to find he was the father of Joan's daughter, despite undisputed scientific evidence to the contrary. By the end of the decade, the combination of the trials, his well-publicized pro-Communist ideology, and his friendships with fellow travelers during the Red Scare was enough to destroy Chaplin in Middle America.

More than thirty years ago, Professor Charles J. Maland, of the University of Tennessee, in *Chaplin and American Culture: The Evolution of a Star Image*, wrote about the way the public's view of Chaplin had changed over the years. "From the mid-1930s through the 1950s, the man's political perspectives, whether in his films or in his public activities, as well as his associations with women, seemed to dominate public attention," Maland wrote. But, Maland explained, a younger generation with liberal ideas about politics and sex who have been exposed to his films in re-releases view Chaplin as "a talented artist rather than as a man with questionable political views and morality."[70] This evolved view of Chaplin led to New York City audiences embracing *Monsieur Verdoux* when it was rereleased in 1964 and to his hero's welcome by the Motion Picture Academy at the 1972 Oscar ceremony.[71]

But after the news of the Weinstein case flooded the media, the #MeToo movement signaled a new era of zero tolerance for sexual misconduct, harassment, or just bad behavior by men in Hollywood. Whether that attitude will prevail or weaken over time remains to be seen. And if Chaplin were alive today, one might ponder how he would be viewed under this sharper lens. There is no doubt that Chaplin's place in history will continue to be endlessly chronicled and debated, because while his landmark films and extraordinary talent will always support his "star image," his personal history with women and his politics will surely be insurmountable to some.

Joan, on the other hand, has long been lost to history. Part of Carol Ann's motivation in cooperating with this book was her small hope that it would help her to better understand the mother she hardly knew. After refusing to assume her mother's care upon Joan's release from the mental hospital more than sixty years ago, Carol Ann lost all contact with her. Her half-brother Stephen hoped that through his cooperation with this book he might find out how his mother died and where she might be buried.

On October 17, 2007, at 12:30 a.m., an eighty-seven-year-old woman named Mary Baker died alone in a hospital in Queens, New York. She had the same Social Security number as Mary Louise Gribble, aka Joan Berry, aka Joan Barry, and the same phony date of birth that Joan gave to the U.S. government when she fled to Mexico in 1952 to avoid testifying against Chaplin. At her death, she was disabled in some unspecified manner and had lived out her final years in a nursing home on Coney Island Avenue in Brooklyn.[72] Only a social worker from the nursing facility was available to identify her body. How she ended up there is anybody's guess.

The body was transferred to the Forest Green Park Cemetery in Morganville, New Jersey, about fifty miles south of Brooklyn. She was buried in an unmarked grave with an American flag to mark the spot for the only two visitors known to have come calling—this author and Joan's son Stephen—in the sixteen years she'd been buried there. After learning of his mother's anonymous burial site, Stephen purchased a flat bronze grave marker reading "Beloved Mother, Mary Louise Seck, Nee Gribble, 'Joan Barry,'" along with her true dates of birth and death. Carol Ann has never visited the grave, and Stephen is unlikely to return often, if at all, because he lives more than fifteen hundred miles away.

A NOTE ON SOURCES

The approximately two thousand pages of Chaplin files amassed by the Federal Bureau of Investigation are available online at "The Vault," https://vault.fbi.gov. Two original Charles Chaplin files, Nos. 31–68496 and 100–127090, have been combined there into a ten-part PDF document, with newly assigned page numbers. Citations to the FBI files are to the file and page numbers of the PDF as created by the FBI and deposited in "The Vault."

The National Archives and Records Administration has no surviving transcript of Charlie Chaplin's federal Mann Act trial, *United States of America v. Charles Spencer Chaplin*, No. 16,617. Quotations from witness testimony or attorney colloquy at the Mann Act trial come primarily from contemporary newspaper accounts. Select papers published line-for-line transcripts of portions of the federal trial testimony. At Chaplin's later civil paternity trials, excerpts of the transcripts of Chaplin's testimony from the Mann Act trial were used by Joseph Scott, counsel for Joan's daughter, to impeach Chaplin's credibility during cross-examination. Those limited transcripts were preserved as part of the record on appeal in Chaplin's paternity trial. Where I've relied on those transcripts, it is reflected in the endnotes. The only full trial transcript that exists is from Chaplin's second paternity trial and it was the source of the quotes in this book about that trial. The second paternity trial, which took place in April 1945, resulted in a verdict against Chaplin. The jury found in favor of Carol Ann on April 17, 1945, and a judgment was entered against Chaplin in the Superior Court on May 2, 1945. Chaplin appealed that judgment to the District Court of Appeal and, when he failed to prevail, to the California Supreme Court. The trial transcript of the second paternity trial became part of the record on appeal and was retained at the California State Archives.

The case files of the federal indictments of Chaplin and his codefendants are available at the National Archives and Records Administration, Riverside, California, in the files of the United States District Court for the Southern Division (Los Angeles) of the Southern District of California, Criminal Case Files, 1907–2005 (NAID 294957), Record Group 21, in boxes 93, 123, 124, 972, and 973. The indictments are numbered 16,616 (*United States of America v. Charles Spencer Chaplin, Thomas Wells Durant, W.W. White, Charles H. Griffin, Robert Arden, Claude Marple, and Jessie Billie Reno*); 16,617 (*United States of America v. Charles Spencer Chaplin*); 16,618 (*United States of America v. Charles Spencer Chaplin, W.W. White, Robert Arden and Charles H. Griffin*); and 16,619 (*United States of America v. Charles Spencer Chaplin, Robert Arden and W.W. White*).

What used to be the Immigration and Naturalization Service created a file of approximately sixty-five hundred pages on Charlie Chaplin. It is available in PDF form and includes files from the investigation about the Chaplin-Barry affair that was conducted in the Spring of 1943 by the Los Angeles County District Attorney's Office.

All references to the United States Census can found on the website Ancestry, www.ancestry.com, but require either a subscription or a visit to a public library.

All references to recent dollar value come from the website Measuring Worth, www.measuringworth.com. At the time of publication, the latest year for which calculations were available was 2020.

Carol Ann Berry, now 81-years-old, spoke with me many times over the course of researching and writing this book. As a condition of her cooperation, I agreed not to reveal her current last name or where she now lives.

NOTES

INTRODUCTION

1. Florabel Muir, *Headline Happy* (New York: Henry Holt, 1950), 62.
2. Adela Rogers St. Johns, *Love, Laughter and Tears: My Hollywood Story* (Garden City, NY: Doubleday, 1978), 86.
3. Charles J. Maland, *Chaplin and American Culture: The Evolution of a Star Image* (Princeton: Princeton University Press, 1989), 32; David Robinson, *Chaplin: His Life and Art* (New York: McGraw-Hill, 1985), 700.
4. GFR Jr. to FBI Director J. Edgar Hoover, memorandum, Aug. 28, 1922, Charlie Chaplin FBI File, Pt. 7, p. 8.
5. Marcia Winn, "Berry-Chaplin Trysts Told; Visited Actor 'Very Often,' Joan Testifies, Relates Details of Trip to N.Y.," *Chicago Daily Tribune*, Mar. 24, 1944.
6. Jan Ransom, "Convicted in New York, Weinstein Will Face Next Rape Trial in Los Angeles," *New York Times*, Feb. 26, 2020; James Queally, Richard Winton and Jenny Jarvie, "Is Harvey Weinstein's California Conviction in Jeopardy After N.Y. Appeals Ruling?" *Los Angeles Times*, Apr. 25, 2024.

PROLOGUE

1. Kevin Thomas, "Parade of Stars: Gloomy Weather Clears, Oscar Event Glitters," *Los Angeles Times*, Apr. 11, 1972.
2. Candice Bergen, *Knock Wood* (New York: Linden Press, Simon & Schuster, 1984), 246.
3. "Double Play: Chaplin to Robeson to Malenkov," editorial, *Saturday Evening Post*, Sept. 4, 1954, 10.
4. Hedda Hopper, "Hollywood's Happy, Says Hedda Hopper," *Daily News* (New York), Sept. 20, 1952.

5. Bob Hope as told to Pete Martin, "This Is On *Saturday Evening Post*, Feb. 13, 1954, 17.

6. Ambassador Davis, U.S. Embassy, Bern, to U.S. Secretary of State, Washington, DC, telegram, Mar. 5, 1971, V/Chaplin, Record Group-59, A1–1613-D, Central Foreign Policy File of the Dept. of State (1970–73) National Archives and Records Administration.

7. Daniel Taradash to Charles Chaplin, Jan. 7, 1972, Daniel Taradash Papers, 9822, Box 92, Folder 7, American Heritage Center, University of Wyoming.

8. Peter Ackroyd, *Charlie Chaplin: A Brief Life* (New York: Nan A. Talese/Doubleday, 2014), 269.

9. McCandlish Phillips, "Chaplin Returns with Silent-Film Style," *New York Times*, Apr. 4, 1972.

10. Phillips, "Chaplin Returns with Silent-Film Style"; Peter Coutros, "Chaplin Returns with a Silent Kiss for America," *Daily News* (New York), Apr. 4, 1972.

11. McCandlish Phillips, "Chaplin to Visit City; Salute Set April 4," *New York Times*, Feb. 8, 1972.

12. Sally Quinn, "'There He Is, There He Is'; Chaos at the Chaplin Reception," *Washington Post*, Apr. 6, 1972.

13. Tom Shales, "Heros' Night in Hollywood," *Washington Post*, Apr. 11, 1972.

14. Jane Fonda, 44th Annual Academy Awards, Apr. 10, 1972.

15. "Hollywood's Shining Hour," *American Cinematographer* (May 1972): 506–7.

16. Steven V. Roberts, "Oscars: 'French Connection' Is Best Film; Jane Fonda and Gene Hackman Top Stars," *New York Times*, Apr. 11, 1972.

CHAPTER 1

1. Frederick C. Othman, "Chaplin Surrenders; Fingerprinted, Mugged," *Long Beach Sun*, Feb. 1, 1944; Theo Hartley, "Sensations of Hollywood: Charlie Chaplin's Day of Shame," *South China Morning Post*, Apr. 5, 1981.

2. R. B. Hood, Special Agent in Charge, Los Angeles, to Mr. Rosen, Identification Division, Feb. 14, 1944, Chaplin FBI File, Pt. 2, p. 94.

3. United Press, "Gay Clothes, Glum Face—Woman Calls Chaplin Rat, but He Ignores Description; Film Associates Say He'll Never Make Another Picture Regardless of Outcome of Charges," *Pittsburgh Press*, Feb. 15, 1944; "Finger Print, Book Chaplin in Berry Case; Nervous and Testy on Appearance," *Chicago Daily Tribune*, Feb. 15, 1944.

4. "Weather Report," *Los Angeles Times*, Feb. 15, 1944.

5. "Charlie Chaplin, Grim Face, Surrenders, Is Fingerprinted: Comic Snaps at 'Photogs,'" *Los Angeles Herald-Express*, Feb. 14, 1944.

6. Jerry Giesler as told to Pete Martin, *The Jerry Giesler Story* (New York: Simon & Schuster, 1960), 182.

7. Associated Press, "Chaplin Goes into Custody; Surrenders under Mann Act and Is Fingerprinted," *Baltimore Sun*, Feb. 15, 1944.

8. *United States of America v. Charles Spencer Chaplin*, No. 16,617, Appearance *Praecipi*, Jerry Giesler, Feb. 11, 1944, Criminal Case Files, 1907–2005, U.S. District Court for the Central District of California, Record Group-21, Box 972, Folder 16,617, NARA; "Order Waives $1000 Bail in Chaplin Case; Writ Obtained by Counsel Quashing Requirement of Bond," *Los Angeles Times*, Feb. 12, 1944.

9. "Finger Print, Book Chaplin in Berry Case."

10. Frederick C. Othman, "'It's a Cinch,' Flynn Lawyer Tells Chaplin," *Chicago Times*, Jan. 14, 1944.

11. A. Rosen to E. A. Tamm, memorandum, Jan. 27, 1944, Chaplin FBI File, Pt. 2, pp. 43–44.

12. "Chaplin Case Girl Cleared; Vagrancy Charge against Joan Berry Dismissed by Court," *Los Angeles Times*, June 12, 1943.

13. Florabel Muir, "Constitutional Rights Befuddle Alien Chaplin at Fingerprinting," *Daily News* (New York), Feb. 15, 1944.

14. "Chaplin Gives Self Up to Face Federal Trial," *Los Angeles Times*, Feb. 15, 1944.

15. Robinson, *Chaplin*, 226, 703–36.

16. John Roeburt, *"Get Me Giesler"* (New York: Belmont Books, 1962), 26–27.

17. Agness Underwood, *Newspaperwoman* (New York: Harper, 1949), 186–87.

18. "Finger Print, Book Chaplin in Berry Case."

19. "Screen Comedian Fingerprinted," *New York Times*, Feb. 15, 1944.

20. "Pasadenan Retires after 30 Years Gov't Service," *Pasadena Independent*, Dec. 28, 1954; 1930 United States Census (George Rossini).

21. "Chaplin Gives Self Up to Face Federal Trial."

22. Muir, "Constitutional Rights Befuddle Alien Chaplin at Fingerprinting."

23. "F.B.I. Queries Justice in Chaplin-Berry Case; Full Investigation Started in 'Vagging' of Young Mother Making Paternity Charge," *Los Angeles Times*, Jan. 6, 1944; Muir, *Headline Happy*, 59.

24. "Jury Indicts Chaplin on Mann Act Charge; Six More Also Accused in Federal Case," *Los Angeles Times*, Feb. 11, 1944

25. "Joan Berry Tells Jury of 'Life with Chaplin,'" *Los Angeles Times*, Jan. 21, 1944.

26. Joyce Milton, *Tramp: The Life of Charlie Chaplin* (New York: HarperCollins, 1996), 412; "Government Jails Radio Commentator; Robert Arden among Five Rounded Up on Illegal-Entry Charges," *Los Angeles Times*, May 20, 1941.

27. "Thomas Durant; '30s Film Figure and Steeplechaser," *Los Angeles Times*, Dec. 16, 1984; Associated Press, "Mrs. Durant Wins Divorce on Cruelty," *Washington Post*, June 30, 1936.

28. Report: "Charles Spencer Chaplin; Mary Louise Gribble, with Aliases . . . Vic-

tim, White Slave Traffic Act," Nov. 9, 1943, Chaplin FBI File, Pt. 1, pp. 94, 130–31.

29. *United States of America v. Charles Spencer Chaplin, et al.*, Record Group 21, No. 16,616, Box 972, Folder 16,616, Pt. 1, NARA.

30. *United States of America v. Charles Spencer Chaplin*, Record Group 21, No. 16,617; *United States v. Chaplin, et al.*, No. 16,616, NARA; "Jury Indicts Chaplin on Mann Act Charge." There were four federal indictments involving Chaplin: Nos. 16,616, 16,617, 16,618, and 16,619. Only 16,617 charged Chaplin alone for violating the Mann Act. The rest alleged conspiracies to violate Joan Berry's civil rights.

31. R. B. Hood to FBI Director, Feb. 14, 1944, Chaplin FBI File Pt. 2, p. 95.

32. Charles Chaplin Jr., with N. and M. Rau, *My Father, Charlie Chaplin* (New York: Random House), 286.

33. "Jury Indicts Chaplin on Mann Act Charge."

34. "Chaplin Is Fingerprinted, Arraignment Next Monday," *Daily Boston Globe*, Feb. 15, 1944; "Charlie Chaplin Fingerprinted," *Daily News* (New York), Feb. 15, 1944; "Charlie Chaplin Fingerprinted," *Daily Home News* (New Brunswick, NJ), Feb. 15, 1944; "Chaplin's No Different from Anybody Else," *Pittsburgh Press*, Feb. 15, 1944.

35. "Flying Fortresses Bomb Mt. Cassino Monastery," *Plainfield (NJ) Courier-News*, Feb. 15, 1944.

36. "Chaplin Gives Self Up to Face Federal Trial."

CHAPTER 2

1. Gertrude McLaren, Certificate and Record of Birth, No. 47406, County and City of New York, State of New York, Dec. 20, 1899, New York City Municipal Archives.

2. 1900 U.S. Census (Robert McLaren); 1910 U.S. Census (Katherine McLaren).

3. Robert McLaren, Certificate and Record of Death No. 34573, Dept. of Health of the City of New York, State of New York, Dec. 5, 1903, New York City Municipal Archives.

4. 1910 U.S. Census (Katherine McLaren).

5. James Gribble, Veterans' Administration Master Index, 1917–1940, Ancestry, www.ancestry.com.

6. 1900 U.S. Census (William Gribbel [sic]).

7. Mary L. Gribbel [sic], Standard Certificate of Death, No. 2016, Dept. of Health of the City of New York, State of New York, Jan. 23, 1914, New York City Municipal Archives.

8. James A. Gribble, Gertrude E. McLaren, Affidavit for License to Marry, No.

24434, County of New York, City of New York, State of New York, Aug. 22, 1919, New York City Municipal Archives.

9. 1920 U.S. Census (James A. Gribble).

10. White Slave Traffic Act Report, Chaplin FBI File, Pt. 1, p. 103.

11. 1925 N.Y. State Census (James Gribble), Ancestry, www.ancestry.com.

12. James Alfred Gribble, Certificate of Death, No. 30455, Dept. of Health of the City of New York, Bureau of Records, State of New York, Dec. 10, 1926, New York City Municipal Archives.

13. John E. Brerry [sic], Gertrude E. Gribble, Affidavit of License to Marry, No. 34685, County of New York, State of New York, Dec. 15, 1927; *Jane P. Resor v. John Barry*, Ind. No. 2816/1948, New York County District Attorney File, New York City Municipal Archives.

14. 1930 U.S. Census (John Berry).

15. White Slave Traffic Act Report, Sept. 2, 1943, Chaplin FBI File, Pt. 1, pp. 20–21.

16. Mary Lou Berry, Newtown High School Yearbook (June 1938), 17, U.S. School Yearbooks, Ancestry, www.ancestry.com.

17. Statement of Joan Berry to Los Angeles County District Attorney, May 29, 1943, Charles Spencer Chaplin Temporary Immigration and Naturalization Service File, A-5653092, Pt. 3, p. 1147.

18. R. B. Hood to FBI Director, Jan. 21, 1944, Chaplin FBI File Pt. 2, p. 24.

19. White Slave Traffic Act Report, Oct. 8, 1943, Chaplin FBI File, Pt. 1, p. 54.

20. Barbara Hayes, "How Tyrone Power Won the Heart of Lonely Janet Gaynor," *Photoplay*, Jan. 1938, 15; Dixie Willson, "The Revealing True Story of Myrna Loy: The Saga of a Beloved Redhead," *Photoplay*, July 1938, 66; "Cal York's Gossip of Hollywood," *Photoplay*, Sept. 1938, 49.

21. Gertrude E. Berry interview, Chaplin FBI File, Pt. 5, pp. 53–58.

22. Violation of Civil Liberties Report, Chaplin FBI File, Pt. 3, p. 167; Amelia Frey interview, Chaplin FBI File, Pt. 5, p. 90.

23. Carol Ann Berry, interview with the author, Apr. 16, 2023.

24. Frey interview, Chaplin FBI File, Pt. 5, p. 90.

25. White Slave Traffic Act Report, Chaplin FBI File, Pt. 1, p. 103; Milton, *Tramp* 389.

26. Gertrude Berry interview, Chaplin FBI File, Pt. 5, p. 58; "Samuel Marx Is Dead; Hollywood Writer, 90," *New York Times*, Mar. 6, 1992; Burt A. Folkart, "Samuel Marx; Hollywood Story Editor, Chronicler," *Los Angeles Times*, Mar. 6, 1992.

27. Kenneth Marx, email to the author, Nov. 23, 2021.

28. Cari Beauchamp, *Without Lying Down: Frances Marion and the Powerful Women of Early Hollywood* (New York: Lisa Drew/Scribner, 1997), 283.

29. Samuel Marx interview, Chaplin FBI File, Pt. 5, pp. 44–50.

30. Samuel Marx interview, Chaplin FBI File, Pt. 5, p. 44.

31. Samuel Marx interview, Chaplin FBI File, Pt. 5, p. 45.

32. Len Martin, *The Republic Pictures Checklist: Features, Serials, Cartoons, Short Subjects and Training Films of Republic Pictures Corporation, 1935–1959* (Jefferson, NC: McFarland, 1998), 1, 62, 222.

33. J. Paul Getty interview, Chaplin FBI File, Pt. 5, p. 33.

34. Russell Miller, *The House of Getty* (London: Bloomsbury, 2018), 166, 179, 185, 204–6.

35. J. Paul Getty, *As I See It* (Los Angeles: J. Paul Getty Museum, 2014), 107.

36. Unknown author to Mr. Ladd, memorandum, "Repatriation of U.S. Citizens Aboard S.S. Drottingholm," May 25, 1942, John Paul Getty FBI File, No. 65–2170, p. 112.

37. Getty, *As I See It*, 112.

38. Jean Paul Getty, Espionage I Report, Nov. 12, 1940, Getty FBI File, p. 9; James Reginato, *Growing Up Getty: The Story of America's Most Unconventional Dynasty* (New York: Gallery Books, 2022), 13.

39. Diaries, J. Paul Getty Institutional Archives (hereafter, Getty Diaries), IA 40009, Getty Research Institute, Aug. 8, 1940–Dec. 26, 1941; Dec. 26, 1941–Dec. 26, 1942.

40. Tom Cameron, "Crowds Swarm around Nominee; Ovation at City Hall Defers Greeting from Acting Mayor Burns," *Los Angeles Times*, Sept. 20, 1940; Getty Diaries, Sept. 19, 1940.

41. Getty Diaries, Sept. 14–Nov. 16, 1940.

42. John Edgar Hoover to Attorney General, Mar. 18, 1944, Chaplin FBI File, Pt. 3, p. 48.

43. Miller, *The House of Getty*, 146–47; Getty Diaries, Nov. 16, 1940.

44. Gertrude Berry interview, Chaplin FBI File, Pt. 5, p. 55.

45. Getty Diaries, Dec. 17–19, 1940.

46. Getty Diaries, Dec. 23, 1940.

47. Florabel Muir, "Chaplin Still Likes 'Em Young: Ma-To-Be Accuses Devotee of Fillies, Busy Wooing Oona," *Sunday News* (New York), May 23, 1943.

48. Getty Diaries, Dec. 23, 1940.

49. Getty interview, Chaplin FBI File, Pt. 5, pp. 33–34.

50. Getty Diaries, Dec. 24–26, 1940.

51. Vanda Krefft, *The Man Who Made the Movies: The Meteoric Rise and Tragic Fall of William Fox* (New York: HarperCollins, 2017), 367, 480–81; "Sues for $600,000 in Theatre Sales," *New York Times*, Oct. 1930.

52. Getty Diaries, Dec. 31, 1940–Jan. 3, 1941.

53. Teddy Getty Gaston, *Alone Together: My Life with J. Paul Getty*, with Digby Diehl (New York: Ecco, 2013), 228–29; Getty interview, Chaplin FBI File, Pt. 5, p. 34.

54. Getty Diaries, Feb. 3–14, 1941.

55. Ann Rork to J. Paul Getty, Feb. 25, 1941, J. P. Getty Family Papers, J. Paul Getty Institutional Archives, 2010. IA.17–01, Getty Research Institute.

56. Robert Lenzner, *The Great Getty: The Life and Loves of J. Paul Getty—Richest Man in the World* (New York: Crown Publishers, 1985), 72–73.

57. Samuel A. Berger, "David S. Hecht," *Year Book 1960* (Association of the Bar of the City of New York), 35; "Kitchin" to J. E. Hoover and Hood (teletype), Nov. 27, 1943, Chaplin FBI File, Pt. 1, pp. 171–74.

58. "Kitchin" teletype.

59. "Kitchin" teletype.

60. Getty Diaries, Feb. 3–Mar. 13, 1941.

61. Getty interview, Chaplin FBI File, Pt. 5, p. 34.

62. "Kitchin" teletype.

63. Getty Diaries, Mar. 1–6, 1941.

64. Getty Diaries, Mar. 13–17, 1941.

65. Getty Diaries, May 17, 26, 30, 1941.

66. Getty Diaries, May 16, 20, 24, 1941.

67. Getty interview, Chaplin FBI File, Pt. 5, p. 34.

CHAPTER 3

1. Milton, *Tramp*, 380–81.

2. Maland, *Chaplin and American Culture*, 75; John Chapman, "Looking at Hollywood," *Chicago Daily News*, Oct. 17, 1940; Kate Cameron, "Chaplin Picture Has Gala Double Opening," *Daily News* (New York), Oct. 16, 1940; Edwin Schallert, "Chaplin Film Shows Flashes of Genius," *Los Angeles Times*, Oct. 15, 1940.

3. "Douglas Fairbanks Dies in His Sleep; Stage and Screen Actor Is Victim of a Sudden Heart Attack at Santa Monica; Saw Football Saturday; Mary Pickford, Lasky, James Roosevelt and Goldwyn Pay Tribute to Famous Star," *New York Times*, Dec. 13, 1939.

4. Samuel Goldwyn, *Behind the Screen* (New York: George H. Doran, 1923), 161.

5. Peter Ackroyd, *Charlie Chaplin: A Brief Life* (New York: Doubleday, 2014), 7.

6. Milton, *Tramp*, 8–11.

7. Charles Chaplin, *My Autobiography* (New York: Plume, 1992), 19.

8. Robinson, *Chaplin*, 10–12.

9. Richard Carr, *Charlie Chaplin: A Political Biography from Victorian Britain to Modern America* (London: Routledge, 2017), 20.

10. Milton, *Tramp*, 2–4.

11. Milton, *Tramp*, 3, 9.

12. Chaplin, *My Autobiography*, 15; Carr, *Charlie Chaplin*, 22.

13. Milton, *Tramp* 14; Carr, *Charlie Chaplin*, 33.

14. Ackroyd, *Charlie Chaplin*, 15, 25.

15. Ackroyd, *Charlie Chaplin*, 15; Scott Eyman, *Charlie Chaplin vs. America: When Art, Sex, and Politics Collided* (New York: Simon & Schuster, 2023), 25–26.

16. Milton, *Tramp*, 12–16.

17. "A Brief History of the Lambeth Workhouse," Kennington Runoff, www.kenningtonrunoff.com/a-brief-history-of-lambeth-workhouse/, accessed May 13, 2021; the full name of the Poor Law Amendment Act of 1834 was "An Act for the Amendment and Better Administration of the Laws Relating to the Poor in England," 4 & 5 Will. 4.c.76; Carr, *Charlie Chaplin*, 32–33.

18. Ackroyd, *Charlie Chaplin*, 11.

19. Chaplin, *My Autobiography*, 31–32.

20. Barry Anthony, *Chaplin's Music Hall: The Chaplins and Their Circle in the Limelight* (London: I. B. Tauris, 2012), 49–50.

21. Ackroyd, *Charlie Chaplin*, 18; Richard Patterson, "The Cost of Living in 1888," The Victorian Web, https://www.victorianweb.org/economics/wages4.html, accessed Nov. 5, 2023.

22. Robinson, *Chaplin*, 29; Milton, *Tramp*, 25.

23. Chaplin, *My Autobiography*, 58.

24. Milton, *Tramp*, 27–28; Ackroyd, *Charlie Chaplin*, 17, 23.

25. Ackroyd, *Charlie Chaplin*, 27, 36–37.

26. Chaplin, *My Autobiography*, 103–7, 263; Richard Schickel, *The Essential Chaplin: Perspectives on the Life and Art of the Great Comedian* (Chicago: Ivan R. Dee, 2006), 18.

27. Mack Sennett, *The King of Comedy*, with Cameron Shipp (San Francisco: Memory House, 1990), 151–52; Chaplin, *My Autobiography*, 139.

28. Chaplin, *My Autobiography*, 138.

29. Sennett, *The King of Comedy*, 88.

30. Gary Krist, *The Mirage Factory: Illusion, Imagination, and the Invention of Los Angeles* (New York: Crown, 2018), 90.

31. Robinson, *Chaplin*, 113.

32. Robinson, *Chaplin*, 700; Chaplin, *My Autobiography*, 145–46.

33. Milton, *Tramp*, 61.

34. Robinson, *Chaplin*, 700–710.

35. Gary A. Rosen, *Adventures of a Jazz Age Lawyer: Nathan Burkan and the Making of American Popular Culture* (Oakland: University of California Press, 2020), 92.

36. Robinson, *Chaplin*, 135.

37. Rosen, *Jazz Age Lawyer*, 93.

38. Schickel, *The Essential Chaplin*, 8.

39. Robinson, *Chaplin*, 267.

40. Robinson, *Chaplin*, 302; Milton, *Tramp*, 361.

41. Mary Pickford, *Sunshine and Shadow* (New York: Doubleday, 1955), 236.

42. Ackroyd, *Charlie Chaplin*, 46, 62, 97–98.

43. Ackroyd, *Charlie Chaplin*, 199.

44. Benjamin De Casseres, "The Hamlet-Like Nature of Charlie Chaplin," *New York Times*, Dec. 12, 1920.

45. Ackroyd, *Charlie Chaplin*, 235.

46. Lita Grey Chaplin, *My Life with Chaplin: An Intimate Memoir*, with Morton Cooper (New York: Bernard Geis Associates, 1966), 259; St. Johns, *Love, Laughter and Tears*, 88.

47. Chaplin, *My Autobiography*, 169.

48. Robinson, *Chaplin*, 711–28.

49. Robinson, *Chaplin*, 141; Chaplin, *My Autobiography*, 203.

50. Chaplin, *My Autobiography*, 203–4.

51. Robinson, *Chaplin*, 246–47.

52. Robinson, *Chaplin*, 247.

53. Chaplin, *My Autobiography*, 475, 480.

54. Maland, *Chaplin and American Culture*, 43; Chaplin, *My Autobiography* 230, 235.

55. Robinson, *Chaplin*, 659.

56. Ackroyd, *Charlie Chaplin*, 62.

57. Georgia Hale, *Intimate Close-Ups*, edited with an introduction and notes by Heather Kiernan (Metuchen, NJ: Scarecrow Press, 1995), 150.

58. St. Johns, *Love, Laughter and Tears*, 88-89

59. Robinson, *Chaplin*, 262.

60. Robinson, 336–37.

61. Lita Grey Chaplin, *My Life with Chaplin*, 95, 127, 134–35; Robinson, *Chaplin*, 348.

62. Rosen, *Jazz Age Lawyer*, 207.

63. Chaplin, *My Autobiography*, 300.

64. Rosen, *Jazz Age Lawyer*, 207.

65. Rosen, *Jazz Age Lawyer*, 214, 220, 224.

66. Rosen, *Jazz Age Lawyer*, 114–16.

67. Rosen, *Jazz Age Lawyer*, 207–8.

68. Rosen, *Jazz Age Lawyer*, 209, 217–18, 220–22.

69. E. J. Fleming, *The Fixers: Eddie Mannix, Howard Strickling and the MGM Publicity Machine* (Jefferson, NC: McFarland, 2005), 78; Scott Eyman, *The Speed of Sound: Hollywood and the Talkie Revolution, 1926–1930* (New York: Simon & Schuster, 1997), 138.

70. Robinson, *Chaplin*, 446.

71. Chaplin, *My Autobiography*, 375.

72. According to her birth certificate, Paulette Goddard, born Marion Goddard Levy, was born on June 3, 1910. (Marion Goddard Levy, Certification of Birth,

Bureau of Records and Statistics, Dept. of Health of the City of New York), located in the Erich Maria Remarque Papers, 1918-2000, MSS. 095, Folder 44, Fales Library and Special Collections, New York University.

73. Chaplin, *My Autobiography*, 375.

74. Milton, *Tramp*, 331.

75. Chaplin Jr., *My Father*, 58.

76. "Former Follies Girl Sues, Paulette Goddard James, Wed Here in 1927, Seeks Reno Divorce," *New York Times*, Jan. 9, 1932; Dan Thomas, "Charlie Chaplin's Three Loves: Paulette Goddard, 21-year-old Blonde Divorcee Will Be Comedian's Third Wife, Hollywood Reports," *Reading (PA) Times*, Nov. 10, 1932.

77. Milton, *Tramp*, 330.

78. George Shaffer, "Chaplin Draws Big Gape with Platinum Blond," *Daily News* (New York), Aug. 16, 1932; Milton, *Tramp*, 330–31. Milton contradicts Chaplin's version about meeting Goddard on Schenck's yacht. She writes that the couple met on the set of her movie *The Kid from Spain*, before the yacht outing, citing to an interview that Chaplin's longtime cameraman, Rollie Totheroh, gave to author Timothy J. Lyons. See Timothy J. Lyons, ed., "Roland H. Totheroh Interviewed. Chaplin Films," *Film Culture*, no. 53-54-55 (Spring 1972): 277.

79. Maland, *Chaplin and American Culture*, 140–43.

80. Edwin Schallert, "'Modern Times' Proves Charlie Chaplin Still King of Screen Comedians," *Los Angeles Times*, Feb. 13, 1936.

81. Chaplin, *My Autobiography*, 378–80; Chaplin Jr., *My Father*, 13.

82. Chaplin, *My Autobiography*, 380.

83. Edwin Schallert, "Chaplin Sets October Dead Line for Start of Goddard Production," *Los Angeles Times*, July 9, 1937; Daily Production Report, Charles Chaplin Film Corp., W/E June 11, 1939, Charlie Chaplin Archive, ECCI00312471, CH018.

84. Edwin Schallert, "Ginger Rogers and James Cagney Will Co-Star in 'On Your Toes'; Miss Goddard Wins Contract with Selznick," *Los Angeles Times*, Feb. 3, 1938.

85. Jennifer Tisdale, "75 Days. 75 Years: Actresses Who Had Screen Tests for the Role of Scarlett O'Hara," *Ransom Center Magazine*, Dec. 13, 2013, www.sites.utexas.edu/ransomcentermagazine/2013/12/13/75-days-75-years-screen-tests-for-role-of-scarlett, accessed July 7, 2023.

86. Chanel Vargas, "A Timeline of Vivien Leigh and Laurence Olivier's Tragic Love Story," *Harper's Bazaar*, www.harpersbazaar.com/celebrity/latest/a/2809242/vivien-leigh-laurence-olivier-relationship, accessed July 18, 2023.

87. Daily Production Report, Charles Chaplin Film Corp., Sept. 9, 1939, Charlie Chaplin Archive, ECCI00312471, CH018.

88. Kaspar Monahan, "All This and Millions, Too, Went into 'Great Dictator,' Chaplin Film Coming to Warner Made in Record Time—For the Producer-Comic," *Pittsburgh Press*, Oct. 19, 1940; Bosley Crowther, "Chaplin at the Premiere; Thousands Cheer Him and Paulette Goddard at Astor and Capitol," *New York Times*, Oct. 16, 1940.

89. Robinson, *Chaplin*, 509; Harrison Carroll, "Behind the Scenes in Hollywood," *Vineland (NJ) Evening Times*, Oct. 31, 1940; Crowther, "Chaplin at the Premiere."

90. Crowther, "Chaplin at the Premiere."

91. Constance Collier to Hedda Hopper, Oct. 21, 1940, in Rocky Lang and Barbara Hall, eds., *Letters from Hollywood: Inside the Private World of Classic American Moviemaking* (New York: Abrams Books, 2019), 101–3.

92. Photo of Paulette Goddard and Charlie Chaplin dancing in New York, *Asbury Park (NJ) Evening Press*, Oct. 18, 1940.

93. Ed Sullivan, "Little Old New York: Men and Maids—and Stuff," *Daily News* (New York), Oct. 21, 1940.

94. Joe Morella and Edward Z. Epstein, *Paulette: The Adventurous Life of Paulette Goddard* (New York: St. Martin's Press, 1985), 108; Chaplin, *My Autobiography*, 400; Robinson, *Chaplin*, 509.

95. Chaplin, *My Autobiography*, 400.

96. Chaplin, *My Autobiography*, 400.

97. Leonard Lyons, "The Lyons Den," *New York Post*, Feb. 6, 1969.

CHAPTER 4

1. "Tribute Paid to Fairbanks; New $40,000 Memorial to Former Film Star Dedicated before 1500," *Los Angeles Times*, May 26, 1941.

2. "Weather Report," *Los Angeles Times*, May 26, 1941; "Sarcophagus Dedicated," *Los Angeles Evening News*, May 26, 1941; Chaplin Jr., *My Father*, 70–71.

3. "Tribute Paid to Fairbanks."

4. "56 Game Hitting Streak by Joe DiMaggio," Baseball Almanac, www.baseball-almanac.com/feats/feats3.shtml, accessed Aug. 20, 2021.

5. Erik Larson, *The Splendid and the Vile: A Saga of Churchill, Family, and Defiance During the Blitz* (New York: Crown, 2020), 484.

6. Chaplin, *My Autobiography*, 407.

7. Robinson, *Chaplin*, 487–88.

8. "Thomas Durant; '30s Film Figure and Steeplechaser," *Los Angeles Times*, Dec. 16, 1984.

9. Thomas Wells Durant, World War II Draft Registration Card, Ancestry, www.ancestry.com.

10. Chaplin, *My Autobiography*, 407.

11. Fleming, *The Fixers*, 50–51.

12. Ackroyd, *Charlie Chaplin*, 263.

13. Joan Berry interviews with FBI, Jan. 7, 10, 11, 1944, Chaplin FBI File, Pt. 3, p. 172.

14. Statement of Thomas Wells Durant to Los Angeles County District Attorney's investigators, June 6, 1943, Chaplin FBI File, Pt. 4, p. 82.

15. Sworn Statement of Thomas Wells Durant to Acting Immigrant Inspector, Oct. 3, 1952, Charles Spencer Chaplin Immigration and Naturalization Service File, Pt. 1, p. 229.

16. Getty Diaries, June 12, 1941.

17. Joan Berry interview, Chaplin FBI File, Pt. 3, pp. 173–74.

18. Chaplin, *My Autobiography*, 407.

19. Joan Berry interview, Chaplin FBI File, Pt. 3, p. 174; Chaplin, *My Autobiography*, 407.

20. Chaplin Jr., *My Father*, 255–56; Chaplin, *My Autobiography*, 407.

21. Chaplin Jr., *My Father*, 252.

22. Getty Diaries, May 26, 1941.

23. Thomas Wells Durant interview with the FBI, Jan. 5, 1944, Chaplin FBI File, Pt. 4, pp. 90–91.

24. Getty Diaries, June 1, 1941.

25. Getty Diaries, June 7, 1941.

26. Chaplin, *My Autobiography*, 407–8; "Weather Report," *Los Angeles Times*, June 12, 1941.

27. Chaplin, *My Autobiography*, 408.

28. Chaplin, *My Autobiography*, 408; Joan Berry interview, Chaplin FBI File, Pt. 3, p. 174.

29. Getty Diaries, June 12, 1941.

30. Chaplin, *My Autobiography*, 408.

31. Getty Diaries, June 19, 1941; Playground to the Stars, "1941: Mocambo Opens," West Hollywood History, www.playgroundtothestars.com, accessed Nov. 6, 2023.

32. Records of Charles Chaplin Studios, Chaplin FBI File, Pt. 2, pp. 176, 181.

33. Joan Berry interview, Chaplin FBI File, Pt. 3, p. 175.

34. Alistair Cooke, *Six Men* (New York: Alfred A. Knopf, 1977), 25.

35. May Reeves and Claire Goll, *The Intimate Charlie Chaplin* (Jefferson, NC: McFarland, 2001), 21, 26.

36. Joan Berry interview, Chaplin FBI File, Pt. 2, p. 152; Daily Production Report, Charles Chaplin Film Corp., W/E July 12, 1941, Charlie Chaplin Archive, ECCI00313439, CHM24.

37. Chaplin Jr., *My Father*, 256; Records of Charlie Chaplin Studios, Chaplin FBI File, Pt. 2, p. 177.

38. Durant interview, Chaplin FBI File, Pt. 4, p. 95.

39. Durant interview, Chaplin FBI File, Pt. 4, p. 97.

40. Joan Berry interview, Chaplin FBI File, Pt. 2, p. 152; Records of Charles Chaplin Studios, Chaplin FBI File, Pt. 2, pp. 176–78.

41. Records of Charles Chaplin Studios, Chaplin FBI File, Pt. 2, pp. 176–78.

42. Getty Diaries, July 12, 1941; Aug. 10, 1941; Aug. 27, 1941; Oct. 4, 1941; Oct. 18, 1941; Oct. 22, 1941; Oct. 30, 1941; Oct. 31, 1941; Dec. 18, 1941.

43. Getty Diaries, Aug. 24, 1941.

44. Gertrude E. Berry interview, Chaplin FBI File, Pt. 5, p. 55.

45. John Berry, Ind. No. 2816/1948, New York County District Attorney File.

46. Getty Diaries, Aug. 8, 1941; Aug. 30, 1941; Oct. 31, 1941.

47. Joan Berry interview, Chaplin FBI File, Pt. 2, p. 155.

48. Joan Berry interview, Chaplin FBI File, Pt. 2, p. 153–54.

49. Statement of Dr. A. M. Tweedy [sic], to Los Angeles County District Attorney investigators, June 5, 1943, Chaplin INS File, Pt. 3, p. 1063.

50. Sworn Statement of Jeanette Voris to INS, Oct. 1, 1952, Chaplin INS File, Pt. 3, p. 732. The name "Jeanette Voris" is blacked out, but her name appears on other documents in connection with Joan's abortions, and the statements and their context indicate she is the speaker. "Probation, Jail Term for Doctor," *Hollywood Citizen-News*, Sept. 17, 1942.

51. Voris statement to INS, Chaplin INS File, Pt. 3, p. 732; Dr. A. M. Tweedy [sic] statement, June 5, 1943, Chaplin INS File, Pt. 3, Pg. 1,062.

52. C. B. Pinkham, M.D., Secretary/Treasurer, State of California Board of Medical Examiners to Los Angeles County Clerk, July 2, 1937; C. B. Pinkham, M.D., to Los Angeles County Clerk, Feb. 17, 1939, Arthur Maurice Tweedie, Dept. of Professional and Vocational Standards, Board of Medical Examiners Physician's Register, California State Archives.

53. Beauchamp, *Without Lying Down*, 221.

54. Marcie Bianco and Merryn Johns, "Classic Hollywood's Secret: Studios Wanted Their Stars to Have Abortions," *Vanity Fair*, July 15, 2016.

55. Dr. Laurie Goldstein, interview with the author, Oct. 25, 2021.

56. Statement of June Wilson to Los Angeles County District Attorney's investigators, June 7, 1943, Chaplin INS File, Pt. 3, p. 1079. As with Jeanette Voris's statement, the name in this report is also blacked out, but her name appears elsewhere in connection with Joan's abortions.

57. *People of the State of California v. Arthur M. Tweedie*, No. 89, 836 (Sup. Ct. L.A. County, 1942).

58. *People v. Tweedie*, No. 89, 836, District Attorney's Recommendation, Aug. 26, 1942.

59. In re: Application for the Revocation of the License of Arthur M. Tweedie, M.D., Minutes of the Meeting of the Board of Medical Examiners, March 10, 1943, F3760:32, California State Archives.

60. Dr. A. M. Tweedy [*sic*] statement, June 5, 1943, Chaplin INS File, Pt. 3, p. 1062.

61. June Wilson statement, Chaplin INS File, Pt. 3, p. 1078.

62. Joan Berry interview, Chaplin FBI File, Pt. 3, p. 177.

63. Voris statement to INS, Chaplin INS File, Pt. 3, p. 735.

64. Statement of employee (name blacked out) of Dr. Tweedie to INS investigators, Oct. 24, 1952, Chaplin INS File, Pt. 3, p. 922.

65. Interview with Edward Charles Chaney, Oct. 30, 1943, Chaplin FBI File, Pt. 2, p. 175.

66. Getty Diaries, Nov. 5, 1941.

67. Joan Berry interview, Chaplin FBI File, Pt. 3, p. 178.

68. Joan Berry interview, Chaplin FBI File, Pt. 3, p. 182.

69. Joan Berry interview, Chaplin FBI File, Pt. 3, pp. 178–79.

70. Joan Berry interview, Chaplin FBI File, Pt. 3, p. 180; interview with Gertrude E. Berry, Nov. 26, 1943, Chaplin FBI File, Pt. 5, p. 56.

71. Voris statement to INS, Chaplin INS File, Pt. 3, p. 734; Joan Berry interview, Chaplin FBI File, Pt. 3, p. 180.

72. Joan Berry interview, Chaplin FBI File, Pt. 2, p. 157.

73. Statement of Jeanette Voris to Los Angeles County District Attorney investigators, June 7, 1943, Chaplin INS File, Pt. 3, pp. 1092–93.

74. Voris statement to INS, Chaplin INS File, Pt. 3, pp. 738–39.

75. Voris statement to LADA, Chaplin INS File, Pt. 3, p. 1094.

76. Joan Berry interview, Chaplin FBI File, Pt. 2, p. 157.

77. Joan Berry interview, Chaplin FBI File, Pt. 2, p. 158.

78. Durant interview, Chaplin FBI File, Pt. 4, p. 96.

79. Joan Barry photographs in costume, Charlie Chaplin Archive, ECCI00028943, SS0006.

80. Daily Production Report, Charles Chaplin, W/E Jan. 24, 1942, and Jan. 31, 1942, Charlie Chaplin Archive, ECCI00313439, CHM24.

CHAPTER 5

1. Paul Vincent Carroll, *Shadow and Substance: A Play in Four Acts* (New York: Random House, 1937).

2. Carroll, *Shadow and Substance*.

3. Joan Berry interview with FBI, Jan. 7, 1944, Chaplin FBI File, Pt. 2, p. 156.

4. Carroll, *Shadow and Substance*, Act 1, 13.

5. Alfred Reeves interview with FBI, Nov. 19, 1943, Chaplin FBI File, Pt. 2, pp. 176–77.

6. Robinson, *Chaplin*, 512.

7. Paul Carroll to Sir Cedric Hardwicke, telegram, 1942, Charlie Chaplin Archive ECCI00008150, CH049.

8. Paul Vincent Carroll and Shadow and Substance, Inc. contract with United Artists Corp., Feb. 25, 1942, Charlie Chaplin Archive, ECCI00008058, CH000.

9. Charles Schwartz to Alfred Reeves, Mar. 4, 1942, Charlie Chaplin Archive, ECCI00008281, CH049.

10. "Reinhardt, Producer, Dies in East; Pneumonia Following Stroke Proves Fatal to Famed Impresario," *New York Times*, Nov. 1, 1943; "History of Theatre of Arts: The Original Hollywood Acting School," Theatre of Arts, www.toa.edu/acting -drama-school-history, accessed Dec. 7, 2021; David Conolly, executive director, Theatre of Arts (the old Max Reinhardt school), interview with the author, Nov. 30, 2021.

11. Robinson, *Chaplin*, 513.

12. Chaplin Jr., *My Father*, 260.

13. Getty Diaries, Jan. 19, 1942.

14. Getty Diaries, Feb. 2, 1942.

15. Getty Diaries, Feb. 20, 1942.

16. Getty Diaries, Dec. 26, 1941–Dec. 26, 1942.

17. Samuel Marx interview with FBI, Mar. 18, 1944, Chaplin FBI File, Pt. 5, p. 46.

18. Joanne Berry to Mr. Reeves, Chaplin FBI File, Pt. 2, p. 185.

19. Gertrude E. Berry interview with FBI, Chaplin FBI File, Pt. 5, p. 56.

20. "Hedda Hopper's Hollywood," *Los Angeles Times*, May 24, 1942.

21. "Hedda Hopper's Hollywood," *Los Angeles Times*, May 24, 1942.

22. George Eells, *Hedda and Louella* (New York: G. P. Putnam's Sons, 1972), 210.

23. Eells, *Hedda and Louella*, 228.

24. Getty Diaries, May 29, 1942,

25. Getty Diaries, June 2, 1942.

26. J. Paul Getty interview with FBI, Nov. 22, 1943, Chaplin FBI File, Pt. 5, p. 35.

27. Marx interview, Chaplin FBI File, Pt. 5, p. 46.

28. Marx interview, Chaplin FBI File, Pt. 5, p. 46.

29. Marx interview, Chaplin FBI File, Pt. 5, p. 47.

30. George Wallach, "Charlie Chaplin's Monsieur Verdoux Press Conference," *Film Comment* 5, no. 4 (Winter 1969): 34, 36.

31. Chaplin, *My Autobiography*, 401–2.

32. Chaplin, *My Autobiography*, 404–5; address of Charles Chaplin, "Support the President Rally for a Second Front Now!" Madison Square Park, July 22, 1942, Berg Collection of English and American Literature, New York Public Library.

33. Gertrude Berry interview, Chaplin FBI File, Pt. 5, p. 57; Harry Mines, "Music Review," *Los Angeles Daily News*, July 22, 1942.

34. Robinson, *Chaplin*, 399.

35. Chaplin, My Autobiography, 409.

36. Chaplin, *My Autobiography*, 409; John McCabe, *Charlie Chaplin* (Garden City, NY: Doubleday, 1978), 236.

37. Chaplin, *My Autobiography*, 409.

38. Joan Berry interview, Jan. 7, 10, and 11, 1943, Chaplin FBI File, Pt. 3, p. 183.

39. Edward Chaney interview with Los Angeles County District Attorney's investigators, June 6, 1943, Chaplin INS File, Pt. 3, p. 1044.

40. Minna Wallis interview with FBI, Dec. 4, 1943, Chaplin FBI File, Pt. 5, p. 25-26.

41. Marx interview, Chaplin FBI File, Pt. 5, p. 48.

42. Records of Charles Chaplin Studios, Chaplin FBI File, Pt. 2, p. 179.

43. Joan Berry interview, Chaplin FBI File, Pt. 2, p. 160; Gertrude Berry interview with FBI, Nov. 26, 1943, Chaplin FBI File, Pt. 2, p. 207.

44. Joan Berry interview, Chaplin FBI File, Pt. 2, p. 160; "Chaplin, et al., White Slave Traffic Act Report," Mar. 18, 1944, Chaplin FBI File, Pt. 3, p. 60.

45. Joan Berry interview, Chaplin FBI File, Pt. 2, p. 160; Richard Severo, "Jinx Falkenburg, Model, Actress, Pioneer of Radio and TV Talk Shows, Dies at 84," *New York Times*, Aug. 28, 2003; History, Miss Rheingold, https://www.missrheingold.com/history, accessed April 1, 2024. The New York Times obituary of Falkenburg reports that she was Miss Rheingold in 1941, company public relations literature places the year as 1940.

46. Joan Berry interview, Chaplin FBI File, Pt. 2, p. 160.

47. David S. Hecht Jr., interview with the author, Oct. 21, 2020; Anthony Hecht, interview with the author, Nov. 1, 2020.

48. Joan Berry interview, Chaplin FBI File, Pt. 2, p. 160.

49. A. Rosen to E. A. Tamm, memorandum, Nov. 5, 1943, Chaplin FBI File, Pt. 2, p. 128; Charles Choquet, Assistant Manager, Hotel Pierre, interview with FBI, Chaplin FBI File, Pt. 2, p. 195.

50. Conroy to Director and SACS, telemeter, Mar. 4, 1944, Chaplin FBI File, Pt. 3, p. 18.

51. Harry Pushman, Chief Accountant, New York Central Railroad, interview with FBI, Chaplin FBI File, Pt. 2, p. 89.

52. W. F. McDermott, Credit Manager, Waldorf Astoria Hotel, interview with FBI Sept. 2, 1943, Chaplin FBI File, Pt. 2, p. 195.

53. Thomas Wells Durant interview with FBI, Jan. 3, 1943, Chaplin FBI File, Pt. 2, p. 200.

54. Joan Berry interview, Chaplin FBI File, Pt. 2, p. 160.

55. Affidavit of Guenther Reinhardt, Chaplin INS File, Pt. 1, pp. 1582, 1594–95.

56. Joan Berry interview, Chaplin FBI File, Pt. 2, p. 160.

57. Joan Berry interview, Chaplin FBI File, Pt. 2, p. 160.

58. Chaplin, *My Autobiography*, 410.

59. Joan Berry interview, Chaplin FBI File, Pt. 2, p. 161.

60. Joan Berry interview, Chaplin FBI File, Pt. 2, pp. 161–62.

61. Daily Production Reports, W/E Nov. 14, 1942, and W/E Jan. 2, 1943, Charlie Chaplin Archive, ECCI00313699, CH131.

62. Chaplin, *My Autobiography*, 412.

63. Joan Berry interview, Chaplin FBI File, Pt. 2, p. 163.

64. "Chatterbox," *Los Angeles Times*, Apr. 19, 1940; "Chatterbox," *Los Angeles Times*, Jan. 12, 1940; Sylvia Weaver, "Max Reinhardt Visions 'Hamlet' as Master Motion Picture Mystery Story; Director Believes Play Can Be More Thrilling on Film; Ambitions Confided to Joine Alderman's Debutante Salon Group," *Los Angeles Times*, Oct. 20, 1935; Barbara Trippet, "Chatterbox," *Los Angeles Times*, Oct. 13, 1940.

65. "Jimmy McHugh," Songwriters Hall of Fame, www.songhall.org/profile/Jimmy _McHugh, accessed Dec. 19, 2021; David Dempsey, "In and Out of Books," *New York Times*, Feb. 19, 1950; Margalit Fox, "Hans Ruesch, 94, Writer and Grand Prix Winner," *New York Times*, Sept. 3, 2007.

66. Joan Barry interview, Chaplin FBI File, Pt. 2, p. 163.

67. Joan Barry interview, Chaplin FBI File, Pt. 2, p. 164–65.

68. Joan Barry interview, Chaplin FBI File, Pt. 2, p. 164.

69. Chaney interview, Los Angeles County District Attorney's investigators, June 6, 1943, Chaplin INS File, Pt. 3, p. 1051.

70. Beverly Hills Hotel to Rosenstein & Gore, Nov. 24, 1942, Chaplin FBI File, Pt. 3, p. 56; Mr. Cortright and Mr. Wilson [first names unclear] interview with FBI, Chaplin FBI File, Pt. 5, pp. 93–95.

71. Edward Nash interview with FBI, Chaplin FBI File, Pt. 3, pp. 42, 54.

72. Beverly Hills Hotel to Rosenstein & Gore, telegram, Nov. 24, 1942; Rosenstein & Gore to Beverly Hills Hotel, Nov. 26, 1942, Chaplin FBI File, Pt. 3, p. 249.

73. Joan Berry interview, Chaplin FBI File, Pt. 2, pp. 164–65.

74. Minna Wallis interview with Los Angeles County District Attorney's investigators, June 5, 1943, Chaplin INS File, Pt. 3, p. 999.

75. "Joan Berry, Weeping, Leaves Witness Stand; Ex-Protégé of Charles Chaplin Breaks Down After Telling Their Relations," Los Angeles Times, Dec. 22, 1944.

76. Kitchin to Director and SAC, teletype, Nov. 27, 1943, Chaplin FBI File, Pt. 1, p. 173.

77. "Joan Berry, Weeping, Leaves Witness Stand."

78. Getty Diaries, Nov. 17–23, 1942.

79. Joan Berry interview, Chaplin FBI File, Pt. 1, p. 108.

80. Joan Berry interview, Chaplin FBI File, Pt. 2 p. 165.

81. Charles Chaplin Daily Production Reports, W/E Nov. 28, Dec. 5, and Dec. 12, 1943, Charlie Chaplin Archive, ECCI00313699, CH131.

82. Ludwig F. Grimstead, Credit Manager, Ambassador Hotel, interview with FBI, Mar. 9, 1944, Chaplin FBI File, Pt. 5, p. 68; Joan Berry interview, Chaplin FBI File, Pt. 2, p. 165; Lionello Vasco Giuseppe Bonini, Declaration of Intention No. 93996, Aug. 24, 1939, United States District Court, Southern District California, Ancestry, www.ancestry.com.

83. Joan Berry interview, Chaplin FBI File, Pt. 2, p. 165.
84. Investigator's Report, Charles Chaplin and Joan Berry, aka Joan Barry, Aug. 4, 1943, Chaplin INS File, Pt. 3, p. 757; Joan Berry interview, Chaplin FBI File, Pt. 2, p. 166.
85. Joan Berry interview, Chaplin FBI File, Pt. 2, p. 166.
86. Joan Berry interview, Chaplin FBI File, Pt. 3, p. 188.

CHAPTER 6

1. Milton, *Tramp*, 407.
2. Jane Scovell, *Oona, Living in the Shadows: A Biography of Oona O'Neill Chaplin* (New York: Warner Books, 1998) 113.
3. Milton, *Tramp*, 407–8.
4. Oona O'Neill interview with Los Angeles District Attorney's investigators, June 4, 1943, Chaplin INS File, Pt. 3, pp. 965–66.
5. Milton, *Tramp*, 407–10.
6. Kenneth S. Lynn, *Charlie Chaplin and His Times* (New York: Simon & Schuster, 1997), 429.
7. Eugene O'Neill to Harry Weinberger, May 12, 1942, in Travis Bogard and Jackson R. Breyer, eds., *Selected Letters of Eugene O'Neill* (New Haven: Yale University Press, 1988), 528.
8. Scovell, *Oona*, 83–84.
9. Eugene O'Neill to Robert Sisk, Feb. 22, 1943, in Bogard and Breyer, *Selected Letters of Eugene O'Neill*, 541–42.
10. Lynn, *Charlie Chaplin and His Times*, 430.
11. Scovell, *Oona*, 93–94.
12. Eugene O'Neill to Harry Weinberger, Sept. 28, 1942, in Bogard and Breyer, *Selected Letters of Eugene O'Neill*, 533.
13. Milton, *Tramp*, 410.
14. O'Neill interview with LADA investigators , Chaplin INS File, Pt. 3, pp. 968–69.
15. Chaplin, *My Autobiography*, 413–14.
16. Lyons, "Roland H. Totheroh Interviewed," 278.
17. Lyons, "Roland H. Totheroh Interviewed," 278.
18. Chaplin Jr., *My Father*, 271–72.
19. The date of Joan's visit to Chaplin's with her gun was a source of confusion. Joan initially told the FBI it was Dec. 19, 1942; Chaplin's oldest son recalled the date as Dec. 23. At trial, Dec. 23 came to be the accepted date.
20. Joan Berry interview, Chaplin FBI File, Pt. 2, p. 166.
21. Joan Berry interview, Chaplin FBI File, Pt. 2, p. 166.
22. Joan Berry interview, Chaplin FBI File, Pt. 2, p. 166.
23. Joan Berry interview, Chaplin FBI File, Pt. 2, pp. 166–67.
24. Joan Berry interview, Chaplin FBI File, Pt. 2, p. 167.

25. Chaplin Jr., *My Father*, 265–66.

26. Charles Chaplin Jr. and Sidney [*sic*] Chaplin interview with LADA investigators, June 7, 1943, Chaplin INS File, Pt. 3, p. 993.

27. Joan Berry interview, Chaplin FBI File, Pt. 2, p. 168.

28. Joan Berry interview, Chaplin FBI File, Pt. 2. p. 168.

29. Joan Berry interview, Chaplin FBI File, Pt. 2., pp. 168–69.

30. Sgt. Claude Marple interview with Los Angeles County District Attorney's investigators, June 4, 1942, Chaplin FBI File, Pt. 4, pp. 61–62. On Nov. 29, 1943, Marple gave another interview to FBI agents about his encounter with Joan on Dec. 31, 1942, Chaplin FBI File, Pt. 4, pp. 51–61. Both interviews are included in the FBI file.

31. Marple interview, Chaplin FBI File, Pt. 4, p. 51.

32. Marple interview, Chaplin FBI File, Pt. 4, p. 52.

33. Joan Berry interview, Chaplin FBI File, Pt. 3, p. 191; Robert Arden interview, Nov. 22, 1943, Chaplin FBI File, Pt. 3, pp. 230–31.

34. Joan Berry interview, Chaplin FBI File, Pt. 3, p. 191.

35. Joan Berry interview, Chaplin FBI File, Pt. 3, p. 191.

36. Joan Berry interview, Chaplin FBI File, Pt. 3, pp. 191–92.

37. Unnamed investigators (probably Herbert Grossman and Philip T. Tower) to Fred H. Howser, District Attorney, memorandum, June 9, 1943, Chaplin INS File, Pt. 3, p. 775.

38. Chaney interview, Chaplin FBI File, Pt. 4, pp. 150–51.

39. Joan Berry interview, Chaplin FBI File, Pt. 3, p. 192.

40. Marple interview with Los Angeles County District Attorney's investigators, Chaplin FBI File, Pt. 4, p. 63.

41. Joan Berry interview, Chaplin FBI File, Pt. 3, p. 193.

42. Joan Berry interview, Chaplin FBI File, Pt. 3, pp. 192–93.

43. Review of Los Angeles County District Attorney's Office File Concerning W. W. White, Nov. 17, 1943, Chaplin FBI File, Pt. 4, p. 12.

44. Muir, *Headline Happy*, 58.

45. Durant interview, Chaplin FBI File, Pt. 4, p. 108.

46. Robert Arden interview with Los Angeles County District Attorney's investigators, June 6, 1943, Chaplin FBI File, Pt. 3, p. 221.

47. Arden interview, Chaplin FBI File, Pt. 3, p. 221.

48. Arden interview, Nov. 22, 1943, Chaplin FBI File, Pt. 3, p. 232.

49. Capt. W. W. White interview, March 1943, Chaplin FBI File, Pt. 4, p. 19.

50. Dale Kibby interview, Jan. 31, 1944, Chaplin FBI File, Pt. 4, p. 115.

51. Judge Charles J. Griffin interview, Nov. 23, 1943, Chaplin FBI File, Pt. 4, pp. 33–34.

52. Muir, *Headline Happy*, 59.

53. B. J. Firminger, Beverly Hills City Clerk, interview, Jan. 28, 1944, Chaplin FBI File, Pt. 4, p. 112.

54. The first public defender office providing legal services without charge to the poor accused of crimes opened in Los Angeles County in 1914. Laurence A. Benner, "The California Public Defender: Its Origins, Evolution and Decline," *California Legal History* (2010): 173, 179, https://scholarlycommons.law.cwsl.edu/fs/148/, accessed Dec. 5, 2023. Today, the right to counsel is part of the California state constitution. Cal. Const. art. I § 15.
55. Joan Berry interview, Chaplin FBI File, Pt. 3, p. 194.
56. Jessie Winifred Reno interview with Los Angeles District Attorney's investigators, June 4, 1943, Chaplin FBI File, Pt. 4. pp. 71–72.
57. Judge Griffin interview, Chaplin FBI File, Pt. 4, p. 35.
58. *Papachristou v. City of Jacksonville*, 405 U.S. 156 (1972); *Kolender v. Lawson*, 461 U.S. 352 (1983).
59. Arden interview, Chaplin FBI File, Pt. 3, p. 243.
60. Arden interview, Chaplin FBI File, Pt. 3, p. 243.
61. Joan Berry interview, Chaplin FBI File, Pt. 3, p. 196.
62. Joan Berry interview, Chaplin FBI File, Pt. 3, p. 197.
63. Beverly Hills Police Chief C. H. Anderson interview, Chaplin FBI File, Pt. 4, pp. 121–23.
64. Joan Berry interview, Chaplin FBI File, Pt. 3, p. 197.

CHAPTER 7

1. Oona O'Neill interview with LADA's investigators, June 4, 1943, Chaplin INS File, Pt. 3, pp. 964, 969.
2. Ed Sullivan, "Little Old New York: Men and Maids, and Stuff," *Daily News* (New York), January 18, 1943.
3. Louella O. Parsons, "Myrna Loy Sought for 'Thin Man' Role; Star Expected to Return to Movies in Old Role Opposite Bill Powell," *Philadelphia Inquirer*, April 8, 1943.
4. Oona O'Neill interview, Chaplin INS File, Pt. 3, p. 975.
5. Background Information on Charles Chaplin and His Association with Berry, Chaplin FBI File, Pt. 1, p. 112.
6. Chaplin, Gribble, WSTA Report, Nov. 20, 1943, Chaplin FBI File, Pt. 1, pp. 156–57.
7. "History, If These Walls Could Talk. . . ." The Paxton Ballroom, www.thepaxtonballroom.com/history, accessed July 25, 2023.
8. Chaplin, Gribble, WSTA Report, Nov. 20, 1943, Chaplin FBI File, Pt. 1, p. 149.
9. "Passenger Service to Be Cut Sharply on Nation's Trains. . . ." *New York Times*, May 3, 1942; Ward Allan Howe, "War Burden Limits Rail Facilities; Vacations Not Forbidden but Essential Trips Get Preference," *New York Times*, June 13, 1943.

10. Gaston, *Alone Together*, 167–72, 187.

11. Getty Diaries, Dec. 25, 1942.

12. Chaplin, Gribble, WSTA Report, Nov. 20, 1943, Chaplin FBI File, Pt. 1, pp. 151–52.

13. Gaston, *Alone Together*, 211.

14. Joan Berry interview, Chaplin FBI File, Pt. 3, p. 197.

15. Joan Berry interview, Chaplin FBI File, Pt. 3, p. 198.

16. Tulsa Police Dept. File No. 150,241 (Joan Berry), Jan. 23, 1943, Chaplin FBI File, Pt. 3, p. 59.

17. Joan Berry interview, Chaplin FBI File, Pt. 3, p. 198; Chaplin, Gribble, WSTA Report, Pt. 1, pp. 151–52.

18. Chaplin, Gribble WSTA Report, Chaplin FBI File, Pt. 1, p. 151.

19. Chaplin, Gribble WSTA Report, Chaplin FBI File, Pt. 1, p. 151.

20. Chaplin, Gribble WSTA Report, Synopsis of Tulsa Police Dept. file on Berry arrest, Mar. 18, 1944, Chaplin FBI File, Pt. 3, p. 53.

21. Getty Diaries, Mar. 4–20, 1943.

22. Joan Berry interview, Chaplin File, FBI Pt. 3, p. 198; "Noble Sells WMCA to Nathan Strauss; Former U.S. Housing Chief to Devote Entire Time to the Station's Management; Price Put at $1,255,000; Ownership of Blue Network With WJZ, Forces Owner to Dispose of 2d Outlet," *New York Times*, Sept. 14, 1943.

23. F. A. Padget, Manager and Vice-President, Pierre Hotel, and Charles Chaquet, Credit Manager, Pierre Hotel, interviews, Chaplin FBI File, Pt. 3, p. 62.

24. Joan Berry interview, Chaplin FBI File, Pt. 3, p. 199.

25. Joan Berry, Note and Release, Chaplin FBI File, Apr. 16, 1943, Pt. 3, p. 57–58.

26. Olga Melton, Proprietor Biltmore Beauty Shop, and Helen Kirk interviews, Chaplin FBI File, Pt. 5, pp. 77–78.

27. Gaston, *Alone Together*, 223–24.

28. Gaston, *Alone Together*, 224–27.

29. Joan Berry interview, Chaplin FBI File, Pt. 3, p. 199; Hadley Mears, "The Chateau Elysee: Scientology's Celebrity Centre Before It Went Clear," PBS SoCal, www.pbssocal.org/history-society/the-chateau-elysee-scientologys-celebrity-centre-before-it-went-went-clear, accessed Nov. 9, 2023.

30. E. L. Hamilton, "When a Hollywood Producer Died Shortly after a Wild Party on William Randolph Hearst's Yacht, There Were Whispers Charlie Chaplin Was Involved," The Vintage News, www.thevintagenews.com/2017/12/06/thomas-inces-death-2/, accessed Nov. 9, 2023.

31. Joan Berry interview, Chaplin FBI File, Pt. 3, p. 199.

32. Joan Berry interview, Chaplin FBI File, Pt. 3, p. 199; "William Castle," IMDb, www.imdb.com/name/nm0145336/bio?ref_=nm_ov_bio_sm, accessed Feb. 19, 2022.

33. Joan Berry interview, Chaplin FBI File, Pt. 3, p. 199.

34. "Wartime Weather," *Los Angeles Times*, May 8, 1943.

35. Milton, *Tramp*, 417.

36. Hedda Hopper interview, Chaplin FBI File, Jan. 8, 1944, Pt. 4, p. 175.

37. Eells, *Hedda and Louella*, 54–55, 61–65, 81.

38. Eells, *Hedda and Louella*, 102–4.

39. Eells, *Hedda and Louella*, 210.

40. Thomas Wells Durant interview with LADA's investigators June 6, 1943, 82, 85.

41. Edward Chaney interview, Dec. 10, 1943, Chaplin FBI File, Pt. 4, pp. 85, 155.

42. Claude Ray Marple interview, Chaplin FBI File, Pt. 4, pp. 51, 56.

43. Marple interview, Chaplin FBI File, Pt. 4, p. 56; Anne Marple, "Eulogy to Claude Ray Marple" (on file with the author).

44. Marple interview, Chaplin FBI File, Pt. 4, p. 66 (This portion of Marple's statement comes from an interview conducted by Los Angeles District Attorney's investigators on June 4, 1943, and provided to the FBI.)

45. Hopper interview, Chaplin FBI File, Pt. 4, p. 70.

46. Muir, *Headline Happy*, 56; Mary Mallory, "Hollywood Heights: The House of Westmore Beautifies Hollywood," *Daily Mirror*, May 20, 2019, www.ladailymirror.com/2019/05/20/mary-mallory-hollywood-heights-the-house-of-westmore-beautifies-hollywood-2/, accessed Feb. 26, 2022.

CHAPTER 8

1. Muir, *Headline Happy*, 56.

2. Muir, *Headline Happy*, 56–57.

3. Muir, *Headline Happy*, 32, 202–3, 209–10.

4. *In re: Joan Berry*, D-2445, Beverly Hills City Court records, Chaplin FBI File, Pt. 4, p. 143; interview with Florabel Muir, Jan. 13, 1944, Chaplin FBI File, Pt. 4. p. 163.

5. Muir interview, Chaplin FBI File, Pt. 4, p. 164.

6. Muir interview, Chaplin FBI File, Pt. 4, p.164.

7. Hopper interview, Chaplin FBI File, Pt. 4, p. 175.

8. Muir interview, Chaplin FBI File, Pt. 4, p. 164.

9. Muir interview, Chaplin FBI File, Pt. 4, p. 164.

10. Muir, *Headline Happy*, 63.

11. Muir interview, Chaplin FBI File, Pt. 4, p. 165.

12. Muir interview, Chaplin FBI File, Pt. 4, pp. 165–66; "Atty. Hahn Dies in Swimming Pool Mystery; Cement Weights on Neck," *Los Angeles Times*, June 26, 1957.

13. Muir interview, Chaplin, FBI File, Pt. 4, p. 166.

14. Capt. White interview, Chaplin FBI File, Pt. 4, p. 29.

15. Cecil Holland interview, Dec. 29, 1943, Chaplin FBI File, Pt. 5, p. 7.

16. "Flynn Promises Not to Hit Fidler Anymore; Film Actor Tells Court His Version of Night Club Row with Gossip Columnist," *Los Angeles Times*, Oct. 1, 1941.

17. "F.B.I. Queries Justice in Chaplin-Berry Case; Full Investigation Started in 'Vagging' of Young Mother Making Paternity Charge," *Los Angeles Times*, June 6, 1944.

18. Durant interview, Chaplin FBI File, Pt. 4, p. 88.

19. Durant interview, Chaplin FBI File, Pt. 4, p. 102.

20. Judge Charles J. Griffin interview, Nov. 23, 1943, Chaplin FBI File, Pt. 4, p. 40.

21. *In re: Joan Berry*, D-2445, Chaplin FBI File, Pt. 4, p. 143; Muir interview, Chaplin FBI File, Pt. 4, p. 163.

22. Griffin interview, Chaplin FBI File, Pt. 4, p. 40.

23. Griffin interview, Chaplin FBI File, Pt. 4, p. 40.

24. Griffin interview, Chaplin FBI File, Pt. 4, p. 41.

25. Arden interview, Chaplin FBI File, Pt. 4, p. 1.

26. Muir interview, Chaplin FBI File, Pt. 4, p. 166.

27. Gertrude Berry interview, Chaplin FBI File, Pt. 5, p. 57.

28. Muir interview, Chaplin FBI File, Pt. 4, p. 168; "Hollywood Publisher Judge Palmer Dies," *Los Angeles Times*, July 26, 1956.

29. "Editorial Comment: Answers," *Hollywood Citizen-News*, May 15, 1943.

30. Muir interview, Chaplin, FBI File, Pt. 4, p. 162.

31. Edith Gwyne, "Rambling Reporter," *Hollywood Reporter*, May 17, 1943.

32. Judge Charles J. Griffin to the Beverly Hills City Council, June 14, 1943, Chaplin FBI File, Pt. 4, pp. 42–49.

33. Judge Charles J. Griffin to Hon. Fred N. Howser, May 27, 1943, Chaplin FBI File, Pt. 4, pp. 49–50.

34. Judge Griffin to City Council, Chaplin FBI File, Pt. 4, pp. 43, 46.

35. Muir interview, Chaplin FBI File, Pt. 4, pp. 166–67.

36. Muir interview, Chaplin FBI File, Pt. 4, pp. 167, 174.

37. Milton, *Tramp*, 421.

38. Muir interview, Chaplin FBI File, Pt. 4, p. 167.

39. Muir interview, Chaplin FBI File, Pt. 4, pp. 167–68.

40. Florabel Muir, "Joan and Chaplin Dine; Ma Visions Bridal Cake," *Daily News* (New York), June 2, 1943.

41. Muir interview, Chaplin FBI File, Pt. 4, p. 168.

42. Muir interview, Chaplin FBI File, Pt. 4, p. 162.

43. Muir interview, Chaplin FBI File, Pt. 4, p. 168.

44. Muir interview, Chaplin FBI File, Pt. 4, p. 169.

45. Muir interview, Chaplin FBI File, Pt. 4, p. 169.

46. John J. Irwin, World War II Draft Registration Card, Ancestry, www.ancestry.com.

47. Myrna Oliver, "John J. Irwin; L.A. Deputy Mayor to Poulson in '50s," *Los Angeles Times*, Mar. 6, 1995.

48. Oliver, "John J. Irwin; L.A. Deputy Mayor to Poulson in '50s"; Joseph R. Irwin, interviews with the author, Dec. 20, 2020; Mar. 6, 2022.

49. Muir interview, Chaplin FBI File, Pt. 4, p. 169.

50. Hedda Hopper, "Looking at Hollywood," *Chicago Daily Tribune*, June 3, 1943.

51. *John Doe Chaplin, an infant by Gertrude E. Berry, Guardian Ad Litem v. Charles Spencer Chaplin*, D-238936, Complaint, June 3, 1943.

52. Frederick C. Othman, "Ex-Protégé Sues Chaplin for Support of Unborn Baby," *Austin Statesman*, June 4, 1943.

53. "Court Orders Chaplin to Answer Suit; Screen Star Served with Papers in Action Brought by Joan Berry," *Los Angeles Times*, June 5, 1943.

54. Associated Press, "Charlie Chaplin Is Sued as Unborn Child's Father; Woman Had Been Jailed for Disturbance at His Home," *New York Herald Tribune*, June 4, 1943.

55. United Press, "Chaplin, 53, Denies Girl's Charge; Tells of Demand for Money," *Press Democrat* (Santa Rosa, CA), June 4, 1943.

56. Hopper interview, Chaplin FBI File, Pt. 4, p. 70.

57. "F.N. Howser New District Attorney; Assemblyman from Long Beach Chosen to Succeed Dockweiler," *Los Angeles Times*, February 2, 1943.

58. "Court Orders Chaplin to Answer Suit."

CHAPTER 9

1. Joan Berry interview with LADA's investigators, May 29, 1943, Chaplin INS File, Pt. 3, pp. 1147, 1171–72.

2. Joan Berry interview, Chaplin INS File, Pt. 3, p. 1149.

3. Joan Berry interview, Chaplin INS File, Pt. 3, p. 1174; Getty Diaries, Nov. 17–23, 1942; Jan. 15, 1943.

4. Joan Berry interview, Chaplin INS File, Pt. 3, p. 1148.

5. Joan Berry interview, Chaplin INS File, Pt. 3, p. 1154.

6. Joan Berry interview, Chaplin INS File, Pt. 3, p. 1167.

7. Oona O'Neill interview with LADA's investigators, Chaplin INS File, Pt. 3, pp. 964, 974.

8. Oona O'Neill interview, Chaplin INS File, Pt. 3, p. 975.

9. Oona O'Neill interview, Chaplin INS File, Pt. 3, p. 985.

10. Dr. Arthur M. Tweedy [*sic*] interview with LADA's investigators, June 5, 1943, at 2:15 a.m., Chaplin INS File, Pt. 3, p. 1059.

11. Tweedy [*sic*] interview, Chaplin INS File, Pt. 3, p. 1060.

12. Tweedy [*sic*] interview, Chaplin INS File, Pt. 3, p. 1061.

13. Tweedy [*sic*] interview, 3:50 p.m., June 5, 1943, Chaplin INS File, Pt. 3, pp. 1063–64.

14. Wallis interview with LADA's investigators, Chaplin INS File, Pt. 3, p. 999.

15. Durant interview with LADA's investigators, Chaplin INS File, Pt. 3, pp. 1003, 1011.

16. Robert Arden interview with LADA's investigators, Chaplin INS File, Pt. 3, p. 1025.

17. Arden interview, Chaplin INS File, Pt. 3, p. 1040.

18. Edward Chaney interview with LADA's investigators, June 6, 1943, Chaplin INS File, Pt. 3, pp. 1057–58.

19. Charles Chaplin Jr. and Sidney [sic] Chaplin interview with LADA's investigators, Chaplin INS File, Pt.3, p. 990.

20. Charles Chaplin Jr. and Sidney [sic] Chaplin interview, Chaplin INS File, Pt. 3, p. 991.

21. Charles Chaplin Jr. and Sidney [sic] Chaplin interview, Chaplin INS File, Pt. 3, p. 991.

22. Charles Chaplin Jr. and Sidney [sic] Chaplin interview, Chaplin INS File, Pt. 3, p. 992.

23. Hood to the Director and SAC, teletype (date blacked out), Chaplin FBI File, Pt. 1, p. 165.

24. "Howser Sifts Report Police Stripped Girl," Los Angeles Times, June 4, 1943.

25. United Press, "Grand Jury Opens Inquiry into Chaplin Girl Charges," Press Democrat (Santa Rosa, CA), June 9, 1943.

26. "Jurors Seek More Facts in Chaplin Case," Chicago Daily Tribune, June 9, 1943.

27. "Grand Jury Opens Inquiry into Chaplin Girl Charges."

28. "Chaplin to Let Science Settle Paternity Suit; Tests to Be Made When Baby Born, Agreement Stipulates," Los Angeles Times, June 11, 1943.

29. "Chaplin Protégé Ready to Deny Vagrancy Plea; Lawyer Due to Make 'Emotionally Distraught' Appeal in Beverly Hills Court Tomorrow," Los Angeles Times, June 10, 1943.

30. "Wartime Weather," Los Angeles Times, June 13, 1943.

31. In re: Joan Berry, D-2445, Chaplin FBI File, Pt. 4, p. 143; "Chaplin Case Girl Cleared; Vagrancy Charge against Joan Berry Dismissed by Court," Los Angeles Times, June 12, 1943.

32. "Chaplin Case Girl Cleared."

33. Fred N. Howser, District Attorney, County of Los Angeles Press Release, June 11, 1943, Chaplin FBI File, Pt. 4, p. 147.

34. Howser Press Release.

35. Kyle Palmer, "The District Attorneyship," Los Angeles Times, April 30, 1944.

36. Adam Saroyan, Trio: Oona Chaplin, Carol Matthau, Gloria Vanderbilt (New York: Linden Press, 1985), 207.

37. Chaplin Jr., My Father, 278; Chaplin, My Autobiography, 415.

38. "Charlie Chaplin Weds Girl of 18, Mimic, 54, Marries Oona O'Neill; News Drives Joan Berry Hysterical," *Los Angeles Times*, June 17, 1943.

39. Robinson, *Chaplin*, 519.

40. Hale, *Intimate Close-Ups*, 177–80.

41. Milton, *Tramp*, 426; R. B. Hood to the Director, memorandum, June 24, 1943, Chaplin FBI File Pt. 1, pp. 5–7. The name of the Chaplin informant is blacked out in the memo, but he is described by Hood as the "long-time" friend who "assisted Chaplin in making preliminary arrangements for the marriage," which was Harry Crocker.

42. Florabel Muir, "Chaplin's Own Little Fellow Is Sore at Him," *Daily News* (New York), June 18, 1943.

43. "54-Year-Old Charlie Chaplin Marries Youthful Oona O'Neil [*sic*]," *Atlanta Constitution*, June 17, 1943.

44. "Charlie Chaplin Weds Girl of 18, Mimic, 54, Marries Oona O'Neill."

45. Jerry Epstein, *Remembering Charlie* (New York: Doubleday, 1989), 221.

46. Winifred Van Duzer, "Fourth Wedding Ring," *Philadelphia Inquirer*, July 11, 1943.

47. "Chaplin Weds Daughter of Playwright; Oona O'Neill, 18, Becomes Bride of Actor-Producer, 54, in Surprise Ceremony on Coast," *Hartford Courant*, June 17, 1943.

48. "'Scoopers' Scooped," *Newsweek*, July 5, 1943; Danton Walker, "Broadway," *Daily News* (New York), June 23, 1943.

49. Muir, *Headline Happy*, 69.

50. Muir interview, Chaplin FBI File, Pt. 4, p. 170.

51. Muir, *Headline Happy*, 69.

52. "Chaplin Accuser Plans to Go into Seclusion," *Los Angeles Times*, June 20, 1943.

53. Lynn, *Charlie Chaplin and His Times*, 431.

54. Eugene O'Neill to Agnes Brennan, June 19, 1943, in Bogard and Breyer, *Selected Letters of Eugene O'Neill*, 544–45.

55. "Charlie Chaplin and Bride in Montecito Home," *Los Angeles Times*, June 19, 1943.

56. Chaplin, *My Autobiography*, 416.

57. "Charlie Chaplin and Bride Visit Hollywood Night Spot," *Los Angeles Times*, July 7, 1943.

58. Muir, *Headline Happy*, 73–74.

59. Muir, *Headline Happy*, 74–75.

60. Florabel Muir, "He Done Right by Wrong Girl," *Los Angeles Daily News*, June 25, 1943.

61. "Chaplin Accuser Plans to Go into Seclusion."

62. T. D. Quinn to the Director, memorandum, March 11, 1934, Richard B. Hood

FBI File, Pt. 1, p. 8; J. Edgar Hoover to Richard B. Hood, Aug. 24, 1934, Hood FBI File, Pt. 1, p. 45.

63. L. R. Pennington to Mr. Rosen, memorandum, Aug. 17, 1943, Chaplin FBI File, Pt. 1, p. 9.

64. A. Rosen to Mr. Tamm, memorandum, Aug. 26, 1943, Chaplin FBI File, Pt. 1, p. 10.

65. Hoover to SAC New York, Aug. 27, 1943, Chaplin FBI File, Pt. 1, p. 12.

CHAPTER 10

1. Carr, Charles H., United States Attorney Los Angeles, Individual Earnings Record, U.S. Department of Justice.

2. Athan Theoharis, "FBI Wiretapping: A Case Study of Bureaucratic Autonomy," *Political Science Quarterly* 107, no. 1 (1992): 101.

3. H. H. Clegg to FBI Director, memorandum, June 19, 1942, FBI Personnel File, Special Agent in Charge Richard B. Hood, Pt. 2, p. 366.

4. The multivolume Chaplin FBI report is replete with reports from these field offices.

5. William C. Sullivan, *The Bureau: My Thirty Years in Hoover's FBI*, with Bill Brown (New York: W. W. Norton, 1979), 17.

6. Charlie Chaplin et al., Los Angeles California, "Communist Activities," Aug. 15, 1922, Chaplin FBI File, Pt. 7, p. 4.

7. Sullivan, *The Bureau*, 35, 37.

8. Order of Attorney General Charles J. Bonaparte, July 26, 1908, FBI, www.fbi.gov/history/brief-history, accessed, July 27, 2023.

9. Fred P. Graham, "J. Edgar Hoover, 77, Dies; Will Lie in State in Capitol," *New York Times*, May 3, 1972.

10. Sullivan, *The Bureau*, 20, 37.

11. John Edgar Hoover to Richard B. Hood, June 22, 1937, Hood FBI Personnel File, Pt. 1, p. 225.

12. Sullivan, *The Bureau*, 20, 26, 80.

13. Richard Gid Powers, *Broken: The Troubled Past and Uncertain Future of the FBI* (New York: Free Press, 2004), 66, 139, 141.

14. Powers, *Broken*, 65.

15. White Slave Traffic Act of June 25, 1910, c. 395, 36 Stat. 825; codified today as 18 USC § 2421 as a gender-neutral law that now makes it a crime to transport an individual in interstate or foreign commerce "with intent that such individual engage in prostitution, or in any sexual activity for which any person can be charged with a criminal offense."

16. 242 U.S. 470 (1917).

17. Powers, *Broken*, 67–69.

18. "CHARLES SPENCER CHAPLIN; MARY LOUISE GRIBBLE WITH ALIASES JOAN BARRY, JOAN BERRY, VICTIM, WHITE SLAVE TRAFFIC ACT," Report, Sept. 2, 1943, Chaplin FBI File, Pt. 1, p. 20.

19. "Changed: Charles Spencer Chaplin: Mary Louise Gribble, etc., White Slave Traffic Act" Report, Oct. 8, 1943, Chaplin FBI File, Pt. 1, p. 38.

20. Undated teletype from FBI agent [name blacked out] to Director, Chaplin FBI File, Pt. 1, p. 14.

21. Chaplin FBI File, Pt. 1, p. 14; Los Angeles FBI office to Director, undated teletype, Chaplin FBI File, Pt. 1 p. 16.

22. Los Angeles FBI office to Director, undated teletype, Chaplin FBI File, Pt. 1, p. 16; R. F. Cartwright to Mr. Rosen, memorandum, Sept. 18, 1943, Chaplin FBI File, Pt. 1, pp. 30–31.

23. "Joan Berry Shows Off Baby to News Reporters," *Evening Vanguard* (Venice, CA), Oct. 4, 1943; "Our Baby," South Van Ness Hospital Commemorative Birthday Book, courtesy Carol Ann Berry to author.

24. Florabel Muir, "'The Kid' Arrives; It's a Girl, 6 Lbs., For Joan and—,"*Daily News* (New York), Oct. 4, 1943.

25. Associated Press, "Daughter Born to Joan Berry; Child Kept under Guard, Pending Outcome of Paternity Test," *Daily Home News* (New Brunswick, NJ), Oct. 4, 1943.

26. "Chaplin Doctor Sees Girl Born to Joan Barry; Infant Put under Guard in Hollywood Hospital," *Chicago Daily Tribune*, Oct. 4, 1943.

27. Unknown author to Director, Chaplin FBI File, Pt. 1, p. 76; "Background Information on Edward C. Chaney, Chaplin's Butler, and His Connections in Instant Case," WSTA Report, Nov. 9, 1943, Chaplin FBI File, Pt. 1, pp. 123–26.

28. Unknown author to Director, undated teletype, Chaplin FBI File, Pt. 1, p. 76; A. Rosen to E. A. Tamm, memorandum, Nov. 5, 1943, Chaplin FBI File, Pt. 2, p. 129.

29. R. F. Cartwright to Mr. Rosen, memorandum, Oct. 27, 1943, Chaplin FBI File, Pt. 1, p. 74.

30. "Background Information Concerning Joan Berry and Her Association with Charles Chaplin," WSTA Report, Nov. 9, 1943, Chaplin FBI File, Pt. 1, p. 104.

31. L.R. Pennington to Mr. Rosen, memorandum, Nov. 9, 1943, Chaplin FBI File, Pt. 1, p. 86.

32. Hood to Director, undated teletype, Chaplin FBI File, Pt. 1, p. 184.

33. L. R. Pennington to Mr. Rosen, memorandum, Nov. 9, 1943, Chaplin FBI File, Pt.1, p. 86; A. Rosen to E.A. Tamm, memorandum, Nov. 13, 1943, Chaplin FBI File, Pt. 1, p. 87.

34. Hoover "Urgent" to FBI Offices in Kansas City, Oklahoma City, New York City, Chaplin FBI File, Pt. 1, p. 89.

35. Hood to Director, undated teletype, Chaplin FBI File, Pt. 1, p. 165.

36. Charlie Chaplin to "Governor Murphy," May 31, 1936, Frank Murphy Autograph Book, 1930–1942, No. 86734 AA, Bentley Historical Library, University of Michigan.

37. R. C. Davis to Mr. Rosen, memorandum, Nov. 9, 1943, Chaplin FBI File, Pt. 1, p. 181.

38. Andy Warhol interview with Paulette Goddard, transcript, Julie Gilbert Papers, MSS 038, Box 4, Folder 71, 00144, Fales Special Collections, Elmer Bobst Library, New York University.

39. R. C. Davis to Mr. Rosen, memorandum, Chaplin FBI File, Pt. 1, p. 181.

40. Lynn, *Charlie Chaplin and His Times*, 437.

41. *Script*, Jan. 8, 1944, Chaplin FBI File, Pt. 2, p. 70.

42. Chaplin Jr., *My Father*, 297.

43. Chaplin Jr., *My Father*, 288.

44. "Flynn Attorney Is to Defend Charlie Chaplin," *Spartansburg (SC) Journal*, January 14, 1944.

45. Chaplin Jr., *My Father*, 289.

46. Rosen, *Jazz Age Lawyer*, 316.

47. Hood to the Director, teletype, Chaplin FBI File, Pt. 1, p. 205.

48. Hood to the Director, teletype, Chaplin FBI File, Pt. 1, p. 228.

49. Conroy teletype to Director and SAC, Chaplin FBI File, Pt. 1, p. 237.

50. United Press, "Federal Officials Enter Chaplin Case," *Harlington (TX) Star*, Jan. 5, 1944; United Press, "F.B.I. Probes Arrest of Girl Mother in Chaplin Case," *Oakland (CA) Tribune*, Jan. 5, 1944.

51. "F.B.I. Queries Justice in Chaplin-Berry Case; Full Investigation Started in 'Vagging' of Young Mother Making Paternity Charge," *Los Angeles Times*, Jan. 6, 1944.

52. J. D. O'Connell to Mr. Rosen, memorandum, Jan. 1, 1944, Chaplin FBI File, Pt. 1, p. 240.

53. Frederick C. Othman, "Joan Sobs Chaplin Story to Jury," *Daily News* (New York), January 21, 1944.

54. In re: Presentation of the Partial Report of the Grand Jury Impaneled September 15, 1943, and Continued for this Term, Feb. 10, 1944, Criminal Case Files, 1907–2005, U.S. District Court for the Central District of California, RG-21, NARA.

55. Mark Kadish, "Behind the Locked Door of an American Grand Jury: Its History, Its Secrecy, and Its Process," *Florida State University Law Review* 24, no. 1 (1996): 5–6.

56. The Hon. Frederick B. Lacey, "Paper: The Power of the Grand Jury," *Antitrust Law Journal* 47, no. 1 (1978): 17, 19.

57. *United States v. Providence Tribune*, 241 F. 524 (D.R.I., 1917).

58. Florabel Muir, "Chaplin Isn't Talking for U.S. Grand Jury," *Daily News* (New York), January 14, 1944.

59. Associated Press, "Grand Jury Probes Joan Berry Incident; To Determine If Chaplin's Accuser Was Deprived of Her Civil Rights," *Springfield (MA) Republican*, Jan. 14, 1944.

60. Milton, *Tramp*, 387–88.

61. Loyd Wright to Edward C. Raftery, telegram, Jan. 27, 1944, Loyd Wright Papers, Series 5A, US Mss 99AN, Box 3, Folder 4, United Artists Records, Wisconsin Historical Society.

62. Hood to Director, teletype, Chaplin FBI File, Pt. 2, p. 6.

63. *United States v. Calandra*, 414 U.S. 338 (1974).

64. Hood to Director, telemeter, Jan. 14, 1944, Chaplin FBI File, Pt. 2, p. 12; "Berry-Chaplin Judge Heard by U.S. Grand Jury," *Los Angeles Times*, Jan. 20, 1944.

65. Hood to Director, Chaplin FBI File, Pt. 2, p. 12.

66. Florabel Muir, "FBI's Chaplin Case Quiz Raises a Political Furor," *Daily News* (New York), Jan. 10, 1944.

67. Muir, "FBI's Chaplin Case Quiz Raises a Political Furor."

68. Hood to Director, telemeter, Jan. 18, 1944, Chaplin FBI File, Pt. 2, p. 15.

69. "Winter's Hottest Day Just Misses January Record," *Los Angeles Times*, Jan. 20, 1944; "Weather Report," *Los Angeles Times*, Jan. 21, 1944; "Joan Berry Tells Jury of 'Life With Chaplin,'" *Los Angeles Times*, Jan. 21, 1944.

70. "Joan Berry Tells Jury of 'Life with Chaplin,'" *Los Angeles Times*, Jan. 21, 1944.

71. Frederick C. Othman, "Joan Barry Gave Picture of Woman Scorned to Jurors," *Erie (PA) Times*, Jan. 21, 1944.

72. Joan Berry Tells Jury of 'Life With Chaplin.'"

73. United Press, "Joan Near Collapse Telling of Chaplin," *New York Journal-American*, Jan. 20, 1944.

74. Frederick C. Othman, "Joan Sobs Chaplin Story to Jury," *Daily News* (New York), Jan. 21, 1944.

75. Othman, "Joan Sobs Chaplin Story to Jury."

76. Report, Charles Spencer Chaplin et al., Violation of Civil Liberties, etc. May 4, 1944, Chaplin FBI File, Pt. 3, p. 169.

77. R. B. Hood to Director, FBI, Jan. 15, 1944, Chaplin FBI File, Pt. 2, p. 27.

78. A. Rosen to E. A. Tamm, memorandum, Jan. 27, 1944, Chaplin FBI File, Pt. 2, p. 46.

79. J. Edgar Hoover to the Attorney General, Chaplin FBI File, Jan. 23, 1944, Pt. 2, pp. 33–34.

80. Hood to Director, telemeter, Jan. 31, 1944, Chaplin FBI File, Pt. 2, p. 55.

81. A. Rosen to E. A. Tamm, memorandum, Feb. 10, 1944, Chaplin FBI File, Pt. 2, p. 98.

82. *United States v. Charles Spencer Chaplin*, No. 16,617; *United States of America v. Charles Spencer Chaplin, Thomas Wells Durant, W.W. White, Charles H. Griffin, Robert Arden, Claude Marple, Jessie Billie Reno*, No. 16,616; *United States of America v. Charles Spencer Chaplin, Robert Arden, W.W. White*, No. 16,619; *United States of America v. Charles Spencer Chaplin, W.W. White, Robert Arden, Charles H. Griffin*, No. 16,618, Criminal Case Files, 1907–2005, U.S. District Court for the Central District of California, Record Group 21, Records of the District Courts of the United States, NARA.

83. Hood to Director, telemeter, Jan. 20, 1944, Chaplin FBI File, Pt. 2, p. 26.

84. Muir, *Headline Happy*, 66.

85. Muir, *Headline Happy*, 66.

CHAPTER 11

1. *United States v. Chaplin*, No. 16,617, Minute Books, 1887–1956, U.S. District Court for the Central (Los Angeles) Division of the Southern District of California, Vol. 38, Feb. 21, 1944, NARA.

2. Hood to Director, telemeter, Jan. 12, 1944, Chaplin FBI File, Pt. 2, p. 7.

3. Jerry Giesler, *The Jerry Giesler Story*, as told to Pete Martin (New York: Simon & Schuster, 1960), 5.

4. Chaplin, *My Autobiography*, 424.

5. Florabel Muir, "Hint Test 'Doctored' in Chaplin Dad Suit," *Daily News* (New York), Feb. 17, 1944; "Chaplin Ruled Out as Berry Child's Father; Clinical Blood Tests Clear Comedian in Paternity Suit," *Los Angeles Times*, Feb. 16, 1944.

6. Newton Evans, Roy W. Hammack, and V. L. Andrews to John J. Irwin and Loyd Wright, Feb. 15, 1944, *John Doe v. Charles Spencer Chaplin*, D. 238936, Cal. Super. Ct., Los Angeles Co. After the birth of Joan's daughter, the case was renamed *Carol Ann Berry v. Charles Spencer Chaplin*.

7. "War's Heaviest Bomb Load Hits Berlin; Americans Breach German Lines on Casino Hill," "Chaplin Wins Paternity Suit," *Ithaca Journal*, Feb. 16, 1944.

8. United Press, "Girl's Counsel Attacks Test of Chaplin's Blood, Won't Drop Paternity Case until He Is Sure Drug Did Not Affect Result," *New York Herald Tribune*, Feb. 17, 1944.

9. "Joan Berry and Mother Drop Fight against Chaplin in Paternity Case; No Move Will Be Made to Replace Attorney Who Withdrew from Action," *Los Angeles Times*, Feb. 19, 1944.

10. Muir, "Hint Test 'Doctored' in Chaplin Dad Suit."

11. "Block Chaplin's Move to Quash Paternity Suit," *Daily Mirror* (New York), Feb. 18, 1944.

12. "Joan Berry's Attorney Quits in Chaplin Paternity Case; Court Denies Plea of Actor's Counsel to Dismiss Suit," *Los Angeles Times*, Feb. 18, 1944.

13. Associated Press, "Girl's Counsel Quits Chaplin Paternity Case; Irwin Withdraws Few Hours after Court Refuses to Grant Dismissal Motion," *New York Herald Tribune*, Feb. 18, 1944.

14. Affidavit of John Irwin, Feb. 17, 1944, *Berry v. Chaplin*, D-238936.

15. Supplemental Affidavit of John Irwin, Mar. 1, 1944, *Berry v. Chaplin*, D-238936.

16. Hood to Director, telemeter, Feb. 17, 1944, Chaplin FBI File, Pt. 2, p. 84.

17. Hood to Director, telemeter, Feb. 17, 1944.

18. Chaplin, *My Autobiography*, 417.

19. Loyd Wright to Jerry Giesler, Dec. 5, 1944, ECCI00015310, CH048, Charlie Chaplin Archive.

20. Giesler, *The Jerry Giesler Story*, 37.

21. See, e.g., N.Y. Crim. Proc. Law § 60.42.

22. Giesler, *The Jerry Giesler Story*, 1.

23. Giesler, *The Jerry Giesler Story*, 94, 243, 249.

24. Adela Rogers St. Johns, *Final Verdict* (Garden City, NY: Doubleday, 1962), 409–10.

25. W. W. Robinson, *Lawyers of Los Angeles: A History of the Los Angeles Bar Association and of the Bar of Los Angeles County* (Los Angeles: Los Angeles County Bar Association, 1959), 151.

26. Giesler, *The Jerry Giesler Story*, 263, 266–70, 273.

27. St. Johns, *Final Verdict*, 11.

28. Alfred Cohn and Joe Chisholm, *"Take the Witness!"* (New York: Frederick A. Stokes, 1934), 85.

29. John A. Farrell, *Clarence Darrow: Attorney for the Damned* (New York: Doubleday, 2011), 236.

30. "Earl Rogers Paid Honors. Funeral Attended by Noted Lawyers and Jurists. Friends Mourn Passing of Brilliant Attorney. Deceased Achieved Fame as Counsel and Educator," *Los Angeles Times*, Feb. 26, 1922.

31. Cohn and Chisholm, *"Take the Witness!"* 272, 280–81.

32. Marcia Winn, "Denies Chaplin Blackmail; Joan Shouts She 'Did Not' Ask $150,000; Actor's Butler Is Witness for Her," *Chicago Daily Tribune*, Mar. 29, 1944.

33. John Roeburt, *"Get Me Giesler"* (New York: Belmont Books, 1962), 19, 100, 187.

34. James Hubbart, "Jerry Giesler, Who Helps Stars Shed Mates, Tells How to Save Marriages," *Los Angeles Times*, Oct. 9, 1957.

35. Giesler, *The Jerry Giesler Story*, 331.

36. Chaplin, *My Autobiography*, 418.

37. Giesler, *The Jerry Giesler Story*, 302.

38. Robinson, *Chaplin*, 703.

39. *United States v. Chaplin et al.*, Nos. 16, 616; 16, 618 and 16, 619, Minute Books, Feb. 21, 1944.

40. Hood to Director, teletype, Chaplin FBI File, Pt. 1, p. 239.

41. "Chaplin Takes Bride and Everyone Take a Burn 'Cept Lolly," *Variety*, June 23, 1943.

42. "Frank Doherty Rites Slated," *Los Angeles Times*, July 26, 1974; "Misconduct Charge on Bowron Quashed; Court Decision Absolves Mayor of Accusation in Wire-Tapping Case and Balks Inquiry," *Los Angeles Times*, Apr. 2, 1942.

43. "Attorney Hahn Dies in Swimming Pool Mystery, Cement Weights on Neck," *Los Angeles Times*, June 26, 1957.

44. "Nightgown Mystery in Taylor Case Ended; Mary Miles Minter Declares Initialed Garment Myth and Detective Backs Story," *Los Angeles Times*, Feb. 4, 1937; "This Day in History, February 2, 1922: Director William Desmond Taylor Is Found Murdered," History, www.history.com/this-day-in-history/murder-in -hollywood-a-tale-of-vice-and-vixens, accessed July 17, 2022.

45. "Ex-Wampus Star Jayne Hazard Wed to Theater Owner," *Hollywood Citizen-News*, May 7, 1947.

46. "Fitts' Pay List Violates Charter, Says Grand Jury, Prosecutor Undisturbed by Report Asserting Favoritism in Wages and 'Political Jobs,'" *Los Angeles Times*, Feb. 10, 1935; "Bates Booth Denies He'll Be Candidate," *Los Angeles Times*, Mar. 5, 1940.

47. Hood to Director, telemeter, Feb. 21, 1944, Chaplin FBI File, Pt. 2, p. 97.

48. "Chaplin Files Demurer to Mann Act Indictment; Contends the Law Does Not Apply to Private Actions," *New York Herald Tribune*, Feb. 26, 1944.

49. *United States v. Chaplin*, No. 16617, Order Overruling Demurrer, Feb. 26, 1944.

50. "Chaplin's Mann Act Trial Is Set to Start Mar. 21; Judge Rejects Demurrer; Actor Pleads Innocent," *New York Herald Tribune*, Feb. 27, 1944.

51. *United States v. Chaplin*, No. 16,617.

52. Hood to Director, telemeter, Mar. 8, 1944, Chaplin FBI File, Pt. 3, p. 31.

53. Hood to Director, telemeter, Mar. 8, 1944.

54. Hood to Director, telemeter, Mar. 8, 1944.

55. Chaplin et al., WSTA Report, Mar. 18, 1944, Chaplin FBI File, Pt. 3, p. 58.

56. Chaplin et al., WSTA Report, Mar. 18, 1944, Chaplin FBI File, Pt. 3, p. 70.

57. 18 U.S.C. § 3161.

58. Hood to Director, telemeter, Mar. 4, 1944, Chaplin FBI File, Pt. 3, p. 20.

59. Hood to Director, telemeter, Mar. 4, 1944.

60. Charged: Charles Spencer Chaplin et al., Violation of Civil Liberties (Conspiracy), May 4, 1944, Chaplin FBI File, Pt. 3, pp. 169–70.

61. Charged: Charles Spencer Chaplin et al., Chaplin FBI File, Pt. 3, p. 212.

62. Charged: Charles Spencer Chaplin et al., Chaplin FBI File, Pt. 3, p. 213.

63. Tom C. Clark to Director, Federal Bureau of Investigation, memorandum, Feb. 29, 1944, Chaplin FBI File, Pt. 3, p. 10; Hoover "Urgent" to SAC Los Angeles, Mar. 1, 1944; Chaplin FBI File, Pt. 3, p. 11.

64. Chaplin et al., WSTA Report, Mar. 21, 1944; Chaplin FBI File, Pt. 3, pp. 90–91.

65. Hood to Director, Mar. 1, 1944, telemeter, Chaplin FBI File, Pt. 3, p. 28.

66. Hood to Director, Mar. 9, 1944, teletype, Chaplin FBI File, Pt. 3, pp. 38–39; Frederick C. Othman, "Chaplin Case Documents Swamp Court," *Long Beach Sun*, Mar. 10, 1944.

67. "Federal Judges Name Successor to Palmer; Leo J. Silverstein Appointed Acting U.S. Attorney Here," *Los Angeles Times*, Sept. 6, 1942.

68. Carr, Charles Hardy, "Biographical Directory of Federal Judges," Federal Judicial Center, https://www.fjc.gov/node/1378866, accessed Nov. 12, 2023.

69. "Carr Resigns Federal Post; Justice Department 'Career Man' Returns to Private Practice," *Los Angeles Times*, Feb. 21, 1940.

70. 1940 U.S. Census (Charles H. Carr).

71. Ralph Fleming "Casey" Shawhan unpublished, untitled manuscript, 4, courtesy Linda Shawhan.

72. Muir, *Headline Happy*, 67.

73. Shawhan, unpublished manuscript, 4; Hedda Hopper, "Looking at Hollywood," *Chicago Daily Tribune*, Apr. 10, 1944.

74. St. Johns, *Love, Laughter and Tears*, 91.

75. Linda Shawhan Shewak, interview with the author, Sept. 28, 2020.

76. Shawhan, unpublished manuscript, 1.

77. Underwood, *Newspaperwoman*, 179; Muir, *Headline Happy*, 67; Shawhan, unpublished manuscript, 1.

78. Hood to Director, Mar. 21, 1944, telemeter, Chaplin FBI File, Pt. 3, p. 73.

79. Shawhan, unpublished manuscript, 6.

80. Shawhan, unpublished manuscript, 6

81. Associated Press, "Denies Chaplin Plea to End Paternity Suit; Court Says Justice Demands 'Full and Fair Trial,'" *New York Times*, Mar. 9, 1944.

82. R. B. Hood to Director, FBI, Mar. 17, 1944, Chaplin FBI File, Pt. 3, p. 87.

83. Getty Diaries, Dec. 7, 1941.

84. R. B. Hood to Director, FBI, Mar. 17, 1944, Chaplin FBI File, Pt. 3, pp. 87–88.

85. R. B. Hood to Director, FBI, Mar. 17, 1944, Chaplin FBI File, Pt. 3, p. 87.

86. R. B. Hood to Director, FBI, Mar. 17, 1944, Chaplin FBI File, Pt. 3, p. 88.

87. John Edgar Hoover to the Attorney General, Mar. 18, 1944, Chaplin FBI File, Pt. 3, p. 48.

88. Act of May 8, 1792, ch. 36, Sec. 11, 1 Stat. 278–79 (1792).

89. Editorial Board, Minn. L. Rev., "Disqualification of a Federal District Judge

for Bias—The Standard under Section 144," *Minnesota Law Review* 57 (1973): 749–53.

90. Rules governing federal criminal procedure were not adopted by the United States Supreme Court until Dec. 26, 1944. They went into effect on March 21, 1946. Over the years, they have been liberalized to provide more information to the accused. See Title 18, U.S.C., Appendix, Historical Note. Today, 18 U.S.C.§ 3500 requires the government to turn over to the defense relevant pretrial statements made by witnesses to law enforcement.

CHAPTER 12

1. William Smith White, "Nazis Move into Bulgaria, Hint Seizure of Rumania as Reds Sweep on Balkans; Horthy Troops Resist," *Philadelphia Inquirer*, Mar. 22, 1944.
2. Ackroyd, *Charlie Chaplin*, 235; Reeves and Goll, *The Intimate Charlie Chaplin*, 47; Lita Grey Chaplin and Jeffrey Vance, *Wife of the Party* (Lanham, MD: Scarecrow Press, 1998), 69.
3. "Chaplin as Villain; Recalling Arbuckle Case Reaction, Hollywood Is Fearful of Scandal," *Newsweek*, Feb. 21, 1944.
4. Michael Schulman, "American Chronicles: Fatty Arbuckle and the Birth of the Celebrity Scandal," *New Yorker*, Oct. 4, 2021, www.newyorker.com/magazine /2021/10/11/fatty-arbuckle-and-the-birth-of-the-celebrity-scandal, accessed Nov. 13, 2023.
5. "Official Weather Report," *Los Angeles Times*, Mar. 22, 1944.
6. Chaplin, *My Autobiography*, 416.
7. John Gardner, "Nassau Man Is Indicted in Charlie Chaplin Case," *Newsday*, Feb. 12, 1944.
8. Daily Production Report, Charles Chaplin, W/E Mar. 18, Mar. 25, Apr. 1, and Apr. 8, 1944, Charlie Chaplin Archive, ECCI00313699, CH131.
9. "Five Women Picked on Jury Trying Chaplin; Father of Clifford Odets Also Tentatively Seated; Film Veteran Is Calm," *New York Herald Tribune*, Mar. 22, 1944.
10. Lynn, *Charlie Chaplin and His Times*, 340.
11. Hubbart, "Jerry Giesler, Who Helps Stars Shed Mates, Tells How to Save Marriages."
12. Giesler, *The Jerry Giesler Story*, 328, 330.
13. "Interstate 10," California Highways, www.cahighways.org/ROUTE010.html, accessed Jan. 3, 2024.
14. Chaplin Jr., *My Father*, 292.
15. "Chaplin Fidgets as Trial Opens; Jury of Seven Men and Five Women Face Challenges Today," *Los Angeles Times*, Mar. 22, 1944.

16. International News Service, "Chaplin Affable as Selection of Jury Starts," *Austin Statesman*, Mar. 22, 1944.

17. Associated Press, "Chaplin Jury Box Tentatively Full; But 7 Men and 5 Women Face Possible Challenges Today in Mann Act Case," *New York Times*, Mar. 22, 1944; Marcia Winn, "Chaplin Begins Nervous Role at Bar of Law; Actor Put on Trial in Mann Act Case," *Chicago Daily Tribune*, Mar. 22, 1944.

18. "Chaplin Fidgets as Trial Opens."

19. Winn, "Chaplin Begins Nervous Role at Bar of Law."

20. "Chaplin Affable as Selection of Jury Starts."

21. Winn, "Chaplin Begins Nervous Role at Bar of Law."

22. "Chaplin Fidgets as Trial Opens."

23. "Chaplin Fidgets as Trial Opens"; Winn, "Chaplin Begins Nervous Role at Bar of Law."

24. "Woman's Mishap Upsets Tranquility of Actor; Chaplin Sketches during Court Proceedings; Spectators Peek through Windows of Door," *Los Angeles Times*, Mar. 23, 1944.

25. *United States v. Chaplin*, No. 16,617 , Minute Books, Vol. 39, Mar. 21, 1944, NARA; Marcia Winn, "Front Views & Profiles," *Chicago Daily Tribune*, Mar. 25, 1944.

26. Susan Cianci Salvatore, Application for National Historic Landmark Nomination, U.S. Post Office and Court House (Central District of California), Mar. 24, 2015, 4.

27. Shawhan, unpublished manuscript, 5.

28. "Dramatic Scenes Mark Opening of Actor's Trial; Chaplin Chats with Giesler as Crowd Looks On and Photographers Use Their Flashbulbs," *Los Angeles Times*, Mar. 22, 1944.

29. Muir, *Headline Happy*, 141.

30. James Bacon, "Hollywood's Top Lawyer Doesn't Fit Film Picture," *Atlanta Journal and Constitution*, Feb. 3, 1952.

31. Giesler, *The Jerry Giesler Story*, 184, 189.

32. Diane Kiesel, "Cameras in Court: Media Appeal for Easing Rule," *American Bar Association Journal* 69, no. 5 (May 1983): 576.

33. Paul Bellamy, Stuart Perry, and Newton D. Baker, "Cooperation between Press, Radio and Bar," *Journal of Criminal Law and Criminology* 28 (1937–38): 641, 652.

34. Fed. R. Crim. P. 53.

35. Hedda Hopper, "In Hollywood," *Hartford Courant*, Mar. 31, 1944.

36. Shawhan, unpublished manuscript, 8.

37. Gene Sherman, "Just a Glimpse of Chaplin—or Giesler, Please," *Los Angeles Times*, Mar. 31, 1944.

38. J. F. T. O'Connor, unpublished autobiography, 1, J. F. T. O'Connor Papers,

Elwyn B. Robinson Department of Special Collections, Chester Fritz Library, University of North Dakota, Grand Forks.

39. J. F. T. O'Connor, unpublished autobiography, passim.

40. "O'Connor, U.S. Judge, Succumbs," *San Bernardino (CA) County Sun*, Sept. 29, 1949.

41. "Judge J.F.T. O'Connor Is Dead," *Bakersfield Californian*, Sept. 28, 1949.

42. "Death Takes O'Connor, U.S. Judge Here," *Hollywood Citizen-News*, Sept. 28, 1949.

43. "F.D.R. Praise on Tombstone," *Bakersfield Californian*, Oct. 6, 1949.

44. "Dramatic Scenes Mark Opening of Actor's Trial."

45. Underwood, *Newspaperwoman*, 94.

46. Marcia Winn Tingly, interview with the author, July 1, 2020.

47. Underwood, *Newspaperwoman*, 9.

48. Underwood, *Newspaperwoman*, 151.

49. Underwood, *Newspaperwoman*, 9.

50. Underwood, *Newspaperwoman*, 94.

51. "Dramatic Scenes Mark Opening of Actor's Trial."

52. Frederick C. Othman, "Chaplin Nervous as His Trial Opens," *Philadelphia Inquirer*, Mar. 22, 1944.

53. Winn, "Chaplin Begins Nervous Role at Bar of Law."

54. Shawhan, unpublished manuscript, 5.

55. Giesler, *The Jerry Giesler Story*, 188.

56. Associated Press, "Chaplin Jury Box Tentatively Full"; Giesler, *The Jerry Giesler Story*, 296, 300–301.

57. Winn, "Chaplin Begins Nervous Role at Bar of Law."

58. "Woman's Mishap Upsets Tranquility of Actor."

59. *United States v. Chaplin*, No. 16,617, Minute Books, Vol. 39, Mar. 21, 1944, NARA.

60. "Chaplin Fidgets as Trial Opens."

61. "Chaplin Fidgets as Trial Opens."

62. Associated Press, "Chaplin Jury Box Tentatively Full."

63. "7 Men, Five Women Seated Tentatively in Jury for Chaplin Trial," Daily *Boston Globe*, Mar. 22, 1944.

64. Chaplin, *My Autobiography*, 422.

65. "Woman's Mishap Upsets Tranquility of Actor."

66. *United States v. Chaplin*, No. 16,617, Minute Books, Vol. 39, Mar. 22, 1944, NARA.

67. Marcia Winn, "7 Women on Chaplin Jury; 1st Testimony on Mann Act Charge Today; Ex-Comedian Gay at Trial Session," *Chicago Daily Tribune*, Mar. 23, 1944.

68. Winn, "7 Women on Chaplin Jury."

69. Winn, "7 Women on Chaplin Jury."

70. "Joan Berry May Take Stand Today; Chaplin Scores Victory as Seven Women Are Selected for Jury," *Los Angeles Times*, Mar. 23, 1944.

71. Hood to Director, telemeter, Mar. 21, 1944, Chaplin FBI File, Pt. 3, p. 73.

72. Nancy Cannon, e-mail to the author, Sept. 26, 2019.

73. Jack Moss (1906–1975), IMDB, www.imdb.com/name/nm0608986, accessed Nov. 14, 2023.

74. United Press, "2 Spinsters, 5 Wives Fill Out Chaplin Jury," *Daily News* (New York) Mar. 23, 1944; Frederick C. Othman, "Seven Elderly Women Placed on Chaplin Jury; Defendant Breathes Sigh of Relief Seeing in Box Persons Who Remember Him as Star," *Pittsburgh Post-Gazette*, Mar. 23, 1944.

75. Frederick C. Othman, "Jury of 7 Women and 5 Men Chosen for Chaplin Trial," *Philadelphia Inquirer*, Mar. 23, 1944.

76. "Woman's Mishap Upsets Tranquility of Actor."

77. Underwood, *Newspaperwoman*, 189.

78. Chaplin, *My Autobiography*, 420; "Seven Women Are Selected on Chaplin Jury; Associated Press, "Comedian Ignores Cameras; Draws Pencil Sketches, Including Famous Shoes," *New York Herald Tribune*, Mar. 23, 1944.

79. Chaplin, *My Autobiography*, 420.

80. Shawhan, unpublished manuscript, 8.

81. "Joan Berry May Take Stand Today"; *United States v. Chaplin*, No. 16,617, Minute Books, Vol. 39, Mar. 22, 1944, NARA.

82. *United States v. Chaplin*, No. 16,617, Minute Books, Vol. 39, Mar. 23, 1944, NARA.

83. Miller, *The House of Getty*, 200.

84. Getty Diaries, Mar. 19–29, 1944.

85. "Carr Outlines Federal Case against Actor," *Los Angeles Times*, Mar. 24, 1944.

86. "Carr Outlines Federal Case against Actor."

87. *United States v. Chaplin*, No. 16,617, Minute Books, Vol. 39, Mar. 23, 1944, NARA.

88. Hubbart, "Jerry Giesler, Who Helps Stars Shed Mates, Tells How to Save Marriages."

89. Marcia Winn, "Berry-Chaplin Trysts Told; Visited Actor 'Very Often' Joan Testifies, Relates Details of Trip to N.Y.," *Chicago Daily Tribune*, Mar. 24, 1944.

90. Winn, "Berry-Chaplin Trysts Told."

91. *United States v. Chaplin*, No. 16,617, Minute Books, Vol. 39, Mar. 23, 1944, NARA.

92. "Chaplin Jury Is Completed; First Witnesses Wait Call," *Asbury Park Evening Press*, Mar. 23, 1944.

93. Winn, "Berry-Chaplin Trysts Told."

94. *United States v. Chaplin*, No. 16,617, Minute Books, Vol. 39, Mar. 23, 1944, NARA; Winn, "Berry-Chaplin Trysts Told."

95. Tom Caton, "Joan Berry Tells of Life with Chaplin; Wanted to Be Star but Instead She Became His Mistress," *Los Angeles Times*, Mar. 24, 1944.

96. Winn, "Berry-Chaplin Trysts Told"; Caton, "Joan Berry Tells of Life with Chaplin."

CHAPTER 13

1. Winn, "Berry-Chaplin Trysts Told."

2. Winn, "Berry-Chaplin Trysts Told."

3. Associated Press, "New York Trip Details: Joan Berry Tells of Series of Intimacies with Chaplin," *Washington Post*, Mar. 24, 1944.

4. Associated Press, "Joan Berry Tells Story on Stand in Chaplin Trial; Swears He Had Her Meet Him in New York after Intimacies in Hollywood," *New York Herald Tribune*, Mar. 24, 1944.

5. Gene Sherman, "Just a Glimpse of Chaplin—or Giesler, Please," *Los Angeles Times*, Mar. 31, 1944.

6. Gilbert Geis and Leigh B. Bienen, *Crimes of the Century: From Leopold and Loeb to O.J. Simpson* (Boston: Northeastern University Press, 1998), 216.

7. Sherman, "Just a Glimpse of Chaplin—Or Giesler, Please."

8. Sherman, "Just a Glimpse of Chaplin—Or Giesler, Please."

9. Hopper, "In Hollywood." *Hartford Courant*, Mar. 31, 1944.

10. Hopper, "In Hollywood." *Hartford Courant*, Mar. 31, 1944.

11. Frank Finch, "Crowd Gathers at 6 a.m. to Fight for Trial Seats; Largest Gathering since Proceedings Began Lured by Giesler's Plan to Requestion Joan," *Los Angeles Times*, Mar. 29, 1944.

12. Chaplin, *My Autobiography*, 419.

13. Chaplin, *My Autobiography*, 418.

14. Caton, "Joan Berry Tells of Life with Chaplin."

15. Hopper, "Hollywood," *Daily News* (New York), Mar. 28, 1944.

16. Winn, "Berry-Chaplin Trysts Told."

17. Winn, "Berry-Chaplin Trysts Told."

18. "Joan Barry Tells of Trip to New York, Seeing Star There; First Met Chaplin at Home of Durant; Visits Nightclubs and His Hotel Related," *Los Angeles Examiner*, Mar. 24, 1944.

19. Winn, "Berry-Chaplin Trysts Told."

20. "Joan Barry Tells of Trip to New York, Seeing Star There."

21. "Joan Barry Tells of Trip to New York, Seeing Star There."

22. "Joan Barry Tells of Trip to New York, Seeing Star There."

23. Winn, "Berry-Chaplin Trysts Told."

24. "Joan Barry Tells of Trip to New York, Seeing Star There."

25. "Joan Barry Tells of Trip to New York, Seeing Star There."

26. Winn, "Front Views & Profiles."

27. Winn, "Front Views & Profiles."

28. Caton, "Joan Berry Tells of Life with Chaplin."

29. "Chaplin Cries as He Tells Own Story; Actor Describes Gun Incident and Denies Joan Berry Charges," *Los Angeles Times*, Mar. 31, 1944.

30. Caton, "Joan Berry Tells of Life with Chaplin." The articles about the trial testimony differed slightly among the reporters who covered the case. Marcia Winn reported that Joan said, "I broke in a door." Winn, "Berry-Chaplin Trysts Told."

31. Winn, "Berry-Chaplin Trysts Told."

32. Winn, "Berry-Chaplin Trysts Told."

33. *United States v. Chaplin*, No. 16,617, Minute Books, Vol. 39, Mar. 23, 1944, NARA.

34. Marvin Miles, "Actor Plays Lonely Role in Federal Court Drama," *Los Angeles Times*, Mar. 30, 1944.

35. Minute Books, Vol. 39, Mar. 23, 1944, NARA.

36. Margaret Buell Wilder, "Court Entry of Comedian's Accuser Dramatic Moment, Declares Margaret Buell Wilder," *Los Angeles Examiner*, Mar. 24, 1944.

37. Winn, "Berry-Chaplin Trysts Told."

38. Winn, "Berry-Chaplin Trysts Told."

39. Roeburt, *"Get Me Giesler,"* 86.

40. Roeburt, *"Get Me Giesler,"* 87.

41. Winn, "Berry-Chaplin Trysts Told."

42. Winn, "Berry-Chaplin Trysts Told."

43. Winn, "Berry-Chaplin Trysts Told"; notes of the court clerk, *United States v. Chaplin*, No. 16,617, Minute Books, Vol. 39, Mar. 23, 1944, NARA.

44. Hood to Director, telemeter, Mar. 24, 1944, Chaplin FBI File, Pt. 3, p. 85.

45. "Weather Report," *Los Angeles Times*, Mar. 25, 1944; "Joan Berry Tells of Life with Chaplin."

46. Gene Sherman, "Joan Weeps on Stand as Tender Letter Read," *Los Angeles Times*, Mar. 25, 1944.

47. Margaret Buell Wilder, "Spectators Crane Necks to View Girl," *Los Angeles Examiner*, Mar. 24, 1944.

48. Sherman, "Joan Weeps on Stand as Tender Letter Read."

49. Marcia Winn, "Judge Shields Joan's Past; Chaplin Dealt 2 Setbacks at Mann Act Trial; Girl's Letters Tell of 'Tortured Love,'" *Chicago Tribune*, Mar. 25, 1944.

50. Winn, "Judge Shields Joan's Past."

51. Winn, "Judge Shields Joan's Past."

52. "Giesler Quizzes Joan on New York Visit; Actress Tells of Meeting With Chaplin in East," *Los Angeles Examiner*, Mar. 25, 1944.

53. "Giesler Quizzes Joan on New York Visit."

54. Winn, "Judge Shields Joan's Past."

55. *United States v. Chaplin*, No. 16,617, Minute Books, Vol. 39, Mar. 24, 1944, NARA.

56. Winn, "Judge Shields Joan's Past."

57. Winn, "Judge Shields Joan's Past."

58. "Here Are Love Missives from Joan to Chaplin," *Los Angeles Times*, Mar. 25, 1944.

59. "Here Are Love Missives from Joan to Chaplin."

60. "Here Are Love Missives from Joan to Chaplin."

61. Sherman, "Joan Weeps on Stand as Tender Letter Read."

62. Sherman, "Joan Weeps on Stand as Tender Letter Read."

63. Winn, "Judge Shields Joan's Past."

64. "Here Are Love Missives from Joan to Chaplin."

65. Winn, "Judge Shields Joan's Past."

66. Sherman, "Joan Weeps on Stand as Tender Letter Read."

67. Sherman, "Joan Weeps on Stand as Tender Letter Read."

68. Hood to Director, telemeter, Mar. 25, 1944, Chaplin FBI File, Pt. 3, p. 84.

69. Winn, "Judge Shields Joan's Past."

70. Getty, As I See It, 177.

71. Getty, As I See It, 190.

72. Giesler, The Jerry Giesler Story, 291.

73. "Joan Barry Admits Breaking into Chaplin Home at Night with Pistol," Los Angeles Examiner, Mar. 25, 1944.

74. "Joan Barry Admits Breaking into Chaplin Home at Night with Pistol."

75. Winn, "Judge Shields Joan's Past."

76. Winn, "Judge Shields Joan's Past."

77. "Joan Berry Ends Chaplin Testimony; She Leaves Stand Smiling after Court Bars Evidence on Her Friendship with Others," New York Times, Mar. 25, 1944.

78. Sherman, "Joan Weeps on Stand as Tender Letter Read."

79. Notes of the court clerk, United States v. Chaplin, No. 16,617, Minute Books, Vol. 39, Mar. 24, 1944, NARA.

80. Winn, "Judge Shields Joan's Past."

81. United States v. Chaplin, No. 16,617, Minute Books, Vol. 39, Mar. 24, 1944, NARA.

82. Tom Caton, "Chaplin May Thrill Fans with Own Love Life Story; Mann Act Trial Principals Get Rest till Tuesday," Los Angeles Times, Mar. 26, 1944.

83. Associated Press, "Russians Shell Rumania; Reach Border at Prut River on 53 Mi. Front; Seize Town on Nazi Escape Route," Chicago Daily Tribune, Mar. 27, 1944; "Address by Prime Minister Churchill on War and Conditions in Britain," New York Times, Mar. 27, 1944.

84. Associated Press, "1,700 U.S. Planes Rip Nazis along Invasion Coast," Chicago Daily Tribune, Mar. 27, 1944.

85. Associated Press, "Dunkirk 'Navy' Ordered to Get Set for Action," Chicago Daily Tribune, Mar. 27, 1944.

86. Caton, "Chaplin May Thrill Fans with Own Love Life Story."

87. Getty Diaries, Mar. 21–24, 1944.

88. Gaston, Alone Together, 232.

89. Getty Diaries, Mar. 24, 1944; Gaston, Alone Together, 232.

90. Getty Diaries, Mar. 25–27, 1944.

91. Winn, "Judge Shields Joan's Past."
92. Associated Press, "Joan Berry Denies Demanding Chaplin Pay Her $150,000," *Atlanta Constitution*, Mar. 29, 1944.
93. Roeburt, *"Get Me Giesler,"* 156.

CHAPTER 14

1. Finch, "Crowd Gathers at 6 a.m. to Fight for Trial Seats."
2. Marcia Winn, "Denies Chaplin Blackmail; Joan Shouts She 'Did Not' Ask $150,000; Actor's Butler Is Witness for Her," *Chicago Daily Tribune*, Mar. 29, 1944.
3. Associated Press, "Joan Berry Denies Demanding Chaplin Pay Her $150,000," *Atlanta Constitution*, Mar. 29, 1944.
4. Tom Caton, "Government Rests Case in Chaplin Trial; Joan Berry Denies Hint of Blackmail; Dismissal Asked," *Los Angeles Times*, Mar. 29, 1944.
5. Caton, "Government Rests Case in Chaplin Trial."
6. "Joan Berry Denies Demanding Chaplin Pay Her $150,000."
7. *United States v. Chaplin*, No. 16,-617, Minute Books, Vol. 39, Mar. 28, 1944, NARA.
8. *United States v. Chaplin*, No. 16,617, Minute Books, Vol. 39, Mar. 28, 1944, NARA.
9. Giesler, The Jerry Giesler Story, 189.
10. Winn, "Denies Chaplin Blackmail," Adding to the uncertainty about how many questions Giesler was permitted to ask Joan on recall, Winn wrote in the third paragraph of her article that Giesler was limited to five relevant questions by the judge, but later in the same piece she wrote that of Giesler's 41 questions for Joan, the judge denied 37, which would indicate he only got to ask four. Tom Caton of the Los Angeles Times reported that Giesler asked five questions of Joan. Caton, "Government Rests in Chaplin Trial." The court Minute Book for March 28 mentions that "a document containing questions which Attorney Giesler desires to propound to the witness Joan Berry," was ordered sealed, but there is no entry about the number of questions that were in the document. Finally, the Minute Book notes only "further cross examination of the witness Joan Berry is granted in some respects."
11. Winn, "Denies Chaplin Blackmail."
12. Giesler, *The Jerry Giesler Story*, 189.
13. Giesler, *The Jerry Giesler Story*, 189.
14. Winn, "Denies Chaplin Blackmail."
15. Winn, "Denies Chaplin Blackmail."
16. Winn, "Denies Chaplin Blackmail."
17. Winn, "Denies Chaplin Blackmail."
18. Winn, "Denies Chaplin Blackmail."
19. Winn, "Denies Chaplin Blackmail."
20. Winn, "Denies Chaplin Blackmail."

21. Winn, "Denies Chaplin Blackmail."

22. Winn, "Denies Chaplin Blackmail."

23. Robinson, *Chaplin*, 188.

24. Robinson, *Chaplin*, 464.

25. "Japanese Americans at Manzanar," National Park Service, www.nps.gov/ma nz/learn/historyculture/japanese-americans-at-manzanar.htm, accessed Oct. 4, 2022.

26. Milton, *Tramp*, 411.

27. "Background Information on Edward C. Chaney, Chaplin's Butler, and His Connections in Instant Case; Statement of Edward C. Chaney, Oct. 30, 1943," Chaplin FBI File, Pt. 1, p. 124; Edward Charley Chaney, World War II Registration Card, Apr. 25, 1942, Ancestry, www.ancestry.com.

28. Winn, "Denies Chaplin Blackmail."

29. Caton, "Government Rests Case in Chaplin Trial."

30. Hood to Director, telemeter, Mar. 25, 1944, Chaplin FBI File, Pt. 3, p. 84.

31. Winn, "Denies Chaplin Blackmail."

32. Winn, "Denies Chaplin Blackmail."

33. Chaney Statement, Chaplin FBI File, Pt. 1, p. 124.

34. Caton, "Government Rests Case in Chaplin Trial."

35. Winn, "Denies Chaplin Blackmail."

36. Caton, "Government Rests Case in Chaplin Trial."

37. Caton, "Government Rests Case in Chaplin Trial"; *United States v. Chaplin*, No. 16,617, Minute Books, Vol. 39, Mar. 28, 1944, NARA.

38. Caton, "Government Rests Case in Chaplin Trial."

39. Caton, "Government Rests Case in Chaplin Trial"; *United States v. Chaplin*, No. 16,617, Minute Books, Vol. 39, Mar. 28, 1944 NARA.

40. Marcia Winn, "Chaplin Takes Stand Today; Defense Fails to Bare Facts in Joan's Past; Prosecution Balks Giesler's Plans," *Chicago Tribune*, Mar. 30, 1944.

41. *United States v. Chaplin*, Ind. No. 16,617, Minute Books, Vol. 39, Mar. 29, 1944, NARA; Winn, "Chaplin Takes Stand Today."

42. Winn, "Chaplin Takes Stand Today." Tom Caton, "Chaplin Ready to Take Stand Today; Alibi Witnesses Called after Pleas for Dismissal Lost," *Los Angeles Times*, Mar. 30, 1944.

43. *United States v. Chaplin*, No. 16,617, Minute Books, Vol. 39, Mar. 29, 1944, NARA.

44. *United States v. Chaplin*, No. 16,617, Minute Books, Vol. 39, Mar. 29, 1944, NARA.

45. Winn, "Chaplin Takes Stand Today."

46. Winn, "Chaplin Takes Stand Today."

47. Winn, "Chaplin Takes Stand Today."

48. Winn, "Chaplin Takes Stand Today."

49. Winn, "Chaplin Takes Stand Today."

50. Getty Diaries, Mar. 29, 1944.

51. Hans Ruesch, World War II Registration Card, Oct. 16, 1940, Ancestry, www.ancestry.com; Margalit Fox, "Hans Ruesch, 94, Writer and Grand Prix Winner," *New York Times*, Sept. 3, 2007; Hans Ruesch, Application for Reentry Permit, Nov. 15, 1945, and Application for Extension of Reentry Permit, Jan. 25, 1949, Alien Registration File A-1640669, Immigration and Naturalization Service, U.S. Citizenship and Immigration Services.

52. Fox, "Hans Ruesch, 94, Writer and Grand Prix Winner."

53. Hans Ruesch, Application for Immigration Visa (Quota), Naples, Italy, Sept. 26, 1939, Alien Registration File A-1640669, U.S. Citizenship and Immigration Services.

54. Carl Greenberg, "Chaplin 'Alibi' Witness Hits Joan's Story of Love Tryst; Writer Describes Meeting with Girl at N.Y. Apartment; Miss Barry Drunk, Charges Defense; J. Paul Getty Testifies," *Los Angeles Examiner*, Mar. 30, 1944.

55. Greenberg, "Chaplin 'Alibi' Witness Hits Joan's Story of Love Tryst."

56. Greenberg, "Chaplin 'Alibi' Witness Hits Joan's Story of Love Tryst."

57. Greenberg, "Chaplin 'Alibi' Witness Hits Joan's Story of Love Tryst."

58. Greenberg, "Chaplin's 'Alibi' Witness Hits Joan's Story of Love Tryst."

59. Margaret Buell Wilder, "Witness Adds Drama with His Diary; Prosecutor's Quiz Confuses Ruesch, Chaplin Witness," *Los Angeles Examiner*, Mar. 30, 1944."

60. James Lindsley, "Defense to Climax Fight with Chaplin on Stand; One Witness Tells How Joan Spent the Night in His Apartment—Went There at 2 A.M.," *Bergen Evening Record* (Hackensack, NJ), Mar. 30, 1944.

61. Winn, "Chaplin Takes Stand Today."

62. Winn, "Chaplin Takes Stand Today."

63. Winn, "Chaplin Takes Stand Today."

64. Lindsley, "Defense to Climax Fight with Chaplin on Stand."

CHAPTER 15

1. Sherman, "Just a Glimpse of Chaplin—or Giesler, Please."

2. *United States v. Chaplin*, No. 16,617, Minute Books, Vol. 39, Mar. 30, 1944, NARA; Marcia Winn, "Chaplin Tells His Story; Denies All; Swears Joan Pursued Him after Meeting; Shows Jury a Sob and Distress," *Chicago Tribune*, Mar. 31, 1944.

3. Sherman, "Just a Glimpse of Chaplin—or Giesler, Please."

4. Underwood, *Newspaperwoman*, 179.

5. Chaplin Jr., *My Father*, 291.

6. Giesler, *The Jerry Giesler Story*, 187.

7. Winn, "Chaplin Tells His Story; Denies All."

8. "Chaplin Describes New York Meeting; Comedian Ends Testimony after Two Days on Stand in Federal Mann Act Trial," *Los Angeles Times*, Apr. 1, 1944.

9. "Questions Giesler Asked Chaplin and His Answers; Defendant in Mann Act

Trial Takes Stand for First Time as Star Witness in Defense," *Los Angeles Times*, Mar. 31, 1944.

10. Associated Press, "Chaplin on Stand, Denies Girl's Story; Chokes Up as He Tells about Night Miss Berry Brought Gun to California Home," *New York Times*, Mar. 31, 1944.

11. "Questions Giesler Asked Chaplin and His Answers."

12. "Joan Berry Story Told by Chaplin as Witness; Comedian Tells Why He Paid Fare for Girl, Mother on New York Trip," *Washington Post*, Mar. 31, 1944.

13. "Questions Giesler Asked Chaplin and His Answers."

14. "Chaplin Cries as He Tells Own Story; Actor Describes Gun Incident and Denies Joan Berry Charges," *Los Angeles Times*, Mar. 31, 1944.

15. "Questions Giesler Asked Chaplin and His Answers."

16. "Questions Giesler Asked Chaplin and His Answers."

17. "Chaplin Cries as He Tells Own Story."

18. Winn, "Chaplin Tells His Story; Denies All."

19. Associated Press, "Chaplin Chokingly Denies Intimacies with Joan," *Boston Daily Globe*, Mar. 31, 1944.

20. "Questions Giesler Asked Chaplin and His Answers."

21. "Questions Giesler Asked Chaplin and His Answers."

22. "Questions Giesler Asked Chaplin and His Answers."

23. "Questions Giesler Asked Chaplin and His Answers."

24. "Questions Giesler Asked Chaplin and His Answers."

25. "Questions Giesler Asked Chaplin and His Answers."

26. "Questions Giesler Asked Chaplin and His Answers."

27. "Chaplin Cries as He Tells Own Story."

28. *United States. v. Chaplin*, No. 16,617, Trial Tr., 1065.

29. Winn, "Chaplin Tells His Story; Denies All."

30. *United States v. Chaplin*, No. 16,617, Trial Tr., 1067

31. *United States v. Chaplin*, No. 16,617, Trial Tr., 1067.

32. "Chaplin Cries as He Tells Own Story."

33. Hood to Director, telemeter, Mar. 30, 1944, Chaplin FBI File, Pt. 3, p. 96.

34. Winn, "Chaplin Tells His Story; Denies All."

35. *United States v. Chaplin*, No. 16,617, Trial Tr., 1067.

36. "Questions Giesler Asked Chaplin and His Answers."

37. "Questions Giesler Asked Chaplin and His Answers."

38. "Questions Giesler Asked Chaplin and His Answers."

39. "Questions Giesler Asked Chaplin and His Answers."

40. "Questions Giesler Asked Chaplin and His Answers."

41. Winn, "Chaplin Tells His Story; Denies All."

42. *United States v. Chaplin*, No. 16,617, Minute Books, Vol. 39, Mar. 30, 1944, NARA.

43. "Weather Report," *Los Angeles Times*, Mar. 31, 1944.

44. Associated Press, "Charlie Chaplin Ends Recital of Romance with Joan Berry," *Baltimore Sun*, Apr. 1, 1944.

45. Marcia Winn, "Joan Tells Chaplin Threat; Asserts Actor Said He Would Blacken Name; Testimony Ended in Mann Act Trial," *Chicago Daily Tribune*, Apr. 1, 1944.

46. Winn, "Joan Tells Chaplin Threat."

47. Winn, "Joan Tells Chaplin Threat."

48. "Chaplin Testifies to Tiffs with Joan, Denies Paying New York Fare," *Los Angeles Examiner*, Apr. 1, 1944.

49. Winn, "Joan Tells Chaplin Threat."

50. "Chaplin Testifies to Tiffs with Joan."

51. "Chaplin Testifies to Tiffs with Joan."

52. *United States v. Chaplin*, No. 16,617, Minute Books, Vol. 39, Mar. 31, 1944, NARA.

53. Winn, "Joan Tells Chaplin Threat."

54. Winn, "Joan Tells Chaplin Threat."

55. Winn, "Joan Tells Chaplin Threat."

56. Winn, "Joan Tells Chaplin Threat."

57. Winn, "Joan Tells Chaplin Threat."

58. Winn, "Joan Tells Chaplin Threat."

59. Tom Caton, "Joan Tells of Marriage Plea to Chaplin; Testimony Concluded and Case Will Go to Jury Next Tuesday," *Los Angeles Times*, Apr. 1, 1944.

60. Winn, "Joan Tells Chaplin Threat."

61. Winn, "Joan Tells Chaplin Threat."

62. Caton, Joan Tells of Marriage Plea to Chaplin."

63. Winn, "Joan Tells Chaplin Threat."

64. Winn, "Joan Tells Chaplin Threat."

65. Caton, "Joan Tells of Marriage Plea to Chaplin."

66. Winn, "Joan Tells Chaplin Threat."

67. *United States v. Chaplin*, No. 16,617, Minute Books, Vol. 39, Mar. 31, 1944, NARA.

68. Shawhan, unpublished manuscript, 9.

69. *United States v. Chaplin*, No. 16,617, Minute Books, Vol. 39, Mar. 31, 1944, NARA.

70. Caton, "Joan Tells of Marriage Plea to Chaplin,"

71. Winn, "Joan Tells Chaplin Threat."

72. Caton, "Joan Tells of Marriage Plea to Chaplin."

73. *United States v. Chaplin*, No. 16,617, Minute Books, Vol. 39, Mar. 31, 1944, NARA.

CHAPTER 16

1. Chaplin, *My Autobiography*, 422.

2. Tom Caton, "Attorneys Prepare Chaplin Arguments for Tomorrow; Jury Will Be Given Mann Act Case on Tuesday," *Los Angeles Times*, Apr. 2, 1944.

3. Chaplin, *My Autobiography*, 422.

4. *United States v. Chaplin*, No. 16,617, Minute Books, Vol. 39, Mar. 31, 1944,

5. Roeburt, *"Get Me Giesler,"* 187.

6. Giesler, *The Jerry Giesler Story*, 308–9.

7. Giesler, *The Jerry Giesler Story*, 164–65, 171.

8. Lewis Wood, "High Court Rules Negroes Can Vote in Texas Primary; Decision, 8 to 1, Holds Denial of Right Because of Race Violates the 15th Amendment; Stand since 1935 Upset; Roberts, in Dissent to Reed, Chides Colleagues for 'Intolerance in the Reversal,'" *New York Times*, Apr. 4, 1944; Drew Middleton, "Russians 11 Miles Past the Prut; Ring 15 Divisions; Drive for Lwow; U.S. Fliers Hit Budapest Rail Hub; Blow in Southeast; Big Bombers From Italy Blast Hungarian Line and Plane Plant; Attack Aids Red Army; Traffic Points in Yugoslavia Also Pounded in Opening of New Air Front," *New York Times*, Apr. 4, 1944; Associated Press, "Roosevelt O.K., President's Condition Declared by Physician Satisfactory," *Bergen Evening Record* (Hackensack, NJ), Apr. 4, 1944; *United States v. Chaplin*, No. 16,617, Minute Books, Vol. 39, Apr. 3, 1944.

9. Gene Sherman, "Two Who Know Law Bid for Jury's Decision," *Los Angeles Times*, Apr. 4, 1944.

10. Tom Caton, "Chaplin Fate Nears Jury as Pleas End; Use Common Sense, Giesler Asks, as Carr Demands Penalty," *Los Angeles Times*, Apr. 4, 1944.

11. "Summing Up the Chaplin Case; Said Prosecutor Carr," *Los Angeles Examiner*, Apr. 4, 1944.

12. "Summing Up the Chaplin Case; Said Prosecutor Carr."

13. *United States v. Chaplin*, Ind. No. 16,617, Minute Books, Vol. 39, Apr. 3, 1944.

14. Marcia Winn, "Chaplin Case Goes to Jury Today; Giesler Raps Joan Berry in Closing Plea; Carr Brings Tears to Courtroom," *Chicago Daily Tribune*, Apr. 4, 1944.

15. Caton, "Chaplin Fate Nears Jury as Pleas End."

16. Winn, "Chaplin Case Goes to Jury Today."

17. Winn, "Chaplin Case Goes to Jury Today."

18. Caton, "Chaplin Fate Nears Jury as Pleas End."

19. "Summing up the Chaplin Case; Said Attorney Giesler."

20. Associated Press, "Final Plea Made for Chaplin; Case Goes to Jury Today," *Rochester (NY) Democrat and Chronicle*, Apr. 4, 1944.

21. *United States v. Chaplin*, No. 16,617, Minute Books, Vol. 39, Apr. 3, 1944.

22. Caton, "Chaplin Fate Nears Jury as Pleas End."

23. "Summing Up the Chaplin Case; Said Attorne Giesler."

24. David Sentner, "Chaplin Lauded Stalin, Says Dies Group Report," *Los Angeles Examiner*, Apr. 4, 1944.

25. Caton, "Chaplin Fate Nears Jury as Pleas End."

26. Caton, "Chaplin Fate Nears Jury as Pleas End."

27. Caton, "Chaplin Fate Nears Jury as Pleas End."

28. Roeburt, *"Get Me Giesler,"* 86–88.

29. Caton, "Chaplin Fate Nears Jury as Pleas End."

30. "Summing Up the Chaplin Case."

31. Caton, "Chaplin Fate Nears Jury as Pleas End."

32. Winn, "Chaplin Case Goes to Jury Today."

33. Margaret Buell Wilder, "Carr Changes Style, Stages Dramatic Finish; Rereading of Joan's Letter to Chaplin Clever Move," *Los Angeles Examiner*, Apr. 4, 1944.

34. Florabel Muir, "War—Not Joan's—Hysteria behind Trial, Chaplin Beefs," *Daily News* (New York), Apr. 4, 1944.

35. James Lindsley, "Chaplin Jury Is Instructed in 5,500-Word Statement; Judge O'Connor Devotes Hour to Having Last Say before Deliberations Are Started," *Bergen Evening Record* (Hackensack, NJ), Apr. 4, 1944.

36. "Chaplin Acquitted in Mann Act Case; Jury Including Seven Women Frees Actor on Both Counts and Court Room Cheers," *New York Times*, Apr. 5, 1944.

37. *United States v. Chaplin*, No. 16,617, Minute Books, Vol. 39, Apr. 4, 1944.

38. *United States v. Chaplin*, No. 16,617, Minute Books, Vol. 39, Mar. 31, 1944.

39. *United States v. Chaplin*, No. 16, 617, Jury Instructions, Government's Instruction No. 14, Folder 3, NARA.

40. *United States v. Chaplin*, No. 16, 617, Jury Instructions, Defense Request No. 1, Folder 2, NARA.

41. *United States v. Chaplin*, No. 16,617, Minute Books, Vol. 39, Apr. 4, 1944; Tom Caton, "Chaplin Not Guilty, Federal Jury Finds; Comedian Acquitted on Both Counts," *Los Angeles Times*, Apr. 5, 1944.

42. *United States v. Chaplin*, No. 16,617, Minute Books, Vol. 39, Apr. 4, 1944.

43. Shawhan, unpublished manuscript, 9; Chaplin, *My Autobiography*, 423.

44. *United States v. Chaplin*, Ind. No. 16,617, Minute Books, Vol. 39, Apr. 4, 1944; Gene Sherman, "'The End' Scene at Trial Outdoes Film Scenario; Confusion Follows Verdict as Spectators Storm Railings to Swarm around Chaplin," Los Angeles Times, Apr. 5, 1944.

45. "Chaplin Acquitted in Mann Act Case," *New York Times*, Apr. 5, 1944.

46. "Chaplin Acquitted in Mann Act Case."

47. Underwood, *Newspaperwoman*, 186.

48. Shawhan, unpublished manuscript, 10.

49. Muir, *Headline Happy*, 68.

50. Underwood, *Newspaperwoman*, 195.

51. Sherman, "'The End' Scene at Trial Outdoes Film Scenario"; Shawhan, unpublished manuscript, 9.

52. Sherman, "'The End' Scene at Trial Outdoes Film Scenario."

53. Shawhan, unpublished manuscript, 10.

54. Chaplin, *My Autobiography*, 423.

55. Sherman, "'The End' Scene at Trial Outdoes Film Scenario."

56. Sherman, "'The End' Scene at Trial Outdoes Film Scenario."

57. "Jury Finds Chaplin Is Not Guilty," *Hartford Courant*, Apr. 5, 1944.

58. Hood to Director, memorandum, Apr. 5, 1944, Chaplin FBI File, Pt. 3 p. 119.

59. Margaret Buell Wilder, "Tears on Chaplin's Face as Verdict Read; Near Collapse as 'Not Guilty' Heard; Later, Smile Emerges," *Los Angeles Examiner*, Apr. 5, 1944.

60. Sherman, "'The End,' Scene at Trial Outdoes Film Scenario."

61. "'Mr. Chaplin, You Are Discharged,' Says Judge; 'There Was Lack of Willful Intent,' Jury's Conclusion," *Los Angeles Examiner*, Apr. 5, 1944; Sherman, "'The End,' Scene at Trial Outdoes Film Scenario."

62. *United States v. Chaplin*, No. 16,617,Verdict of the Jury, Minute Books, Vol. 39, Apr. 4, 1944.

63. Wilder, "Tears on Chaplin's Face as Verdict Read."

64. Caton, "Chaplin Not Guilty, Federal Jury Finds."

65. Sherman, "'The End,' Scene at Trial Outdoes Film Scenario."

66. Sherman, "The End,' Scene at Trial Outdoes Film Scenario."

67. Wilder, "Tears on Chaplin's Face as Verdict Read."

68. 'Mr. Chaplin, You Are Discharged,' Says Judge."

69. Caton, "Chaplin Not Guilty, Federal Jury Finds."

70. "'Mr. Chaplin, You Are Discharged,' Says Judge."

71. Hood to Director, telemeter, Apr. 4, 1944, Chaplin FBI File, Pt. 3, p. 115.

72. Caton, "Chaplin Not Guilty, Federal Jury Finds."

73. Chaplin, *My Autobiography*, 424.

74. Caton, "Chaplin Not Guilty, Federal Jury Finds."

75. Muir, *Headline Happy*, 67.

76. Chaplin Jr., *My Father*, 292.

77. "Jurors Tell Views of Case; Report No Friction in Arriving at Verdict," *Los Angeles Examiner*, Apr. 5, 1944.

78. Caton, "Chaplin Not Guilty, Federal Jury Finds"; "'Mr. Chaplin, You Are Discharged,' Says Judge"; Chaplin, *My Autobiography*, 424.

79. Wilder, "Tears on Chaplin's Face as Verdict Read."

80. Wilder, "Tears on Chaplin's Face as Verdict Read."

81. Chaplin, *My Autobiography*, 424–25.

82. "Paternity Suit Unaffected," *Los Angeles Examiner*, Apr. 5, 1944.

83. "No Comment from Joan Barry on Outcome," *Los Angeles Examiner*, Apr. 5, 1944.

84. "'He Looks Happy,' Joan's Only Comment on Case," *Los Angeles Times*, Apr. 5, 1944.

85. Sherman, "'The End,' Scene at Trial Outdoes Film Scenario."

CHAPTER 17

1. "Chaplin Prosecutor's Mother Dies in Memphis," *Bakersfield Californian*, Apr. 7, 1944.
2. Chaplin, *My Autobiography*, 426.
3. Chaplin, *My Autobiography*, 425.
4. "Chaplins Look for Stork in August," *Los Angeles Times*, Feb. 20, 1944.
5. United Press, "Conspiracy Suit Attorney Asks Carr for Dismissal," *Bakersfield Californian*, Apr. 5, 1944.
6. Associated Press, "Chaplin Is Facing Trial on Civil Rights Charge; U.S. to Press Case Based on Miss Berry's Arrest," *New York Herald Tribune*, Apr. 6, 1944.
7. Eyman, *Charlie Chaplin vs. America*, 15–16.
8. "Chaplin Vindication Is Appeaser Defeat," *Daily Worker*, May 21, 1944.
9. "Mann Act," *Washington Post*, Apr. 6, 1944.
10. "The Chaplin Mystery," *Chicago Daily Tribune*, May 11, 1944.
11. Westbrook Pegler, "Fair Enough," *Washington News*, Feb. 19, 1944.
12. John A. Olmsted, "No Use for Charlie—Or the Girls," *Petaluma (CA) Argus-Courier*, Apr. 5, 1944.
13. R. B. Hood to Director, May 1, 1944, Chaplin FBI File, Pt. 3, p. 150.
14. *United States v. Chaplin*, Ind. No. 16,617, Minute Books, Vol. 39, Apr. 11, 1944; "Chaplin Sick; Case Put Off," *Los Angeles Times*, Apr. 12, 1944.
15. 18 U.S.C. Sec. 371.
16. John Edgar Hoover to Mr. Tolson, Mr. Tamm, and Mr. Rosen, memorandum, Apr. 11, 1944, Chaplin FBI File, Pt. 3, p. 112.
17. Hood to the Director, telemeter, Chaplin FBI File, Apr. 4, 1944, Pt. 3 p. 115.
18. "Bicentennial Celebration of the United States Attorneys, 1789–1989," U.S. Department of Justice, www.justice.gov/sites/default/files/usao/legacy/2011/11/23/bicn_celebration.pdf, accessed Nov. 20, 2023.
19. R. B. Hood to Mr. A. Rosen, Apr. 14, 1944, Chaplin FBI File, Pt. 3, p. 125.
20. Hood to Director, teletype, date blacked out, Chaplin FBI File, Pt. 3, p. 134.
21. *United States v. Charles Spencer Chaplin, et al.*, No. 16,616 and 16,618, Opinion, J. F. T. O'Connor, Judge, pp. 35, 47, Apr. 14, 1944, Criminal Case Dockets, 1907–1993, U.S. District Court for the Central District of California, Record Group 21, Records of the District Courts of the United States, NARA.
22. *United States v. Charles Spencer Chaplin, et al.*, Nos. 16,616 and 16, 618, Partial Reporter's Transcript of Proceedings, pp. 5–6, Apr. 14, 1944.
23. R. B. Hood to A. Rosen, Apr. 14, 1944, Chaplin FBI File, Pt. 3 p. 126.
24. Hood to Director, telemeter, Apr. 26, 1944, Chaplin FBI File, Pt. 3, p. 137.
25. R. B. Hood to Mr. Rosen, May 9, 1944, Chaplin FBI File, Pt. 3, pp. 157–59.
26. R. B. Hood to Mr. Rosen, May 9, 1944.
27. Charles H. Carr to J. Edgar Hoover, Apr. 27, 1944, Chaplin FBI File, Pt. 5, p. 142.

28. *United States v. Charles Spencer Chaplin, et al.*, Nos., 16,616, 16,618, and 16,619, NARA.

29. R. B. Hood to Mr. Rosen, May 11, 1944, Chaplin FBI File, Pt. 3, pp. 152–54, Charlie Chaplin Archive, Charles Chaplin Daily Production Reports, W/E May 6 and 20, 1944, ECCI00313699, CH131.

30. R. B. Hood to Director, FBI, May 26, 1944, Chaplin FBI File, Pt. 5, p. 143.

31. Jerry Giesler to the Hon. J. F. T. O'Connor, May 16, 1944; "Letters from Friends, 1944," J. F. T. O'Connor Archive, MSS C-B 549, v. 20, Bancroft Library, University of California at Berkeley.

32. "Biddle to Renew Battle on Trusts; Cabinet Member, Here, Also Talks about Problem of Handling Aliens," *Los Angeles Times*, Aug. 22, 1944.

33. "13 Named in Drive on Black Market; Jury Indictments Follow Inquiry; Night Clubs, Cafes to Get Attention," *Los Angeles Times*, July 19, 1945.

34. "Chain Letter Scheme Nipped," *Los Angeles Times*, June 9, 1945.

35. "Chiseling on Servicemen Charged to Four Suspects," *Los Angeles Times*, Aug. 12, 1944.

36. "More Gasoline Sellers Indicted; Black Market Arrests Expected; Government Keeps Names Secret," *Los Angeles Times*, Mar. 15, 1945.

37. "Tokyo Rose May Stand Trial Here; U.S. Atty. Carr Asks Washington for Her Return to Los Angeles for Prosecution," *Los Angeles Times*, Sept. 14, 1945.

38. "Tokyo Rose Trial Here Doubted," *Los Angeles Times*, Sept. 15, 1945.

39. "Mikhail Kalatozov," Movie Data Base, www.themoviedb.org/person/108764 -mikhail-kalatozov?language=en-US, accessed Nov. 20, 2023.

40. Hood to Director, telemeter, Apr. 19, 1944, Chaplin FBI File, Pt. 3, p. 135.

41. Charles Chaplin Daily Production Report, W/E June 3, 1944, Charlie Chaplin Archive, ECCI00313699, CH131.

42. Chaplin, *My Autobiography*, 426.

43. Charles Chaplin Daily Production Reports, W/E July 1 and 15, 1944, Charlie Chaplin Archive, ECCI00313699, CH131.

CHAPTER 18

1. Farrell, *Clarence Darrow: Attorney for the Damned*, 214–16.

2. "3-Day Rites Set for Joseph Scott; Requiem Mass in Cathedral to Climax Church Ceremonies," *Los Angeles Times*, Mar. 26, 1958.

3. "1930 Nobel Prize in Physiology or Medicine (Karl Landsteiner)," Rockefeller University, www.rockefeller.edu/our-scientists/karl-landsteiner/2554-nobel -prize/, accessed Dec. 16, 2023.

4. "Chaplin Ruled Out as Berry Child's Father; Clinical Blood Tests Clear Comedian in Paternity Suit," *Los Angeles Times*, Feb. 16, 1944.

5. Florabel Muir, "Hint Test 'Doctored' in Chaplin Dad Suit," *Daily News* (New York), Feb. 17, 1944.

6. "Joan Berry's Attorney Quits in Chaplin Paternity Case; Court Denies Plea of Actor's Counsel to Dismiss Suit," *Los Angeles Times*, Feb. 18, 1944.

7. "Joan Berry and Mother Drop Fight against Chaplin in Paternity Case; No Move Will Be Made to Replace Attorney Who Withdrew from Action," *Los Angeles Times*, Feb. 19, 1944.

8. Associated Press, "Joseph Scott, Noted Attorney, Enters Chaplin Case as Counsel for Joan Barry Baby in Paternity Claim," *Oakland Tribune*, Feb. 22, 1944.

9. "Attorney Scott to Fight Chaplin Paternity Suit Dismissal Today," *Los Angeles Times*, Feb. 23, 1944.

10. Barbara Jaqua (Joseph Scott's granddaughter), interview with the author, Aug. 6, 2023.

11. Robinson, *Lawyers of Los Angeles*, 129, 144, 274.

12. Father Alfonso A. Scott, interview with the author, Jan. 11, 2023.

13. Jaqua, interview with the author, Aug. 6, 2023

14. John Sharpe, "Joseph Scott (1867–1958): Devout English Emigrant to Fame and Fortune in Los Angeles, Part One," *The Homestead Blog*, Feb. 12, 2022, www.homesteadmuseum.blog/2022/02/12/joseph-scott-1867-1958-devout-english-emigrant-to-fame-and-fortune-in-los-angeles, accessed Nov. 21, 2023.

15. "Joseph Scott to Nominate President; State Republican Chiefs Honor Pasadenan; Mr. Hoover Wants Californian; Leader May Come West to Receive Word," *Pasadena (CA) Star-News*, May 25, 1932; Joseph Scott to Lawrence Richey, Feb. 7, 1933, President Hoover Personal File, Joseph Scott, 1930–33, Herbert Hoover Presidential Library and Museum.

16. "Calls Ireland Beacon Light of Democracy; Leader of Rally Backs Homeland's Fight upon Alien 'Isms,'" *Chicago Daily News*, May 20, 1939; Richard M. Nixon to Bertha Scott, Mar. 27, 1958, Condolence Folder, Scott, Mrs. Joe, Richard Nixon Presidential Library and Museum.

17. Loyd Wright to Jerry Giesler, Dec. 5, 1944, Charlie Chaplin Archive, ECCI00015310, CH048.

18. Chaplin Jr., *My Father*, 296.

19. Loyd Wright to Edward C. Raftery, telegram, Jan. 27, 1944, Loyd Wright Papers, Series 5A, US Mss 99AN, Box 3, Folder 4, United Artists Records, Wisconsin Historical Society.

20. Loyd Wright III, interview with the author, Jan. 11, 2021. Associated Press, "Fields in Court as Suit Retried," *Hollywood Citizen-News*, Sept. 13, 1939; "Move to Dismiss Swanson Suit Is under Advisement," *Los Angeles Daily News*, Dec. 2, 1932; United Press, "Marx Brothers to Talk over Appeal of Fine," *Oakland Tribune*, Apr. 13, 1938.

21. Wright, interview with the author, Jan. 11, 2021.

22. "Loyd Wright Dies; Coast Lawyer, 81; Ex-Chairman of A.B.A. Led Commission on Government," *New York Times*, Oct. 24, 1974; C.P. Trussell, "12 Chosen for U.S. Panel to Study Loyalty Program," New York Times, Nov. 11, 1955

23. "Kiwanis Urge Deportation," *Chico (CA) Record*, June 20, 1939; "Charles English Millikan and Gertrude Eileen Pentland," Return of Marriage Certificate No. 36899, Portland, Oregon, July 6, 1918, Ancestry, www.ancestry.com.

24. "Charles English Millikan," World War II Draft Registration Card, Charles Millikan, 1940 U.S. Census, Ancestry, www.ancestry.com.

25. "'Shell Game' with Joan Barry Baby Denounced by Her New Lawyer," *Washington Daily News*, Feb. 22, 1944.

26. "Joseph Scott, New Joan Berry Lawyer, Opens Fight for Baby," *Los Angeles Times*, Feb. 22, 1944.

27. Stanley Mosk to his brother, Edward, *California Legal History* 4 (2009): 12.

28. Jacqueline R. Braitman and Gerald F. Uelmen, *Justice Stanley Mosk: A Life at the Center of California Politics and Justice* (Jefferson, NC: McFarland, 2013), 9–15, 21–24.

29. Braitman and Uelmen, *Justice Stanley Mosk*, 5.

30. Braitman and Uelmen, *Judge Stanley Mosk*, 122–23.

31. Braitman and Uelmen, *Justice Stanley Mosk*, 123–26; Gerald F. Uelman, interview with the author, July 3, 2020.

32. "Light Rains Visit Southland; More Predicted for Today," *Los Angeles Times*, Mar. 1, 1944; "Chaplin Assailed in Paternity Suit; Lawyers Clash over Blood Test; Decision Delayed on Trial of Actor," *Los Angeles Times*, Mar. 2, 1944.

33. Frederick C. Othman, "Scott Lashes Chaplin's Plea for Dismissal," *Long Beach Sun*, Mar. 2, 1944; "Chaplin Assailed in Paternity Suit."

34. "Chaplin Assailed in Paternity Suit."

35. Associated Press, "Sizzling Record Studied by Judge in Chaplin Case," *Long Beach Press Telegram*, Mar. 2, 1944.

36. United Press, "Joan's Lawyer Bases Plea on Eyes' Color; Chaplin Denounced in Battle over Baby's Paternity," *Stockton (CA) Daily Evening Record*, Mar. 1, 1944.

37. International News Service, "Lawyers Fume in Chaplin Suit Fight," *Long Beach Independent*, Mar. 2, 1944; "Chaplin Assailed in Paternity Suit;" Othman, "Scott Lashes Chaplin's Plea for Dismissal.

38. Othman, "Scott Lashes Chaplin's Plea for Dismissal."

39. "Chaplin Assailed in Paternity Suit."

40. Florabel Muir, "Judge 'No Solomon,' Delays Rule on Chaplin Blood," *Daily News* (New York), Mar. 2, 1944.

41. "Joan's Lawyer Bases Plea on Eyes' Color."

42. Othman, "Scott Lashes Chaplin's Plea for Dismissal"; Muir, "Judge 'No Solomon.'"

43. "Dismissal of Berry Child Suit Denied; Chaplin Faces Court Action in Case; Stipulation Which Called for Blood Tests Voided," *Los Angeles Times*, Mar. 9, 1944.

44. "Dismissal of Berry Child Suit Denied."

45. "Court Orders Chaplin Trial in Paternity Case; Rejects Actor's Dismissal Plea Despite Blood Test Indication Baby Is Not His," *New York Herald Tribune*, Mar. 9, 1944.

46. Transcript of Record at 11, *Berry v. Chaplin*, No. D-238936, Dept. 23, California Superior Court, Los Angeles County, Apr. 4–18, 1945.

47. 10 Cal. 2d 428, 433–34 (1937).

48. Uelmen, interview with author.

49. Prof. Andrea Roth, interview with the author, July 18, 2020.

50. Judge Stanley Mosk to Edward Mosk, Mar. 27, 1944, reprinted in Richard M. Mosk, "Stanley Mosk's Letters to His Brother Overseas during World War II," *California Legal History* 4 (2009): 3, 12.

51. "Eastside Journal Political Page; Judge Mosk," *Eastside (Los Angeles) Journal*, Apr. 26, 1944.

52. Braitman and Uelmen, *Justice Stanley Mosk*, 62.

53. Florabel Muir, "Chaplin Freed in Federal Case; Civil Suit Stands," *Washington Times-Herald*, May 16, 1944.

54. United Press, "Chaplin Case Appeal Filed," *Press Democrat (Santa Rosa, CA)*, Mar. 10, 1944.

55. "Chaplin Loses Another Round," *Hollywood Citizen-News*, Mar. 17, 1944.

56. "Chaplin Petitions Court to Quash Paternity Suit; Cites Blood Test in Request to State Supreme Court," *New York Herald Tribune*, Apr. 18, 1944.

57. Associated Press, "Chaplin Loses, Wins in Court Decisions," *Stockton (CA) Daily Evening Record*, May 15, 1944.

58. "Chaplin Loses Plea to Avoid Paternity Suit; Civil Rights Case Is Dismissed," *Chicago Daily Tribune*, May 16, 1944; "Government Voids Chaplin Charges; Remaining Criminal Indictments Dismissed, but State Court Upholds Civil Suit," *New York Times*, May 16, 1944.

59. *Berry v. Chaplin*, No. D-238936, Answer to Complaint, May 25, 1944.

60. *Berry v. Chaplin*, No. D-238936, Complaint by Unborn Infant by Guardian Ad Litem, June 3, 1943.

61. "Chaplin Case Baby Declared Destitute," *Los Angeles Times*, June 3, 1944.

62. "Chaplin Wants to Know How $11,700 Was Spent," *Washington Post*, June 9, 1944.

63. Associated Press, "Chaplin Agrees to Support Joan's Baby," *Oakland Tribune*, June 14, 1944.

64. *Berry v. Chaplin*, No. D-238936, Minute Order, Hon. Myron Westover, June 16, 1944.

CHAPTER 19

1. "Chaplin Trial Nears," *New York Sunday News*, Dec. 10, 1944.

2. "Court Jam May Delay Start of Chaplin Trial," *Los Angeles Times*, Dec. 13, 1944.

3. Tom Caton, "Chaplin to Blame Others for Baby; Comedian Maps Defense in Trial for Paternity of Joan Berry Child," *Los Angeles Times*, Dec. 14, 1944.

4. *Berry v. Chaplin*, No. D-238936, Affidavit of Charles E. Millikan, Dec. 12, 1944.

5. Millikan Affidavit, 5–6.

6. Millikan Affidavit, 6.

7. Caton, "Chaplin to Blame Others for Baby."

8. Caton, "Chaplin to Blame Others for Baby."

9. Associated Press, "Chaplin Defense in New Attempt to Halt Hearing; Will Cite Alleged Baby Case Agreement Not to Prosecute," *San Bernardino (CA) County Sun*, Dec. 14, 1944.

10. "Chaplin Case Goes On—But Blood Test Hit," *Los Angeles Daily News*, Dec. 15, 1944.

11. "Chaplin Jolted Twice in Court Pleas; Selection of Joan Berry Jury Begins; Court Declines Comedian's Move for Trial by Judge," *Los Angeles Times*, Dec. 15, 1944.

12. Marcia Winn, "Chaplin Loses First Rounds in Baby Suit," *Chicago Daily Tribune*, Dec. 15, 1944.

13. Winn, "Chaplin Loses First Rounds in Baby Suit."

14. Winn, "Chaplin Loses First Rounds in Baby Suit."

15. "Judge Henry M. Willis," *Los Angeles Bench and Bar, Centennial Edition 1949–50* (Los Angeles: Wilson & Sons, 1950), 20; "M'Cormick's Assistant Is Not Yet Appointed," *Los Angeles Express*, May 15, 1909; James Carey, "Judge Willis' Career Full of Activity," *Los Angeles Daily News*, Feb. 29, 1932; "Order to Show Cause," *San Bernardino Daily Courier*, Apr. 16, 1887.

16. Henry M. Willis III, e-mail to the author, Jan. 21, 2023; "Judge Willis, Once State Senator for S.B. County, Dies," *San Bernardino (CA) County Sun*, Apr. 16, 1960.

17. Ruth McClintock, "Women's Clubs," *Los Angeles Evening Express*, July 4, 1930.

18. *Berry v. Chaplin*, No. D-238936, Minute Order, Dec. 14, 1944; "Judge Decides Jury Must Hear the Chaplin Case," *Boston Globe*, Dec. 15, 1944.

19. Cal. Civ. Proc. Code § 631.

20. *Berry v. Chaplin*, No. D-238936, Minute Order, Dec. 14, 1944; "Weather Report," *Los Angeles Times*, Dec. 15, 1944.

21. "Berry-Chaplin Legal Battle Fails to Stir Baby Carol Ann; Child over Whom Big Lawsuit Rages Plays at Her Home," *Los Angeles Times*, Dec. 17, 1944.

22. Marcia Winn, "Defense Grills 12 Prospective Chaplin Jurors," *Chicago Daily Tribune*, Dec. 16, 1944.

23. "Berry-Chaplin Legal Battle Fails to Stir Baby Carol Ann."

24. Associated Press, "Chaplin Shouts He Is Not Guilty of Any 'Crime'; On Stand He Says Counsel for Miss Berry Tries to Paint Him as 'Monster,'" *New York Herald Tribune*, Dec. 20, 1944.

25. "Chaplin Case Legal Words Stump Juror," *Los Angeles Daily News*, Dec. 16, 1944.

26. "Selection of Chaplin Jury Finished; Case Opens Today," *Los Angeles Daily News*, Dec. 19, 1944.

27. "Jury Chosen in Chaplin Paternity Case," *Atlanta Constitution*, Dec. 19, 1944.

28. "Selection of Chaplin Jury Finished."

29. "Our Baby," South Van Ness Hospital Commemorative Birthday Book, courtesy Carol Ann Berry to author.

30. "Chaplin Testifies in Paternity Trial; Comedian Describes Night Visit of Girl, with Gun, to His Home," *Los Angeles Times*, Dec. 20, 1944; Dr. Laurie Goldstein, interview with the author, Oct. 25, 2021

31. Cal. Civ. Proc. Code § 2055; "Chaplin Testifies in Paternity Trial; Comedian Describes Night Visit of Girl."

32. "Chaplin Shouts He Is Not Guilty of Any 'Crime.'"

33. Marcia Winn, "Chaplin Bangs Witness Chair; Shouts Denials," *Chicago Daily Tribune*, Dec. 20, 1944.

34. Transcript of Record at 43–44, *Berry v. Chaplin*, No. D-238936 (Dept. 23, California Superior Court, Los Angeles County, Apr. 4–18, 1945). Chaplin testified at the first paternity trial that began in December 1944. He chose not to attend the second trial, which occurred Apr. 4–18, 1945. Therefore, the judge allowed Joseph Scott to introduce the transcript of Chaplin's testimony from the first paternity trial as evidence in the second trial. Accordingly, Chaplin's testimony from the two trials was exactly the same. No transcript exists from the first trial; so citations to the transcript pages are from the second one.

35. Transcript of Record at 104.

36. Transcript of Record at 105.

37. Transcript of Record at 44.

38. Transcript of Record at 44.

39. Transcript of Record at 45.

40. Transcript of Record at 46.

41. Transcript of Record at 48.

42. Transcript of Record at 48.

43. Transcript of Record at 111–12.

44. Transcript of Record at 56.

45 Transcript of Record at 57.

46. Transcript of Record at 57.

47. Transcript of Record at 57.

48. Transcript of Record at 57.

49. Transcript of Record at 57.

50. Transcript of Record at 57.

51. Transcript of Record at 82.

52. Transcript of Record at 82, 87.

53. Transcript of Record at 88.

54. Transcript of Record at 92.

55. Transcript of Record at 93.

56. Transcript of Record at 95.

57. Transcript of Record at 96.

58. Transcript of Record at 96.

59. Transcript of Record at 99.

60. "Joan Berry Asks Jurors to Name Chaplin Father; Actress Calls Herself 'Forgotten Woman' in Tearful Plea to Decide Paternity of Child," *Los Angeles Times*, Dec. 21, 1944.

61. Lucille Leimert, "Confidentially," *Los Angeles Times*, Dec. 26, 1944.

62. Associated Press, "Miss Berry Tells Court Chaplin Is Child's Father; Comedian's Lawyer Tries to Block Testimony, but Objection Is Overruled," *New York Herald Tribune*, Dec. 21, 1944.

63. "Chaplin Stands Beside Baby Before Jurors; Suspense Marks Scene in Courtroom Battle; Comedian Makes Mute Appeal to Talesmen," *Los Angeles Times*, Dec. 27, 1944.

64. "Joan Berry, Weeping, Leaves Witness Stand; Ex-Protégé of Charles Chaplin Breaks Down after Telling Their Relations," *Los Angeles Times*, Dec. 22, 1944.

65. Associated Press, "Miss Berry Tells Court Chaplin Is Child's Father."

66. "Joan Berry Asks Jurors to Name Chaplin Father."

67. "Joan Berry Asks Jurors to Name Chaplin Father."

68. "Joan Berry Asks Jurors to Name Chaplin Father."

69. Marcia Winn, "Joan Breaks, Flees Witness Chair in Tears," *Chicago Daily Tribune*, Dec. 22, 1944.

70. "Joan Berry, Weeping, Leaves Witness Stand."

71. "Joan Berry, Weeping, Leaves Witness Stand."

72. "Joan Berry, Weeping, Leaves Witness Stand."

73. "Joan Berry, Weeping, Leaves Witness Stand."

74. Associated Press, "Collapses at Trial: Joan Berry Admits Trying to Slay Self," *Washington Post*, Dec. 22, 1944.

75. "Joan Berry, Weeping, Leaves Witness Stand."

76. "Chaplin on Stand Denies Most of Joan's Testimony," *Los Angeles Daily News*, Dec. 27, 1944.

77. "Chaplin on Stand Denies Most of Joan's Testimony."

78. "Chaplin Stands Beside Baby Before Jurors."

79. "Chaplin Stands Beside Baby Before Jurors."

80. "Chaplin Stands Beside Baby Before Jurors." The article states that Joan was in Tulsa in January 1942, which is clearly a typographical error. She was there in January 1943.

81. Tom Caton, "Chaplin Assailed in Scott Tirade; Attorney Scathing in Criticism; Actor and Joan Berry Absent," *Los Angeles Times*, Dec. 30, 1944.

82. "Two Doctors Aid Chaplin Defense; Complicated Medical Testimony Introduced in Paternity Suit over Joan Berry's Baby," *Los Angeles Times*, Dec. 28, 1944.

83. "Chaplin Trial Expected to Wind Up Early Next Week," *Los Angeles Daily News*, Dec. 29, 1944.

84. "Two Doctors Aid Chaplin Defense."

85. "Film Comedian Called 'Menace' and 'Crucified'; Chaplin's Case Expected to Go to Jury Today," *Los Angeles Times*, Jan. 3, 1945.

86. Associated Press, "Calls Chaplin 'Buzzard'; Joan Berry's Counsel Denounces Defendant in Court," *New York Times*, Dec. 30, 1944.

87. Florabel Muir, "Chaplin Jury Mulls Over Verdict," *Daily News* (New York), Jan. 4, 1945.

88. Florabel Muir, "Charlie Betrayed at Gunpoint?" *Daily News* (New York), Jan. 3, 1944.

89. Associated Press, "Chaplin Called 'Runt' and 'Cad' in Baby Trial; Attorney for Miss Berry Quotes from Bible and Classics in Summation," *New York Herald Tribune*, Dec. 30, 1944.

90. Caton, "Chaplin Assailed in Scott Tirade."

91. "Chaplin Called 'Runt' and 'Cad' in Baby Trial."

92. Caton, "Chaplin Assailed in Scott Tirade."

93. Caton, "Chaplin Assailed in Scott Tirade."

94. Florabel Muir, "Feet That Made Millions Couldn't Kick in a Door," *Daily News* (New York), Jan. 1, 1945.

95. Florabel Muir, "Chaplin Suit a Draw; Gals for Charlie," *Daily News* (New York), Jan. 5, 1945.

96. "Film Comedian Called 'Menace' and 'Crucified.'"

97. Muir, "Charlie Betrayed at Gunpoint?"

98. "Film Comedian Called 'Menace' and 'Crucified.'"

99. "Film Comedian Called 'Menace' and 'Crucified.'"

100. Associated Press, "Chaplin's Case Will Be Given to Jury Today; Miss Berry's Lawyer Calls Him 'Wretched Specimen,' as Argument Is Ended," *New York Herald Tribune*, Jan. 3, 1945.

101. Associated Press, "Chaplin's Case Will Be Given to Jury Today."

102. "Film Comedian Called 'Menace' and 'Crucified.'"

103. "Chaplin Jurors Recess for Night without Verdict; Will Resume Deliberations

Today after Failing to Agree in First 4½ Hours," *New York Herald Tribune*, Jan. 4, 1945.

104. Muir, "Chaplin Jury Mulls Over Verdict."

105. "Jury in Chaplin Case Deadlocked; Hung Jury in Chaplin-Joan Baby Dispute," *Los Angeles Daily News*, Jan. 5, 1945.

106. Muir, "Chaplin Suit a Draw."

107. Muir, "Chaplin Suit a Draw."

108. United Press, "Chaplin Jurors Fail to Agree; Suit a Mistrial; Court Dismisses Panel after Long Deadlock Favors Actor, 7 to 5," *New York Herald Tribune*, Jan. 5, 1945.

109. "Deadlock Forces Chaplin Mistrial; Jurors in Paternity Case Split 7 to 5 in Favor of Comedian," *Los Angeles Times*, Jan. 5, 1945.

110. Associated Press, "Joan Is Suing Again, Date to Be Set Soon; Hearing Is Called Thursday as Scott Presses for Action," *Binghamton (NY) Press*, Jan. 5, 1945.

111. Associated Press, "Joan Is Suing Again, Date to Be Set Soon."

CHAPTER 20

1. *Monsieur Verdoux*, Daily Production Reports, Charles Chaplin, W/E Jan. 20, 1945, to Apr. 7, 1945, Charlie Chaplin Archive, ECCI00313699, CH131.

2. Louella O. Parsons, "Film to Star Joan Barry; Monogram Signs Chaplin Case Girl for Mystery Movie," *Los Angeles Examiner*, Feb. 12, 1945.

3. Ted Okuda, *The Monogram Checklist: The Films of Monogram Pictures Corporation, 1931–1952* (Jefferson, NC: McFarland, 1987), 5; "Monogram, the Big Little Studio," *Vienna's Classic Hollywood* (blog), www.dancinglady39.wordpress.com/2014/01/21/monogramthe-big-little-studio/ accessed Nov. 25, 2023.

4. Okuda, *The Monogram Checklist*, 1.

5. Ivan Spear, "Hollywood Report: Litigant in le Affaire Chaplin Will Be Starred in a Picture," *Boxoffice*, Feb. 17, 1945.

6. "Rejects Barry Film," *Motion Picture Daily*, Feb. 27, 1945.

7. "Chaplin Case Retrial's Start Set for May 2," *Los Angeles Times*, Jan. 12, 1945.

8. "Chaplin Case Retrial's Start Set for May 2."

9. Associated Press, "Chaplin-Berry Case Set for Trial April 4," *Baltimore Sun*, Feb. 20, 1945.

10. United Press, "Chaplin Deportation Is Asked in Bill," *Knoxville News-Sentinel*, Feb. 16, 1945.

11. Chesly Manly, "Langer's Trial for Turpitude Opens in Senate; Lucas, as 'Prosecutor,' Finds Rough Going," *Chicago Daily Tribune*, Mar. 10, 1942.

12. United Press, "Chaplin Says He's a Victim of a Smear Plot; Not a Communist, but an Internationalist, Film Comedian Explains," *Anniston (AL) Star*, Feb. 22, 1945.

13. S. B. 536, 79th Cong., 1st Sess. (1945).

14. United Press, "Blood Test Motion Opens Chaplin Trial," *Stockton (CA) Daily Evening Record*, Apr. 4, 1945.

15. Cal. Civ. Proc. Code §597.

16. Transcript of Record at 5–6, 11, *Berry v. Chaplin*, No. D-238936, Dept. 23, California Superior Court, Los Angeles County, Apr. 4–18, 1945.

17. "Offer Made to Waive Jury in Chaplin Case," *Los Angeles Times*, Apr. 5, 1945.

18. "Judge Kincaid Will Retire at End of Month," *Los Angeles Times*, Jan. 17, 1963.

19. Clarence Leslie Kincaid, World War II Draft Registration Card, Ancestry, www.ancestry.com.

20. Transcript of Record, 18.

21. "Chaplin Testimony Starts Monday," *Long Beach Independent*, Apr. 8, 1945.

22. Associated Press, "Chaplin Juror Given Bounce," *Daily News* (New York), Apr. 19, 1945.

23. "Eleven Women on Chaplin Jury," *Los Angeles Times*, Apr. 7, 1945; "Jury Holds Charlie Chaplin Father of Joan Berry Child; Former Protégé Wins Two-Year Fight with Actor," *Los Angeles Times*, Apr. 18, 1945. Further information about the jurors' backgrounds was obtained from U.S. Census records, available at www.ancestry.com.

24. "The Weather," *Los Angeles Times*, Apr. 9, 1945.

25. Transcript of Record, 18.

26. Transcript of Reccord, 16.

27. Transcript of Record, 16.

28. Transcript of Record, 17.

29. Transcript of Record, 19.

30. Transcript of Record, 21.

31. Transcript of Record, 40.

32. Transcript of Record, 41.

33. Transcript of Record, 131.

34. See Rose Eveleth, "Smart News: Lysol's Vintage Ads Subtly Pushed Women to Use Its Disinfectant as Birth Control; As If That Wasn't Bad Enough, Lysol Isn't Even an Effective Contraceptive," *Smithsonian Magazine*, Sept. 30, 2013, https://www.smithsonianmag.com/smart-news/lysols-vintage-ads-subtly-pushed-women-to-use-its-disinfectant-as-birth-control-218734/, accessed Dec. 31, 2023.

35. Transcript of Record, 166–67.

36. Transcript of Record, 139–40.

37. Transcript of Record, 171, 177, 186, 193, 198, 202.

38. Transcript of Record, 329.

39. Transcript of Record, 330.

40. Transcript of Record, 336.

41. Transcript of Record, 336.

42. Transcript of Record, 402.

43. Transcript of Record, 402.

44. Transcript of Record, 403.

45. Transcript of Record, 412–13.

46. Transcript of Record, 263.

47. Transcript of Record, 271.

48. Transcript of Record, 356–72.

49. Transcript of Record, 365–66.

50. Transcript of Record, 366.

51. Transcript of Record, 366.

52. Millikan affidavit, 5, *Berry v. Chaplin*.

53. Transcript of Record, 449; "The Weather," *Los Angeles Times*, Apr. 12, 1945.

54. Transcript of Record, 462–63, 466–67, 473.

55. Transcript of Record, 498.

56. Transcript of Record, 498–99.

57. Transcript of Record, 499.

58. Transcript of Record, 486.

59. Transcript of Record, 554.

60. Transcript of Record, 558.

61. Transcript of Record, 573–74.

62. Transcript of Record, 579, 590, 605.

63. Transcript of Record, 626.

64. Transcript of Record, 628–29.

65. Getty Diaries, Apr. 13, 1945.

66. Transcript of Record, 630.

67. Transcript of Record, 631–33.

68. Transcript of Record, 635.

69. Associated Press, "Chaplin Suit Near Jury," *Daily News* (New York), Apr. 17, 1945; Transcript of Record, 643–44.

70. Transcript of Record, 641, 644.

71. Transcript of Record, 644.

72. Transcript of Record, 644.

73. Transcript of Record, 660.

74. Gaston, *Alone Together*, 323. Teddy Getty Gaston, like Joan, was red haired. Photos of Timothy Getty, who died in 1958 at age twelve, are included in Gaston's autobiography.

75. Transcript of Record, 657.

76. Transcript of Record, 658.

77. Transcript of Record, 670–71.

78. Verdict, *Berry v. Chaplin*, No. D-238936, Apr. 17, 1945; Associated Press, "Chaplin Ruled Father of Baby of Joan Berry; Jury at Second Hearing Votes 11 to 1, Reversing 7-to-5 Ballot at Mistrial," *New York Herald Tribune*, Apr. 18, 1945.

79. "Jury Holds Charlie Chaplin Father of Joan Berry Child."

80. "Jury Decrees Chaplin Is Father of Joan Berry's Baby; Call Hearing to Decide Sum He Must Pay," *Chicago Daily Tribune*, Apr. 18, 1945.

81. "Jury Holds Charlie Chaplin Father of Joan Berry Child."

82. "Jury Decrees Chaplin Is Father of Joan Berry's Baby."

83. "Jury Holds Charlie Chaplin Father of Joan Berry Child."

84. "Jury Decrees Chaplin Is Father of Joan Berry's Baby."

85. Transcript of Record, 710.

86. Transcript of Record, 685–86.

87. Transcript of Record, 684–85.

88. Transcript of Record, 688.

89. Transcript of Record, 696.

90. Transcript of Record, 701.

91. Transcript of Record, 705–6.

92. Transcript of Record, 706.

93. Transcript of Record, 712–13.

94. Transcript of Record, 713.

95. Transcript of Record, 721.

96. Transcript of Record, 727–43.

97. Transcript of Record, 719–20.

98. Transcript of Record, 743.

99. "Court Orders Chaplin to Pay $75 Weekly till Carol's 21," *Los Angeles Times*, Apr. 19, 1945.

100. Florabel Muir, "Chaplin Must Pay $75 a Week; and Are Joan and Lawyer Sore!" *Daily News* (New York), Apr. 19, 1945; Associated Press, "Rule Chaplin Must Pay $75 Week to Baby," *Chicago Daily Tribune*, Apr. 19, 1945.

101. Associated Press, "Rule Chaplin Must Pay $75 Week to Baby."

102. Muir, "Chaplin Must Pay $75 a Week."

103. United Press, "All Unhappy in Chaplin Case," *Oroville (CA) Mercury Register*, Apr. 20, 1945.

CHAPTER 21

1. Daily Production Report, Charles Chaplin, W/E Apr. 28, 1945, Charlie Chaplin Archive, ECCI00313699, CH131.

2. Hedda Hopper, "Looking at Hollywood," *Chicago Daily Tribune*, May 11, 1945.

3. Associated Press, "New Trial Denied Chaplin," *New York Times*, June 7, 1945.

4. *Berry v. Chaplin*, No. D-238936, Notice of Appeal, June 29, 1945.

5. United Press, "Chaplin Ordered to Pay $75 a Week for Baby; also Must Give Joan Berry $3,250 for Attorneys," *New York Herald Tribune*, July 17, 1945.

6. Associated Press, "Chaplin Must Bare Fortune; Court Orders Him to Produce Records and Data July 16," *Baltimore Sun*, July 5, 1945.

7. "Order Chaplin to Pay Joan $75 a Week," *Chicago Daily Tribune*, July 17, 1945; Transcript of Record, 704.

8. "Order Chaplin to Pay Joan $75 a Week."

9. Associated Press, "Chaplin Admits Millions; Support of Carol Ann to Be Determined," *Evening Vanguard* (Venice, CA), July 17, 1945.

10. "Chaplin Says He Has 'in Vicinity of $3,000,000,'" *Los Angeles Times*, July 17, 1945.

11. "Order Chaplin to Pay Joan $75 a Week."

12. "Worth $3,000,000 Chaplin Must Pay," *New York Times*, July 17, 1945.

13. "Order Chaplin to Pay Joan $75 a Week."

14. Associated Press, "Chaplin, Worth $3,000,000, to Pay Joan $75 Weekly," *Hartford Courant*, July 17, 1945.

15. United Press, "Chaplin Ordered to Pay $75 a Week for Baby."

16. "Gene Kelly, Fine Arts Man; U. of Pittsburgh Hoods Its Dancing Alumnus," *Variety*, Oct. 11, 1961.

17. "Joan Barry Studying Nitery Singing in Pitt," *Variety*, Oct. 10, 1945.

18. Associated Press, "Joan Barry Takes Singing Lessons," *Los Angeles Times*, Oct. 3, 1945.

19. "Joan Berry Back from Singing Tour," *Los Angeles Daily News*, Oct. 31, 1945.

20. "Girl Who Sued Chaplin, Now Wed, Settles Here; Joan Barry, Central Figure in Paternity Suit, Retires from Stage, Weds Pittsburgh Man," *Pittsburgh Post-Gazette*, Jan. 20, 1947.

21. Ad for "Riviera," *Pittsburgh Post-Gazette*, Oct. 15, 1945.

22. Danton Walker, "Broadway," *Daily News* (New York), Nov. 13, 1945.

23. The Square, "Strictly Ad Lib," *Downbeat*, Dec. 15, 1945.

24. "Even a Stable or a Silo Is Home for Off-Broadway's Theatres," *New York Times*, Nov. 9, 1958.

25. "4th Street," New York Songlines, www.nysonglines.com/4st.htm, accessed Nov. 26, 2023.

26. "New Acts: Joan Barry," *Variety*, Dec. 12, 1945.

27. "Transition: Jitters," *Newsweek*, Dec. 17, 1945.

28. Jack Gaver, "Broadway," *Dunkirk (NY) Evening Observer*, Dec. 7, 1945.

29. "Night Club Reviews; Brown Derby, Chi," *Variety*, Feb. 13, 1946.

30. Rod Reed, "Blue Notes," *Downbeat*, Feb. 25, 1946.

31. Associated Press, "Joan Berry Files Appeal," *New York Herald Tribune*, Sept. 28, 1945.

32. *Carol Ann Berry v. Charles Spencer Chaplin*, Civ. No. 15135, District Court of Appeal, Second Appellate District, State of California, Appellant's Opening Brief, Jan. 10, 1946.

33. *Berry v. Chaplin*, 74 Cal. App. 2d 669 (Cal. Ct. App, 1946).

34. "Chaplin-Berry Appeal Argued," *Los Angeles Times*, Apr. 25, 1946.

35. *Berry v. Chaplin*, 74 Cal. App. 2d 652, 668 (Cal. Ct. App. 1946). This was the Chaplin appeal of the jury's finding that he was the legal father of Joan Berry's child.

36. "Emmet H. Wilson," California Courts, https://www.courts.ca.gov/documents/WilsonE.pdf, accessed Dec. 19, 2023.

37. 74 Cal. App. 657.

38. 74 Cal. App. 658.

39. 74 Cal. App. 665.

40. 74 Cal. App. 661.

41. 74 Cal. App. 666.

42. *Berry v. Chaplin*, 74 Cal. App. 2d 669, 674 (Cal. Ct. App. 1946). This was Carol Ann's appeal of the judge's finding she deserved only $75 a week and her lawyer only $5,000.

43. 74 Cal. App. 2d 675.

44. 74 Cal. App. 677.

45. 74 Cal. App. 680–81.

46. 74 Cal. App. 681.

47. Associated Press, "Chaplin Petitions in Child Case," *New York Times*, July 4, 1946; *Berry v. Chaplin*, Civ. No. 15135, Petition for Hearing in the Supreme Court, Wright and Millikan, July 2, 1946.

48. *Berry v. Chaplin*, Civ. No. 15135, Answer to Petition for Hearing in the Supreme Court, Joseph Scott et al., July 12, 1946.

49. *Berry v. Chaplin*, Civ. No. 15135, Order Denying Hearing, California Supreme Court, July 24, 1946.

50. Gene Blake, "Ex-Chief Justice Traynor Dies," *Los Angeles Times*, May 17, 1983; "Rites for Retired Justice Schauer Set," *Los Angeles Times*, Mar. 7, 1977; Rule 8.512, Ordering Review, California Rules of Court.

51. "Lawyers Ask $75,000 Fees from Chaplin," *Los Angeles Times*, Dec. 17, 1946.

52. "Three Fix $60,000 Up as Fair Chaplin Fee," *Los Angeles Times*, Dec.18, 1946.

53. "Chaplin Case Attorney Wins $42,706 in Fees," *Los Angeles Times*, Dec. 21, 1946.

54. Robinson, *Chaplin*, 737–38.

55. Robinson, *Chaplin*, 549.

56. United Press, "Wants Finger in Joan's Pay," *Daily News* (New York), Jan. 17, 1946.

57. "Pitt Agent Attaches Joan Barry's Salary at Detroit Night Spot," *Variety*, Jan. 23, 1946.

58. "Salary Released by Court," *Variety*, Jan. 23, 1946.

59. "Pitt Agent Attaches Joan Barry's Salary at Detroit Night Spot."

60. "Joan Barry's 50–50 Contract with Agent Ordered Abrogated by AGVA," *Variety*, Jan. 2, 1946.

61. "Joan Barry's 50–50 Contract with Agent Ordered Abrogated by AGVA."

62. Ricky Riccardi, *What a Wonderful World: The Magic of Louis Armstrong's Later Years* (New York: Pantheon Books, 2011), 12.

63. Simon Hodgson, "A Hell of a Businessman: A Biography of Joe Glaser," American Conservatory Theater, Jan. 29, 2016, http://blog.act-sf.org/2016/01/a-hell-of-businessman-biography-of-joe.html, accessed Mar. 26, 2023.

64. "Joan Barry Bows Out of Detroit Nitery after Heckling Re Chaplin," *Variety*, Jan. 30, 1946.

65. "Joan Barry in $50,000 Damage Suit Filed by Pitt Agent in Philly," *Variety*, Mar. 27, 1946.

66. United Press, "Agent Sues Joan Barry for $50,000," *Los Angeles Times*, Mar. 23, 1946.

67. "Joan Barry Sued by Agent, Contract Breach Charged," *Philadelphia Inquirer*, Mar. 23, 1946.

68. "Joan Barry Bows Out of Detroit Nitery after Heckling Re Chaplin."

69. "Joan Barry Still Creating Nitery Stir," *Variety*, May 29, 1946.

70. "Joan Barry Tagged by AGVA in Contract Jump," *Variety*, July 17, 1946.

71. United Press, "Joan Berry Happy That She's Brakeman's Bride," *Los Angeles Times*, Jan. 20, 1947.

72. Associated Press, "Joan Berry Discloses She's Mother Again," *Los Angeles Times*, July 27, 1947.

73. *Mary Louise Seck v. Russell Charles Seck*, D-433807, Complaint for divorce, Superior Court, State of California, County of Los Angeles, May 27, 1952.

74. "Girl Who Sued Chaplin, Now Wed, Settles Here."

CHAPTER 22

1. "The Weather in the Nation," *New York Times*, Apr. 15, 1947.

2. George Wallach, "Charlie Chaplin's *Monsieur Verdoux* Press Conference," *Film Comment* 5, no. 4 (Winter 1969): 34. Wallach was a radio-TV producer. *Film Comment* placed the date of the press conference as April 12, as did Chaplin's biographer, David Robinson, in *Chaplin: His Life and Art*, 538. Charles Maland, in "The Strange Case of *Monsieur Verdoux*: Comedy, Ideology, and the Dynamics of Reception," *Film Criticism* 13, no. 1 (Fall 1988), writes that the news conference took place on April 14. Contemporary newspaper accounts reported that the conference took place on Monday, April 14. International News Service, "Charlie Chaplin Hedges on Sympathy to Reds," *Knoxville (TN) Journal*, Apr. 15, 1947.

3. Wallach, "Charlie Chaplin's *Monsieur Verdoux* Press Conference," 35.

4. When the film was rereleased in New York in 1964, it was a box-office hit. Maland, "The Strange Case of *Monsieur Verdoux*," 59–60.

5. Chaplin, *My Autobiography*, 412.

6. Robinson, *Chaplin*, 538.

7. Robinson, *Chaplin*, 538.

8. Bosley Crowther, "The Screen: 'Monsieur Verdoux' New Film Starring Charles Chaplin, Has World Premiere at Broadway," *New York Times*, Apr. 12, 1947.

9. Howard Barnes, "On the Screen: 'Monsieur Verdoux, Broadway," *New York Herald Tribune*, Apr. 12, 1947.

10. Wallach, "Charlie Chaplin's *Monsieur Verdoux* Press Conference," 35.

11. Wallach, "Charlie Chaplin's *Monsieur Verdoux* Press Conference, 35-36.

12. Wallach, "Charlie Chaplin's *Monsieur Verdoux* Press Conference," 36.

13. Wallach, "Charlie Chaplin's *Monsieur Verdoux* Press Conference," 36.

14. Maland, "The Strange Case of *Monsieur Verdoux*," 58.

15. "Statement of Sen. Langer," *Congressional Record*, 80th Cong. 1st Sess. (Mar. 7, 1947), 1792.

16. "More Funds Favored for Red Probers," *Washington Post*, Apr. 1, 1947.

17. Victor Navasky, *Naming Names* (New York: Viking Press, 1980), 78.

18. "Film Industry to Ban All Reds; Official Announcement Due Today Barring Them from Employment in Pictures," *Hollywood Reporter*, Nov. 25, 1947.

19. Chaplin, *My Autobiography*, 428.

20. Chaplin, *My Autobiography*, 429.

21. "Chaplin Tells Red Prober to Phone Collect," *Detroit Free Press*, July 21, 1947.

22. "Chaplin, Eisler to Be Called First in House 'Red Probe,'" *Hollywood Reporter*, July 11, 1947.

23. "Subpena [sic] Served Eisler by House Red Probers," *Hollywood Reporter*, July 15, 1947.

24. "Inside Washington; Charlie Chaplin Is Next Hollywood Probe Figure," *Courier-Gazette* (McKinney, TX), Aug. 26, 1947.

25. "Collection Overview," Russell Birdwell Papers, LSC.0114, UCLA Library Special Collections, Charles E. Young Research Library.

26. "Chaplin Tells Just Where He Stands," *Hollywood Reporter*, July 21, 1947.

27. "Chaplin Tells Just Where He Stands."

28. "Chaplin Tells Red Prober to Phone Collect."

29. "Press Release from the Committee on Un-American Activities, U.S. House of Representatives," Sept. 19, 1947, Records of the United States House of Representatives, Record Group 233, NARA.

30. Robert E. Nichols, "43 from Hollywood Subpoenaed by House Un-American Inquiry; Committee to Hear Both Sides on Communism, Parnell Thomas Says; Gary Cooper, Goldwyn, Disney, Eric Johnston among Those Called," *New York Herald Tribune*, Sept. 21, 1947.

31. "House Group to Ask Chaplin to Testify on Communism," *Washington Post*, Dec. 7, 1946.

32. Associated Press, "Doubt Chaplin Will Be Called in Red Inquiry," *Chicago Daily Tribune*, Oct. 18, 1947.

33. Maland, *Chaplin and American Culture*, 261.

34. Westbrook Pegler, "As Pegler Sees It," *Decatur (AL) Daily*, Jan. 7, 1949.

35. Russell Charles Seck, Certificate of Death, No. 0509, Dept. of Health, State of Washington, Feb. 11, 2013; Associated Press, "Joan Berry a Mother for 2d Time—A Boy," *Atlanta Constitution*, July 27, 1947.

36. Associated Press, "Joan Berry's New Son Poses for First Photo," *Chicago Tribune*, Aug. 8, 1947.

37. "Variety Bills; Week of December 31," *Variety*, December 31, 1947; Carol Ann Berry, interview with the author, Oct. 17, 2020.

38. Stephen Seck, interview with the author, June 20, 2023.

39. "Joan Berry Baby Support Hiked," *Los Angeles Times*, Jan. 15, 1948.

40. "Chaplin's Accuser Reported in Mexico," *Pittsburgh Post-Gazette*, May 12, 1948.

41. "Joan Berry Says She's Just Visiting Mexico," *Los Angeles Times*, May 13, 1948; Carol Ann Berry, interview with the author, Jan. 1, 2021.

42. Stephen Seck, interview with the author June 20, 2023.

43. Stephen Irving Seck, Certificate of Live Birth, Certification of Vital Record No. 44036, County of Los Angeles, State of California.

44. *Seck v. Seck*, D-433807; Stephen Seck, interview with the author, Nov. 6, 2021.

45. 1950 U.S. Census (Gertrude E. Berry); Carol Ann Berry, interview with the author, Aug. 1, 2023

46. *People v. John Barry*, Ind. No. 2816/1948, Supreme Court of the State of New York, County of New York, New York City Municipal Archives.

47. 1950 U.S. Census (Eleanor Jericho); Carol Ann Berry, interview with the author, Sept. 5, 2020

48. "3 Lots," Advertisement, Marcus C. Lovelady, Agnes Clark, Brokers, *Redondo Reflex*, Jan. 17, 1947.

49. 1920 U.S. Census (Eleanor Jericho).

50. 1950 U.S. Census (Eleanor Jericho).

51. Charles Spencer Chaplin Report, Aug. 6, 1947, Chaplin FBI File, Pt. 7, p. 71.

52. Charles Spencer Chaplin Report, Chaplin FBI File, Pt. 7, p. 71.

53. Charles Spencer Chaplin Report, Chaplin FBI File, Pt. 7, p. 73.

54. Charles Spencer Chaplin Report, Chaplin FBI File, Pt. 7, p. 77.

55. Examination of Max Eastman at Martha's Vineyard, MA, Oct. 22, 1952, Charles Chaplin File INS File Pt. 4, pp. 417, 418.

56. Charles Spencer Chaplin Internal Security Report- R, Oct. 28, 1948, Chaplin FBI File, Pt. 7, p. 210.

57. Maland, *Chaplin and American Culture*, 266.

58. D. W. Ladd to Director, memorandum, Aug. 6, 1947, Chaplin FBI File, Pt. 7, pp. 70–94.

59. Charles Spencer Chaplin, Internal Security Report—R, Chaplin FBI File, Pt. 7, pp. 210, 212–13.

60. Robinson, *Chaplin*, 548.

61. Interview with Charles Spencer Chaplin, Apr. 17, 1948, Chaplin INS File, Pt. 1, pp. 148–69.

62. Interview with Chaplin, Chaplin INS File, Pt. 1, p. 151.

63. Interview with Chaplin, Chaplin INS File, Pt. 1, p. 151.

64. Interview with Chaplin, Chaplin INS File, Pt. 1, p. 151.

65. Interview with Chaplin, Chaplin INS File, Pt. 1, p. 152.

66. Interview with Chaplin, Chaplin INS File, Pt. 1, p. 155.

67. Interview with Chaplin, Chaplin INS File, Pt. 1, p. 155

68. Interview with Chaplin, Chaplin INS File, Pt. 1, p. 160.

69. Memorandum (sender's and recipient's names blacked out), "Charles Chaplin—A-5653092," July 3, 1947, Chaplin INS File, Pt. 1, p. 198.

70. Memorandum, Charles Chaplin –A-5653092, Chaplin INS File, Pt. 1, p. 198.

71. Memorandum, Charles Chaplin –A-5653092, Chaplin INS File, Pt. 1, p. 198.

72. Robinson, *Chaplin*, 548.

73. Robinson, *Chaplin*, 550.

CHAPTER 23

1. Loyd Wright Jr. to INS District Director, July 31, 1952, Chaplin INS File, Pt. 1, p. 5; Associated Press, "Chaplin Plans Return to U.S. in Six Months," *Chicago Daily Tribune*, Sept. 23, 1952.

2. "The Weather," *Los Angeles Times*, Sept. 6, 1952; Robinson, *Chaplin*, 570.

3. Chaplin, *Autobiography*, 452; Robinson, *Chaplin*, 570–71.

4. John Durniak, "Camera: Richard Avedon Recalls a Life behind the Lens, Where He Brought His Subjects to Life," *New York Times*, Sept. 15, 1991.

5. Queen Elizabeth Ship Movement Book, Sept. 17, 1952, D42/GM1/29, Cunard Archive, Special Collections and Archives, University of Liverpool Library.

6. Robinson, *Chaplin*, 570–71.

7. Queen Elizabeth Ship Log Book, Sept. 17, 1952, D42/GM 12/2/10, p. 1432, Cunard Archive.

8. Chaplin, *My Autobiography*, 455.; Robinson, 570.

9. Queen Elizabeth Log Book, D42/GM 12/2/10.

10. Queen Elizabeth Log Book, D42/GM 12/2/10; Harry Crocker Papers, 1895–1952, "Charlie Chaplin: Man and Mime," unpublished manuscript, folder 19, chap. 16, p. 9, Margaret Herrick Library, Academy of Motion Picture Arts and Sciences.

11. Crocker, "Charlie Chaplin: Man and Mime," chap. 16, pp. 9–10.

12. Associated Press, "Charlie Chaplin Barred from U.S. Pending Quiz; Comedian, on Trip Abroad, Still Not Citizen after Living Here for 40 Years," *Los Angeles Times*, Sept. 20, 1952.

13. Mike Connolly, "Rambling Reporter," *Hollywood Reporter*, Sept. 23, 1952.

14. "Nixon Checkers Speech," *American Experience*, PBS, www.pbs.org/wgbh/americanexperience/features/eisenhower-checkers, accessed June 24, 2023.

15. Queen Elizabeth Ship Movement Book, Sept. 19, 1952, D42/GM1/29.

16. Crocker, "Charlie Chaplin: Man and Mime," chap. 16, p. 16.

17. "Charlie Chaplin in Cherbourg (1952)," British Pathé, www.britishpathe.com/asset/75337, accessed Dec. 24, 2023.

18. Chaplin, *My Autobiography*, 456.

19. Robinson *Chaplin*, 574; "Charlie Chaplin in Cherbourg (1952)."

20. Associated Press, "Chaplin to Return Here, He Declares; Comedian, in France, Says He Cabled Lawyers to Find Why McGranery Threatened Ban," *New York Times*, Sept. 23, 1952.

21. "Charlie Chaplin in Cherbourg (1952)."

22. Queen Elizabeth Ship Movement Book, Sept. 22, 1952, D42/GM1/29.

23. Associated Press, "1000 Hail Chaplin on London Return," *Los Angeles Mirror*, Sept. 23, 1952.

24. Queen Elizabeth Ship Movement Book, Sept. 23, 1952, D42/GM1/29; "Film Making in Britain? Mr. Chaplin's Plans," *Manchester Guardian*, Sept. 23, 1952.

25. Associated Press, "1000 Hail Chaplin on London Return."

26. United Press, "Chaplin Insists He Will Return to United States," *Ventura County (CA) Star-Free Press*, Sept. 23, 1952.

27. Associated Press, "Chaplin Weeps as Britons Mob Him," *Los Angeles Times*, Sept. 24, 1952; International News Service, "Chaplin Says He Is No Red, Never Was," *Stockton (CA) Daily Evening Record*, Sept. 23, 1952.

28. Westbrook Pegler, "Fair Enough," *Times-Herald* (Washington, DC), Sept. 23, 1952.

29. "Catching Up with Chaplin," *Evening Outlook*, Sept. 22, 1952.

30. Bosley Crowther, "Under Suspicion: The Dilemma of Charlie Chaplin and Some Other Artists in Hollywood," *New York Times*, Sept. 28, 1952.

31. Sworn statement of Mrs. Joan Seck, Sept. 30, 1952, Chaplin INS File, Pt. 1, p. 268.

32. Statement of Joan Seck, Chaplin INS File, Pt. 1, p. 269.

33. Statement of Joan Seck, Chaplin INS File, Pt. 1, p. 270.

34. Statement of Joan Seck, Chaplin INS File, Pt. 1, p. 285.

35. Memorandum for file (author's name blacked out), Subversive Alien Branch, Investigations Division, In re: Charles Chaplin, A-5653092, Oct. 6, 1952, Chaplin INS File, Pt. 1, p. 363–364

36. Commissioner of Immigration and Naturalization to Attorney General,

undated memorandum, Chaplin INS File, Pt. 1, p. 1355; Acting District Director memorandum to the file, Oct. 28, 1952, Chaplin INS File, Pt. 2, p. 710.

37. Memorandum for file (author's name blacked out), In re: Charles Chaplin, A-5653092, Oct. 6, 1952.

38. Sworn statement of Thomas Wells Durant, Oct. 3, 1952, Chaplin INS File, Pt. 1, pp. 221–34.

39. Sworn statement of Yoshito Yonemori, Oct. 6, 1953, Chaplin INS File, Pt. 1, pp. 235, 244.

40. Handwritten memorandum to file (author's name blacked out), Oct. 17, 1952, Chaplin INS File, Pt. 2, p. 506.

41. Sworn statement of Marion Douras Brown (Marion Davies), Nov. 17, 1952, Chaplin INS File, Pt. 1, pp. 1,199, 1201.

42. Statement of Marion Douras Brown (Marion Davies), Nov. 17, 1952, Chaplin INS File, Pt. 1, p. 1,203.

43. Statement of Marion Douras Brown (Marion Davies), Nov. 17, 1952, Chaplin INS File, Pt. 1, p. 1,203.

44. Associated Press, "M'Granery Lashes Comedian Chaplin; 'Unsavory Character if What Has Been Said about Him Is True,' Attorney General Declares," *Los Angeles Times*, Oct. 3, 1952.

45. Robert E. Clark, "Ike Charges Faint-Hearted Foreign Policy to Stevenson," *Los Angeles Examiner*, Sept. 23, 1952.

46. United Press, "Princess Margaret Hails Chaplin," *New York Times*, Oct. 17, 1952.

47. Robinson, *Chaplin*, 578.

48. "Chaplin Film Ban Praised," *Los Angeles Examiner*, Jan. 16, 1953.

49. Robinson, *Chaplin*, 580; Milton, *Tramp*, 488.

50. Louella O. Parsons, "Chaplin Wife Visits L.A. on Secret Trip," *Los Angeles Examiner*, Dec. 6, 1952.

51. Press Release, Department of Justice, Apr. 15, 1953, Chaplin INS File, Pt. 2, p. 14.

52. Chaplin, *My Autobiography*, 465; Robinson, *Chaplin*, 581.

53. Charles Spencer Chaplin, No. 1600–41933, Re-Entry Permit, Potential Applicant for Re-admission, June 11, 1953, Chaplin INS File, Pt. 4, p. 314.

54. "Chaplin 'Proud' as Oona Turns Her Back on U.S.," *New York Post*, Feb. 11, 1954.

55. "Chaplin Sells Studio Here to N.Y. Firm," *Los Angeles Times*, Oct. 1, 1953.

56. *Seck v. Seck*, D-433807, Superior Court, Los Angeles County, Complaint for Divorce, p. 2.

57. "PKSW" to unknown recipient, Re: "Information received from Mr. [name blacked out] Central Office," Oct. 17, 1952, Chaplin INS File, Pt. 2, p. 497.

58. Subpena [sic] for Mrs. Joan Barry Seck, Dept. of Justice, Immigration and Naturalization Service, Los Angeles, Oct. 14, 1952, Chaplin INS File, Pt. 2, p. 542.

59. Act'g INS District Director, Los Angeles to E. DeWitt Marshall, Attaché, American Embassy, Mexico, Oct. 28, 1952, Chaplin INS File, Pt. 2, p. 740.

60. Act'g INS District Director, Los Angeles to E. DeWitt Marshall, Attaché, American Embassy, Mexico, Oct. 28, 1952; E. DeWitt Marshall to District Enforcement Officer, Los Angeles, Oct. 23, 1952, Chaplin INS File, Pt. 1, p. 772.

61. Act'g INS District Director, Los Angeles to E. DeWitt Marshall, Attaché, American Embassy, Mexico, Oct. 28, 1952, Chaplin INS File, Pt. 2, p. 740.

62. "Joan Berry Gets Mental Test at Own Request," *Los Angeles Times*, June 28, 1953.

63. Carol Ann Berry, interview with the author, Aug. 2, 2023

64. Marshall telegram to INS District Director, Los Angeles, Mar. 17, 1953, Chaplin INS File, Pt. 2, p. 1,035.

65. District Director (name blacked out) to E. DeWitt Marshall, Chaplin INS File, Mar. 18, 1953, Pt. 2, p. 1,034.

66. Louella O. Parsons, "Chaplin Home as Subdivision: 8 Lots Go on Sale; Carpets, Furniture Going to London," *Los Angeles Examiner*, Feb. 10, 1953; "Chaplin May Buy Modest Villa on French Riviera," *Los Angeles Times*, Mar. 8, 1953.

67. Eyman, *Charlie Chaplin vs. America*, 176–77.

68. "Joan Berry Gets Mental Test at Own Request."

69. "Joan Berry Keeps Silence in Hospital," *Los Angeles Times*, June 29, 1953.

70. "Joan Berry Gets Mental Test at Own Request"; "Joan Berry Goes Home after Mental Checkup; 'No Evidence of Psychotic Condition,' Say Doctors after Tests She Requested," *Los Angeles Times*, June 30, 1953.

71. International News Service, "Mental Hospital Frees Joan Berry," *Philadelphia Inquirer*, June 30, 1953.

72. "Science & Tech, Insulin Shock Therapy," Britannica, www.britannica.com/science/insulin-shock-therapy, accessed Dec. 25, 2023; "Science & Tech, Lobotomy," Britannica, www.britannica.com/science/lobotomy, accessed Dec. 25, 2023.

73. Carol Ann Berry, interview with the author., July 21, 2023.

74. "Mental Hospital Frees Joan Berry."

75. International News Service, "Joan Barry Released from Mental Ward; Protégé of Chaplin," *Morning Call* (Allentown, PA), June 30, 1953.

76. "Joan Berry Goes Back to Psychiatric Ward," *Los Angeles Times*, July 31, 1953; "Joan Berry Found in Daze, Hospitalized," *Long Beach Independent*, July 31, 1953.

77. Carol Ann Berry, interview with the author, Aug. 2, 2023 "Joan Berry Goes Back to Psychiatric Ward."

78. "Hospital Stay Turned Down by Joan Berry," *Los Angeles Times*, Aug. 1, 1953.

79. Associated Press, "Papers Filed to Have Joan Berry Placed in Mental Institution," San Bernardino County (CA) Sun, Aug. 2, 1953.

80. Associated Press, "Joan Berry Sent to Mental Hospital," Redwood City (CA) Tribune, Aug. 6, 1953.

EPILOGUE

1. United Press International, "Rusk, Charlie Chaplin Win Oxford Degrees," *Washington Post–Times Herald*, June 28, 1962.

2. Robinson, *Chaplin*, 590.

3. "Critics Are Cool to Chaplin Film; 'A King in New York' Fails to Impress London Writers—Comedian's Son in Movie," *New York Times*, Sept. 11, 1957.

4. Nora Sayre, "Film: 'A King in New York' at Last," *New York Times*, Dec. 22, 1973.

5. Bosley Crowther, "Screen: 'A Countess from Hong Kong'; New Movie by Chaplin Opens at the Sutton; Miss Loren and Brando in an Antique Farce," *New York Times*, Mar. 17, 1967.

6. Milton, *Tramp*, 497; "U.S. Grants Chaplin Cut Rate on Taxes," *Chicago Daily Tribune*, Dec. 30, 1958.

7. Michael Chaplin, *I Couldn't Smoke the Grass on My Father's Lawn* (New York: G. P. Putnam's Sons, 1966), 79; Robinson, *Chaplin*, 581.

8. Milton, *Tramp*, 492.

9. James P. O'Donnell, "Charlie Chaplin's Stormy Exile, Conclusion" *Saturday Evening Post*, Mar. 22, 1958, 36.

10. Carol Matthau, *Among the Porcupines* (New York: Turtle Bay Books, 1992), 41.

11. Chaplin Jr., *My Father*, 284.

12. Scovell, *Oona, Living in the Shadows*, 130.

13. Julie Gilbert, *Opposite Attraction: The Lives of Erich Maria Remarque and Paulette Goddard* (New York: Pantheon Books, 1995), 430–31.

14. M. Chaplin, *I Couldn't Smoke the Grass on My Father's Lawn*, 1.

15. Scovell, *Oona, Living in the Shadows*, 204.

16. United Press International, "'Little Tramp' Dubbed Sir Chaplin, in Wheelchair, Knighted at Buckingham Palace," *Los Angeles Times*, Mar. 4, 1975.

17. Lt. Col. George Rowland Stanley Baring, 3rd Earl of Cromer to GMF Stow, Protocol and Conference Dept., Foreign and Commonwealth Office, Sept. 16, 1971, British National Archives, FCO 57/291, p. 18

18. Chaplin, *My Autobiography*, 458.

19. M. Chaplin, *I Couldn't Smoke the Grass on My Father's Lawn*, 11.

20. J. Y. Smith, "Comedy Genius Chaplin Is Dead," *Boston Globe*, Dec. 26, 1977.

21. Scovell, *Oona, Living in the Shadows*, 266.

22. See, e.g., Clyde Gilmour, "Chaplin: World Mourns Immortal Clown," *Toronto Star*, Dec. 26, 1977; Alden Whitman, "The 'Little Tramp' Leaves the Stage," *Times of India*, Jan. 8, 1978; "The Little Tramp Who Was King of Comedy," *Jerusalem Post*, Dec. 26, 1977; Penelope McMillan, "Charlie Chaplin, 88, the 'Little

Tramp,' Dies in Sleep; Movie-Making Career Spans 52 Years, Ends at Switzerland Home," *Los Angeles Times*, Dec. 26, 1977.

23. Alden Whitman, "Chaplin's Little Tramp, an Everyman Trying to Gild Cage of Life, Enthralled World," *New York Times*, Dec. 26, 1977. The obituary continues on a second page with the headline "The Comedian Had Crises with Women, the Talkies, Taxes and Cold War Politics."

24. Lynn, *Charlie Chaplin and His Times*, 538–39; Scovell, *Oona, Living in the Shadows*, 278.

25. Scovell, *Oona, Living in the Shadows*, 180.

26. Scovell, *Oona, Living in the Shadows*, 42, 149.

27. Scovell, *Oona, Living in the Shadows*, 228.

28. Scovell, *Oona, Living in the Shadows*, 267–68.

29. Scovell, *Oona, Living in the Shadows*, 274.

30. Patrice Chaplin, *Hidden Star: A Memoir* (London: Richard Cohen Books, 1995), 186.

31. Kenneth S. Lynn, *Charlie Chaplin and His Times*, 540.

32. Burt A. Folkart, "Oona Chaplin; Fourth and Last Wife of Comedian," *Los Angeles Times*, Sept. 28, 1991; Scovell, *Oona, Living in the Shadows*, 315.

33. Sidney B. Schatkin, "Law and Science in Collision: Use of Blood Tests in Paternity Suits," *Virginia Law Review* 32, no. 4 (1945–46): 886, 891.

34. Schatkin, "Law and Science in Collision," 888.

35. Arthur John Keeffe, William B. Landis Jr., and Robert B. Shaad, "Sense and Nonsense about Judicial Notice," *Stanford Law Review* 2, no. 4 (July 1950): 664, 670.

36. Keeffe, Landis, and Shaad, "Sense and Nonsense about Judicial Notice," 670–71.

37. Jule B. Greene, "Comments: 'Blood Will Tell!'", *Mercer Law Review* 1, no. 2 (Spring 1950): 266, 274. The states that had statutes specifically addressing the admissibility of blood tests were Maine, Maryland, New Jersey, North Carolina, Ohio, South Dakota, and Wisconsin. Greene, "Blood Will Tell!," 273.

38. Greene, "Blood Will Tell!," 274.

39. Andrea Roth, interview with the author, July 18, 2020.

40. Andrea Roth, "Defying DNA: Rethinking the Role of the Jury in an Age of Scientific Proof of Innocence," *Boston University Law Review* 93 (2013): 1643, 1647.

41. Uniform Law Commission, www.uniformlaws.org/home#:~:text=Uniform%20Law%20Commission%20The%20Uniform,areas%20of%20state%20statutory%20law, accessed Sept. 1, 2023.

42. Prefatory Note: "Uniform Act on Blood Tests to Determine Paternity," *Handbook of the National Conference of Commissioners on Uniform State Laws and Proceedings of the Annual Conference Meeting* 61 (1952): 434.

43. Cal. Civ. Proc. Code § 1980.6, Uniform Act on Blood Tests to Determine Paternity, Sec. 4; Edward M. Ford Jr., "Procedure: Discovery: California and Federal Civil Procedure: Physical Examination of Parties: Admission of Facts and Genuineness of Documents," *California Law Review* 42, no. 1 (Spring 1954): 187, 190 n. 26. . The law governing the admission at trial of the results of paternity testing to determine parentage in California is found today at Cal. Fam. Code § 7554(a)(b).

44. Roth, "Defying DNA," 1669.

45. Jill Adams, "Paternity Testing: Blood Types and DNA," *Nature Education* 1, no. 1 (2008): 146, www.nature.com/scitable/topicpage/paternity-testing-blood-ty pes-and-dna-374/#, accessed Sept. 2, 2023.

46. Associated Press, "Court Orders Chaplin to Deposit $10,000 for Protégé's Child," *Boston Globe*, Apr. 28, 1954.

47. Carol Ann Berry, interview with the author, Jan. 1, 2021; April 16, 2023.

48. Carol Ann Berry, interview with the author, Aug. 2, 2023

49. Carol Ann Berry, interview with the author, Aug. 2, 2023.

50. Carol Ann Berry, interview with the author, Aug. 1, 2023.

51. Carol Ann Berry, interview with the author, Jan. 1, 2021; July 21, 2023; April 28, 2024.

52. Carol Ann Berry, interview with the author, April 28, 2024.

53. Carol Ann Berry, interview with the author, May 26, 2023.

54. Carol Ann Berry, interview with the author, April 28, 2024.

55. Carol Ann Berry, interview with the author, Oct. 17, 2020.

56. Carol Ann Berry, interview with the author, April 28, 2024.

57. Carol Ann Berry, interview with the author, Oct. 17, 2020

58. Carol Ann Berry, interview with the author, April 28, 2024.

59. Complaint, *Eleanor Jericho v. Carol Ann Berry*, No. INGL C 2458 (Cal. Sup. Ct., Los Angeles, Mar. 13, 1959); Order of Dismissal, *Jericho v. Berry*, No. INGL C 2458 (Mar. 20, 1967).

60. Complaint to Quiet Title and to Set Aside the Deed, *Josephine Fossette and Lorene E. Perkins v. Carol Ann Berry*, No. SW C8435 (Cal. Sup. Ct. Los Angeles, Mar. 21, 1966); Judgment, *Fossett and Perkins v. Berry*, No. SW C8435 (Nov. 20, 1968); Carol Ann Berry, interview with the author, April 28, 2024.

61. Carol Ann Berry, interview with the author, April 28, 2024.

62. Carol Ann Berry, interview with the author, April 28, 2024.

63. Stephen Seck, interview with the author, Aug. 19, 2020.

64. Chaplin, *My Autobiography*, 409.

65. Beauchamp, *Without Lying Down*, 9, 11, 146.

66. Marilyn Beck, "Hollywood's Changing Morals: Notoriety No Longer Means Disgrace—It Means Success," *Austin American Statesman*, Nov. 6, 1977. Beck's

article erroneously refers to Joan as "the 16-year-old aspiring actress with whom he would later be involved in a spectacular paternity suit."

67. Jodi Kantor and Megan Twohey, "Sexual Misconduct Claims Trail a Hollywood Mogul; Oscar-Winning Producer Has Quietly Settled at Least 8 Complaints in 3 Decades," *New York Times*, Oct. 6, 2017.

68. Jan Ransom, "In Defining #MeToo Case, 23 Years for Weinstein; a First Conviction, but 'Not a First Offense,'" *New York Times*, Mar. 12, 2020; Lauren Herstik, "Harvey Weinstein Sentenced to 16 Years for Los Angeles Sex Crimes: The Former Film Producer Was Convicted in December of Raping and Sexually Assaulting a Woman in 2013," *New York Times*, Feb. 23, 2023; People v. Harvey Weinstein, No. 24-2024, slip op. (N.Y. Ct. of Appeals, April 25, 2024)

69. Jodi Kantor and Rachel Abrams, "Big-Name Actresses Say They Were Harassed by Weinstein," *New York Times*, Oct. 11, 2017.

70. Maland, *Chaplin and American Culture*, 371–72.

71. Eugene Archer, "Chaplin 'Failure' Is a Hit Here Now; 'Monsieur Verdoux' Pays Off after 17 Years on Shelf," *New York Times*, July 7, 1964.

72. Mary Baker, Certificate of Death No. 156-07-044817, Department of Health and Mental Hygiene., City of New York.

BIBLIOGRAPHY

ARCHIVAL SOURCES

Bancroft Library, University of California Berkeley
J. F. T. O'Connor Papers

Boston University
Sir Cedric Hardwicke Collection

California State Archives
Berry v. Chaplin, Civ. No. 15135 (paternity case on appeal)
California Un-American Activities Committee Records

California State University Dominguez Hills Gerth Archives and Special Collections
Herbert McClain Photo Collection

California State University Northridge Special Collections and Archives
Agness M. Underwood Collection

California Superior Court Archives and Records Center, Los Angeles
Berry v. Chaplin, D-238936
Fossette v. Berry, SW-C-8435
Jericho v. Berry, INGL-C-2458
Seck v. Seck, D-433807

Charlie Chaplin Archive

Federal Bureau of Investigation Files
Charles Spencer Chaplin
J. Paul Getty
R. B. Hood

Getty Research Institute
J. Paul Getty Family Papers
J. Paul Getty Family Photos

Herbert Hoover Presidential Library and Museum, West Branch, Iowa
President's Personal File, Joseph Scott, 1930–33

Immigration Naturalization Service Files
Charles Spencer Chaplin

Los Angeles Public Library
Special Collections

Margaret Herrick Library, Los Angeles
44th Annual Academy Awards Broadcast Script
44th Annual Academy Awards Photographs
Alf Reeves Scrapbook
Charlie Chaplin Interview Transcript
Harry Crocker Papers
Hedda Hopper Papers

Museum of Modern Art, New York
Charlie Chaplin Clipping File
Paulette Goddard Clipping File

National Archives and Records Administration, Riverside, California
United States v. Chaplin et al. Court Files for Indictments 16,616; 16,617; 16,618;
    and 16,619.

New York City Municipal Archives

New York Public Library for the Performing Arts
Billy Rose Theatre Collection—Max Eastman Papers
Charlie Chaplin Clipping File

New York University Fales Library and Special Collections
Erich Maria Remarque Papers
Julie Gilbert Papers

Richard Nixon Presidential Library and Museum, Yorba Linda, California

Seaver Center for Western History Research, Los Angeles, California
Charlie Chaplin Studio Collection
Motion Picture Photograph Collection
Rollie Totheroh Collection

Smithsonian Museum of American History
Lili St. Cyr Papers

UCLA Library Special Collections
Howard Bellew Oral History
Jim Tully Papers
Russell Birdwell Papers

University of Liverpool
Cunard Archives

University of North Dakota Special Collections
J. F. T. O'Connor Papers, 1906–54

University of Southern California Doheny Memorial Library
Hearst Examiner Photo Collection

University of Wyoming
Daniel Taradash Papers

Wisconsin Historical Society, Madison
Loyd Wright Legal Files
O'Brien Legal Files
Paul Lazarus Jr. Files
United Artists Corp. Press Books

BOOKS

Ackroyd, Peter. *Charlie Chaplin: A Brief Life*. New York: Doubleday, 2014.

Allen, Woody. *Apropos of Nothing*. New York: Arcade Publishing, 2020.

Anderson, Clinton H. *Beverly Hills Is My Beat*. Englewood Cliffs, NJ: Prentice-Hall, 1960.

Anger, Kenneth. *Hollywood Babylon*. New York: Delta Publishing, 1975.

Auletta, Ken. *Hollywood Ending: Harvey Weinstein and the Culture of Silence*. New York: Penguin Press, 2022.

Barbas, Samantha. *Confidential Confidential: The Inside Story of Hollywood's Notorious Scandal Magazine*. Chicago: Chicago Review Press, 2018.

Barrymore, Elaine, and Sandford Dody. *All My Sins Remembered*. New York: Appleton Century, 1964.

Basinger, Jeanine, and Sam Wasson. *Hollywood: The Oral History*. New York: HarperCollins, 2022.

Beauchamp, Cari. *Without Lying Down: Frances Marion and the Powerful Women of Early Hollywood*. New York: Lisa Drew/Scribner, 1997.

Begley, Adam. *Houdini: The Elusive American*. New Haven: Yale University Press, 2020.

Bergen, Candice. *Knock Wood*. New York: Linden Press/Simon & Schuster, 1984.

Bloom, Claire. *Limelight and After: The Education of an Actress*. New York: Harper & Row, 1982.

Bogard, Travis, and Jackson R. Bryer, eds. *Selected Letters of Eugene O'Neill*. New Haven: Yale University Press, 1988.

Braitman, Jacqueline R., and Gerald F. Uelmen. *Justice Stanley Mosk: A Life at the Center of California Politics and Justice*. Jefferson, NC: McFarland, 2013.

Brownlow, Kevin. *The Parade's Gone By . . .* Berkeley: University of California Press, 1968.

Capote, Truman. *Portraits and Observations: The Essays of Truman Capote*. New York: Random House, 1993.

Carr, Richard. *Charlie Chaplin: A Political Biography from Victorian Britain to Modern America*. London: Routledge, 2017.

Carroll, Paul Vincent. *Shadow and Substance: A Play in Four Acts*. New York: Random House, 1937.

Chaplin, Charlie. *My Trip Abroad*. New York: Harper & Brothers, 1922.

Chaplin, Charles. *My Autobiography*. New York: Simon and Schuster, 1964.

Chaplin, Charles, Jr., with N. and M. Rau. *My Father, Charlie Chaplin*. New York: Random House, 1960.

Chaplin, Lita Grey. *My Life with Chaplin: An Intimate Memoir*. With Morton Cooper. New York: Bernard Geis Associates, 1966.

Chaplin, Lita Grey, and Jeffrey Vance. *Wife of the Party*. Lanham, MD: Scarecrow Press, 1998.

Chaplin, Michael. *I Couldn't Smoke the Grass on My Father's Lawn*. New York: G. P. Putnam's Sons, 1966.

Chaplin, Patrice. *Hidden Star: A Memoir*. London: Richard Cohen Books, 1995.

Chiasson, Lloyd, Jr., ed. *The Press on Trial: Crimes and Trials as Media Events*. Westport, CT: Greenwood Press, 1997.

Cohn, Alfred, and Joe Chisholm. *"Take the Witness!"* New York: Frederick A. Stokes, 1934.

Cotes, Peter, and Thelma Niklaus. *The Little Fellow: The Life and Work of Charles Chaplin*. New York: Citadel Press, 1965.

Curtis, James. *Buster Keaton: A Filmmaker's Life*. New York: Alfred A. Knopf, 2022.

Davies, Marion. *The Times We Had: Life with William Randolph Hearst*. Edited by Pamela Pfau and Kenneth S. Marx. New York: Ballantine Books, 1975.

Davis, Nanette J. *From Crime to Choice: The Transformation of Abortion in America*. Westport, CT: Greenwood Press, 1985.

Davis, Nick. *Competing with Idiots: Herman and Joe Mankiewicz, a Dual Portrait*. New York: Alfred A. Knopf, 2021.

Eatwell, Piu. *Black Dahlia, Red Rose*. New York: Liveright Publishing, 2017.

Eells, George. *Hedda and Louella*. New York: G. P. Putnam's Sons, 1972.

Epstein, Jerry. *Remembering Charlie*. New York: Doubleday, 1989.

Eyman, Scott. *The Speed of Sound: Hollywood and the Talkie Revolution, 1926–1930*. New York: Simon & Schuster, 1997.

Eyman, Scott. *Charlie Chaplin vs. America: When Art, Sex, and Politics Collided*. New York: Simon & Schuster, 2023.

Farrell, John A. *Clarence Darrow: Attorney for the Damned*. New York: Doubleday, 2011.

Fleming, E. J. *The Fixers: Eddie Mannix, Howard Strickling and the MGM Publicity Machine*. Jefferson, NC: McFarland, 2005.

Frankel, Glenn. *High Noon: The Hollywood Blacklist and the Making of an American Classic*. New York: Bloomsbury, 2017.

Frankel, Glenn. *Shooting Midnight Cowboy: Art, Sex, Loneliness, Liberation, and the Making of a Dark Classic*. New York: Farrar, Straus & Giroux, 2021.

Franks, Jill. *Woody Allen and Charlie Chaplin: Little Men, Big Auteurs*. Jefferson, NC: McFarland, 2019.

Friedrich, Otto. *City of Nets: A Portrait of Hollywood in the 1940's*. New York: Harper & Row, 1986.

Gaston, Teddy Getty. *Alone Together: My Life with J. Paul Getty*. With Digby Diehl. New York: HarperCollins, 2013.

Gehrig, Lou. *The Lost Memoir*. New York: Simon & Schuster, 2020.

Geis, Gilbert, and Leigh B. Bienen. *Crimes of the Century: From Leopold and Loeb to O.J. Simpson*. Boston: Northeastern University Press, 1998.

Getty, J. Paul. *As I See It*. London: W. H. Allen, 1976.

Giesler, Jerry. *The Jerry Giesler Story*. As told to Pete Martin. New York: Simon and Schuster, 1960.

Gilbert, Julie. *Opposite Attraction: The Lives of Erich Maria Remarque and Paulette Goddard*. New York: Pantheon Books, 1995.

Goldwyn, Samuel. *Behind the Screen*. New York: George H. Doran, 1923.

Griffin, Mark. *All That Heaven Allows: A Biography of Rock Hudson*. New York: HarperCollins, 2018.

Hale, Georgia. *Intimate Close-Ups*. Edited with an introduction and notes by Heather Kiernan. Metuchen, NJ: Scarecrow Press, 1995.

Hayes, Kevin J., ed. *Charlie Chaplin Interviews*. Jackson: University Press of Mississippi, 2005.

Higham, Charles, and Joel Greenberg. *Hollywood in the Forties*. London: Tantivy Press, 1968.

Hodel, Steve. *Black Dahlia Avenger: The True Story*. New York: Arcade Publishing, 2003.

Jobb, Dean. *The Case of the Murderous Dr. Cream*. Chapel Hill, NC: Algonquin Books, 2021.

Joffe, Carole. *Doctors of Conscience: The Struggle to Provide Abortion before and after Roe v. Wade*. Boston: Beacon Press, 1995.

Johnson, Nelson. *Darrow's Nightmare: The Forgotten Story of America's Most Famous Trial Lawyer, Los Angeles 1911–1913*. New York: Rosetta Books, 2021.

Jung, Patricia Beattie, and Thomas A. Shannon, eds. *Abortion and Catholicism: The American Debate*. New York: Crossroad, 1988.

Kaplan, James. *Irving Berlin: New York Genius*. New Haven: Yale University Press, 2019.

Kornhaber, Donna. *Charlie Chaplin, Director*. Evanston, IL: Northwestern University Press, 2014.

Krist, Gary. *The Mirage Factory: Illusion, Imagination, and the Invention of Los Angeles*. New York: Crown, 2018.

Lamarr, Hedy. *Ecstasy and Me: My Life as a Woman*. Bartholomew House Publishing, 1966.

Larcher, Jerome. *Masters of Cinema: Charlie Chaplin*. Paris: Cahiers du Cinema, 2011.

Larson, Erik. *The Splendid and the Vile: A Saga of Churchill, Family, and Defiance during the Blitz*. New York: Crown, 2020.

Lenzner, Robert. *The Great Getty: The Life and Loves of J. Paul Getty—Richest Man in the World*. New York: Crown Publishers, 1985.

Levy, Shawn. *The Castle on Sunset*. New York: Doubleday, 2019.

Lewis, Jon. *Hard Boiled Hollywood: Crime and Punishment in Postwar Los Angeles*. Oakland: University of California Press, 2017.

Louvish, Simon. *Chaplin: The Tramp's Odyssey*. New York: Thomas Dunne Books, 2009.

Lynn, Kenneth S. *Charlie Chaplin and His Times*. New York: Simon & Schuster, 1997.

Maland, Charles J. *Chaplin and American Culture: The Evolution of a Star Image*. Princeton: Princeton University Press, 1989.

Maraniss, David. *A Good American Family: The Red Scare and My Father*. New York: Simon & Schuster, 2019.

Marx, Sam. *Mayer and Thalberg: The Make-Believe Saints*. New York: Random House, 1975.

Matthau, Carol. *Among the Porcupines*. New York: Turtle Bay Books, 1992.

McCabe, John. *Charlie Chaplin*. Garden City, NY: Doubleday, 1978.

McLean, Adrienne L., and David A. Cook, eds. *Headline Hollywood: A Century of Film Scandal*. New Brunswick: Rutgers University Press, 2001.

Menjou, Adolphe, and M. M. Musselman. *It Took Nine Tailors*. New York: McGraw-Hill, 1948.

Merritt, Greg. *Room 1219: The Life of Fatty Arbuckle, the Mysterious Death of Virginia Rappe, and the Scandal That Changed Hollywood*. Chicago: Chicago Review Press, 2013.

Milanich, Nara B. *Paternity: The Elusive Quest for the Father*. Cambridge, MA: Harvard University Press, 2019.

Miller, Russell. *The House of Getty*. London: Bloomsbury Reader, 2018.

Milton, Joyce. *Tramp: The Life of Charlie Chaplin*. New York: HarperCollins, 1996.

Morella, Joe, and Edward Z. Epstein. *Paulette: The Adventurous Life of Paulette Goddard*. New York: St. Martin's Press, 1985.

Moss, Robert F. *Charlie Chaplin*. New York: Pyramid Publishers, 1975.

Muir, Florabel. *Headline Happy*. New York: Henry Holt, 1950.

Nabokov, Vladimir. *Lolita*. New York: G. P. Putnam's Sons, 1955.

Paris, Barry. *Louise Brooks*. New York: Alfred A. Knopf, 1989.

Parsons, Louella O. *Tell It to Louella*. New York: G. P. Putnam's Sons, 1961.

Pickford, Mary. *Sunshine and Shadow*. New York: Doubleday, 1955.

Powers, Richard Gid. *Broken: The Troubled Past and Uncertain Future of the FBI*. New York: Free Press, 2004.

Rayner, Richard. *A Bright and Guilty Place: Murder, Corruption, and L.A.'s Scandalous Coming of Age*. New York: Doubleday, 2009.

Reagan, Leslie J. *When Abortion Was a Crime: Women, Medicine, and Law in the United States, 1867–1973*. Berkeley: University of California Press, 1997.

Reeves, May, and Claire Goll. *The Intimate Charlie Chaplin*. Jefferson, NC: McFarland, 2001.

Richardson, James H. *For the Life of Me: Memoirs of a City Editor*. New York: G. P. Putnam's Sons, 1954.

Robinson, David. *Chaplin: His Life and Art*. New York: McGraw-Hill, 1985.

Robinson, W. W. *Lawyers of Los Angeles: A History of the Los Angeles Bar Association and of the Bar of Los Angeles County*. Los Angeles: Los Angeles Bar Association, 1959.

Roeburt, John. *"Get Me Giesler."* New York: Belmont Books, 1962.

Rooney, Andy. *My War*. New York: Public Affairs, 2000.

Rosen, Gary A. *Adventures of a Jazz Age Lawyer: Nathan Burkan and the Making of American Popular Culture*. Berkeley: University of California Press, 2020.

Ross, Lillian. *Moments with Chaplin*. New York: Dodd, Mead, 1980.

Ross, Steven J. *Hollywood Left and Right: How Movie Stars Shaped American Politics*. New York: Oxford University Press, 2011.

Rucker, Phillip, and Carol Leonnig. *A Very Stable Genius*. New York: Penguin Press, 2020.

Saroyan, Aram. *Trio: Oona Chaplin, Carol Matthau, Gloria Vanderbilt: Portrait of an Intimate Friendship*. New York: Linden Press/Simon & Schuster, 1985.

Schickel, Richard. *The Essential Chaplin: Perspectives on the Life and Art of the Great Comedian*. Chicago: Ivan R. Dee, 2006.

Scovell, Jane. *Oona, Living in the Shadows: A Biography of Oona O'Neill Chaplin*. New York: Warner Books, 1998.

Sennett, Mack. *King of Comedy*. With Cameron Shipp. San Francisco: Memory House, 1990.

Smith, David T., ed. *Abortion and the Law*. Cleveland: Press of Western Reserve University, 1967.

Sobel, Raoul, and David Francis. *Chaplin: Genesis of a Clown*. London: Quartet Books, 1977.

St. Johns, Adela Rogers. *Final Verdict*. Garden City, NY: Doubleday, 1962.

St. Johns, Adela Rogers. *The Honeycomb*. Garden City, NY: Doubleday, 1969.

St. Johns, Adela Rogers. *Love, Laughter and Tears: My Hollywood Story*. Garden City, NY: Doubleday, 1978.

Sullivan, William C. *The Bureau: My Thirty Years in Hoover's FBI*. With Bill Brown. New York: W. W. Norton, 1979.

Summers, Anthony. *Official and Confidential: The Secret Life of J. Edgar Hoover*. New York: G. P. Putnam's Sons, 1993.

Thomas, Evan. *The Man to See: Edward Bennett Williams: Ultimate Insider; Legendary Trial Lawyer*. New York: Simon and Schuster, 1991.

Thomson, David. *Sleeping with Strangers: How the Movies Shaped Desire*. New York: Alfred A. Knopf, 2019.

Tye, Larry. *Demagogue: The Life and Long Shadow of Senator Joe McCarthy*. Boston: Houghton Mifflin Harcourt, 2020.

Underwood, Agness. *Newspaperwoman*. New York: Harper & Brothers, 1949.

Vanderbilt, Gloria. *It Seemed Important at the Time: A Romance Memoir*. New York: Simon & Schuster, 2004.

Von Ulm, Gerith. *Charlie Chaplin, King of Tragedy*. Caldwell, ID: Caxton Printers, 1940.

Wasson, Sam. *The Big Goodbye: Chinatown and the Last Years of Hollywood*. New York: Flatiron Books, 2020.

Weiner, Tim. *Enemies: A History of the FBI*. New York: Random House, 2012.

Wetstein, Matthew E. *Abortion Rates in the United States: The Influence of Opinion and Policy*. Albany: State University of New York Press, 1996.

Wilson, Earl. *The Show Business Nobody Knows*. Chicago: Cowles, 1971.

DOCUMENTARY

Kindleberg, Oliver, Peter Middleton, and James Spinney. *The Real Charlie Chaplin*. Showtime, 2021.

THEATRICAL PRODUCTION

Curtis, Christopher, and Thomas Meehan. *Chaplin: The Musical*. Ethel Barrymore Theatre, New York, Sept. 10, 2012–Jan. 6, 2013.

INDEX